ONCE UPON A F

NANZAN STUDIES IN ASIAN RELIGIONS

Paul L. Swanson, General Editor

1. Jan NATTIER, *Once Upon a Future Time: Studies in a Buddhist Prophecy of Decline,* 1991.
2. David REID, *New Wine: The Cultural Shaping of Japanese Christianity,* 1991.
3. Minor and Ann ROGERS, *Rennyo: The Second Founder of Shin Buddhism,* 1991.

ONCE UPON A FUTURE TIME

Studies in a Buddhist Prophecy of Decline

Jan Nattier

ASIAN HUMANITIES PRESS
Berkeley, California

ASIAN HUMANITIES PRESS

Asian Humanities Press offers to the specialist and the general reader alike the best in new translations of major works and significant original contributions to our understanding of Asian religions, cultures, and thought.

The map on page xviii is reprinted with the kind permission of the University of California Press, Berkeley, California.

Printed in the United States of America

Library of Congress Cataloging-in-Publication Data

Nattier, Jan, 1949–
Once upon a future time: studies in a Buddhist prophecy of decline / Jan Nattier.
p. cm. – (Nanzan studies in Asian religions; 1)
Revision of the author's doctoral dissertation (Harvard University).
Includes bibliographical references (p.) and index.
ISBN 0-89581-925-2 (cloth). – ISBN 0-89581-926-0 (paper)
1. Saddharmavipralopa. 2. History (Buddhism). 3. Prophecy–Buddhism. I. Title. II. Series.
BQ4480.N38 1992
291.2'3 – dc20

91-42549
CIP

To the members of my dissertation committee:

Masatoshi Nagatomi, Francis W. Cleaves,
John R. McRae, and Richard N. Frye

with gratitude and affection

Contents

PART 2 – CASE STUDY: THE KAUŚĀMBĪ PROPHECY

Acknowledgements

The number of those who have contributed to the completion of this project surely exceeds that of the proverbial sands of the Ganges River. Friends, colleagues and cohorts far and near have offered comments, encouragement, and advice without which this study (if it were completed at all) would surely be much poorer.

I must begin with my first teachers in the Inner Asian field, at Indiana University in Bloomington. John (Gombojab) Hangin and John Krueger, who introduced me to the study of Mongolian; Helmut Hoffmann, who awakened my interest in Classical Tibetan and in materials from Tun-huang in particular; and Larry Clark, who introduced me to the fascinating and perplexing religious literature of Old Uighur, combined forces to set me on a path from which there has been no turning back. Together they aroused an unquenchable curiosity about things Inner Asian, and managed to convey their sense that working with these materials can be as rewarding as it is sometimes baffling.

This book was begun as a doctoral dissertation, written for the Committee on Inner Asian and Altaic Studies at Harvard University. During my graduate studies there it was my great privilege to study the Mongolian language with Francis Cleaves, whose erudition and high standards of scholarship are exceeded only by the warmth of his concern for his many students. Though the Mongolian portion of the dissertation has not been included here (as it is being prepared for publication elsewhere), the influence of his thorough and exacting scholarship has had an impact on every page of this manuscript. Richard Frye was responsible for introducing me to the Iranian language family, and for providing many valuable insights into the important (and still so little known) role of "greater Iran" in the expansion of Buddhism across Central Asia. He has answered my many questions on things Sogdian, Bactrian and Khotanese with energy and enthusiasm, and has saved me from many an error on the Iranian front. John McRae served as a fount of information on a wide variety of Chinese Buddhist topics, and has provided detailed answers and invaluable leads in response to my seemingly endless questions. My summaries of the content of the Chinese versions of the Kauśāmbī prophecy could not have been done without his generosity in reading through these texts with me. Finally, Masatoshi Nagatomi has been my academic advisor and friend throughout my long and sometimes trying years at Harvard, and has served as an unfailing source of information, encouragement, and good advice. That his vast knowledge of the history of Buddhism serves to inspire his students rather than to intimidate them is a testimony to his great humanity.

In addition to these four members of my dissertation committee, many other friends and colleagues have actively assisted with this project. Judy Boltz supplied valuable references to materials in Chinese, and conversations with Raoul Birnbaum helped me to clarify my ideas on Buddhist decline terminology in East Asia. On the South Asian front Michael Witzel provided timely information and bibliography on current work in Prakrit studies, Richard Salomon offered helpful comments on some of my more out-on-a-limb theories concerning the use of the Kharoṣṭhī script, and Gary Tubb provided useful insights into Sanskrit metrics. Bill Boltz offered cautionary advice on the pronunciation of Chinese loan words in Tibetan, Şinasi Tekin supplied valuable references on Uighur vocabulary in Mongolian, and Chris Beckwith opened the door to the methodology of Greek and Latin textual criticism while serving as a tough but friendly critic on all things Tibetan.

Others have contributed to the sheer survival of this writer in ways that only those who have lived through the final months of dissertation-writing can appreciate. Long-distance encouragement (and reminders that not *everyone* believes the Dharma is declining) came from Alan Sponberg, Jean Pietarinen, and Maida Uhlig, while in Minnesota my department chairman at Macalester College, Calvin Roetzel, managed to create an atmosphere in which a junior visiting lecturer could manage to teach four new courses, write large chunks of a dissertation, and maintain some degree of sanity all in the same year. Without his sympathetic encouragement and unfailing sense of humor the dissertation would surely not have been completed on schedule. On the grueling home stretch Juanita Garciagodoy, Irit Averbuch, and Kevin Reinhart provided vital moral support, while friends and former coworkers at M.I.T. offered ongoing encouragement, the much-appreciated use of a laser printer, and that refreshing change of perspective that comes from trying to explain one's research on Buddhist decline theory to an audience of genuinely interested geophysicists.

In the course of converting the dissertation into book form I have benefited from the expertise of yet another group of friends, foremost among them Jim Heisig, who instigated my collaboration with the Nanzan Institute and created the customized characters used here to romanize numerous obscure writing systems; and Paul Swanson, surely the world's kindest series editor, whose expertise on Chinese and Japanese topics provided valuable fine-tuning on more than one occasion. Comments from Jan Van Bragt, offered during the course of seminars given at Nanzan University, were especially helpful in broadening the perspective of this study beyond that of the Buddhist Studies realm; and conversations with Jamie Hubbard during the final typesetting process at Nanzan provided both a welcome respite from hours at the computer and numerous insightful observations (some of which I actually managed to incorporate without unduly endangering the margins). A last-minute suggestion from Paul Harrison sent me back into the Tibetan canon for one final round of investigations, saving me from a moderately grievous error in the process, and comments from John McRae on the penultimate draft (offered even as he was contending with deadlines of his own) resulted in a number of stylistic and conceptual improvements. The manuscript has also benefited greatly from the sharp editorial eye of Ed Skrzypczak, whose ability to spot inconsistencies, computer blips, and stylistic infelicities is legendary. Any remaining errors, whether of content or of style, are naturally the responsibility of the author.

In the financial realm, support from the Nanzan Institute made possible the first of three trips to Nagoya for editorial consulting, and partial funding from the Center for East Asian Studies at Stanford University contributed to the third. On all three occasions accommodations provided by Nanzan made my stays not only possible, but pleasurable.

Finally, an unrepayable debt of gratitude is owed to my parents, Clayton and Jean Nattier, who would probably rather I had studied something else, but have always let me know they're on my side.

Transliteration Conventions

TIBETAN

For the Tibetan text I have employed the system proposed by T. V. Wylie (*HJAS* 22 (1959), 261-167), with the following emendations: (1) the *'a-chung* (འ་) is transcribed by an apostrophe wherever it appears (even at the end of a word, where Wylie does not transcribe it at all); (2) the reversed letter *i* (ྀ), so common in Old Tibetan texts, has been underlined wherever it occurs (*i̲*); (3) wherever a letter could be misconstrued in Wylie's transcription as an abbreviated subscript or as part of another letter, I have inserted a period before the doubtful letter to indicate that it is written separately (i.e., in its full form, though this may be subscripted) in the Tibetan script; and (4) wherever a nasal letter has been replaced by an *anusvāra* in the Tibetan script, I have marked the presence of the *anusvāra* with a small raised circle (e.g., *rna°s* in place of *rnams*).

I have followed Wylie's method of distinguishing between the subscript and full forms of the letter *y* in the combinations *gy-* གྱ and *g-y-* གཡ , replacing his hyphen by a period (since the hyphen is used for other purposes in Tibetan transcription) and extending it to include other ambiguous letters, most commonly the letter *h*, as well. In most cases these ambiguities appear in the Tibetan transcriptions of foreign (especially Sanskrit) words, but occasionally they arise in native Tibetan terms as well. The following examples should illustrate the method used:

gyag གྱག་ *g.yag* གཡག་

**gslo* གསློ་ *gs.lo* གསལོ་[1]

---

[1] See the transcription of the Tun-huang version, p. 257 below, §3, line 2.

sho ཤོ་ *s.ho* སྷོ་

shu ཤུ་ *sh.hu* ཤྷུ་[2]

CHINESE

Following the lead of the majority of scholars in Buddhist Studies (and the logic of David Pollack, who states in the introduction to his recent book that he will adopt the *pin-yin* system "the day I find the layman who can pronounce the name of Ts'ao Hsüeh-ch'in . . . more accurately in its Pinyin rendering of Cao Xueqin"[3]), I have retained the traditional Wade-Giles system for the transcription of Chinese. In addition I have made frequent use of Karlgren's reconstructions of the Ancient Chinese pronunciations (6th c. CE) for characters used to transcribe proper names. In all such instances I have provided the number of the entry in Karlgren's *Analytic Dictionary of Chinese and Sino-Japanese*.

OTHER LANGUAGES

For the romanization of other languages I have followed standard conventions, as exemplified in the following sources:

Japanese:	Nelson, *Japanese-English Dictionary*
Khotanese:	Emmerick, *The Book of Zambasta*
Mongolian:	F. W. Cleaves and A. Mostaert, in *The Harvard Journal of Asiatic Studies*
Pāli:	Pali Text Society, *Pali-English Dictionary*
Sanskrit:	Whitney, *Sanskrit Grammar*
Sogdian:	Benveniste, *Vessantara Jātaka*
Uighur:	von Gabain, *Alttürkische Grammatik*

---

[2] See the Tun-huang version, §19, line 5.

[3] David Pollack, *The Fracture of Meaning: Japan's Synthesis of China from the Eighth through the Eighteenth Centuries* (Princeton: Princeton University Press, 1986), xiv.

Special Symbols

TIBETAN TEXT

< >	letters or words found in the original manuscript or xylograph, but which are erroneous and should be removed
└ ┘	indicates material originally omitted, but later inserted below the line by the copyist
[ ]	letters omitted from (or invisible in) the manuscript or xylograph, but which should be supplied
. . .	letters that are present, but totally illegible
–	used to mark passages where the Tun-huang manuscript lacks entire phrases or sentences found in the later xylograph editions

ENGLISH TRANSLATION

[ ]	words not found in the original Tibetan text, but which are necessary to convey the sense in English
( )	equivalents of a proper name or Buddhist technical term in another language (ordinarily Sanskrit)
{ }	words found in some but not all copies of the text

ANNOTATIONS

~	alternates with
<	is derived from
<<	is ultimately derived from (at a considerable remove)
→	becomes

Abbreviations

Apte	V. Sh. Apte, *The Student's English-Sanskrit Dictionary*
BHSD	F. W. Edgerton, *Buddhist Hybrid Sanskrit Dictionary*
D	Derge edition (Tibetan canon)
Das	S. C. Das, *Tibetan-English Dictionary*
ER	M. Eliade, ed., *The Encyclopedia of Religion*
ERE	J. Hastings, ed., *Encyclopedia of Religion and Ethics*
K.	B. Karlgren, *Analytic Dictionary of Chinese and Sino-Japanese*
Khot.	Khotanese
L	Lhasa edition (Tibetan canon)
Mo.	Mongolian
Mvy.	R. Sakaki et al., eds., *Mahāvyutpatti*
MW	M. Monier-Williams, *A Sanskrit-English Dictionary*
N	Narthang edition (Tibetan canon)
Pek.	Peking edition (Tibetan canon)
Pkt.	Prakrit
PTSD	Pali Text Society, Pali English Dictionary
Rerikh	Yu. N. Rerikh, *Tibetsko-russko-anglĭiskĭi slovar'*
Skt.	Sanskrit
Sogd.	Sogdian
SOR	Serie Orientale Roma
T	*Taishō shinshū daizōkyō*
Tib.	Tibetan
Uig.	Uighur

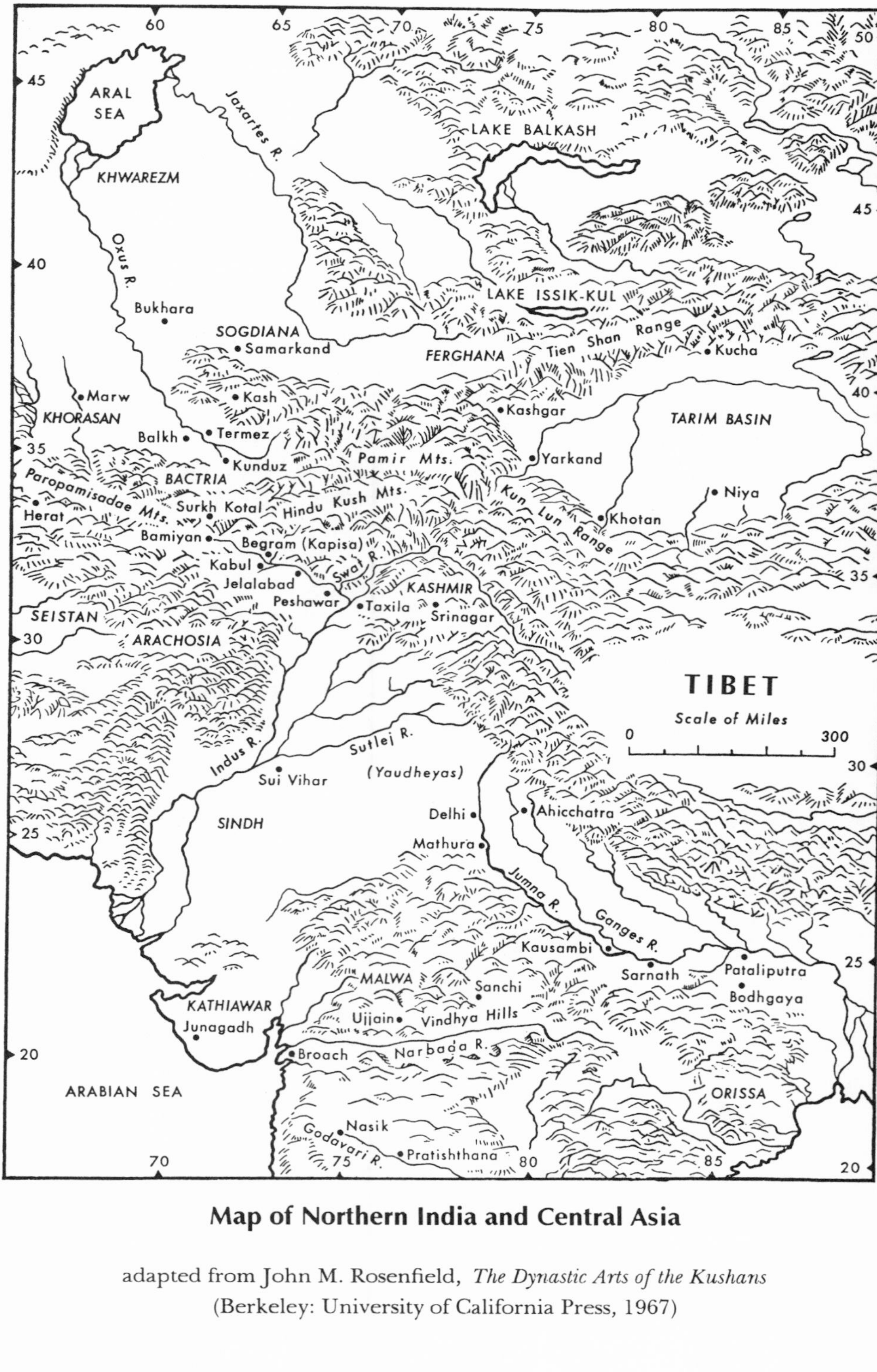

Map of Northern India and Central Asia

adapted from John M. Rosenfield, *The Dynastic Arts of the Kushans*
(Berkeley: University of California Press, 1967)

Part One

Buddhist Concepts of History: An Overview

Chapter One

The Death of the Dharma: Preliminary Considerations

ONCE UPON A TIME, at an uncertain point in the future, the Buddhist religion will come to an end. A combined force of Greeks, Sakas, and Parthians will invade northwest India, destroying stūpas and temples along their way. After causing tremendous destruction they will finally be defeated by a Buddhist king who is ruling at the city of Kauśāmbī. Then the king, fearing the karmic consequences of his bloody military campaigns, will turn to his Buddhist preceptor for advice. Anxious to gain merit, the king will follow his advice, inviting all the Buddhist monks in the known inhabited world to a great religious feast. They accept his invitation and converge in vast numbers on the city of Kauśāmbī. But by bringing together monks from many separate lineages, the king will inadvertently create conflict in the sangha. On the occasion of a great religious assembly, this conflict escalates into open warfare, resulting in the death of the last remaining arhat. The monks in turn all kill one another, leaving not a single one of their number alive. And with that, the history of the Buddhist religion on earth comes to an end, leaving the good king to mourn the results of his well-intentioned actions.

Such, in outline form, is the story contained in the Buddhist prophecy of the death of the Dharma that will be the central focus of this study. Composed not later than the 2nd century CE, in all probability in northwest India, the story circulated in numerous languages and in a variety of recensions, of which over a dozen examples (in such languages as Chinese, Khotanese, Tibetan, and Mongolian) have survived. The quantity of these texts and the number of divergences in their content raise intriguing questions concerning their development from the now lost original. A portion of this study, therefore, will be devoted to examining the relationships among these various recensions and to establishing the probable content of the original prophecy.

A second question concerns the relationship of the "Kauśāmbī story" (as we may call it, after the city where these events are to take place) to actual historical events. To what extent is this tale—with its concrete plot and specific characters—the product of a mythological imagination, and to what extent is it a reflection of genuine historical fact? Was there indeed once a conflict within the monastic community that led to the death of one or more of its members, or was this story simply invented in order to convey a truth of another kind? A separate but related question is whether those Buddhists who handed down this tradition considered the story to be purely a prophecy, or to contain (at least in part) a record of events that had already taken place. (We are led to suspect the latter in at least some cases, when we encounter versions of the story in which the editor or copyist inadvertently fluctuates between past and future tense.)

Even more intriguing, however, are the questions raised by the main themes of the prophecy itself. To the Western ear (and indeed to many Buddhist ones) such a story seems startling, even incomprehensible. What could possibly have motivated a Buddhist writer—for there is no doubt that the story was both produced and transmitted by Buddhists, and not their competitors—to predict the annihilation of his or her own religion? And how could subsequent generations of Buddhists have been content to leave the story as it is, resisting the temptation to counter its unhappy ending by adding a more edifying conclusion?

But resist they did, and they preserved and transmitted the text with enthusiasm. For more than a millennium this prophecy was held in the highest esteem among Buddhists in India, Central Asia, and China, and the number of its surviving translations and recensions serves as an index of its ongoing popularity.

Even this popularity, however, was not to be eternal, for roughly a millennium after its composition the prophecy seems to have been abandoned by all the Buddhist communities that had previously shown it favor. Replaced by other prophetic and historical traditions, the Kauśāmbī story eventually sank into oblivion, ignored by Buddhists of all schools and only recently rediscovered by modern scholars. The final question we must answer is thus an ironic one: Why should this prophecy, which so uncompromisingly predicted the eventual eclipse of the Buddhist religion, have finally suffered from the same eclipse itself?

To approach these questions in context we will begin in Part One with an overview of the variety of Buddhist concepts of history. Our first task will be to establish that such concepts exist, for it is a commonplace of much scholarly writing on Buddhism that for Buddhists history simply does not matter. After reviewing the major time schemes found in Buddhist literature, we will narrow our focus to the specific category to which our prophecy belongs—that is, the traditions concerning the decline and disappearance of the Buddhist Dharma.[1] Within this category, too, we will find a variety of traditions, which have a variety of implications for Buddhist practice.

With this background in mind, we then turn in Part Two to an exploration of the Kauśāmbī story itself. The variety of the extant versions of this tale allows us to construct a genealogical stemma of their relationships, which in turn provides the basis for an examination of the gradual evolution of the story. We then offer some suggestions for identifying both the historical circumstances that gave rise to the text and those that subsequently stimulated its reappropriation.

Finally, we return to a consideration of the impact of the expectation of the disappearance of the Dharma on Buddhist thought and practice. A comparison of the functions of this myth in South and Inner Asia, on the one hand, and in East Asia on the other, reveals two strikingly different patterns, which have led in turn to very different uses of the imagery of decline in these two parts of the Buddhist world.

---

[1] In the phrase "decline of the Dharma" the word *dharma* refers to the Buddhist teachings (as well as Buddhist religious practices and institutional forms), and not to *dharma* in the sense of the underlying order of the universe—what Hindus would call the *sanātana-dharma*, or "eternal Dharma." Both Hindus and Buddhists agree that the overall structure of the cosmos (that is, the rules by which it operates) will remain unchanged.

This, then, is a study of Buddhist attitudes toward time. Not the time of the philosophers—for there are many abstract questions concerning the nature of time in Buddhist metaphysical reflections that will not concern us here—but the everyday sense of one's location in history, as experienced by ordinary men and women, both lay and monastic. In attempting to grasp the sense of time that these Buddhist believers have held, we will be dealing with issues that are relevant not only to the study of Buddhism, but to the historical and comparative study of other religious traditions as well. What impact does it have on a member of a given religious community, for example, to believe that the tradition that expresses his or her religious faith will one day disappear from the earth? Why does the expectation of the potential demise of one's values lead to the anticipation of a future "golden age" in one context, but only to a resigned acceptance of a "degenerate age" in another? Finally, in the most general terms, what impact does an individual's sense of "what time it is" have on the configuration of priorities in his or her religious faith and practice?

The conclusions offered below are based on a detailed textual analysis of the surviving versions of the Kauśāmbī story, focused in particular on the Tibetan version, which provided the original impetus for this study. I have therefore included a romanized edition of the Tibetan text itself (in both xylograph and Tun-huang manuscript versions) together with an English translation in the ninth chapter of this book. The text is thus offered for use by other scholars, who may well wish to use it to construct interpretations other than my own.

Chapter Two

Frameworks of Buddhist Historical Thought

THE BUDDHIST religious tradition — indeed, Indian religious thought in general — is often described as lacking a true sense of history. Because the Indian view of time is cyclic rather than linear, so it is argued, no single historical event is decisive, no turning point unrepeatable, and no progress or decline in human culture truly significant. In short, the Buddhists, like the Hindus, simply have no interest in history. The contribution of Buddhism to human thought is thus not to be sought primarily in the realm of the historical, but in its perception of a reality transcending time, or of an unchanging pattern of flux.

It is true, we should concede at the outset, that Buddhism is not a "historical religion" in the sense that applies to the monotheistic faiths of the Semitic world. What the Buddha discovered in his experience of enlightenment, so the Buddhist scriptures tell us, was not any new revelation irrupting into the world for the first time, but a timeless truth about the nature of reality, identical to the truth discovered by all other enlightened sages before him. Thus even the central event of Buddhist mythology — the Buddha's experience of illumination under the Bodhi tree — is not viewed as a decisive historical event in the sense that Jews, Christians, or Muslims might use to speak of the receipt of the ten commandments by Moses, the incarnation of God in the person of Jesus, or the revelation of the *Qur'ān* to Muhammad. Indeed, it is a central contention of virtually all schools of Buddhism that the Buddha's experience is by definition repeatable and is accessible (at least in theory) to all human beings.

On a macrocosmic scale, too, Buddhists have shared with their Hindu counterparts a sense of the incomprehensible vastness of the cosmos. The astronomical distances and immense time scales envisioned in Hindu and Buddhist cosmology have few counterparts, if any, prior to the development of modern physics and astronomy. That many languages of Central and East Asia use terms borrowed from Sanskrit for these mind-boggling numbers demonstrates India's primacy in thinking in these terms.

This entire cosmos, moreover, is seen as passing through an ongoing series of cycles, just as do events on our earth. Periods of manifestation and non-manifestation occur in continuing sequence, with each phase lasting for an unimaginable period of time. Since these cycles recur ad infinitum, the universe cannot properly be described as having a "beginning" or an "end." Such a view of the cosmos is anything but linear, and events taking place within such a world can be described as teleological only on the smallest of scales.

All this does not imply, however, that Indian thought lacks any concept of history. Though neither Hindus nor Buddhists have devoted much attention to mere chronological record-keeping (much to the distress of modern historians), we can find at least certain aspects of historical consciousness within both of these religious traditions. Both Hindus and Buddhists, as I hope to demonstrate, have viewed time as neither irrelevant nor homogeneous, and have drawn clear and qualitative distinctions between one era and another. To take an obvious example, Śākyamuni's experience of enlightenment is portrayed in Buddhist sources as having radically transformed the age in which he lived. By opening up the possibility of replicating this experience (for the spiritual élite) or of earning merit by contributing to the Buddhist community (for the ordinary lay people), the Buddha transformed his own time into one filled with new possibilities for human experience, an age subsequently referred to in Buddhist literature as the *bhadrakalpa* (good eon).

This single example, however, only begins to suggest the depths of the Buddhist concern with history. I would even go so far as to suggest that for most of the Buddhists most of the time, the question of history—of where we are in the evolution of the cosmos, and of how much time remains in the world as we know it—has been of central, not peripheral, importance. And at certain times in history, under pressure from particular circumstances, these questions have become not only central, but decisive.

We will begin, then, with a review of the variety of attitudes toward history that can be found in the Buddhist tradition. With this context in hand, we will turn to the central issue of this study: the significance of Buddhist expectations of decline.

* * *

NOWHERE IN THE earliest layers of the surviving Buddhist literature—whether in the Nikāyas of the Theravāda school preserved in the Pāli canon or in the Āgamas of the Sarvāstivāda, Mahāsāṃghika, and Dharmaguptaka schools preserved in the Chinese—do we find any indication that primitive Buddhism[1] had a systematic concept of history. And this is hardly surprising, for the historical Buddha appears to have described such reflections as "not conducive to liberation," leading only to abstract philosophical speculation and not to the release from the bondage of craving that was the object of his path.[2] Though such speculations were thus not the focus of attention, Buddhists did formulate (or adopt from their immediate environment) certain basic notions concerning the overall nature of time and of history.

These traditions may conveniently be divided into two categories: the cosmological, on the one hand, and the Buddhological on the other. In the cosmological traditions the focus is on the origin, duration, and destruction of the universe as a whole, and little or no attention is paid to the activities of the Buddhas. (Indeed, such

---

[1] The term "primitive" refers to the original, pre-sectarian tradition, in the sense used in Reginald H. Fuller's English translation of Rudolf Bultmann's *Das Urchristentum im Rahmen der antiken Religionen* (1949) as *Primitive Christianity in its Contemporary Setting* (New York: Meridian Books, 1951). For sectarian Buddhism (the so-called "Eighteen Schools") I follow the usage of HIRAKAWA Akira, adopting the term "Nikāya" (sectarian) Buddhism in place of the pejorative (and inaccurate) "Hīnayāna."

[2] Speculations concerning the dimensions and duration of the universe are among the futile preoccupations criticized in the *Brahmajāla-sutta*, generally considered to be one of the earliest texts in the Pāli canon. See *Dīghanikāya*, vol. I, text no. 1, chapter 2; English translation by T. W. Rhys Davids in *Sacred Books of the Buddhists*, vol. 2 (London: Pali Text Society, 1899), 30–45.

traditions are, as we shall see in the following discussion, characterized by their relative lack of references to Buddha figures.) In the Buddhological traditions, by contrast, the evolution of the cosmos is viewed in terms of the appearance, or non-appearance, of enlightened beings. The two categories have in common, however, a vast scale of time, for both are framed in terms of incalculable eons.

Within each of these two categories, in turn, we find traditions of different varieties. The cosmological traditions appear both in narrative accounts, in which the plot and characters are carefully delineated, and in more schematic scholastic accounts where only the overall framework is described. The scholastic accounts are thus both more comprehensive (in terms of their overall scope) and less complete (in terms of delineation of characters and actions) than their narrative counterparts. The buddhological traditions, by contrast, are almost always schematic in format, offering genuine narrative detail only in the case of the historical Buddha, Śākyamuni. These accounts can best be sorted according to the number of Buddhas they include, and according to their (primarily) past or future orientation.

COSMOLOGICAL TRADITIONS

We may begin with the traditions that offer the broadest perspective, dealing with the appearance and evolution of the cosmos as a whole. In this category we will find both narrative and schematic traditions, in which certain differences of emphasis can be discerned. Since the narrative traditions appear to be earlier—emerging perhaps a century or two after the time of the Buddha, while the schematic accounts are several centuries later—we will begin with the narrative accounts, and then turn to the later literature in which they are systematized.

NARRATIVE TRADITIONS

As we have already seen, the Buddha appears to have discouraged his followers from indulging in cosmological speculation. Nonetheless, such topics seem to have been of interest to many Buddhists, and two texts that deal directly with these issues succeeded in gaining acceptance in the Pāli canon. In both of these sūtras the central focus of attention is on a period of decline or "devolution," though the second contains a narration of an evolutionary period as well.

The *Aggañña-suttanta* ("Primeval Sūtra")[3]

This sūtra opens with a discussion of the insignificance of caste status, and portions of the narrative are clearly intended to undercut the pretensions of the Brahman class. The main theme of the story, however, is the repopulation of this universe after the most recent period of non-manifestation.[4] When the world as we know it begins to take shape, the Buddha tells his followers, beings are reborn on earth from a heavenly realm known as the "world of radiance" (Pāli *ābhassaraloka*, Skt. *ābhāsvaraloka*).[5] At that time there is no sun, no moon, no stars, no distinctions of gender, and—most important—no food. The beings born into this world are of such sublime nature that they do not need physical nourishment to survive. As

---

[3] *Dīghanikāya*, sutta no. 27 (English translation by T. W. Rhys Davids in *Sacred Books of the Buddhists*, vol. 4, *Dialogues of the Buddha, Part 3* [London: Pali Text Society, 1957], 77–94). The same story appears in the *Mahāvastu* (i, 338–48), where it is titled the *Rājavaṃśa* (History of Kings), and continues with a discussion (not found in the Pāli version) of the successors of the primordial ruler. The Chinese canon contains three translations of the text, in the Taishō edition nos. 1[5] (part of the *Dīrghāgama*), 26[154] (part of the *Madhyamāgama*), and 10 (an independent translation done in the 11th century). The fact that the text thus appears in works belonging to the Theravāda, Mahāsāṃghika, Sarvāstivāda, and Dharmaguptaka schools (the latter if the affiliation of the Chinese *Dīrghāgama* with the Dharmaguptaka school is accepted) offers strong evidence that the story had already been accepted into the Buddhist canon prior to the division of the Buddhist community into separate sectarian groups. The text is absent from the Tibetan canon, which contains no equivalent of the Pāli Nikāyas or the Āgamas of the Sarvāstivāda and other schools. For the translation of *aggañña* as "primeval" see Edgerton, *Buddhist Hybrid Sanskrit Dictionary*, 4a–b, s.v. *agninya*.

[4] It is striking that the first part of this speech is a verbatim parallel to a passage that occurs in the *Brahmajāla-sutta* (cited above, n. 2). In the latter, however, the context is quite the opposite, as the Buddha is there represented as discouraging his followers from thinking about such cosmological issues, while here he himself discusses them in considerable detail.

[5] Though the scholastic tradition describes this period as the "kalpa of the duration of destruction" (discussed below), it is apparent that the world is not entirely unmanifest during this period, since this heavenly realm is maintained. Some scholastic texts also note that those beings whose karma is insufficient to allow rebirth in the *ābhāsvara* heaven during a period of non-manifestation may be reborn instead in another world-system.

the earth cools, however (and here the text shifts into the past tense), a milky scum formed on top of the water, which eventually became the earth's surface. One of those beings put in his finger, licked it, and found the earth tasty, and—so the sūtra tells us—"craving entered into him." With increasing consumption of this coarse earthly food the sentient beings on earth became gross, progressively losing the inherent luminosity they had earlier possessed. Because they were no longer luminous, the stars, sun, and moon came into being to provide light. In the wake of these changes many negative practices came about, including the hoarding of food, belittling of others, and competition.

The more these beings ate, the more solid (and less ethereal) they became. And in the process they began to look very different from one another. Worst of all, distinctions of gender emerged, and these beings began to desire one another. In the end the chaos and suffering increased so much that the people (for they had now become truly human) were forced to elect a king to rule over them, so that disorder could be kept to a minimum.

Returning at last to the theme with which it began, the text now reveals its own agenda: the *kṣatriya*s (warriors or nobles) are here portrayed as the highest class, second only to the ruler himself. After them come the *brahman*s (priests, who are here subdivided into meditators and "repeaters" of texts), the *vaiṣya*s (tradesmen or merchants), and *śudra*s (ordinarily described as farmers, but here said to make their living by hunting). The text closes by stating that one who has become an arhat—no matter what his class origins—is the highest of all human beings.

When this story is retold in Buddhist literature, in countries as distant as Mongolia,[6] it is usually with a focus on the idea of kingship. For this first king, selected by the people themselves to help keep their own evil proclivities in check, has been honored as the prototype of all good Buddhist rulers. What is important for our purposes, however, is that the sūtra presents a clear-cut scenario of a portion of the process of cosmic devolution, from the appearance

[6] The story appears, for example, at the beginning of the *White History* of the Mongols, composed early in the Yüan dynasty (c. 14th century). For the text and German translation see Karl Sagaster, ed. and trans., *Die Weisse Geschichte* (Leipzig: Otto Harrassowitz, 1981).

of luminous beings in the world at the beginning of the kalpa to their metamorphosis into human beings near its end.

The *Cakkavatti-sīhanāda-suttanta* ("Sūtra on the Lion's Roar of the Wheel-Turning King")[7]

This sūtra, like the *Aggañña-suttanta*, opens with an introductory section that seems remote from the course of its main narrative. Here the Buddha counsels his followers to rely on themselves, to rely on the Dharma, and to "walk in the haunts where your fathers roamed." He then turns to the story that is of interest to us here, the tale of a series of great rulers of the past, the so-called *cakravartins* or "wheel-turning" kings.[8]

The sūtra begins at the peak of a cycle, with a wheel-turning king on the throne. This king, picturesquely translated by Rhys Davids as "Strongtyre," has already ruled for thousands of years when we meet him, as he asks his advisor to let him know when the "Celestial Wheel" slips from its place. Just what this wheel represents is a matter of controversy; most scholars have seen in it an image of the solar disk. What it signifies in this context, however, is quite clear: it is the symbol of the Wheel-Turning King's power, controlling all four directions not by might, but by righteousness. When the wheel slips from its place (signifying the end of his reign) the king renounces his throne, turns over the kingdom to his son, and becomes a mendicant. The son is distressed that when he takes over the realm the wheel disappears entirely, until his father explains that he must earn the reappearance of the wheel by ruling

---

[7] *Dīghanikāya*, sutta no. 26 (English translation by T. W. Rhys Davids in *Sacred Books of the Buddhists*, vol. 4, *Dialogues of the Buddha, Part 3* [London: Pali Text Society, 1957], 59–76). The sūtra also appears in two places in the Chinese canon (T Nos. 1[6] and 26[70]), where it comprises part of the *Dīrghāgama* and *Madhyamāgama* sections, respectively. The text is not included in the Tibetan canon. Once again the sūtra clearly transcends sectarian boundaries (cf. above, n. 3), though the absence of a Mahāsāṃghika version of the text suggests a slightly later date than that of the *Aggañña-suttanta*.

[8] The motif of the *cakravartin* is surely non-Aryan. It is absent from the early Vedic literature, emerges suddenly (without any evidence of gradual evolution) in the *Upaniṣads*, and appears only sporadically in the early Buddhist literature. It is central, however, to Jaina mythology, where the ancient *cakravartins* comprise a series parallel to that of the enlightened sages, or *Tīrthaṅkaras*. See Walther Schubring, *The Doctrine of the Jainas*, trans. Wolfgang Beurlen (Delhi: Motilal Banarsidass, 1962), 21–23.

as his father has done. And so he does, ruling according to Dharma, while the magical wheel rolls from one end of his kingdom to the other.

This succession continues through a series of kings, each ruling according to the Dharma like his father. At a certain point, however, one such ruler neglects to follow tradition, and decides instead to rule as he himself sees fit. Poverty, crime, and disorder are the result, and the wheel eventually disappears altogether. At this point "both the span of life in those beings and their comeliness" begin to decline, with the life span sinking from 80,000 years (its original length) to only 40,000. As the cycle continues and kings go on ruling by their own whims, the situation continues to deteriorate, resulting in an ever-shortened life span. Finally, human beings live for only ten years, all semblance of morality has disappeared, and greed and hostility run rampant. At last some of these beings take refuge in caves, where they wait out a final seven days of fighting. At this point the cycle shifts: so glad are the survivors to see one another that they resolve to take up morality once again, and their life span and comeliness begin to increase. Gradually the cycle returns to its zenith, the world is filled with prosperity and morality, and the human life span again attains its maximum duration of 80,000 years. Once again a wheel-turning king, known as Śaṅkha, will arise—the first to be given a name since "King Strongtyre" at the outset. Ruling at Ketumatī (the future name of Benares), he will once again carry out his duties according to Dharma.

Up to now there has been nothing in this story that is peculiarly Buddhist: no Buddhist teachings have been given, no Buddhist community appears to exist, and no Buddha (historical or otherwise) has made his appearance. Now we hear for the first time of the future Buddha, Maitreya (Pāli Metteyya), who will attain enlightenment during King Śaṅkha's rule. His teachings will attract a huge congregation of followers, and at last even Śaṅkha himself will abandon his throne. He, too, will attain full enlightenment, and with this the narrative portion of the sūtra ends.[9]

[9] The story of King Śaṅkha and Maitreya also occurs in the (Sarvāstivādin) *Divyāvadāna*, the (Theravāda) *Anāgatavaṃsa*, and the *Maitreyavyākaraṇa* (whose sectarian identity is unclear). For further details on these and other versions of the Maitreya story see Jan Nattier, "The Meanings of the Maitreya Myth: A

At this point the sūtra returns to its initial formulas, advising the monks to live as islands and refuges unto themselves. Cultivating mindfulness, morality, and restraint, and "walking in the haunts where their fathers roamed," the monks will eventually accomplish the highest goal. Here the only note of unity that is sounded between the narrative and its frame is in this reference to following in the paths of their fathers, for it is through innovation in the art of kingship that the process of degeneration began, and through a return to tradition that it is brought to an end.

What is important here for our purposes is not the moral of the story, but the overall sweep of its plot. For this sūtra — whatever its moralistic intentions — is constructed with the assumption of cosmic evolution and devolution in mind. As we shall see in the following section, both of the narrative traditions considered here can easily be placed within the more systematic scenario found in the scholastic literature, representing individual segments of the overall cosmic drama.

THE SCHOLASTIC TRADITION

While the composers of the Pāli sūtras were content to describe only a portion of the history of the cosmos, in the later scholastic tradition such a topic had to be dealt with in a more comprehensive fashion. It is in the commentary literature that we find the most explicit accounts of the evolution of the cosmos, and of these the most detailed is that presented in the *Abhidharmakośa*.[10]

As we have seen, Buddhists share with their Hindu counterparts the idea that we live in an oscillating universe. In the *Abhidharmakośa* this general idea was systematized into a time scheme consisting of four *asaṃkhyeya* (innumerable) kalpas:

Typological Analysis" in Alan Sponberg and Helen Hardacre, eds., *Maitreya, the Future Buddha* (Cambridge: Cambridge University Press, 1988), 23–47.

[10] The *Abhidharmakośa*, composed by Vasubandhu in approximately the 5th century, follows in general the perspectives the Sarvāstivāda school, though Vasubandhu often introduces the ideas of the Sautrāntika school as well. The discussion of Buddhist cosmology is contained in chapter 3, §89d–102. For a French translation see Louis de La Vallée Poussin, *L'Abhidharmakośa de Vasubandhu* (Paris: Paul Geuthner, 1926), vol. 2, 181–207. The Theravāda views on cosmology are mentioned in passing by such great commentators as Buddhaghosa, but are not systematically collected in any single text.

1. a kalpa of destruction, during which the world as we know it is progressively destroyed;
2. a kalpa of the duration of destruction, during which the universe is entirely non-manifest;
3. a kalpa of renovation, in which the universe gradually reappears and is repopulated; and
4. a kalpa of the duration of renovation, during which the universe remains manifest and filled with sentient life.

Each of these four kalpas, moreover, is further subdivided into twenty intermediate eons or sub-kalpas (*antarakalpa*). These sub-kalpas are rather meaningless during the kalpa of destruction, when the world is entirely unmanifest (and there is presumably no change that these boundaries could serve to mark); nor is there much discussion in the scholastic literature of their significance during the periods of destruction and renovation. During the kalpa of the duration of renovation, however, these sub-periods take on particular importance, as they mark the boundaries between the periods of decline (when the human life span grows progressively shorter) and those of advance (when the reverse of this process takes place). This can best be illustrated by the following diagram, showing this process of repeated devolution and evolution.[11]

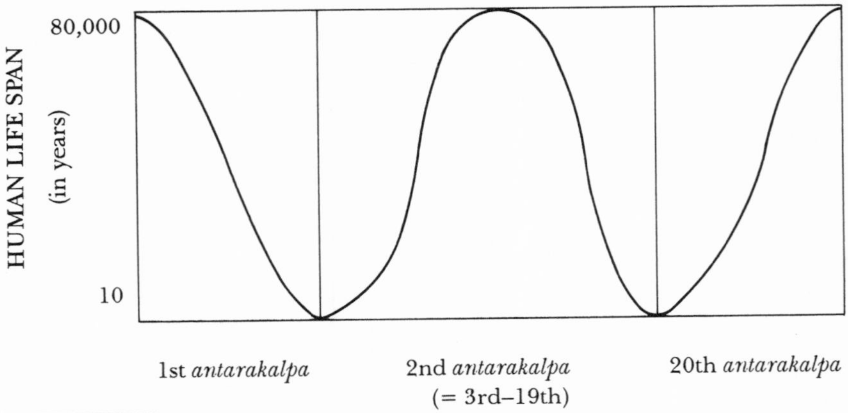

[11] Strictly speaking, the Buddhist model should be described as consisting of eighteen complete phases and two partial ones, since the first *antarakalpa* involves only the second half of the curve (the descent from the peak of the cycle to the nadir), while the twentieth involves only the reverse (the ascent from the nadir to the peak).

The kalpa begins at the zenith, with the life span of human beings at its height (80,000 years).[12] By the end of the first *antarakalpa*, however, the process has reached its nadir, and human life expectancy is reduced to just ten years. Conditions in the physical world evolve in tandem, ranging from ease and abundance at the zenith to war and starvation at the bottom. What is noteworthy in this scheme is that the Buddhist system—unlike the Hindu one—involves alternating phases of improvement and degeneration. The Buddhist system is thus genuinely an "oscillating" one, involving periods of both progress and decline.[13]

A comparison with the corresponding Hindu diagram is instructive, for the two schemes are strikingly different:

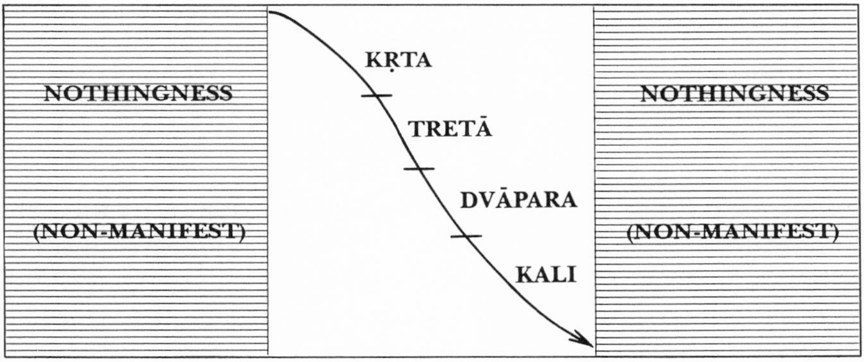

Unlike its Buddhist counterpart, the Hindu model consists exclusively of periods of decline, comprising a series of four phases or *yugas* at the end of which the world is destroyed.[14] A period of

---

[12] The *Abhidharmakośa* (ch. 3, §91a–b) states that the human life span at the beginning of the kalpa of the duration of renovation is infinite in duration; at subsequent peaks within that kalpa, however, it reaches a maximum of only 80,000 years (§91b–92b).

[13] The Jaina cosmology is similar to that of the Buddhists, involving phases of both rise and decline. For an overview of the system see Padmanabh S. Jaini, *The Jaina Path of Purification* (Berkeley: University of California Press, 1979), 30–32.

[14] The names of these ages are said to be based on the names of the four possible throws in an Indian dice game, from the best throw (*kṛta*) to the worst (*kali*). On the meaning of the term *yuga* and the names of these four periods as denoting gambling throws see Mahāmahopādhyāya Pandurang Vaman Kane, *History of Dharmaśāstra*, vol. 3 (Poona: Bhandarkar Oriental Research Institute, 1946), 886ff.

nothingness (or non-manifestation) follows, succeeded by another period of continual decline.[15]

With these models in mind we can return to our two narrative traditions, which can easily be accommodated within the overall Buddhist scheme. In the *Aggañña-suttanta* we have an account that corresponds to the beginnings of the *kalpa* of renovation, from the time of the repopulating of this universe to the election of the first human king. In the *Cakkavatti-sīhanāda-suttanta*, by contrast, we enter the story with a *kalpa* of the duration of renovation already in progress, and a wheel-turning king on the throne. Though the *Aggañña-suttanta* could theoretically fit within either the Hindu or the Buddhist model (since it deals only with a period of decline), the *Cakkavatti-sīhanāda-suttanta* can be accommodated only within the Buddhist framework, as its story proceeds in continuous fashion from the peak of one cycle to the nadir and then gradually upward, culminating at the peak of the next.

All three of these Buddhist traditions relate (either in whole or in part) a tale of the progressive evolution and devolution of the cosmos. What is surprising, however—since these are, after all, Buddhist texts—is that they are singularly devoid of Buddhist imagery. In particular, it is striking that not one of these texts includes any reference to the historical Buddha Śākyamuni. The *Aggañña-suttanta* makes no mention of *any* Buddha, while in the *Cakkavatti-sīhanāda-suttanta* only Maitreya makes an appearance at the end. In the cosmology section of the *Abhidharmakośa* the appearance of Buddhas in general is considered, but the historical Buddha himself is not mentioned. One is tempted to conclude that even the life of an enlightened being is simply dwarfed by events on this scale.

This cosmological scheme is not, however, the only framework within which Buddhists have formulated their understanding of history. Far more common in the Buddhist literature is another

---

[15] The diagram given here is based on the older of two systems found in Hindu sources, that of the epic literature (*Rāmāyaṇa* and *Mahābhārata*). In the later *purāṇa* literature a series of 1,000 *mahāyuga* (great *yuga*)—each consisting of the series of four *yuga*s listed above—before the world is finally destroyed. This system thus presupposes a sudden shift from the nadir (*kali yuga*) to the zenith (golden age, or *kṛta yuga*) at the end of each four-*yuga* cycle, a possibility that would seem to have offered fuel for apocalyptic speculations. This possibility was apparently not realized, however, in Hindu cosmological thought.

organizing framework: the sequential appearance of Buddhas in the world.

BUDDHOLOGICAL TRADITIONS

The earliest Buddhist tradition may well have known of only one Buddha. The charismatic presence of the historical Buddha Śākyamuni no doubt overshadowed, during his own lifetime, both the memory and the anticipation of other enlightened beings. Within a century or two after his death, however, a group of "previous Buddhas" had been assimilated into his lineage. Thus by the time of King Aśoka (r. circa 268–232 BCE) at the latest we find evidence that Śākyamuni was believed to have been preceded, albeit in the distant past, by others of his kind. In one of his inscriptions Aśoka refers to enlarging the stūpa of the Buddha Konākamana (Skt. Konākamuni or Kanakamuni),[16] providing our first datable reference to the existence of such beliefs. A variety of lists of Buddhas of the past—some belonging to particular Buddhist schools, some crossing sectarian boundaries—can be found in the canonical sources. The following are the best known of these lineage accounts.

SEVEN BUDDHAS OF THE PAST

One of the most widespread traditions concerning the existence of other Buddhas holds that Śākyamuni had six predecessors like himself. The *locus classicus* for this tradition is the *Mahāpadāna-suttanta*, a text found in the Pāli canon as well as in a number of Chinese translations.[17] Here the careers of these seven Buddhas

---

[16] See Jules Bloch, ed. and trans., *Les inscriptions d'Asoka* (Paris: Société d'Édition "Les Belles Lettres," 1950), 158.

[17] Translated as "The Sublime Story" by Rhys Davids, though the precise meaning of the term *apadāna* (Skt. *avadāna*) remains a matter of dispute. (For an early discussion of this issue see J. S. Speyer, ed., *Avadānaçataka, Bibliotheca Buddhica*, vol. 3 [1902–06, repr. Osnabrück: Biblio Verlag, 1970], vol. 3(2), i–xiv.) The Pāli text is contained in the *Dīghanikāya* (text no. 14), and has been translated into English by T. W. Rhys Davids, *Dialogues of the Buddha, Part 2*, 4–41. Chinese translations are found in the *Dīrghāgama* (T No. 1[1]), in the *Ekottarikāgama* (T No. 125 [48.45]) and in three independent translations (T Nos. 2, 3, and 4). Once again we have versions of this text that span sectarian boundaries, for in addition to the Pāli version of the Theravāda school we have versions that can probably be assigned

are related in terms that are virtually identical, from the manner of their birth to the nature of their enlightenment. Only in minor details—e.g., the names of their parents and the span of their lives—can these figures be individually distinguished. A detailed chart of their life stories is provided by Rhys Davids;[18] we may use only a schematic one below. This list is well attested in the Pāli canon,[19] and is represented in Indian inscriptions and artwork as well.[20] The list subsequently gained some currency in East Asian Buddhism, despite the availability of later Mahāyāna alternatives.[21]

NAME[22]	PERIOD OF EXISTENCE	LIFE SPAN
Vipaśyin	91 kalpas ago	80,000 years
Śikhin	31 kalpas ago	70,000 years
Viśvabhū	31 kalpas ago	60,000 years
Krakucchanda	in the present kalpa	40,000 years
Kanakamuni	in the present kalpa	30,000 years
Kāśyapa	in the present kalpa	20,000 years
Śākyamuni	in the present kalpa	100 years

to the Dharmaguptaka (*Dīrghāgama*) and Mahāsāṃghika (*Ekottarikāgama*) schools. The text is not included in the Tibetan canon.

[18] In his translation of the *Mahāpadāna-suttanta* (see above, n. 17), 6–7.

[19] In addition to the *Mahāpadāna-suttanta* the list appears in the *Āṭānāṭiya-sutta* (*Dīghanikāya*, iii, 195–96; for the English see Rhys Davids, *Dialogues of the Buddha*, vol. 3, 189–90).

[20] For an analysis of this list see J. Vogel, "The Past Buddhas and Kāśyapa in Indian Art and Epigraphy," in *Asiatica, Festschrift Friedrich Weller* (Leipzig: Harrassowitz, 1954), 808–16.

[21] See INAGAKI Hisao, *A Dictionary of Japanese Buddhist Terms* (Kyoto: Nagata Bunshōdō, 1984), 164 s.v. *kako shichibutsu*. This list should not be confused with another list of seven Buddhas, also current in East Asia (but only in Mahāyāna traditions), who represent various forms of Bhaiṣajya-guru (see Mochizuki, *Bukkyō daijiten*, vol. 2, 1919–1920 s.v. *shichibutsu yakushi hō*).

[22] The names are given here in their Sanskrit forms. The standard Pāli spellings are: Vipassi, Sikhi, Vessabhu, Kakusandha, Konāgamana, Kassapa, and Gotama.

TWENTY-FIVE BUDDHAS OF THE PAST

An extended version of this list, totalling twenty-five Buddhas in all, subsequently appeared in the Pāli tradition. In the *Buddhavaṃsa* we find an account of the careers of each of them, from Dīpaṃkara to Gotama, the historical Buddha.[23] This list of twenty-five Buddhas, however, appears to be unknown outside the Theravāda school, and may well have been formulated in competition with the Jainas. Since the latter had a well-established list of twenty-four enlightened teachers or *Tīrthaṅkaras*,[24] we are tempted to conclude that this aberrant list of twenty-five was the fruit of a Buddhist attempt at keeping up with the Jainas.

Whatever the origins of the list of twenty-five Buddhas, however, it is structurally identical to the list of seven: that is, all the Buddhas included in the list are located in the past, with the final place given to Śākyamuni. The center of gravity of the tradition thus remains firmly in the past, with no attention to the future whatsoever.

FIVE BUDDHAS OF THE *BHADRAKALPA*

Sometime afterwards, however, at a point that is difficult to date with precision, the standard list of seven Buddhas was subjected to a far more significant and widely accepted alteration. The first three—Vipaśyin, Śikhin, and Viśvabhū—were removed from the list, and a future Buddha, Maitreya, was added. This new list, then, consisted of Krakucchanda, Kanakamuni, Kāśyapa, and Śākyamuni, together with the future Buddha Maitreya. At the same time a new qualifier was added, for these five were now described as the Buddhas of the "good eon," or *bhadrakalpa*.

This list, like that of the original seven, appears to have been accepted across sectarian boundaries, for it became standard in the Theravāda tradition[25] and also appears in the *Mahāvastu*, a work of

---

[23] For an English translation see I. B. Horner, trans., *Buddhavaṃsa* (London: Pali Text Society, 1975).

[24] For a discussion of the historicity of this list see Padmanabh S. Jaini, *The Jaina Path of Purification*, 32–34. A complete list of the names of the twenty-four *Tīrthaṅkaras* is given in Walther Schubring, *The Doctrine of the Jainas*, 23.

[25] See G. P. Malalasekera, *A Dictionary of Pali Proper Names* (London: Luzac & Co., 1960), vol. 2, 349.

the Lokottaravādin branch of the Mahāsāṃghika.[26] Moreover, this list was to become the basis for the construction of a much longer Mahāyāna lineage, which suggests that it once had currency in Mahāyāna circles as well.[27]

While the Theravāda list of twenty-five Buddhas represented simply an extension of the earlier list of seven, the innovations that produced the list of five Buddhas were far more radical. What we see here, in fact, is the product of three simultaneous shifts: the change from an exclusively past-oriented list to one including both past and future Buddhas; the *abbreviation* of the pantheon (a very unusual event in the history of religions) from seven Buddhas to five; and the positive valuation of the present age, which is described as a good or "auspicious" eon (*bhadrakalpa*). Any one of these changes, taken alone, would be striking; the fact that all three occurred together represents a significant revolution in Buddhist thinking.[28]

---

[26] *Mahāvastu* iii, 243, 279, 330. For an English translation see J. J. Jones, trans., *The Mahāvastu*, vol. 3 (London: Luzac, 1956), 233, 267, 321. In the first of these instances the five *bhadrakalpika* Buddhas are embedded within a much longer (and quite chaotic) list; in the second, the text clearly contained a straightforward reference to the five Buddhas of the *bhadrakalpa*, but has been emended to state (after a description of the appearance of five Buddha-seats) "in an auspicious *kalpa* [*bhadrakalpa*] a thousand Buddhas must arise" (322). For a discussion of the problems with the text at this point see Jones, p. 321, n. 7, and p. 322, nn. 1–2.

[27] See the following section for a discussion of the "one thousand Buddhas of the *bhadrakalpa*."

[28] The source(s) of the idea of the five Buddhas of the *bhadrakalpa* will probably never be known with certainty. Several possible clues to its origins, however, are worth our attention. First of all, the optimism inherent in the term *bhadrakalpa* itself is uncharacteristic of Indian thought, which—as we have seen—generally describes the present as a degenerate age, on a downward course from the golden age that existed in the distant past. Second, the inclusion of a future Buddha in the list indicates a greater orientation toward the future than was typical of Indian religion before this time. While the Hindus, like the Buddhists, eventually added a future figure to their list—in this case, a future avatar of the deity Viṣṇu—there is every reason to believe that they did so in imitation of the Buddhists, whose future-oriented system thus remains to be explained. Finally, while the number seven has a long history of use in religious contexts in India (e.g., as the number of the ancient sages or *ṛṣi*), the number five is far less common in religious formulations. The fact that ancient Iranian religion (at least from the time of Zoroaster) is characterized by a positive attitude toward this world and an explicit orientation toward the future (including the expectation of a religious teacher to appear in a future golden age) suggests that we might consider the possibility of Iranian input into the *bhadrakalpa* scheme. (Maitreya himself has long been suspected of Iranian

ONE THOUSAND BUDDHAS OF THE *BHADRAKALPA*

With the introduction of the future Buddha Maitreya, the lineage of Buddhas was for the first time freed of any historical limitations. Now completely open-ended—at least with respect to the future—the *bhadrakalpa* system was free to expand with the addition of other Buddhas to the list.

And expand it did. In the hands of the Mahāyānists the system of five Buddhas was transformed (apparently all at once, for we have no evidence of any intermediate developments) into a list of one thousand, all but four of whom were still to appear in this age.[29] The center of gravity of the system, once planted so firmly in the past, has now shifted definitively into the future. The well-known "cave of the thousand Buddhas" at Tun-huang and the countless references to the "one thousand *bhadrakalpika* Buddhas" in the Mahāyāna sūtras are evidence of the widespread acceptance of this new formulation.[30]

---

ancestry by some scholars; for references to this controversy see Nattier, "The Meanings of the Maitreya Myth," 45, n. 51.) Finally, the number five is used far more often in Iranian than in Indian religious imagery (though this is most prominent in the Manichaean system, which is too late for our purposes). The system of five Buddhas reappears much later in the list of the so-called *dhyāni*-Buddhas of Vajrayāna Buddhism, who are likewise suspected of being influenced by an Iranian milieu.

[29] Hence the enigmatic references to the "996 bodhisattvas of the *bhadrakalpa*" found in some Mahāyāna texts, when the emphasis is placed only on those (future) Buddhas who are still to come.

[30] The major text detailing the careers of each of these Buddhas is the *Bhadrakalpika-sūtra*, no longer extant in Sanskrit but preserved in Tibetan (Peking No. 762) and Chinese (T No. 425) translations. A polyglot listing (in Manchu, Chinese, Sanskrit, Tibetan, and Mongolian) of the names of the 1,000 Buddhas has been edited by Friedrich Weller as *Tausend Buddhanamen des Bhadrakalpa* (Leipzig: Asia Major, 1928). A peculiar variant of this Mahāyāna tradition is seen in the *Karuṇāpuṇḍarīka-sūtra*, in which 1,004 (not 1,000) Buddhas of the *bhadrakalpa* are anticipated (see YAMADA Isshi, ed., *Karuṇāpuṇḍarīka, The White Lotus of Compassion* [New Delhi: Heritage Publishers, 1989], vol. 1, 95 and vol. 2, 210, lines 13–14). The Tibetan tradition apparently had access to a version of the *Karuṇāpuṇḍarīka-sūtra* in which 1,005 Buddhas of the *bhadrakalpa* were mentioned; see Bu-ston's *Chos-'byung*, E. Obermiller, trans., *History of Buddhism (Chos-hbyung) by Bu-ston*, Part I (Heidelberg: Otto Harrassowitz, 1931, 91). The same tradition was apparently known in Khotan, for it appears in a text that is preserved only in Tibetan but is certainly of Khotanese origin (see "The Prophecy of the Arhat of Khotan," translated in F. W. Thomas, *Tibetan Literary Texts and Documents Concerning Chinese Turkestan*, vol. 1 [London: Royal Asiatic Society, 1935], 79). Yet another variant

Even in this greatly elaborated system, however, it is striking that the basic concept of what a "Buddha" is has remained unchanged. For the Buddhas of the *bhadrakalpa* system—whether five or one thousand in number—are not in any sense transcendent, but simply repetitions (even clones) of Śākyamuni himself. They are, in other words, simply human beings, who will rediscover the same truths in the distant future as have other Buddhas in the past. The system is thus still a lineage of historical (i. e., earthly) Buddhas, with no celestial Buddhas or bodhisattvas whatsoever.

Thus while it is typical of the Mahāyāna to expand the number of Buddhas, no distinctively Mahāyāna ideas concerning "Buddha-nature" have been introduced. We find here no reference to the *dharmakāya* or *sambhogakāya*, for example, nor are any of these Buddhas (past or future) seen as emanations from other worlds. Nor do we find anything to suggest that more than one of these Buddhas can function simultaneously; rather, they are clearly sequential, with many eons separating the appearance of one Buddha from the next. In this sense the *bhadrakalpa* scheme is continuous with its predecessors, assuming the appearance of only one (quite human) Buddha at a time.

COSMOS AND BUDDHOLOGY: INTEGRATING THE SYSTEMS

It is likely that the stories of the rise and decline of the cosmos, on the one hand, and of the appearance of Buddhas, on the other, arose in quite separate places and times. Yet for the living Buddhist communities that inherited both of these frames of reference, the

---

appears almost exclusively in Sarvāstivādin works from Central Asia. Here we have a list of five hundred Buddhas of the *bhadrakalpa*, of which 496 are yet to come. See for example Şinasi Tekin, ed. and trans., *Maitrisimit*, vol. 1 (Berlin: Akademie Verlag, 1980), 44, lines 11–16. The same figure appears in a group of Buddhist confession fragments from the same region; see Jan Nattier, ed. and trans., "*Kšanti qïlmaq nom bitig*, An Uighur Buddhist Confession Text for Laity" (unpublished manuscript, 1974). The only non-Uighur text in which the figure of 500 Buddhas has yet been identified is the *Ch'i fo fu-mu hsing-tzu ching* 七佛父母姓字經, translated into Chinese during the Former Wei dynasty (240–254 CE); see T No. 4, 1.159b14–15, where it is stated that "in this *bhadrakalpa* there will be a full five hundred Buddhas" (是披地羅劫中當有兩五百佛, where the character *liang* 兩 is certainly an error for *man* 滿).

task was to integrate the two. There is no single result of this process, but two major variants can be distinguished: the Nikāya Buddhist model, on the one hand, and the Mahāyāna model on the other.

For the Mahāyānists, we are now in the first *antarakalpa* of a kalpa of the duration of renovation. From the beginning of that kalpa (when human life was at its peak) until the present, four Buddhas (including Śākyamuni) have appeared. The fifth, Maitreya, will appear at the peak of the next (second) *antarakalpa*; the remaining 995 will presumably appear during the following cycles. The Nikāya Buddhist sources, by contrast, assume that the evolution of the present kalpa of the duration of renovation is considerably farther along. According to the Chinese *Dīrghāgama* (generally associated with the Dharmaguptaka school), the Sanskrit *Avadānaśataka* (a Sarvāstivāda text), and the (Theravādin) *Dīghanikāya* (ii,3), the first four Buddhas of the *bhadrakalpa* have appeared during the ninth, not the first, *antarakalpa*. Others place Krakucchanda in the sixth, Kanakamuni in the seventh, Kāśyapa in the eighth, and Śākyamuni in the ninth *antarakalpa* (the first five *antarakalpa*s thus being devoid of Buddhas). Maitreya, in any case, appears in the tenth.[31] For both Nikāya and Mahāyāna Buddhists, then, the immediate context in which we find ourselves is the following:

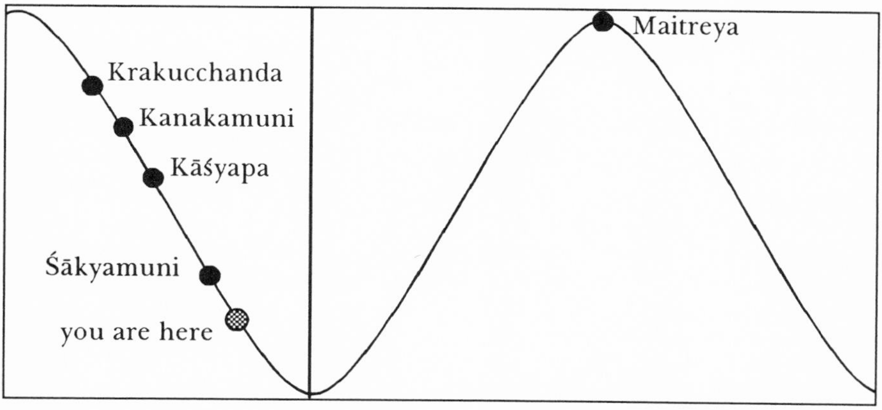

[31] All references given in this paragraph are taken from La Vallée Poussin's notes to chapter 3 of the *Abhidharmakośa*, in vol. 2 of his translation, 192–93, note 2.

Thus while there has been no unanimity among Buddhist scholars as to our exact location within the current *mahākalpa*, there is a consensus as to at least two things: first, that several Buddhas have already appeared during the present kalpa of the duration of renovation, of whom the most recent is Śākyamuni; and second, that we are now in the lower reaches of a decline cycle, which must be completed before the upward cycle can begin. In the distant future we can look forward to the appearance of Maitreya, when the next peak of the cycle has been reached.[32] In the meantime, however, what awaits us is an extended period of decline.

---

[32] The date of his advent is placed at approximately 5.6 billion years from now (variant: 560 million years) by Buddhist commentators.

Chapter Three

The Timetables of Decline

GIVEN THE ASSUMPTIONS outlined in the preceding chapter, it is perhaps not surprising that most Buddhists since the time of Śākyamuni have seen themselves as living in a period of decline. What *is* surprising, however—at least to the outside observer—is that Buddhist writers have also predicted not just the decline, but the eventual demise, of the Buddhist religion itself.[1]

One could argue, of course, that such a decline is implicit not only in the grand theories of cosmic devolution that we have just examined, but in the basic teachings of Buddhism themselves. For it is one of the cardinal tenets of the Buddhist religion that all compounded things are inherently transitory (*anitya*), and from this perspective the Buddhist anticipation of the decline of the Dharma

---

[1] There is an extensive secondary literature on the origins and development of the Buddhist concept of decline. Some of the most important studies, in chronological order, are Jean Przyluski, *La légende de l'empereur Açoka* (Paris: Paul Geuthner, 1923), 161–85; YAMADA Ryūjō, "Mappō shisō ni tsuite," *Indogaku bukkyōgaku kenkyū*, 4/2 (1956), 361–70; Étienne Lamotte, *Histoire du bouddhisme indien* (Louvain: Institut Orientaliste, 1958), 210–22; YAMADA Ryūjō, "Kōki kyōten no haikei," in his *Daijō bukkyō seiritsu ron josetsu* (Kyoto: Heirakuji Shoten, 1959); KAZUE Kyōichi, *Nihon no mappō shisō* (Tokyo: Kōbundō, 1961), 1–38; KUMOI Shōzen, "Hōmetsu shisō no genryū," in ŌCHŌ Enichi, ed., *Hokugi bukkyō no kenkyū* (Kyoto: Heirakuji Shoten, 1970), 287–97; David W. Chappell, "Early Forebodings of the Death of Buddhism," *Numen* 27 (1980), 122–53; James B. Hubbard, "Salvation in the Final Period of the Dharma: The Inexhaustible Storehouse of the San-chieh-chiao" (Ph.D. thesis, University of Wisconsin, 1986), 10–48; Jackie Stone, "Seeking Enlightenment in the Last Age: *Mappō* Thought in Kamakura Buddhism," *The Eastern Buddhist*, n.s. 18/1 (1985), 28–56 (Part 1) and 18/2, 35–64 (Part 2); and KAJIYAMA Yūichi, *Shinran*, vol. 22 of NAGAO Gajin, YANAGIDA Seizan, and KAJIYAMA Yūichi, eds., *Daijō butten (Chūgoku Nihon)* (Tokyo: Chūō Kōronsha, 1987), 314–34.

is not at all unexpected. Rather, it is merely a corollary, a "special theory" of the transitoriness of Buddhism, derived from the general theory of the transitoriness of everything.

Whatever the source of their primary inspiration, Buddhist beliefs in the finite duration of Buddhism are quite evident in the canonical scriptures. With relentless consistency, Buddhist writers have predicted the eventual disappearance of their own religion, offering explicit timetables for its extinction. In this chapter we will survey some of the forms these predictions have taken, beginning with the chronologies offered by Buddhist writers for their religion's eventual demise.

Forebodings of the eventual extinction of the Dharma are found even in the earliest layers of Buddhist literature. Doubtless the first distinction made by followers of the Buddha was between the "golden age" of their teacher's own lifetime and the less-than-ideal period following his death. Before long, however, there arose the belief that the Dharma would endure only for a fixed period of time, after which the Buddhist teachings would disappear from the face of the earth. The timetables associated with this tradition have varied widely, ranging from a minimum of five hundred years to a maximum of more than 10,000. We will survey them here in the order of their duration, considering for each one in turn the evidence for the date of its appearance.

500 YEARS

The earliest traditions offering specific figures for the duration of the Dharma predict that the Buddhist religion will endure for only five hundred years after the Buddha's death. This statement is generally intertwined with a story that the Buddhist teachings would have survived for a full 1,000 years, were it not for the Buddha's decision to admit women to the monastic order. One of the best known of these passages is found in the Theravādin canon, in the section dealing with Buddhist monastic rules:

> If, Ānanda, women had not retired from household life to the houseless one, under the Doctrine and Discipline announced by the Tathāgata, religion, Ānanda, would long endure; a thousand years would the Good Doctrine abide. But since, Ānanda, women have now retired from household life to the houseless one, under the Doctrine and Discipline announced by the

Tathāgata, not long, Ānanda, will religion endure; but five hundred years, Ānanda, will the Good Doctrine abide.[2]

The Buddha goes on to make a number of unflattering analogies, comparing the effect on the sangha of the presence of women to that of mildew on a field of rice, or rust on the sugarcane plant.

Were this story an isolated occurrence found only in a single version of the Buddhist canon, we might be tempted to dismiss it as representing the views only of a single disgruntled (and misogynist) monk. The story is anything but isolated, however: in addition to several occurrences in the Theravāda literature,[3] it appears in texts belonging to the Dharmaguptaka,[4] Mahīśāsaka,[5] Haimavata,[6] and Sarvāstivāda[7] schools, as well as in two sūtras whose sectarian affinity is uncertain.[8]

What is noteworthy about this story — in addition to the rather disheartening information it conveys about the status of women in at least some segments of the early Buddhist community[9] — is that the reference to the nuns as the source of the shortened life span of the Dharma and the figure of five hundred years for its total duration virtually always occur together.[10] We may surmise, therefore, that these two elements entered the Buddhist tradition together.

---

[2] *Vinaya, Cullavagga* X, 1, 6. English translation from Henry Clarke Warren, *Buddhism in Translations* (1896; repr. New York: Atheneum, 1968), 447.

[3] In addition to the version of the story found in the Theravāda Vinaya (cited in the previous note), this tradition occurs in the Pāli *Aṅguttara-nikāya* (IV, 278) and in the *Milindapañha* (IV, i, 55–61).

[4] Found in the Dharmaguptaka Vinaya, preserved only in Chinese translation (T No. 1428, 22.923c9).

[5] In the Mahīśāsaka Vinaya, preserved only in Chinese (T No. 1421, 22.186a14).

[6] In the **Vinaya-Mātṛkā* (*P'i-ni mu ching* 毘尼母經, T No. 1463, 24.818c4). The text is generally associated with the Haimavata school (see Lamotte, *Histoire du bouddhisme indien*, 212).

[7] In the Sarvāstivādin *Madhyamāgama* (*Chung a-han ching* 中阿含經), preserved only in Chinese translation (T No. 26, 1.607b9).

[8] See the *Ch'ü-t'an-mi chi-kuo ching* 瞿曇彌記果經 (T No. 60, 1.857c29) and the *Chung pen-ch'i ching* 中本起經 (T No. 196, 4.159b8). Both texts exist only in Chinese translation.

[9] For a recent discussion of this issue see Alan Sponberg, "Attitudes toward Women and the Feminine in Early Buddhism," in José Ignacio Cabezón, ed., *Buddhism, Sexuality and Gender* (forthcoming, 1991).

[10] The only exception seems to be a Mahāyāna scholastic text, the *Ta chih-tu lun* 大智度論 attributed to Nāgārjuna, in which the figure of five hundred years occurs without any mention of the nuns (T No. 1509, 25.68a16).

What, then, can we say about the chronology of this tradition? Are we to assume that it should be attributed to the Buddha himself, or was it introduced some centuries later? Modern scholars have generally been reluctant to accept this pronouncement as representing the words of the Buddha, finding it more reasonable to assume that it emerged in misogynist circles sometime well after the Buddha's death.[11] Until now, however, no one has succeeded in marshalling any concrete evidence to support this preference.

A close look at the extant versions of this story, however, provides important evidence concerning its date. As we have seen, the story is contained in scriptures belonging to a number of the Nikāya schools. It does not, however, appear in all of them. In the diagram on the following page, showing the genealogy of the early Buddhist schools, those schools in whose scriptures the nuns are blamed for the diminished life span of the Dharma are underlined.[12] It is immediately evident that the results are asymmetrical: all the extant versions of this story belong to schools on the

[11] A notable exception is I. B. Horner, who appears to accept the authenticity of this tradition. See her *Women Under Primitive Buddhism* (New York: E.P. Dutton and Co., 1930), 103–13. For the majority view—that these words are not those of the Buddha—see for example Edward J. Thomas, *The Life of the Buddha as Legend and History* (New York: Alfred A. Knopf, 1927), 109–10, with further reference to M. E. Lulius van Goor, *De Buddhistische Non* (Leiden, 1915). A more recent treatment of the subject, focusing primarily on the Mahāyāna sources, is Diana Paul's *Women in Buddhism*, 2nd ed. (Berkeley, CA: Asian Humanities Press, 1985).

[12] As Kajiyama has recently pointed out (*Shinran*, 321), all versions of the story save one agree that the nuns were responsible for an abbreviation of the life span of Buddhism from 1,000 to 500 years. The Dharmaguptaka version alone claims simply that "if women had not become nuns [lit. 'left home in the Buddha-Dharma'], the Dharma would have lasted long, [i.e.,] five hundred years" (T No. 1428, 22.923c9–11), thus implying that the actual duration will be even shorter, though no figure for this abbreviated duration is given. According to Kajiyama the Dharmaguptaka version should therefore be considered the oldest, since the life span it proposes is shorter (and therefore presumably more primitive) than that contained in the other versions. The diagram given on p. 31, however, suggests that we should regard this proposal with some skepticism. A more reasonable explanation might be that the extant Dharmaguptaka account is the result of an error in textual transmission, in which an original version reading "if women had not become nuns, the Dharma would long endure, [for 1,000 years; but because women have become nuns, the Dharma will only endure] for 500 years" was shortened by the inadvertent omission of the material in brackets. The use of repetition and parallelism in the Indian versions of this tradition (cf. the passage from the *Cullavagga* cited above, pp. 28–29) could easily lead to such a copying error.

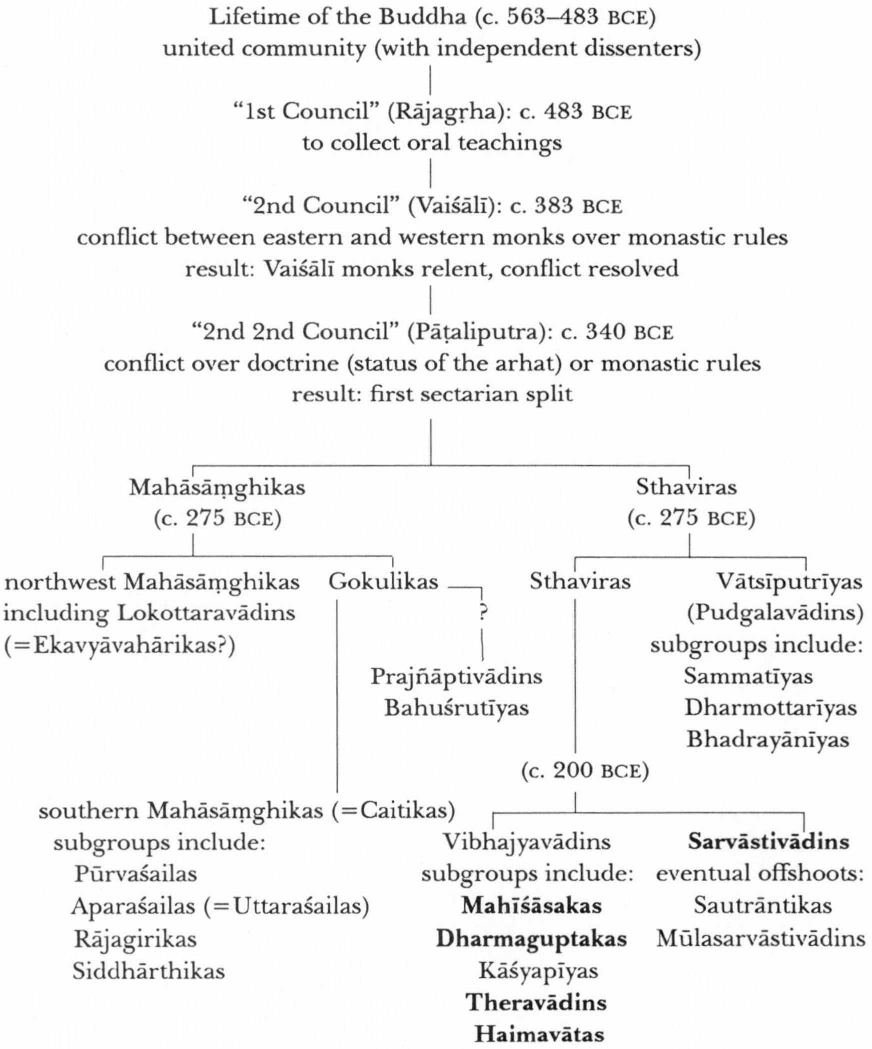

Schematic diagram of the filiation of Buddhist sects (the so-called "Eighteen Schools"). Schools in bold print are those in whose surviving literature a version of the tradition blaming the community of nuns for the shortened lifespan of the Dharma has been identified. (No literature from the undifferentiated Sthavira group has survived.) Data in this diagram is based on Edward Conze, *Buddhist Thought in India* (1962; repr. Ann Arbor: University of Michigan Press, 1970), especially pp. 119 and 195, and André Bareau, *Les sectes bouddhiques du petit véhicule* (Saigon: École Française d'Extrême-Orient, 1955). All dates are tentative, and are based on the "long chronology" that places the Buddha's death in 483 BCE.

Sthavira side of the family tree. Not a single occurrence of this tradition has been identified in the surviving literature of any of the Mahāsāṃghika schools.

This is, of course, to some extent an argument from silence, since only a small percentage of the literature of the Nikāya schools has come down to us.[13] Nonetheless, the striking pattern exhibited by the surviving literature does suggest that the idea of blaming the early demise of the Dharma on the nuns developed sometime after the initial sectarian division between the Sthavira and Mahāsāṃghika schools, but before any further subdivisions within the Sthavira branch had taken place.[14] According to the best estimates of modern scholarship, this initial division took place roughly a century and a half after the death of the Buddha, while the division between the Vibhajyavādin and Sarvāstivādin branches occurred nearly a century and a half later.[15] The date of the emergence of

---

[13] In addition to the Buddhist Hybrid Sanskrit *Mahāvastu*, which refers to itself (despite its evidently non-regulatory content) as a "Vinaya text of the Lokottaravādin school" (see Jones, *The Mahāvastu*, vol. 1, pp. xi, 3), extant Mahāsāṃghika literature includes a (genuine) Vinaya text preserved in Chinese (T No. 1425), Sanskrit fragments of the same text discovered in Tibet in 1937 (translated in Charles S. Prebish, *Buddhist Monastic Discipline* [University Park/London: Pennsylvania State University Press, 1975], 42–112), and a portion of the sūtra section of the canon, the *Ekottarikāgama*, likewise preserved only in Chinese (T No. 125). These are precisely the types of literature in which we do find the story of the nuns connected with the decline of the Dharma in the canons of other schools; thus the absence of this tradition from the extant Mahāsāṃghika sources is an important indication that such a tradition was not current in these schools.

[14] The quantity of the surviving literature does not allow us to determine whether the story emerged before or after the split that resulted in the emergence of the Vātsīputrīya branch (c. 275 BCE). The only surviving texts that can be attributed with certainty to a sect of the Vātsīputrīya group are an Abhidharma text found in Tibet (announced as forthcoming by G. Tucci in *Serie Orientale Roma*, vol. 9a, but apparently never published) and two documents preserved only in Chinese: a short doctrinal text (T No. 1649) and a brief treatise on Vinaya matters (T No. 1641). Since these are not the sort of writings in which we would expect to find such a tradition preserved, we are not in a position to determine whether the story of the nuns being responsible for the premature demise of the Dharma arose before or after the emergence of the Vātsīputrīya schools.

[15] On the dates of the first sectarian schisms see André Bareau, *Les premiers conciles bouddhiques* (Saigon: École Française d'Extrême-Orient, 1955); Charles S. Prebish, "A Review of Scholarship on the Buddhist Councils," *Journal of Asian Studies*, 33/2 (1974), 239–54; and Charles S. Prebish and Janice J. Nattier, "Mahāsāṃghika Origins: The Beginnings of Buddhist Sectarianism," *History of Religions*, 16 (1977), 237–72.

this tradition should therefore be placed during the period from 340–200 BCE.[16]

"FIVE HUNDRED AFTER-YEARS"

The diversity of sources in which the five-hundred-year timetable occurs shows that this number was long accepted—at least by the Nikāya schools of the Sthavira branch—as the standard one. The number five hundred also appears, however, in certain Mahāyāna texts, where it has been interpreted by East Asian Buddhists (and by a number of modern scholars) in a strikingly different fashion.

One of the best known of these texts is the Sanskrit *Diamond Sūtra* (*Vajracchedikā-prajñāpāramitā-sūtra*), where we find three virtually identical references to a period of five hundred years. In the first of these the Buddha's disciple Subhūti asks (in the translation of Edward Conze) whether there will be any beings who will understand teachings such as those contained in this sūtra "in the future period, in the last time, in the last epoch, in the last five hundred years, at the time of the collapse of the good doctrine."[17]

---

[16] A different date has recently been proposed by Kajiyama, who argues that the tradition blaming the early disappearance of Buddhism on the nuns should be dated (at least in its present form) to approximately five hundred years after the Buddha's death, i.e., around the turn of the millennium (*Shinran*, 321–22). Kajiyama's reasoning is that the story represents an *ex post facto* prophecy, composed at the time of the events it predicts—i.e., at a time when Buddhism was considered to have disappeared, some five hundred years after the Buddha's death. A careful reading of the content of these prophecies, however, suggests that they are directed not toward explaining an already actualized disappearance of Buddhism, but rather toward executing the rather complicated maneuver of simultaneously accounting for the perceived decadence of the sangha and justifying the existence of the increasingly problematic institution of the community of nuns. (For further discussion see Sponberg, "Attitudes toward Women and the Feminine.") Even more telling, though, are two other pieces of data: first, the evidence presented above for the existence of a common Sthavira version of this story prior to the Vibhajyavāda-Sarvāstivāda division (see the diagram on p. 31), which would require a date no later than around 200 BCE; and second, the fact that there is no known instance of a Buddhist writer having composed a text suggesting that the Dharma had already completely disappeared. In fact, all the datable texts attempt to place this disastrous event at a time well in the future, ordinarily at least a few hundred years from the time of composition.

[17] Edward Conze, *Buddhist Wisdom Books* (1958; repr. New York: Harper & Row, 1972), 30. The Sanskrit text reads *anāgate 'dhvani paścime kāle paścime samaye paścimāyāṃ pañcaśatyāṃ saddharmavipralopakāle vartamāne*; see Edward Conze,

The Buddha replies that such beings will indeed exist, and goes on to describe the merits of these bodhisattvas. Three other passages are virtually identical in wording,[18] conveying the same sense of anxiety concerning the "last five hundred years."

But what is meant by the phrase Conze has rendered as "in the last five hundred years" (Skt. *paścimāyāṃ pañcaśatyām*)? In the commentary to his translation Conze states that this figure refers to a timetable consisting of a series of five-hundred-year periods, of which the "last five hundred years" is the fifth:

> It is well known from the scriptures of all schools that after the Buddha's nirvāṇa the Dharma will progressively decline, and that every five hundred years a decisive change for the worse takes place. . . . "The last five hundred years" are the fifth five hundred years, when the Buddhists will be strong in nothing but fighting and reproving, and the Dharma itself becomes practically invisible.[19]

According to Conze, in other words, these passages were composed with a 2,500-year timetable in mind.

Vajracchedikā, Serie Orientale Roma, 13 (Rome, 1957), 30–31 (§6). The corresponding passage in the earliest Chinese translation of the text, done by Kumārajīva at the beginning of the 5th century CE, occurs in T No. 235, 8.749a28.

[18] Conze, *Buddhist Wisdom Books*, 53, 57, 61. For the corresponding Sanskrit text see Conze, *Vajracchedikā*, p. 40, lines 4–5 (§14b), p. 45, lines 13–14 (§16b) and p. 53, lines 16–17 (§21b). Kumārajīva, however, renders these four passages very differently: for the first he has 如來滅後後五百歲 "after the Buddha's extinction, during the five hundred after-years" (8.749a28), for the second 來世後五百歲 "in the future age, during the five hundred after-years" (8.750b5), for the third 於後末世 "in the latter final age" (8.751a1), and for the fourth simply 於未來世 "in the future age" (8.751c17). While it is quite possible that Kumārajīva was improvising beyond the bounds of his Indian text, it is important to point out that the earliest Indian manuscripts (the Gilgit manuscript and the Pargiter manuscript found in Xinjiang) do not agree with the most developed Sanskrit text, upon which Conze's translation is based. In particular, the references to the "latter age" in §§14b and 21b are absent from the Gilgit version (for which see the transcription and translation by Gregory Schopen in Luis O. Gómez and Jonathan A. Silk, eds., *Studies in the Literature of the Great Vehicle: Three Mahāyāna Buddhist Texts* [Ann Arbor: Collegiate Institute for the Study of Buddhist Literature, 1989], 89–131). In §16b the Gilgit manuscript reads *carime kāle paścimāyāṃ paṃcāśatyāṃ varttamānāyām* (see Schopen, 101, folio 7b:1), which may be translated as "in the final time, in the latter fifty- (NB: not 'five hundred') year period." For further discussion of these passages see below, p. 91, n. 89.

[19] Conze, *Buddhist Wisdom Books*, 31.

A number of parallel passages occur in the *Lotus Sūtra* (*Saddharmapuṇḍarīka-sūtra*), in language considerably more varied than that found in the Sanskrit *Diamond Sūtra*.[20] The version of this passage that occurs with the greatest frequency has been translated by H. Kern as follows: "at the end of time, at the end of the period, in the second half of the millennium."[21] In translating the expression *paścimāyāṃ pañcaśatyām* as "in the second half of the millennium," Kern is clearly assuming a timetable different from Conze's. His explanation is the following:

> According to the declaration of the Buddha in *Cullavagga*, X, 1, 6, the true law (*saddhamma*) is to stand a millennium, though at the same time, owing to the institution of female monks, the number of one thousand years should be reduced to half.[22]

For Kern, in other words, this expression refers to a timetable not of 2,500 years, but of 1,000.

Which of these translators, then—if either—is correct? A close look at their sources reveals that there are serious problems with both interpretations. Kern's reading relies on a very loose interpretation of the *Cullavagga*, an interpretation never found (to the best of my knowledge) in the Theravāda commentary literature. Conze's interpretation, on the other hand, is based—though he never says so explicitly—on a timetable found in only one Buddhist sūtra, which in all probability postdates the composition of the *Diamond Sūtra* by at least a century.[23] A more cautious approach

---

[20] One indication, perhaps, of its greater antiquity, since the phrasing has not yet become formulaic.

[21] Skt. *paścime kāle paścime samaye paścimāyāṃ pañcaśatyām vartamānāyāṃ*. For the English translation see H. Kern, *Saddharmapuṇḍarīka or the Lotus of the Good Law* (1884; repr. New York: Dover, 1963), 391, 433, 438, and 439. For the Sanskrit see H. Kern and B. Nanjio, *Saddharmapuṇḍarīka*, Bibliotheca Buddhica, vol. X (1912; repr. Osnabrück: Biblio Verlag, 1970), 420 (lines 13–14), 474 (lines 3–4), 481 (line 6), and 481 (line 10)–482 (line 1). The same phrase (but without the term *vartamānāyāṃ*) appears on p. 475 (line 10) of the Sanskrit text, and is translated identically into English by Kern (434).

[22] See Kern, *Saddharmapuṇḍarīka*, 268, n. 2. The passage in question is the one cited on pp. 28–29 above.

[23] In his commmentary (*Buddhist Wisdom Books*, 31) Conze refers the reader to his *Buddhism: Its Essence and Development* (New York: Harper & Row, 1951), 114–16 for further details. In the latter, however, he does not cite his source, but refers only to "another scripture" in that laconic fashion so exasperatingly familiar to students of Indian and Tibetan Buddhist commentary literature. A careful text-

would begin by considering only what is found in these two texts themselves, before turning elsewhere for clues to their interpretation.

In the *Diamond Sūtra* we have little to go on, for in all four instances this passage appears suddenly, with no necessary connection to the surrounding text. One gets the impression, at least from the Sanskrit texts, that the composer of this sūtra was merely repeating a set of stock phrases adopted from another source.[24]

In the *Lotus Sūtra*, by contrast, references to the "latter age" are phrased in a variety of different ways, and in several cases this phrase is preceded by a mention of the Buddha's entrance into nirvāṇa. In this context another possibility seems evident: that the expression "five hundred years" refers to the period immediately after the death of the Buddha. And in fact the word *paścima* (understood as "last" or "final" by both Conze and Kern) can mean simply "that which follows" something else.[25] Thus in interpreting these passages there is no need to read back into the texts any of the later formalized schemes (to be discussed below) according to which the Dharma will pass through a series of five-hundred-year periods (as Conze has done), or to stretch the meaning of the *Cullavagga* passage beyond what the text seems to allow (as did Kern). Rather, we can retranslate the two texts as follows:

> *Diamond Sūtra*: "in the future time, in the latter age, in the latter period, in the latter five hundred years, when the True Dharma is in the process of decay"

---

critical reading of Conze's discussion, however, reveals that it is based on Lamotte's *Histoire du bouddhisme indien* (214–15), which in turn is a description of the timetable presented in one part of the Chinese *Candragarbha-sūtra* (*Yüeh-tsang fen* 月藏分, T No. 397[15], 13.363a29–b5). This sūtra, however, was not translated into Chinese until the second half of the 6th century, and is unlikely to have been composed much earlier than the 5th. We can therefore discount the possibility that the composer of the *Diamond Sūtra* had such a system in mind. At a later date, however, the *Candragarbha-sūtra* gained such influence (especially in East Asia) that its 2,500-year system was often read back into the *Diamond Sūtra*, the *Lotus Sūtra*, and other such works by commentators. For further discussion see below, pp. 54–56.

24 It is noteworthy that these references to a period of five hundred years are not found in the rest of the Prajñāpāramitā sūtras (in particular, those such as the *Aṣṭasāhasrikā-prajñāpāramitā-sūtra* and the *Ratnaguṇasaṃcayagāthā*, which are known to be older than the *Diamond Sūtra*).

25 See M. Monier-Williams, *Sanskrit-English Dictionary*, 2nd ed. (1899; repr. Oxford: Clarendon, 1964), 612b.

Lotus Sūtra: "after the Tathāgata's death (*parninirvāṇa*), in the latter age, in the latter period, in the latter five hundred years"

In other words, what is probably meant by the expression *paścimāyāṃ pañcaśatyām* in the early Mahāyāna literature is simply "during the five hundred after-years"—or, to borrow an expression used by Sukumar Dutt in another context, "five after-centuries."[26] If this reading is correct, we still find in the early Mahāyāna literature an echo of the earliest timetable for the Dharma's decline. Only five hundred years in all are envisioned, all of which (since this time follows the death of the Buddha) can be viewed in a certain sense as a period of decline.[27]

700 YEARS

The prolonged acceptance of this 500-year timetable in a number of the Nikāya schools (and apparently also in some segments of the Mahāyāna) may be reflected in the fact that virtually all other timetables for the duration of the Dharma are based on the simple multiplication of this figure. Two anomalous traditions, however, seem to deviate from this pattern: the Mahāyāna *Mahāparinirvāṇa-sūtra* and the *Sūtra on the Seven Dreams of Ānanda* both appear to predict that the Dharma will die out after seven hundred years.

Mahāparinirvāṇa-sūtra. There are three versions of the Mahāyāna *Mahāparinirvāṇa-sūtra* in the Chinese Buddhist canon and two

---

[26] See Sukumar Dutt, *The Buddha and Five After-Centuries* (London: Luzac & Co., 1957).

[27] It is also possible, though in my view less likely, that this expression refers to the second of two five-hundred-year periods, as formalized in some of the 1,000-year timetables discussed below. In this case Kern's verdict—though not his line of reasoning—would be vindicated. If this is the case, however, we would have to explain why not a single one of these references to the "five hundred after-years" is ever accompanied by a mention of the longer timetable. A final conclusion on this issue must await the thorough comparative study of all extant versions (in all languages) of the *Diamond* and *Lotus* sūtras, and of other texts that can be identified in which this expression occurs. For a list of all such references to the "latter age" in the *Lotus Sūtra* of Kumārajīva (T No. 262), with parallels in Sanskrit and in the two other Chinese translations, see Jan Nattier, "The *Candragarbha-sūtra* in Central and East Asia" (Ph.D. thesis, Harvard University, 1988), 340–47. Note in particular that there are several interesting divergences in the Chinese translation of Dharmarakṣa (late 3rd–early 4th c. CE).

in the Tibetan;[28] all of them mention events that are to take place seven hundred years after the Buddha's nirvāṇa. It is not entirely clear, however, that what is meant here is the actual demise of the Buddhist Dharma and not merely its decline (a distinction which, as we shall see below, is of considerable importance). The passages in question are the following:

Version 1

> Chinese: "Seven hundred years after my death (*parinirvāṇa*), sinful Māra[29] will gradually ruin (*chü-huai* 沮壞) my True Dharma (*saddharma*)."[30]
>
> Tibetan: "After seven hundred years have passed since my death, the True Dharma will be broken, decayed, and brought to ruin by sinful Māra."[31]

Version 2

> Chinese: "Seven hundred years after my death, sinful Māra will gradually destroy (*huai-luan* 壞亂) my True Dharma."[32]
>
> Tibetan: no equivalent.

Version 3

> Chinese: "Seven hundred years after my death, the Tathāgata's Dharma-teaching will gradually become extinct (*mieh* 滅) in

---

[28] T No. 374 (cf. Pek. No. 787 in the Tibetan canon), translated by Dharmakṣema in the period 414–421 and generally referred to as the "northern edition"; No. 375, a reorganized version of Dharmakṣema's translation produced by Hui-yen and others during the period 424–435, and referred to as the "southern edition"; and No. 376, translated by Fa-hsien during the period 410–418 CE. T No. 377 (translated by Jñānabhadra in 664–665) is not a different version of the sūtra as a whole, but simply a translation of five additional chapters. In the Tibetan translation the content of T No. 377 has been incorporated into Pek. No. 787, which shows that by the time this translation was made these chapters were regarded as an integral part of the sūtra. (Note that Pek. No. 787 was translated into Tibetan from the Chinese; see the colophon in *mdo-sna-tshogs ñu*, 355a4.) One other sūtra by the same name (T No. 390, Pek. No. 789) is an entirely different work, and contains a 1,000-year timetable to be dealt with below.

[29] Māra is the Buddhist devil, though considerably less sinister than his Western counterparts. For a study of his role in Buddhist mythology see Alex Wayman, "Studies in Yama and Māra," *Iranian Journal* 3 (1959), 44–73 (Part 1) and 112–113 (Part 2).

[30] T No. 374, 12.402c26.

[31] Pek. No. 787, *mdo-sna-tshogs ju*, 105b2–3.

[32] T No. 375, 12.643b25–26.

> the following [way]. Māra-made monks will destroy (*huai-luan* 壞亂) the True Dharma."[33]
>
> Tibetan: "When seven hundred years have passed since my death, my teaching will be altered and subverted. At the time when the True Dharma is dying out . . ."[34]

All three of these texts clearly suggest that seven hundred years after the death of the Buddha the Dharma will be in decay, and at first glance it would appear that they are predicting the demise of the Dharma at this point. A closer reading, however, shows that all three versions go on to describe various activities of both evil and good Buddhist believers, suggesting that the Buddhist community will continue to exist for some time. What we have here is certainly a decline prophecy, but these texts should not be construed as offering a clear-cut scenario for the Dharma's demise.

If the figure of seven hundred years is not intended as the date of the Dharma's extinction, what is its function in these texts? Every indication is that what we have here is a genuine *ex post facto* prophecy of the development of problems within the Buddhist sangha. What is particularly interesting in this regard is what these texts identify as evidence of Māra's activities. Though certain moral failings (especially on the part of the monks) are mentioned, issues of doctrine are given greater attention. For the author of this sūtra, belief in the eternity of the Buddha, his exemption from any earthly desires, and the validity of the *vaipulya* sūtras[35] are the litmus-test of the genuine Buddhist. Those who see things otherwise—arguing that the Buddha was born of human parents, enjoyed carnal love with his wife, was subject to change, and did not preach the Mahāyāna sūtras—are no better than devils in disguise. What we have here, in other words, is a fervent defense of the docetic view of the Buddha, introduced by the northwestern Mahāsāṃghika schools and subsequently inherited by certain Mahāyānists.[36]

---

[33] T No. 376, 12.880a23-24.

[34] Pek. No. 788, *mdo-sna-tshogs tu*, 94b2. The Tibetan text reads *dam-pa'i chos nub-pa'i tshe*, which could refer either to the time when the *saddharma* is in the process of declining or to the time when such a decline has already taken place.

[35] The *vaipulya* or "extensive" sūtras are those belonging to the Mahāyāna. The main issue, of course, is not their length, but their distinctive doctrinal content.

[36] In its insistence that the Buddha is eternal and not subject to change and that he only "manifested" a human form (which he had long since transcended) the *Mahāparinirvāṇa-sūtra* is reminiscent both of the *Mahāvastu* (a work of the

Sūtra on the Seven Dreams of Ānanda. If the seven-hundred-year figure does not indicate a prediction of the extinction of the Dharma in the *Mahāparinirvāṇa-sūtra*, there is one little-known text where it would seem that it does. YAMADA Ryūjō has drawn attention to the presence of a seven-hundred-year timetable in the *A-nan ch'i-meng ching* 阿難七夢經 , which contains a timetable for the lifetime of the Dharma consisting of seven periods of one hundred years each.[37]

In this brief and enigmatic text Ānanda experiences a series of seven symbolic dreams and turns to the Buddha for an explanation of their contents. He is told that the seven dreams refer to a variety of events that will take place after the Buddha's death. In order, the significance of the seven dreams is said to be as follows:

1. The good thoughts of the monks will decrease, evil thoughts will increase, and the monks will injure and kill one another.
2. The Buddha's main disciples will follow him into nirvāṇa (here probably meaning simply death rather than enlightenment), and the Buddhist community will be deprived of its leadership (literally, "the eye of sentient beings will be extinguished").
3. Monks will increasingly live in impure places, and will harbor jealousy toward one another; the lay people will observe this and will remonstrate with the monks. The monks will be reborn in hell after their death; the lay people, by contrast, will be reborn in heaven.
4. Lay people will come into the stūpas and monasteries and will criticize the monks; they will destroy stūpas and damage temples.
5. Ānanda will be able to recite all the sūtras without forgetting a single line.

Lokottaravādin, or "transcendentalist," wing of the Mahāsāṃghika school) and of the *Lotus Sūtra*. For a translation of the "southern edition" (T No. 375) of this sūtra into rather choppy English see YAMAMOTO Kosho, *The Mahayana Mahaparinirvana-Sutra*, 3 vols. (Ube City: The Karinbunko, 1973–75). For the prophecy of the decline of the Dharma after 700 years see vol. 1, 159–72.

[37] Cited in his "Mappō shisō ni tsuite," 368. For the text itself see T No. 494, 14.758a–b.

6. False views will become prevalent and will destroy the Buddha-Dharma.
7. 1,470 years after the Buddha's nirvāṇa the mind with which the Buddha's disciples cultivate virtue cannot be shaken by all the evil demons. "The 'seven hairs' [of a lion referred to in the seventh dream]," the text then states, "refers to matters [to take place] after seven hundred years" (七毫者七百歲後事).

And with that, the sūtra comes to a close.

It is easy to see why Yamada concluded that this text contained a prediction of the death of the Dharma after seven hundred years, for that figure is explicitly mentioned in the text and the format of the seven dreams certainly suggests a chronological sequence of seven centuries. Yet the content of the seven dreams makes it clear that they are not arranged in anything resembling chronological order. The death of the Buddha's major disciples (*śrāvaka*s) is mentioned in the second dream, while Ānanda's recital of the sūtras (ordinarily considered to have taken place immediately after the Buddha's death) is not mentioned until the fifth. A decrease in good thoughts among the monks is mentioned in the first dream, yet the explanation of the seventh states that the virtue-cultivating minds of the Buddha's disciples will still be unshaken after 1,470 years. It is not possible, therefore, to interpret these dreams as a series of consecutive one-hundred-year periods.

Neither the *Mahāparinirvāṇa-sūtra* nor the *Sūtra on the Seven Dreams of Ānanda*, then, actually predicts that the Dharma will die out after seven hundred years. That this figure occurs in both texts may well be significant, but it is difficult at this point to recover its meaning. At most, we may speculate that it represents an *ex post facto* prophecy, describing certain elements of decadence and decline that were present in the Buddhist community at a time believed to be seven hundred years after the Buddha's death.[38]

---

[38] If we take this approach, however, it is difficult to explain the reference to "1,470 years after the Buddha's nirvāṇa" in the *A-nan ch'i-meng ching*. Such a specific figure carries all the markings of an *ex post facto* prophecy in itself, and may represent a subsequent revision of an earlier 700-year tradition. If so, it is a revision that also serves to reintroduce an element of optimism into the text, for it points to a time not of decadence in the Buddhist community, but of the unthwarted cultivation of virtue.

1,000 YEARS

In the early years of the Buddhist community the figure of five hundred years given for the duration of the Dharma in a number of scriptural sources must have seemed reasonably generous. Around the first century CE, however—that is, around five hundred years after the death of the Buddha—we begin to find a new version of the prophecy of decline. In certain Sarvāstivāda and Mahāyāna texts the life span of the Dharma is now given not as a mere five hundred years, but rather one thousand, a total sometimes treated as consisting of two "sub-periods" of five hundred years each.

There are some significant differences, however, between the treatment of this new timetable in the Nikāya Buddhist literature, on the one hand, and in Mahāyāna texts on the other. We will begin with a review of the non-Mahāyāna (Nikāya) Buddhist literature in which this timetable occurs, and then compare these formulations with their Mahāyāna counterparts.

NON-MAHĀYĀNA TRADITIONS

Mentions of a 1,000-year life span of the Dharma have been identified to date in ten Nikāya Buddhist texts, most of which are preserved only in Chinese translation. Of these, six are of Sarvāstivādin or Mūlasarvāstivādin authorship,[39] while the sectarian affinity of the remaining four has not been established.[40] Thus,

---

[39] The 1,000-year timetable is found in the *A-yü wang chuan* 阿育王傳 (**Aśokarājāvadāna*, T No. 2042, 50.126b26), translated into Chinese by An Fa-ch'in in 306 CE; the *Tsa a-han ching* 雜阿含經 (*Saṃyuktāgama*, T No. 99, 2.177b23), translated by Guṇabhadra in 435–443; the *Gen-pen shuo i-ch'ieh yu-pu p'i-na-yeh tsa-shih* 根本說一切有部毘奈耶雜事 (the *Vinayakṣudrakavastu* of the Mūlasarvāstivāda school, T No. 1451, 24.405a7), translated by I-ching in 710; the *A-p'i-ta-mo p'i-p'o-sha lun* 阿毘達磨大毘婆沙論 (**Abhidharma-mahāvibhāṣā-śāstra*, T No. 1545, 27.918a6–17), translated by Hsüan-tsang in 656–659; the *Karmaśataka* (preserved only in Tibetan translation; see Pek. No. 1007, *mdo-sna-tshogs su*, 279b1–290b4; and the *Abhidharmakośa*, chapter 8, §39 (for a French translation see La Vallée Poussin, *L'Abhidharmakośa*, vol. 5, 218–21).

[40] The other Nikāya Buddhist texts containing this timetable are the *Chia-she chieh ching* (*Kāśyapa-saṃgīti-sūtra*, T No. 2027, 49.6a7), translated by An Shih-kao during the period 148–170 CE; the *Fo-shih pi-ch'iu Chia-chan-yen shuo fa mei-chin chieh* ("Sūtra on the Extinction of the Dharma, Taught by the Bhikṣu Kātyāyana at the Buddha's Request," T No. 2029, 49.12b26–c1), translator unknown, but the text is mentioned in the *Hsi Chin lu* (265–317 CE); the *Chüan-chi san-tsang chi tsa-*

while it is possible that other Nikāya groups may have made use of this timetable, it clearly had the greatest currency in Sarvāstivādin circles.

In the Sarvāstivāda literature[41] the 1,000-year timetable appears in texts of a wide variety of genres, including the sūtra, vinaya, and *avadāna* literature, as well as in the scholastic commentaries. This wide diffusion assures us that the tradition was indeed well established in Sarvāstivāda circles, regardless of its acceptance by other schools.

In all but one of these Sarvāstivāda sources the number 1,000 appears without reference to any other timetable, including the five-hundred-year prophecy that occurs elsewhere in the Sarvāstivādin canon.[42] In the *Mahāvibhāṣā*, however, the writer acknowledges the currency of that timetable. After citing the story of how the overall duration of the Dharma is to be reduced from 1,000 to 500 years due to the admission of women into the monastic community, the writer continues:

> *Question*: If the *saddharma* will last instead for 1,000 years, why did the Lord give this explanation?
> *Answer*: This really refers to the solidity (*chien-ku* 堅固) of liberation. That is, if women had not been allowed to leave home the solidity of liberation would have lasted for a thousand years. As it is, after five hundred years there will be the solidity

---

tsang chuan ("Account of the Compilation of the Tripiṭaka," T No. 2026, 49.2a16), likewise by an unknown translator, but listed in the *Tung Chin lu* (317–420 CE); and the smaller *Mahāparinirvāṇa-sūtra*, preserved in both Chinese and Tibetan translations (for the Chinese text see T No. 390, 12.1112b–1113c, translated by Hsüan-tsang in 652 CE; for the corresponding Tibetan text see Pek. No. 789, *'Phags-pa yongs-su mya-ngan-las 'das-pa chen-po'i mdo, mdo-sna-tshogs tu,* 157a1–158b8, translated by Kamalagupta and Rin-chen bzang-po (late 10th/early 11th century CE). Of these the last has been characterized by Lamotte as "un petit *Mahāparinirvāṇa* mahāyāniste" (*Histoire du bouddhisme indien*, 213), but these peripheral Mahāyāna elements are found only in the Chinese and not the Tibetan version of the text (see T 12.1112c, 21–22). Since it is virtually certain that these elements are late additions to the text (indeed the entire introductory section in which they are found has no counterpart in the Tibetan), we may conclude that the text was originally produced in a non-Mahāyāna environment.

41 The precise nature of the relationship between the Sarvāstivādins and the Mūlasarvāstivādins has yet to be established. In the following discussion I have dealt with the two schools together, referring to them under the general heading of "Sarvāstivādins."

42 See above, n. 7.

> of precepts, learning (lit. "hearing"), and so on, but not the solidity of liberation.[43]

The text then goes on to offer a second opinion on the meaning of the old tradition concerning the nuns: according to other teachers, what the Buddha meant was that if women were allowed to enter the monastic order but did not obey the eight additional rules (*gurudharmas*) imposed upon them—rules clearly designed to keep them in a subordinate position with respect to men[44]—the *saddharma* would have lasted for only five hundred years. Since these rules were implemented, however, the *saddharma* will remain in the world for a full 1,000 years. It is clear from this discussion that the author of the *Mahāvibhāṣā* was keenly aware of the canonicity of the 500-year timetable, and felt obligated to defend his advocacy of the 1,000-year timetable against this well-established tradition.

The author of the *Mahāvibhāṣā* is alone, however, in confronting this earlier tradition directly. All the other Nikāya Buddhist sources containing the 1,000-year timetable refer to it alone, without opening the Pandora's box of other alternatives. Thus, while there are some interesting variations in these traditions,[45] none of

---

[43] T No. 1545, vol. 27, 918a9–12.

[44] For the Theravāda version of these eight rules see the *Cullavagga*, X,1,4, translated in T W. Rhys Davids and Hermann Oldenberg, *Vinaya Texts*, Part 3 (1885; repr. Delhi: Motilal Banarsidass, 1975), 322–25.

[45] The *Saṃyuktāgama* portrays the Buddha as reflecting, "If I entrust my teachings just to human beings, or just to the gods, they will not last long; but if I entrust them to *both* gods and men, my teachings will endure for a thousand years." This tradition also occurs in the closely related *Karmaśataka*; both texts then go on to relate the prophecy contained in the "Kauśāmbī story," to be described below. The *Abhidharmakośa* appears to entertain the possibility that the Dharma may endure for more than 1,000 years, for it states that "It is said in a general manner that the *saddharma* will last for 1,000 years. But this refers only to the *adhigama* [accomplishment of results]; the *āgama* [scriptures] will last longer." The **Kāśyapa-saṃgīti-sūtra* appears to have reinterpreted the story of the nuns, stating that "the Buddha's *saddharma* was originally supposed to have lasted for a long time, but because [the Buddha] allowed women to leave home and become *śramanas*, it will last for only 1,000 years." The *Aśokāvadāna* states only that when a full 1,000 years have passed, the Dharma will be on the point of becoming extinct; it then launches into the Kauśāmbī story, as in the *Saṃyuktāgama* and *Karmaśataka* accounts. The Mūlasarvāstivāda *Vinaya-kṣudraka-vastu* simply states that the *saddharma* will remain in the world for a full 1,000 years, while the *Chüan-chi san-tsang chi tsa-tsang chuan* states that "the Buddha's Dharma will lessen [*chien* 減 ; could this be a mis-

them offers any other numbers, or any justification for the choice of this figure.

Particularly striking, when we compare these Nikāya Buddhist traditions with their Mahāyāna counterparts, is the fact that only three of them offer any periodization of the 1,000-year timetable. Only the *Mahāvibhāṣā*, the *Prophecy of Kātyāyana*, and the shorter *Mahāparinirvāṇa-sūtra* offer any subdivisions of this total. And no two of these subdivisions are alike. The *Mahāvibhāṣā*, as we have seen, divides the 1,000-year total into two 500-year periods. In the *Prophecy of Kātyāyana*, by contrast, we have a sequence of three 300-year periods, supplemented (apparently) by a final segment of 100 years:

> During [the first] 300 years, many will be liberated; during [the following] 300 years, [they will be able to maintain] learning (*śruta*), precepts (*śīla*), and meditation (*samādhi*); during the [next] 300 years [they will build] Buddha-temples. When 1,000 years have passed [lit. "when one enters 1,000 years"], there will be anger and fighting.[46]

Yet another periodization system is given in the shorter *Mahāparinirvāṇa-sūtra*, where the duration of the Dharma is divided into ten 100-year periods, each of a quality inferior to its predecessor. While the Chinese and Tibetan versions differ in some particulars,[47] the overall outline offered by both versions is as follows. During the first several periods believers are still devoted to the practice and preservation of the Dharma, but as time goes on they become more preoccupied with the externals of the Buddhist tradition rather than its essence. A turn for the worse begins during the seventh and eighth centuries, and during the ninth and tenth periods Buddhist monks turn their attention almost exclusively to worldly activities.

What is striking about these three periodization schemes is that they have nothing at all in common: neither the duration of

---

take for *mieh* 滅 ?] in 1,000 years." For full references to these texts see note 40 above.

[46] T No. 2029, 49.12b25–28. For the last line I have adopted the reading given in note 9 by the Taishō editors; the reading given in the main text, "blue garden preaching" 青宛説 , seems to make little sense.

[47] In general the Tibetan text is more concise and appears to represent an earlier Sanskrit recension than that which served as the basis of the Chinese. For references to the texts themselves see note 40 above.

the sub-periods themselves (one built on 500-year units, another on 300-year units, and the third on units of only a century) nor their contents are the same. We can safely conclude, therefore, that there was no standard system in Nikāya Buddhist circles for subdividing this 1,000-year timetable.

MAHĀYĀNA TRADITIONS

In the Mahāyāna scriptures, by contrast, precisely the opposite is the case. In all four of the Mahāyāna scriptures containing this timetable that have been identified to date,[48] the total figure of 1,000 years appears to be divided into two 500-year periods. Most striking of all, these texts all use the same language to refer to these subdivisions: the first 500-year-period (when it is named at all) is described as that of the true Dharma (*saddharma*), while the second is the period of its semblance (*saddharma-pratirūpaka*). The origin and meaning of these terms will be discussed in detail below;[49] here we will only point out the contexts of their occurrence.

Two of the Mahāyāna texts containing this timetable are sūtras, while the other two occurrences are in the commentary literature. (Interestingly, in this case it is the sūtras that discuss this timetable most explicitly.) What they tell us is the following:

> *Hsien-chieh ching* 賢劫經 (*Bhadrakalpika-sūtra*): "The *saddharma* will last for five hundred years, and likewise the *saddharma-pratirūpaka*."[50]

---

[48] A fifth example of this usage, identified just as this book was going to press, is contained in the *Fo pen-hsing chi ching* 佛本行集經 (T No. 190), translated by Jñanagupta in 587–595 CE; see T 3.672a5–6. While in its present form this text appears to be a Mahāyāna composition, certain resemblances between its content and that of the *Mahāvastu* suggest that parts of the text, at least, may be of Mahāsāṃghika origin. For further discussion see below, chapter 4, note 70.

[49] See chapter 4, "The East Asian Tripartite System."

[50] T No. 425, 14.21a25. Cf. the Tibetan version (Pek. No. 762, vol. 27, *mdo snatshogs* 62 (*i*), 112b2–3: "the *saddharma* [of Śākyamuni Buddha] will remain for a period of five hundred years. And as for [another] period of five hundred years, it will appear as an artifice, like the *saddharma*" (*dam-pa'i chos ni lo lnga-brgya'i bar-du gnas-so // lo lnga-brgya'i bar-du ni dam-pa'i chos ltar bcos-par snang-ngo //*). The intrusive nature of this second period is shown here by the fact that none of the other Buddhas listed has such a second period or dispensation in the lifetime of their teachings; for all of them, only the *saddharma* is mentioned. (Note also that the Tibetan translator was apparently unfamiliar with this second term; the usual Tibetan

Ta-sheng san-chü ch'an-hui ching 大乘三聚懺悔經 ("Mahāyāna Three-Part Repentance Sūtra"); "After my nirvāṇa, the *saddharma* will last for five hundred years; then the *saddharma-pratirūpaka* will last for five hundred years."[51]

Ta chih-tu lun 大智度論 (**Mahāprajñāpāramitā-śāstra*): "Five hundred years after the Buddha's nirvāṇa, during [the time of] *saddharma-pratirūpaka*"[52]

Chung lun 中論 (**Madhyamaka-śāstra*): "after the Buddha's extinction, during the five-hundred-year period of *saddharma-pratirūpaka*"[53]

Here the sūtras specify the length of both periods, while the commentaries tell us only that the period of the *saddharma-pratirūpaka* will be in effect five hundred years after the death of the Buddha (in the case of the *Ta chih-tu lun*), or that it will endure for five hundred years (according to the *Chung lun*). What is consistent throughout this Mahāyāna group, though, is the use of the term *saddharma-pratirūpaka* (Ch. *hsiang-fa* / Jpn. *zōbō* 像法) to refer to the second of two periods of time.[54]

In sum, while the one-thousand-year timetable appears in both Sarvāstivāda and Mahāyāna literature (as well as in other Nikāya Buddhist works whose sectarian origins are uncertain), the practice of dividing this total into two five-hundred-year periods described as the times of the *saddharma* and the *saddharma-pratirūpaka*, respectively, appears to be restricted to the Mahāyāna texts. This suggests, as we shall see in detail below, that the origins of this terminology should be sought in a Mahāyāna milieu.[55]

---

translation of Skt. *saddharma-pratirūpaka*—the presumed original of this expression—is *dam-pa'i chos-kyi gzugs-brnyan*, "reflection of the True Dharma," but here he seems to have understood this expression rather as meaning "an artifice like the True Dharma." For a discussion of the meaning of *saddharma-pratirūpaka* see below.

[51] T No. 1493, 24.1094a16–18.

[52] T No. 1509, 25.681b7–8.

[53] T No. 1564, 30.1b29–c1.

[54] It must be admitted, however, that the text of the *Chung lun* is somewhat ambiguous. It would also be possible to interpret this passage as meaning that the total duration of the Dharma after the Buddha's death—all of which is labeled the *saddharma-pratirūpaka*—will be five hundred years.

[55] That is, the origins of the term *saddharma-pratirūpaka* and its pairing with the term *saddharma* should be sought in Mahāyāna circles. As we shall see (chapter 4), the term *saddharma* had long been in currency before the emergence of *saddharma-*

Both the Mahāyānists and the Sarvāstivādins seem to have been well aware of the earlier orthodoxy of the five-hundred-year tradition. This did not prevent them, however, from going beyond it, and the new 1,000-year timetable clearly had gained wide circulation during the first half of the first millennium CE.[56] By reinterpreting the meaning of the original five-hundred-year figure and incorporating it within a larger timetable, Buddhists were able to accomplish two things at once. First, they were able to justify the ongoing existence of the Buddhist community well beyond its originally allotted life span. And second, at least in the Mahāyāna texts and in the passage contained in the *Mahāvibhāṣā* (in which the latter half of the 1,000-year period is portrayed as considerably worse than the first), they were able to explain the perceived decline, or even decadence, to which certain elements of the Buddhist community were apparently subject.

Once the figure of 1,000 years for the total duration of the Dharma was surpassed, a variety of new timetables came into being. Virtually all of these were constructed as multiples of the original five-hundred-year figure, and appear only in Mahāyāna texts. The sole exception, a 5,000-year timetable belonging to the Theravāda school, will be examined in detail below.

1,500 YEARS

Four Buddhist sūtras, all of Mahāyāna origins, contain predictions that the Dharma will last for 1,500 years. Though the timetables these texts offer are identical in length, their treatments of this figure are quite different. We will examine each of these timetables in turn.

In the *Yüeh-tsang fen* 月藏分 (*Candragarbha-sūtra*) section of the *Ta chi ching* 大集經 (*Mahāsaṃnipāta-sūtra*), the timetable is presented as follows:

> After my nirvāṇa, the True Dharma (*saddharma*) will remain in the world for five hundred years. Sentient beings will extinguish

---

pratirūpaka as its counterpart.

[56] This timetable appears in a number of texts translated into Chinese from the mid-2nd to the mid-5th centuries. It also occurs in scholastic and vinaya texts that were translated later (e.g., by Hsüan-tsang and I-ching), but were certainly composed several centuries before their translation. For the specific translation dates in question see above, notes 39 and 40.

> the *kleśas*, and the bodhisattva with *vīrya* will achieve fulfillment in the six *pāramitās*. Those who practice [the Dharma] will be able to enter quickly into the peaceful city [of nirvāṇa] which is without *āsravas*. And the *saddharma-pratirūpaka* will remain in the world for a full one thousand years.[57]

Here the overall duration of the Dharma is subdivided, in a manner reminiscent of the Mahāyāna 1,000-year timetables, into an earlier period of *saddharma* lasting five hundred years, followed by a period of *saddharma-pratirūpaka* lasting for one thousand. The qualitative distinction between the two periods is quite clear: the first five hundred years are an ideal period for practicing the Buddha's teachings, while the period of the *saddharma-pratirūpaka* is considerably less auspicious. The sūtra then goes on to relate the Kauśāmbī story, culminating in the demise of the Dharma. A related (but not identical) account of the Kauśāmbī story is contained in a Khotanese anthology in verse dating from around the beginning of the 8th century CE, where the same figure of 1,500 years is given, but without any mention of subdivisions.[58]

Just the inverse of the subdivisions found in the Chinese *Candragarbha-sūtra* is given in another Mahāyāna text, preserved in the original Sanskrit as well as in Chinese and Tibetan translations. According to the *Karuṇāpuṇḍarīka-sūtra* the period of *saddharma* is to last for 1,000 years, while the *saddharma-pratirūpaka* endures for only five hundred. The context, however, is not a pronouncement made by the Buddha Śākyamuni, but a vow he is said to have made while still a bodhisattva in the distant past. To quote the Sanskrit version of the text,

> And after my death (*parinirvāṇa*), may the *saddharma* endure (*tiṣṭhet*) for a thousand years, and again may the *saddharma-pratirūpaka* endure for five hundred years.[59]

---

[57] T No. 397[15], 13.379c5–9.

[58] See R. E. Emmerick, ed. and trans., *The Book of Zambasta, a Khotanese Poem on Buddhism* (London: Oxford University Press, 1968), 410–11, line 462. Khotanese is a Middle Iranian language once spoken in the southwestern part of modern Xinjiang (P.R.C.).

[59] Skt. *parinirvṛtasya ca me varṣasahasraṃ saddharmas tiṣṭhet, pañcapunar-varṣaśatāni saddharmapratirūpakas tiṣṭhet* (YAMADA Isshi, *Karuṇāpuṇḍarīka* [London: School of Oriental and African Studies, 1968], vol. 2, 262, lines 9–11). The Tibetan text reads *bdag yongs-su mya-ngan-las 'das-nas kyang lo stong-du dam-pa'i chos gnas-par gyur-cig // yang lo lnga-brgyar ni dam-pa'i chos-kyi gzugs-brnyan gnas-par gyur-cig //* (Pek. No. 780,

Since a vow made by a bodhisattva (especially the one who became the Buddha Śākyamuni) is not to be taken lightly, this timetable should probably be included in our list, as Lamotte has done.[60] It is important to note, however, that the phrasing of this statement is not in the simple future, but in the optative.

One final version of the 1,500-year timetable still remains to be examined. In the *Mo-ho-mo-yeh ching* 摩訶摩耶經 (*Mahāmāyā-sūtra*) we find a quite different periodization of the Dharma. Here the overall figure of 1,500 years is broken down not into two sub-periods, but fifteen, each lasting for a hundred years. The story is cast in the form of a prophecy, culminating in the destruction of the Dharma at Kauśāmbī.[61]

The timetable begins with a lineage of patriarchs, ranging from Mahākāśyapa and Upagupta in the first century through Śīlānanda in the second, "Blue-Lotus" and Puṣpanetra in the third, Gomukha in the fourth, and Ratnadeva in the fifth. All of them contribute to the spread of the Dharma (assisted by King Aśoka, who appears at the end of the first period), yet at the close of the fifth century the *saddharma* comes to an end. Two important Buddhist teachers are still to come, however, for the sūtra places Aśvaghoṣa in the sixth century and Nāgārjuna in the seventh. After this point no further Buddhist teachers are mentioned, and the situation continues to deteriorate as monks and nuns violate the precepts and take part in secular activities. At the end of the fifteenth period the events narrated in the Kauśāmbī story take place, and the Buddha-Dharma comes to an end.

That this is another Mahāyāna version of the 1,500-year timetable is quite clear, given the presence of such teachers as Aśvaghoṣa and Nāgārjuna. Yet the division of this total into fifteen separate periods is unique. Moreover, though Lamotte states that

---

mdo-sna-tshogs cu, 269a6–7). The Tibetan text can be translated in the same way, though here the humble language used by the speaker underscores the fact that the speaker is not yet a Buddha. For the corresponding Chinese passage (of which two translations are extant) see T No. 157, 3.211b26–27, and T No. 158, 3.270.a3–4. Of these the former was translated by Dharmakṣema during the period 414–421 CE, while the latter was executed during the Ch'in dynasty (350–431) by a translator whose name has not been preserved.

[60] *Histoire du bouddhisme indien*, 214.

[61] This sūtra is preserved only in Chinese translation. For the timetable for the decline of the Dharma see T No. 383, 12.1013b14–1014a11.

this scripture is another example (like the Chinese *Candragarbha-sūtra*) of a five-hundred-year period of *saddharma* followed by one thousand years of *saddharma-pratirūpaka*, the latter term (Ch. *hsiang-fa*) is nowhere mentioned in this section. It is possible that the author intended to say that the latter thousand years was the period of *hsiang-fa*, but this is nowhere made explicit.

And in fact the fifteen sub-periods described in the text do not seem very well integrated even with the notion of the *saddharma* itself. We are told that the True Dharma comes to an end at the end of the fifth century, yet Aśvaghoṣa and Nāgārjuna are consigned to the less desirable period that follows. Moreover, the sūtra tells us that Aśvaghoṣa overcame the heretics who destroyed the *saddharma* during the sixth period (when it should already be extinct), and Nāgārjuna "lit the lamp of the *saddharma*" in the seventh. In sum, there is every indication that this list was originally formulated without reference to the categories of *saddharma* and *saddharma-pratirūpaka*, and that the reference to the end of the *saddharma* after five hundred years was a later interpolation.

The 1,500-year timetables, then, can be described as follows. All of them are found in Mahāyāna texts,[62] and all (at least in their present forms) state that the *saddharma* will endure for only a portion of this time. Both the *Candragarbha-sūtra* and the *Karuṇā-puṇḍarīka-sūtra* make explicit the division between *saddharma* and *saddharma-pratirūpaka*, but differ as to the extent of their relative duration.

In the majority of 1,500-year timetables, then, we seem to find at least some reference to the *saddharma/saddharma-pratirūpaka* distinction. In timetables of 2,000 years and over, however, this distinction disappears from view. Insofar as these concepts played a role in the formulation of such chronological timetables, they seem to have done so only for the "middle-length" formulations of 1,000 and 1,500 years.

---

[62] Lamotte (*Histoire du bouddhisme indien*, 214) suggests that there may be an implicit 1,500-year timetable in the *Milindapañha*, which mentions only one five-hundred-year period, but goes on to describe two other periods of decline as well. By analogy, Lamotte suggests, these two periods might be understood as consisting of five hundred years as well. This is an interesting suggestion, but the absence of any reference to a 1,500-year timetable elsewhere in the Theravāda literature makes it rather doubtful.

2,000 YEARS

Four extant texts, all belonging to the *Candragarbha-sūtra* corpus, contain timetables of 2,000 years. Two of these are versions of the sūtra itself (one in Chinese and another in Tibetan), while the other two are elaborations of the sūtra produced in Khotan but preserved only in Tibetan translation. All are closely related in content, and each culminates in a version of the Kauśāmbī prophecy.

Both the Chinese and Tibetan translations of the *Candragarbha-sūtra* contain explicit timetables, subdivided into four 500-year periods. As we have just seen, the Chinese version of this text also contains a 1,500-year timetable, in addition to a 2,500-year system to be discussed below. In both the 2,000-year and the 2,500-year formulations the total figure is not stated explicitly, but is implied by the enumeration of its sub-periods. We may begin with the Chinese version of this sūtra, where these periods are described as follows:

> [As to] the *saddharma*, after my death (*mieh* 滅) liberation will be well established. During the [next] five hundred years, meditation (*ch'an* 禪) and recitation (*sung* 誦) [will be well established]. For [another] five hundred years, the building of stūpas and temples [will be well established]. And in the latter five hundred years, quarreling and debate will be well established.[63]

The Tibetan translation contains the same 2,000-year timetable, but described in much greater detail. The first two periods seem identical to those cited in the Chinese, but the subsequent periods diverge in content. According to the Tibetan text the lifetime of the Dharma will consist of the following periods:

1. During the first five hundred years, many sentient beings will attain liberation by practicing the Buddha's teachings.
2. During the second five hundred years, many will practice meditation (*samādhi*).
3. During the third five hundred years, many teachers of the Dharma will appear, but there will be only a few *śrāvaka*s and arhats. Kings, ministers, and ordinary people will merely listen passively to the teaching and will not take it

[63] T No. 397[15], 13.370b8–11.

to heart and practice it. Kings will compete with one another, and warfare will break out.

4. The fourth five hundred years is divided into two sub-periods of three hundred years and two hundred years, respectively.
   (a) During the first sub-period the *dharmapālas* (gods and spirits who safeguard the Dharma) will abandon this world in disgust and will go elsewhere to spread the Dharma. The few Dharma practitioners who remain will make only half-hearted efforts, and accordingly will make little progress. Famine and disease will break out.
   (b) During the second sub-period even monks will not practice the Dharma in accordance with the Buddha's teachings. They will engage in worldly pursuits, occupying themselves in a variety of secular trades. Kings and officials will appropriate the goods belonging to the sangha, and will gradually destroy Buddhist stūpas and statues. At the end of this fourth and final period the events to take place at Kauśāmbī are related, and the Dharma comes to an end.

Two other Tibetan texts, both translations from lost Khotanese originals, also include timetables of 2,000 years. *The Prophecy of the Arhat Saṃghavardana*[64] and the *Prophecy of* [*the Arhat of*] *Khotan*[65] both give this figure without further subdivisions, and in many respects represent abbreviations of the tradition. The core of their content, however, is clearly derived from the Kauśāmbī story as contained in the *Candragarbha-sūtra*.

The 2,000-year timetable, then, appears to be restricted to texts related to the *Candragarbha-sūtra* (and, accordingly, appears only in Mahāyāna texts).[66] Even so, what we do *not* find in these

---

[64] *Dgra-bcom-pa Dge-'dun 'phel-gyis lung-bstan-pa*, Pek. No. 5698, *mdo-'grel* (*spring-yig*) *nge*, 435a8–444a2.

[65] *Li'i yul* [*-gyi dgra-bcom-pas*] *lung bstan-pa*, Pek. No. 5699, *mdo-'grel* (*spring-yig*) *nge*, 444a2–468a8. In this text the xylograph copies (Peking, Derge, Narthang, and so on) have apparently been emended to read "1,000 years." All three Tun-huang manuscript copies of this work, however, read "2,000 years" (according to Thomas, *Tibetan Literary Texts and Documents*, vol. 1, 78 and n. 4).

[66] The Tibetan text, however, contains no Mahāyāna elements except in the

2,000-year timetables is the use of the term *saddharma-pratirūpaka* to designate a later portion of the life span of the Dharma, in contrast to an earlier period of *saddharma*. In fact, in most of the texts containing mentions of this timetable, the term *saddharma-pratirūpaka* does not appear at all; in the Tibetan version of the *Candragarbha-sūtra* it does appear, but apparently without any special technical meaning.[67] The term *saddharma-pratirūpaka*, then, does not appear to be used in conjunction with any 2,000-year timetable to subdivide this overall figure into two parts.[68] Indeed, the two Khotanese (abbreviated) versions preserved in Tibetan do not offer any subdivisions, while both the Chinese and Tibetan versions of the *Candragarbha-sūtra* itself are based on four subdivisions of five hundred years each. It seems likely, therefore, that the 2,000-year timetable was originally formulated with a set of four, rather than two, periods in mind.

2,500 YEARS

One final timetable found within the *Candragarbha* corpus still remains to be examined. As we have seen, the Chinese translation of the *Candragarbha-sūtra* contains a 1,500-year timetable, as well as another version enumerating a total of 2,000 years. The most influential of its formulations, however, was yet another timetable, enumerating five periods of five hundred years each. Widely quoted in East Asian commentaries, it was subsequently read back into earlier sūtras, including the passages concerning the "five hundred after-years" in the *Diamond* and *Lotus* sūtras.

In the Chinese *Candragarbha-sūtra* the Buddha sets forth the 2,500-year timetable as follows:

1. During the first five hundred years, many people will be established in liberation.

---

mention of the bodhisattva Candragarbha as the interlocutor (in itself not necessarily an indication of its Mahāyāna provenance).

[67] For a discussion of the emergence of *saddharma-pratirūpaka* in the "technical" sense, see below, pp. 78-86.

[68] The sole exception is a late interpolation found in the Chinese (but not the Sanskrit or Tibetan) *Karuṇāpuṇḍarīka-sūtra* (see T No. 157, 3.219c20–22 and T No. 158, 3.277b12–14). Elsewhere in the same text, however, the figure of 1,500 years is given (see above, pp. 49–50 and note 59).

2. During the second five hundred years, they will be well established in meditation (*ch'an ting san-mei* 禪定三昧).
3. During the third five hundred years, they will be well established in study, recitation, and erudition (多聞 , lit. "much hearing," Skt. *bahuśruta*).
4. During the fourth five hundred years, they will be well established in the building of stūpas and temples.
5. During the fifth five hundred years, there will be quarreling and debate, and the disappearance and destruction of the "white Dharma" (白法) will be well established.[69]

The five periods outlined here are essentially the same as those described in the 2,000-year timetable found elsewhere in the Chinese *Candragarbha-sūtra*; the only difference is that here the practices of meditation and study are assigned to separate five-hundred-year periods, while in the 2,000-year system both are included in the second period. The Tibetan text follows this sequence during the first two periods (those of liberation and meditation, respectively); its third period could be construed as a reference to study, though other issues are mentioned as well. The fourth and final period (which is subdivided in the Tibetan text into two periods of three hundred and two hundred years, respectively) contains no mention of the building of stūpas and temples, however, and references to "quarrel and debate," while perhaps present, are buried within a mass of other material.

In sum, while these three timetables are clearly related to one another, the connection between the 2,000-year version found in the Tibetan and its two Chinese counterparts is not straightforward. In fact, the Chinese 2,000-year timetable is considerably closer to the list given in the Chinese 2,500-year list than to its 2,000-year Tibetan counterpart.[70]

One other point should be mentioned with respect to the

---

[69] T No. 397[15], 13.363a29–b5.

[70] Curiously, the Chinese commentator Chi-tsang describes the *Candragarbha-sūtra* as containing a six-period timetable, totalling 3,000 years in all (T No. 1824, 42.18a23–26). His description of these six periods corresponds fairly closely to that contained in the 2,500-year timetable, though with the second (meditation) and third (erudition) reversed and with the addition of a sixth 500-year period. Nowhere in the extant version of this sūtra, however, is such a sixth period mentioned, nor does a total figure of 3,000 years appear.

2,500-year scheme. Nowhere, in this context, does the Chinese *Candragarbha-sūtra* contain a mention of a period of *saddharma-pratirūpaka*, nor is any subdivision of the five 500-year periods into two subsets anywhere implied. In fact, the only mention of the term *saddharma* (Ch. *cheng-fa*) occurs in reference to the second of these five periods of time.[71] Elsewhere, the Buddha speaks only of "my Dharma" (我法) and not of the True Dharma (*saddharma*) or any other technical term. The concept of a period of *saddharma-pratirūpaka* thus does not seem to be taken into consideration in the formulation of these timetables.

5,000 YEARS

With a single exception, all the chronologies for the duration of the Dharma that exceed 1,000 years are found only in Mahāyāna sources. That exception is a 5,000-year timetable, made popular by the great 5th-century commentator Buddhaghosa and subsequently accepted as standard in Theravāda countries.

Buddhaghosa's formulation of this periodization scheme is contained in the *Manorathapūraṇī*, his commentary on the *Aṅguttaranikāya*.[72] His timetable is based on the gradual disappearance of each aspect of the Dharma during successive 1,000-year periods, which are described in the following terms:

Period 1:

> Disappearance of attainments (Pāli *adhigama*). At first the Buddha's followers will be able to attain arhatship, as well as the lower levels of attainment en route to complete liberation. As time goes on, however, this ability will be lost, and the death of the last disciple to attain the status of stream-winner (Pāli *sotāpanna*) will mark the end of the first 1,000 years.

---

[71] T 13.363b2.

[72] See Max Walleser, ed., *Manorathapūraṇī* (London: Oxford University Press, 1924), I, 87–91. This portion of Buddhaghosa's text (i.e., the prophecy of the decline and destruction of the Dharma) was subsequently reproduced in an extra-canonical Theravāda text titled the *Anāgatavaṃsa*, where it was sometimes (but not always) paired with a verse account, originally an entirely separate text, of the future appearance of the Buddha Metteyya (Skt. Maitreya). For an English translation of some portions of the *Anāgatavaṃsa* and a synopsis of others see Henry Clarke Warren, *Buddhism in Translations* (Cambridge: Harvard University Press, 1896), 481–86.

Period 2:

Disappearance of the method (*paṭipatti*). At first the disciples of the Buddha will be able to attain meditative trance states and will keep the precepts. But as time goes on these abilities will be lost. The death of the last precept-keeping monk (or the breaking of the precepts by the last such person) marks the end of the second 1,000-year period.

Period 3:

Disappearance of learning (*pariyatti*). At the beginning of this period the scriptures and commentaries will still exist, but gradually these will be lost.[73] When the last book of the Tripiṭaka has disappeared, the third 1,000-year period will have come to an end.

Period 4:

Disappearance of signs (*nimitta*). At the beginning of this period the monks will still wear their proper monastic robes and carry only the objects that are permitted to them. Later on, however, they will give up wearing the saffron robe and will enter into secular occupations and ordinary family life. (Though the text does not say so explicitly, we are given to understand that when the last monk abandons the true monastic life, this period will come to an end.)

Period 5:

Disappearance of relics (*dhātu*). At the beginning of this period, the Buddha's relics will still be worshipped and honored, but as time goes on people will no longer treat them with respect. Then the relics will all come together in one place, where only the gods are in attendance. The gods will realize that the Dharma will disappear in only seven days and will weep, saying, "From now on we shall be in darkness." Then the relics will burst into flame, and will be consumed without remainder. At this point all vestiges of the

---

[73] Here the text contains a complete listing of the major sections of the Theravāda canon in reverse order, from the end (the *Paṭṭhāna* section of the *Abhidhamma-piṭaka*, which is to disappear first) to the beginning (the *Vinaya-piṭaka*). This portion of the text was to cause great difficulty to its Tibetan translators, who would have been unfamiliar with most of the names in this list (as their convoluted attempts at translation demonstrate) and who must surely have concluded that the disappearance of the Dharma was already well under way!

Dharma will have disappeared, and one can truly speak of its destruction.

Buddhaghosa's figure of 5,000 years was to become the standard timetable in Theravāda Buddhism, and it appears in a number of historical chronicles and commentaries.[74] Not all of these sources, however, describe the content of these five periods in the same fashion. In the *Samantapāsādikā*, another commentary written by Buddhaghosa, it is stated that during the first thousand years Buddhists will be able to gain insight into the truths (*pratisaṃvid*), as well as gain the four fruits of the religious life (the state of being an arhat, a once-returner, a non-returner, and a stream-enterer). During the second millennium, only the four fruits can be attained. During the third millennium, it will no longer be possible to attain arhatship, but the other three attainments are still possible. During the fourth, one can only attain the fruit of the non-returner and the stream-enterer; and during the fifth, only the state of the stream-enterer can be attained. Finally, at the end of 5,000 years all these fruits will be inaccessible, and Buddhism will for all practical purposes have disappeared.[75] The text goes on to say, however, that some of the external signs (*liṅga*) of the Buddhist religion will still linger, though the life has gone out of the tradition.[76]

It is rare for a work of the Theravāda school—or indeed of any Nikāya Buddhist school—to be preserved in Tibetan translation. In the early years of Tibetan Buddhist history an official decision was made to translate only Mahāyāna and Vajrayāna scriptures,[77] making a few exceptions for works belonging to the Mūlasarvāstivāda school.[78] The result has been the almost total exclusion of non-Mahāyāna sūtra and abhidharma texts from the Tibetan

---

[74] See the *Mahāvaṃsa* (III, 38), the *Sumaṅgalavīlāsinī* (I, 25), the *Atthasālinī* (27), and the *Samantapāsādikā* (I, 30).

[75] *Samantapāsādikā*, I, 30.

[76] *Samantapāsādikā*, VI, 1291.

[77] I have been unable to locate a textual reference to document this assertion, which is based on information conveyed in lectures at Harvard University by Masatoshi Nagatomi. Nonetheless, I have every reason to believe that it is accurate, as the actual contents of the canon do indeed correspond to this description.

[78] E.g., the Vinaya, which is necessary to the formation of any legitimate Buddhist monastic community.

canonical collections.[79] Thus only a handful of texts known to the Theravāda tradition can be matched with equivalents in the Tibetan Kanjur.[80] One of these, however, whose Theravādin origins were overlooked by the cataloguers of the Peking Kanjur, is a composite of an extracanonical verse prediction of the coming of Maitreya and the commentary of Buddhaghosa just described. Titled the *Byams-pa'i mdo* (**Maitreya-sūtra*, but given in the Tibetan texts themselves as *Maitrī-sūtra*), it exists in the Tibetan canon in two separate translations.[81] Thus, in this strange hybrid creation the Tibetans had access to a timetable that would eventually become their standard figure.

5,104 YEARS

Although the 5,000-year timetable is generally cited as the orthodox figure by Tibetan Buddhists, two other systems have competed for their attention in recent centuries. One, allotting to the Dharma a total life span of 4,500 years, appears to have no canonical basis.[82] The other, founded on the apocalyptic prophecy given in the *Kālacakra-tantra*, has been calculated as allowing 5,104 years.[83]

---

[79] The Tibetan canon does, of course, contain a vast number of Mahāyāna sūtras, but it generally has not preserved any of the works contained in the Theravāda Nikāyas or in the Āgamas of the Sarvāstivāda and other Nikāya schools.

[80] Exceptions listed in the Ōtani catalogue (Tokyo-Kyoto: Tibetan Tripitaka Research Institute, 1961) include Pek. Nos. 747, 748, 749, 750, 752, 754, 755, 756, 757, 758, 759, 955, 956, 957, 958, 962, 963, 966, 982, 997, 1005.

[81] Pek. Nos. 751, *sher-phyin tsi*, 278b6–286a4, and 1010, *mdo-sna-tshogs hu*, 304a5–312a3. Neither of these has been recognized, apparently, as based on a Pāli original. (There is internal evidence within these texts, however, for the existence of a Sanskrit intermediary.) That the prophecy they contain is based on a Theravāda text can be seen in the fact that the order of the sections of the Buddhist canon cited within the text conforms only to the Theravāda version. The Tibetan translators, needless to say, had great difficulty with this portion of the text.

[82] Cited by Geshe Nornang (University of Washington) of the Sakya (*sa-skya*) school, and the Ven. Tulku Thondup (Cambridge, Mass.) of the Nyingma (*rnying-ma*) school. Neither cited any textual reference for this figure.

[83] For the Tibetan text of the *Kālacakra-tantra* see Pek. No. 4, *rgyud oṃ*, 23b1–141b8. For a recent edition see Biswanath Banerjee, ed., *A Critical Edition of the Śrī Kālacakratantra-rāja (Collated with the Tibetan Version)* (Calcutta: The Asiatic Society, 1985). The Sanskrit text has also been preserved. The text is not included in the Chinese canon. For a discussion of its content see Tenzin Gyatso (the current Dalai Lama), *The Kālachakra Tantra*, edited and translated by Jeffrey Hopkins (London: Wisdom Publications, 1985). A thorough scholarly examination of the historical

The *Kālacakra-tantra* is the only genuinely apocalyptic text that has ever been accepted into any Buddhist canon.[84] Born out of the traumatic encounter between the Hindu and Buddhist inhabitants of northwest India and the Muslim invaders who first penetrated the subcontinent in 712 and returned with a vengeance under Mahmūd of Ghaznī (who carried out annual raids into the Punjab from 997–1030), the text incorporates a range of themes rarely encountered in Buddhist literature. The prophetic portion of the text culminates in an apocalyptic battle between Muslims and Buddhists, in which—contrary to all realistic historical expectation—the Buddhists emerge victorious. The ancestry of the text is a matter of controversy; while the Tibetan tradition (and the testimony of the text itself) would have us believe that it was preached by the historical Buddha Śākyamuni to King Sucandra, ruler of the mysterious kingdom of Śambhala, who then took it home with him for safekeeping,[85] all available evidence suggests that the text first appeared in India early in the 11th century.[86]

The time scheme envisioned in the *Kālacakra-tantra* is the following. A series of seven kings of Śambhala, of whom the first is the above-mentioned Sucandra, will be followed by twenty-five "lineage-holders" (Skt. *kūlika*, Tib. *rigs-ldan*), each ruling for a period of one hundred years. Finally, in the 98th reign-year of the last lineage-holder (in 2425 CE by modern Tibetan calculations[87]) there will be a great war between the Buddhist forces, based at Śambhala, and the barbarians. The barbarians (Skt. *mleccha*, Tib. *kla-klo*, a term

---

data and prophetic traditions contained in the text are given in John R. Newman, "The Outer Wheel of Time: Vajrayāna Buddhist Cosmology in the Kālacakra Tantra" (Ph.D. thesis, University of Wisconsin, 1987). For the figure of 5,104 years see Tenzin Gyatso, *The Kālachakra Tantra*, 65, where the author notes that this figure is "104 years longer than the Sūtra system." The sūtra system in question is apparently that of the *Maitrī-sūtra*, where 5,000 years are allotted.

[84] By "apocalyptic" I mean a worldview that anticipates the radical overturning of the present religio-political order as a result of action by forces operating on a cosmic (i.e., transhuman) level. For an extended discussion of this usage and related issues see Nattier, "The Meanings of the Maitreya Myth," especially pp. 42–44, notes 41–46.

[85] For the Tibetan (Gelugpa) view see Tenzin Gyatso, *The Kālachakra Tantra*, 59–65. On the kingdom of Shambhala itself see Edwin Bernbaum, *The Way to Shambhala* (Garden City, NJ: Anchor Books, 1980).

[86] See Newman, *The Outer Wheel of Time*, 75.

[87] Tenzin Gyatso, *The Kālachakra Tantra*, 65.

that can safely be translated as "Muslims" throughout the text) will be defeated, and Buddhism will again flourish throughout the world. Finally, 5,104 years after Śākyamuni's nirvāṇa, the Buddhist teachings will disappear from the face of the earth, and the Dharma will come to an end.

10,000 YEARS AND BEYOND

It is probable that no Buddhist timetable constructed in India ever exceeded a total of 5,000 years.[88] Yet in one case we find a text preserved in the Chinese canon, and based on an Indian original, in which the figure of 10,000 years is given. The *Shan-chien lü p'i-po-sha* 善見律毘婆沙, translated into Chinese by Saṅghabhadra in 488, is apparently a Chinese version of Buddhaghosa's *Samantapāsādikā*.[89] As we have seen, however, in Buddhaghosa's text the total life span of the Dharma is said to be 5,000 years, not 10,000, and the figure of 5,000 years regularly appears in Theravādin sources. Thus it is possible (and in my view quite likely) that the change from 5,000 to 10,000 was made by a Chinese editorial hand.[90]

Other timetables extend this figure to 11,500 and 12,000 years, respectively.[91] Yet these figures are unknown outside East Asia,

---

[88] The *Kālacakra-tantra* does not mention any overall figure for the duration of the Dharma. The number 5,104 is the result of Tibetan calculations, based on the idea that the Buddha was born in 880 BCE (see Tenzin Gyatso, *The Kālachakra Tantra*, 484, n. 88).

[89] According to Lamotte, *Histoire du bouddhisme indien*, 215–16, and according to L. Lancaster, *The Korean Buddhist Canon: A Descriptive Catalogue* (Berkeley: University of California Press, 1979), 337, K 937 (= T No. 1462).

[90] The number 10,000 has overtones of infinity in China that it lacks in India, where far larger numbers were available. Thus to say that Buddhism will last for 10,000 years, in a Chinese context, is to say in essence that it will last forever. Since no example of an Indian text containing the number 10,000 has ever been identified, we are justified in suspecting that this figure is the result of a modification made in China. In fact, we may have evidence for this change (and perhaps even the date of the change) within the Chinese canon itself. In the course of his review of timetables for the disappearance of the Dharma, Chi-tsang (549–623) cites the *Shan-chien lü p'i-po-sha*, but states only that it predicts a total duration of 5,000 years (T No. 1824, 42.18a27–b2). Since Chi-tsang's aim in this passage is to provide a complete overview of available timetables, it seems certain that he was not aware of the existence of a 10,000-year figure in the version(s) of the *Shan-chien lü p'i-po-sha* then available.

[91] The figure of 11,500 years appears in a text attributed to Hui-ssu (T No. 1933, 46.786c4–6), while a total of 12,000 years is given by Chi-tsang (T No. 1824,

and appear only in connection with a three-part scenario (to be discussed in the following chapter) that appears to have been constructed in China. That they appear only in the commentary literature (and never in the sūtras themselves) confirms the impression that these numbers are a late and extracanonical development.

OVERVIEW: THE EVOLUTION OF BUDDHIST TIMETABLES OF DECLINE

As we have seen, once the concept of extending the lifetime of the Dharma beyond one thousand years was introduced, new periodization schemes begin to appear in a bewildering variety of forms. We find systems consisting of 1,500 years, 2,000 years, 2,500 years, and 5,000 years, as well as other more anomalous figures.[92] And in fact it is the sheer variety of these schemes that strikes the reader at the outset. The material does indeed seem chaotic at first, and one is tempted to agree with YAMADA Ryūjō that in the Indian context, at least, there was simply no normative length for the duration of the Dharma.[93]

Yet a closer look does reveal an underlying pattern. First, it is possible to establish at least a minimal chronological stratification of these traditions. The five-hundred-year tradition, which appears to date from a period two centuries or more before the Common Era, is clearly the oldest. And it may well have been precisely the

---

42.18b2–5), Huai-kan (T No. 1960, 47.48c7–8), and Liang-p'i (T No. 1709, 33.520c10).

[92] Some scholars have seen other timetables in the figures contained in the *Humane Kings Sūtra* (*Jen-wang ching* 仁王經, T Nos. 245 and 246, translations attributed to Kumārajīva and Amoghavajra, respectively). Here the Buddha says (according to the translation of Kumārajīva) "after my nirvāṇa, during 80, 800, [or] 8,000 years there will be no Buddha, Dharma, and Sangha, and no male and female believers" (T 8.833b13–15). Amoghavajra's translation reads "after my nirvāṇa, when the True Dharma is about to expire, in the latter 50 years, the latter 500 years, [and] the latter 5,000 years there will not be any Buddha, Dharma, and Sangha" (T 8.844b6–7). These figures may not imply a specific timetable, however, but simply a general sense that the world will be devoid of the Buddhist teachings for a prolonged period of time.

[93] More specifically, Yamada argues that the "constant fluctuation" in the figures given for the duration of *shōbō* 正法 and *zōbō* 像法 demonstrates that Indian Buddhists felt free to "think quite freely" about their duration ("Mappō shisō," 367).

normative status of this tradition—at least among certain sectarian groups—that led to a crisis in the first or second century CE, when the allotted time had expired and a reinterpretation of the earlier tradition to allow for the continued existence of the Buddhist community was suddenly seen as vital.[94]

The 1,000-year traditions, I would argue, are the product of this crisis in historical self-consciousness. By reinterpreting the original figure of five hundred years to refer only to the duration of the "True Dharma" (that is, the Dharma in its pristine condition), and not of the Dharma as a whole, Buddhist thinkers were able to rationalize the continued existence of the Buddhist community beyond its originally allotted time span without repudiating the earlier tradition altogether. Following this line of reasoning (and assuming that the 1,000-year tradition may have enjoyed a period of trans-sectarian orthodoxy), we would expect the more extended traditions—those predicting a total duration of the Dharma of more than 1,000 years—to have arisen sometime around a thousand years after the time of the Buddha. And the available (albeit rather skimpy) data would seem to support such a hypothesis. Not a single text translated into Chinese before the early 5th century, for example, predicts that the Dharma will endure for a period longer than 1,000 years.[95]

It is at this point, I would suggest—that is, around the late 5th or early 6th century—that the loss of even a minimal consensus on the duration of the Dharma took place. Indian Buddhism was, of course, never subject to any centralized authority capable of ruling on such matters; yet, as we have seen, there is some evidence that the figures of five hundred and one thousand years were accepted in turn as orthodox, across at least some sectarian boundaries. Once the figure of one thousand years was breached, however, no easy solution (such as the simple doubling of the original five-hundred-year figure) was available. Thus, it is not altogether sur-

---

[94] The arguments advanced in the *Mahāvibhāṣā* (T 27.918a9–17) in favor of a 1,000-year timetable, for instance, appear to show a keen awareness of the previously normative status of the five-hundred-year tradition.

[95] The earliest Chinese translations of texts containing timetables exceeding 1,000 years are the *Karuṇāpuṇḍarīka-sūtra* (T No. 157), translated by Dharmakṣema during the period 414–421; T No. 158, an anonymous translation of the same work, completed during the period 350–431, and the *Mahāmāyā-sūtra* (T No. 383), translated during the period 479–502.

prising that a wide variety of longer time schemes—the products, perhaps, of different sectarian groups[96]—should have arisen.

The seemingly wild proliferation of timetables that appears during this third phase, then, may be viewed as a response by the Buddhist community to a problem brought about precisely by the normative quality of the earlier time schemes. Once a certain timetable had attained the status of an orthodox tradition, it was inevitable that—when the predicated number of years had elapsed—the Buddhist community would eventually face the threat of the sudden and total undermining of its own legitimacy. The greater the normative status assigned to the existing tradition, in other words, the more urgent was the demand for a response. The very creation of such fixed timetables, then—however expansive they may have seemed at the outset—guaranteed that new and more extensive chronologies would eventually be required.

---

[96] A clear majority of the five-hundred-year traditions belong to schools of the Nikāya group (i. e., to non-Mahāyāna sects), while the 1,000-year traditions are more evenly divided among Mahāyāna and non-Mahāyāna sources. Timetables exceeding 1,000 years are found almost exclusively in Mahāyāna works.

Chapter Four

The East Asian Tripartite System: *Cheng-fa*, *Hsiang-fa*, and *Mo-fa*

TO THE SPECIALIST in East Asian Buddhism, one of the most striking features of the texts reviewed in the previous chapter is that not a single one of them contains any reference to the concept of *mo-fa* (Jpn. *mappō*), lit. "end-dharma" or "final Dharma." For it was not any of the timetables discussed above, but rather a three-part system culminating in a prolonged period of *mo-fa*, that was to become the most influential historical frame of reference in the Buddhist schools of China, Korea, and Japan. Building on the concepts of *saddharma* ("True Dharma") and *saddharma-pratirūpaka* ("semblance of the True Dharma") that we have already met in the Indian sources, East Asian Buddhists formulated a system of three periods in the history of the Buddhist religion, which were expected to occur in the following sequence:

- a period of the "True Dharma" (Ch. *cheng-fa* / Jpn. *shōbō* 正法, corresponding to Skt. *saddharma*) immediately following the death of the Buddha, during which it is possible to attain enlightenment by practicing the Buddha's teachings;
- a period of the "Semblance Dharma" (Ch. *hsiang-fa* / Jpn. *zōbō* 像法, a term patterned on but not identical to Skt. *saddharma-pratirūpaka*[1]), during which a few may still be able

[1] Most notably, the Chinese term *hsiang-fa* contains no equivalent of the Sanskrit prefix *sad-* "true." For further details see below, p. 89.

to reach the goal of enlightenment, but most Buddhists simply carry out the external forms of the religion; and

- a period of the "Final Dharma" (Ch. *mo-fa* / Jpn. *mappō* 末法, a term for which no proper Sanskrit equivalent exists[2]), during which traditional religious practice loses its effectiveness and the spiritual capacity of human beings reaches an all-time low.

While this system is known only in East Asian Buddhist sources, it is clearly constructed with reference to elements that were already known in India. We will begin, therefore, with an examination of the individual components that make up this system, and their significance in the Indian Buddhist context.

THE TRUE DHARMA AND ITS SHADOW: *SADDHARMA* AND *SADDHARMA-PRATIRŪPAKA*

The term *saddharma* (Pāli *saddhamma*) occurs in some of the earliest layers of Buddhist literature. It appears in numerous passages in the Pāli canon, a fact that suggests it had entered the mainstream of Buddhist vocabulary well before the closing of the canonical corpus.[3] At leat one scholar has argued that the very use of this term implies that Buddhists already had begun to sense that their religion was in a state of decline.[4] It seems more likely, however, that the term was introduced simply because the word *dharma*, used alone, has a great number of meanings, including (but not limited to) the teachings of the Buddha.[5] Moreover, the word *dharma* was

---

[2] Despite the fact that a number of eminent Buddhologists have equated the term *mo-fa* with Skt. *saddharma-vipralopa* ("destruction of the True Dharma"), this equivalence does not seem to hold. For a detailed discussion of this issue see below, pp. 91–95.

[3] The Theravāda canon was first set down in writing around 30 BCE (see Lamotte, *Histoire*, 403-405); the orally transmitted canon, however, had already attained a fixed form well before that date.

[4] See Yamada, "Mappō shisō ni tsuite," 364-65.

[5] For a discussion of the term *saddhamma* in Pāli literature see Magdalene and Wilhelm Geiger, "Pāli Dhamma: Vornehmlich in der kanonischen Literatur," *Abhandlungen der Bayerischen Akademie der Wissenschaften*, Philosophisch-philologische und historische Klasse, Band XXXI, 1, May 1920 (München: Verlag der Bayerischen Akademie der Wissenschaften, 1920). A recent overview of the

not an exclusive possession of the Buddhists, for it has been used by virtually all schools of Indian religion and was even used by Buddhists themselves to refer to the teachings of other (non-Buddhist) leaders.[6] Thus there was a need for a term that would refer specifically to "the teachings of the Buddha Śākyamuni," and it is in precisely this sense that the term *saddharma* first begins to appear.

Once it had been introduced into Buddhist vocabulary, the term *saddharma* quickly gained wide circulation, and by around the 1st century BCE it was sufficiently well established to be able to serve in turn as the basis for the construction of another compound, the expression *saddharma-pratirūpaka*, in which the second element refers to the "semblance," "image," or "shadow" of the True Dharma. In current scholarship one encounters a number of commonly held assumptions concerning the usage and significance of this term:

1. that the concept of *saddharma-pratirūpaka* was part of the common intellectual property of Indian Buddhists, shared widely among believers regardless of sectarian affiliation;
2. that the term continued to function as a basic element in the Indian Buddhist conceptual repertoire from the time it was first introduced (shortly after the Buddha's death) until the disappearance of Buddhism from India around 1200 CE;
3. that the term has consistently been used in reference to a second period or "dispensation" in Buddhist history, which was expected to follow immediately after a period of *saddharma*; and
4. that the connotations of the term are strongly negative (as expressed in the commonly used English translation "counterfeit Dharma"), implying the emergence of a Dharma that is false (or at best, a second-rate imitation) in

uses of the term in the Theravāda tradition of Sri Lanka is given in John Ross Carter, *Dhamma: Western Academic and Sinhalese Buddhist Interpretations, A Study of a Religious Concept* (Tokyo: The Hokuseido Press, 1978), 165-70.

[6] For examples of the use of the word *dharma* in Buddhist literature in reference to non-Buddhist teachings see J. J. Jones, trans., *The Mahāvastu*, vol. 2, 114-15 (§118) and 186 (§195).

contrast to the original Dharma in its pristine condition (*saddharma*).

As we shall see, however, not a single one of these assumptions is supported by the actual occurrences of the expression *saddharma-pratirūpaka* in Indian Buddhist literature. Rather, our understanding of the original significance of the term has been distorted by assumptions based on its uses in East Asian commentaries, on the one hand, and on its sole (and extremely atypical) occurrence in the Pāli canon, on the other. We will begin, therefore, by attempting to gain a general picture of the occurrences and significance of the term in the Buddhist literature of India.

SECTARIAN DISTRIBUTION

To evaluate the first of these assumptions—that the idea of *saddharma-pratirūpaka* was part of the shared conceptual repertoire of all Indian Buddhists, regardless of sectarian affiliation—we must first review the actual occurrences of this term in Indian Buddhist texts. Since so few of these texts have survived in the original Indian languges, however—and of these, many represent extremely late recensions—we must also include in our survey scriptures of Indian origin that are preserved only in Chinese or Tibetan translation.[7] Even a preliminary survey of the Buddhist canonical literature, however, reveals that the occurrences of *saddharma-pratirūpaka* are far from being uniformly distributed in Buddhist texts. Rather, what we find instead is a striking degree of asymmetry: most noticeably, the virtually total absence of this term from the surviving sūtra literature of the Nikāya schools,[8] where only a single passage containing this expression has been documented.[9] Even in the Mahāyāna texts, however, the uses of the

[7] It is important to bear in mind, of course, the possibility that such works (particularly those preserved in Chinese) may have undergone substantial alteration outside the Indian environment.

[8] For the term "Nikāya Buddhism" (used to refer to the so-called "Eighteen Schools" of non-Mahāyāna Buddhism) see above, chapter 2, note 1.

[9] On the single occurrence of this term in the Pāli canon (*Saṃyutta-nikāya* II, 224) and its Chinese parallels see below, pp. 87–88. Even more important, perhaps, is the fact that the term does not seem to enter the conceptual repertoire of these schools in the later (post-canonical) period. No occurrences of the term are registered, at any rate, in the Taishō index volumes (vol. 14[1] and [2]; see follow-

term *saddharma-pratirūpaka* are strikingly asymmetrical in distribution. A survey of the occurrences of the term in the Mahāyāna sūtras preserved in Chinese translation (the only version of the canon, aside from the Pāli, for which an index of any kind is available[10]) reveals the following pattern: while the term occurs in a substantial number of sūtras classified by the Taishō editors as "miscellaneous" 經集 ,[11] it occurs only once in the voluminous Prajñāpāramitā corpus[12] and only twice in the Avataṃsaka literature.[13] Again, there are a handful of occurrences in the Ratnakuṭa texts,[14] but none at all in the Nirvāṇa[15] or Pure Land[16] sūtras.

The relatively abundant (if unevenly distributed) occurrences of *saddharma-pratirūpaka* in the Mahāyāna literature, in contrast to its sole (and, as we shall see below, extremely atypical) appearance in the Nikāya Buddhist literature, leads us to a further corollary: i.e., the strong probability that the term itself was coined in Mahāyāna circles. If this is indeed the case, it carries certain implications

ing note) containing the abhidharma literature of the Nikāya schools. In the Nikāya Buddhist vinaya literature the term appears in only one text, a Sarvāstivādin vinaya work translated by a variety of scholars including Kumārajīva; see T No. 1435, 23.358c.

[10] All statements made in this section concerning the appearance or non-appearance of certain Buddhist technical terms in the Chinese canon are made on the basis of the entries contained in the index volumes to the Taishō edition of the Tripiṭaka (*Taishō Shinshū Daizōkyō Sakuin* [Tokyo: Research Association for the Terminology of the Taishō Tripiṭaka, 1964–]). These indices represent a massive work of scholarship and have contributed directly to the far greater advancement of research on the Chinese canon than on its Tibetan counterpart, which remains to date entirely unindexed. The Taishō indices are by no means, however, a complete concordance of all terms appearing in the canon. Thus, while a survey of the appearances of a given term in the Taishō index can provide a good general indication of the patterns of its appearance, all conclusions drawn on this basis must remain provisional until a machine-readable version of the canon, which will allow for comprehensive searches of terminology, becomes available.

[11] T vols. 14-17. A total of 29 occurrences of the term in this section are listed in the Taishō index (see vol. 8[1], p. 263b and vol. 8[2], p. 266a).

[12] The term appears twice in one passage of Mokṣala's late 3rd-century translation of the *Pañcaviṃśati-prajñāpāramitā-sūtra* (T No. 221, 8.87a29-b1), but not elsewhere in the Prajñāpāramitā corpus.

[13] T No. 291, 10.604c and No. 294, 10.859b.

[14] T Nos. 310[12] (11.284c), 316 (11.838a, 861c), 320 (11.935c), 329 (12.63b), 342 (12.148c, 153a), and 345 (12.165c)

[15] T Nos. 374-378.

[16] T Nos. 360-373.

for the date of origin of the term, for if it appears almost exclusively in Mahāyāna texts it seems highly unlikely that it was in wide circulation prior to the 1st century BCE. The available sources, then, suggest both a Mahāyāna environment and a relatively late date for the emergence of this term.[17]

HISTORICAL RANGE

When we turn to the second commonly-held assumption concerning *saddharma-pratirūpaka* — the idea that the term, once it had been coined, remained influential throughout the history of Indian Buddhism — we again find that the sources do not confirm our expectations. As we have already seen, the term first appears well after the Buddha's time, in all probability some four or five centuries after his death. But rather than remaining at a constant level of usage throughout the remainder of Buddhist history, the term seems to reach a peak of popularity early in the first millennium CE, and to undergo a gradual decline in popularity after that time. Such a broad generalization is, of course, difficult to substantiate; yet evidence pointing in this direction is available from at least three different sources. First of all, to sketch the picture in broad sectarian terms, the expression *saddharma-pratirūpaka* is essentially absent from the earliest (Nikāya Buddhist) literature, occurs frequently (but by no means universally) in the literature of the Mahāyāna schools, and recedes noticeably in prominence with the rise of the Vajrayāna literature.[18] Second, while the term is abun-

---

[17] Given the paucity of surviving Indian Buddhist sources at our disposal, the possibility still remains that the concept of *saddharma-pratirūpaka* first appeared in a Nikāya school whose literature has not come down to us, and was subsequently adopted by (at least some of the) Mahāyāna schools. Nonetheless, the most likely possibility is that the idea was a Mahāyāna invention, and that it never gained significant currency outside Mahāyāna circles.

[18] The term *hsiang-fa* occurs in forty-seven Mahāyāna sūtras, according to the Taishō index, but in only nine texts in the *mi-chiao* (tantric) volumes. In the latter, *hsiang-fa* is clearly outpaced by *mo-fa* (with twenty occurrences) and by the closely related term *mo-shih* (with fourteen), whose significance will be discussed below. To treat the Nikāya, Mahāyāna, and Vajrayāna movements as strictly sequential would of course be far too simplistic; most of the Nikāya schools continued to exist and flourish well after the appearance of the Mahāyāna, and non-tantric Mahāyāna teachings and practices likewise continued to hold a following even after advocates of the Vajrayāna had appeared. Nonetheless, the clearly disproportionate representation of the term *saddharma-pratirūpaka* in the literature of these

dantly represented in Chinese translations of Indian Buddhist texts[19] (and even more widely distributed in the Chinese commentary literature), in the Tibetan canon—and this statement must remain only an impressionistic one, pending the completion of a machine-readable version of the canon or a usable set of indices—it is considerably less common. And we can state with certainty that in the Tibetan realm the idea of *saddharma-pratirūpaka* never entered the mainstream of commentary literature.[20] Since the bulk of the Indian Buddhist literature in the Chinese canon was imported during the 2nd to 8th centuries CE, while the Tibetan Buddhist tradition is considerably later (drawing mainly on the currents of Buddhist thought circulating in India during the 7th to 12th centuries), this again suggests that Indian interest in the term must have peaked sometime before the 7th century. Third, corroborative evidence for the rise and subsequent fall in the popularity of this concept can be seen in the materials discussed in the previous chapter. As we have seen, the expression *saddharma-pratirūpaka* occurs in conjunction with timetables for the duration of the Dharma

three major wings of the Buddhist tradition is evident enough to be chronologically instructive.

[19] In this connection it may be significant that a disproportionate number of these occurrences are in works translated by Dharmarakṣa (active c. 265-313 CE). His contribution is even more striking when we look only at those translations produced prior to 309 CE, in which case we find 16 texts containing the term *hsiang-fa*, of which all but one were produced by Dharmarakṣa. (The sole exception, T No. 156, is listed as the work of an unknown translator of the latter Han period. Internal evidence, however, suggests that the translation is considerably later, dating from perhaps the 4th or 5th century CE. If this later date is accepted, this would leave Dharmarakṣa as the only known user of this term in China prior to the 4th century.) It seems quite safe to assume, then, that it was primarily through the translations of Dharmarakṣa that Chinese Buddhists first became acquainted with the term *hsiang-fa*.

[20] The lack of importance of *saddharma-pratirūpaka* as a Buddhist technical term in later Indian Buddhism (as adopted by the Tibetans) can be seen in the fact that the term is not even registered in the *Mahāvyutpatti*, the standard dictionary of Sanskrit-Tibetan equivalents compiled in Tibet during the first half of the 9th century. The word *saddharma* is of course registered, but never in combination with the term *pratirūpaka*, and when the latter is listed (nos. 6688 and 6689) it is in compound with other terms (*mārga-pratirūpaka* and *śramaṇa-pratirūpaka*, respectively). Likewise the term is never discussed by the great 14th-century scholar Buston in his review of traditions concerning the decline of the Dharma (see his *Chos-'byung*, trans. E. Obermiller, Part 2, 171-80).

ranging from 1,000 to 1,500 years, but not with the longer or shorter versions. If the historical arguments outlined above are correct, it would follow that the concept of *saddharma-pratirūpaka* reached a peak of importance during the second half of the millennium following the death of the Buddha—that is, from around the first to the sixth centuries CE.[21]

In the Indian environment, then, the idea of *saddharma-pratirūpaka* seems to have emerged approximately four centuries after the death of the Buddha, and to have remained influential (in at least certain Mahāyāna circles) for another half a millennium or so. Afterwards it declined in importance, disappearing almost entirely from the Buddhist conceptual repertoire by the latter part of the first millennium CE. In East Asia, by contrast, the term *hsiang-fa* was accepted into the mainstream of Buddhist thinking, where it achieved a place of prominence from which it was never to be dislodged.

SIGNIFICANCE OF THE TERM

The third widely held assumption concerning the idea of *saddharma-pratirūpaka* is that this expression has consistently been used in reference to a second period in the history of the Buddhist Dharma, to follow an earlier period known as that of the *saddharma* or "True Dharma." And, indeed, a number of the texts in which this expression occurs do use it in precisely this sense. Yet a review of the actual occurrences of the term in Buddhist literature reveals that this is by no means always the case. Since only a small fraction of the Buddhist literature that once existed in Sanskrit has survived, and since no index to the Tibetan canon is yet available, we will rely heavily on the texts preserved in Chinese translation, for which a useful (though hardly comprehensive) index is available.[22] In the following discussion we will therefore begin by reviewing the occurrences of the term *hsiang-fa*, the usual Chinese translation of *saddharma-pratirūpaka*, as represented in the index to the Taishō canon.

---

[21] It is perhaps significant in this regard that in both the Prajñāpāramitā and the Avataṃsaka texts the term *hsiang-fa* occurs only in the earliest (3rd–4th century) Chinese translations, disappearing from the later versions of these same works.

[22] On the uses and limitations of the Taishō index see above, note 10.

We may begin with a group of sūtras, all translated by Dharmarakṣa 竺法護 (fl. 265–313 CE), in which the term *hsiang-fa* occurs in a fixed phrase that would seem to mean "such a *saddharma-pratirūpaka* as this" 如是像法 . In these passages it seems evident that the term *hsiang-fa* is not being used in reference to a chronological period, but simply to the Buddhist Dharma as such. For example:

> If [one] listens to a Dharma such as this (*ju-shih hsiang-fa*), which is profound, wonderful, and difficult to understand, rarely heard in the entire world, [which is] empty, signless, and wishless, one's fears will be quieted and eliminated.[23]

> A Dharma such as this (*ju-shih hsiang-fa*) is ultimately penetrating. Believe and take joy [in it]. Having practiced this Dharma, one will finally and completely attain the Buddha-way [i.e., Buddhahood].[24]

> The Buddha said to Ānanda, "If there is someone who receives and accepts a Dharma such as this (*ju-shih hsiang-fa*)—a pure and unalloyed scripture-text 純淑經巻 —and upholds, recites, chants, and reads it, and if there is a monk or nun, layman or laywoman, who is able to believe,[25] explain, receive, uphold, recite, chant, and read it, their merit will be immeasurable, and their benefits unlimited.[26]

There are a number of other such occurrences in Dharmarakṣa's translations, all of which are essentially the same in tone as those cited above.[27]

That this usage is reflected only in the works of Dharmarakṣa may strike us as peculiar, but it does not necessarily minimize the value of these sources. On the contrary, for as one of the earliest and most prolific Chinese translators,[28] Dharmarakṣa was in a

---

[23] T No. 342, 12.148c19-20.

[24] T No. 399, 13.467c9.

[25] Ordinarily one would translate the character *ts'ung* 從 as "follow"or "obey" (see Mathews no. 6919). In the present context, however, it seems clear that the implication is that of "conforming" to the text in the sense of conforming one's thoughts to its content—that is, believing in its message.

[26] T No. 477, 14.596b27-29.

[27] See T No. 481, 14.627c9–10, c17, c20, 628b12, 629b20, 630b12, and 638a20; T No. 585, 15.9a25; T No. 598, 15.136c1; and T No. 635, 15.492a8, 494a10, and 498c21.

[28] He is credited with 95 separate translations by the editors of the Taishō

unique position to be familiar with the terminology used in the wide variety of Indian Mahāyāna texts that were arriving in China during the late 3rd and early 4th centuries CE. His understanding of the term could therefore be representative of its significance in Indian Buddhism at a relatively early stage of its development.

If we are to use these translations as evidence for the early significance of the term *saddharma-pratirūpaka* in Indian Buddhism, however, we must be certain that this was indeed the term underlying Dharmarakṣa's translations. Unfortunately, not a single one of the Chinese translations in which the expression *ju-shih hsiang-fa* occurs has an extant original in Sanskrit. Thus it is impossible to compare Dharmarakṣa's phrasing directly with the Sanskrit to be sure that we are indeed dealing with a rendering of *saddharma-pratirūpaka*.

We still have another recourse, however, for several (though not all) of the texts in which this expression occurs have corresponding translations in Tibetan. And a review of these texts demonstrates that not one of them contains any expression that could be construed as a translation of *saddharma-pratirūpaka*. Instead, they contain only the word "Dharma" (Tib. *chos*), together with an expression meaning "such as this" (*'di-lta-bu* or, in one instance, *'di 'dra-ba*).[29] The Tibetan texts thus force us to conclude that these passages are not translations of a phrase meaning "a *saddharma-pratirūpaka* such as this," but some other Sanskrit expression.

What this might be quickly becomes evident if we follow the suggestion of Paul Harrison that the Taishō indexers have simply divided the phrase incorrectly, and that the correct reading is *ju-shih-hsiang fa*, "a Dharma having an appearance like this."[30] For both the Chinese expression *ju-shih-hsiang* and the Tibetan *'di-lta-bu* (or *'di 'dra-ba*) are predictable translations of the Sanskrit phrase *evaṃ-rūpa*, "such as this" (or more literally, "of such a form as this"). The original Sanskrit expression, in other words, was almost cer-

---

canon (see the *Hōbōgirin* catalogue, p. 259, s.v. Jiku Hōgo).

[29] See Pek. No. 760[3], *dkon-brtsegs zi*, 345a, corresponding to T No. 342; Pek. No. 836, *mdo-sna-tshogs phu*, 309b7, corresponding to T No. 399; Pek. No. 841, *mdo-sna-tshogs bu*, 17a5, a7, and b2, corresponding to T No. 481; Pek. No. 823, *mdo-sna-tshogs pu*, 224a5, 228b2, and 241a7-8, corresponding to T No. 635.

[30] Personal communication, July 1991.

tainly *evaṃ-rūpa-dharma,* "a dharma such as this," rendered into Chinese by Dharmarakṣa (and by Dharmarakṣa alone) as *ju-shih-hsiang fa*. This group of "occurrences" of the term *hsiang-fa* listed in the Taishō index are thus figments of incorrect word division, and should be deleted from the list of genuine occurrences of *hsiang-fa* as a translation of *saddharma-pratirūpaka*.

Type 1: Inclusive Uses

Having eliminated these spurious examples from our list, we come to the first group of genuine occurrences of the term *hsiang-fa*, found in the works of a variety of translators whose works span a number of centuries. In passages of this type the expression *hsiang-fa* occurs in a set phrase meaning "after the death of [Buddha So-and-so], during *saddharma-pratirūpaka*."[31] Examples include the following:

> In the past there was a Buddha named Vipaśyin. After he had entered nirvāṇa 入涅槃後 , during *saddharma-pratirūpaka* 於像法中 . . . .[32]

> Ninety-one kalpas ago, in the world there was a Buddha named Vipaśyin. After his extinction 滅度之後 , during *saddharma-pratirūpaka* 於像法中 . . . .[33]

> In the past there was a Buddha named Vipaśyin Tathāgata. He was worthy of offerings,[34] [possessing] right and universal knowledge.[35] He made his appearance in the world, taught and converted sentient beings, and liberated people everywhere. After his *parinirvāṇa* 般涅槃後 , during *saddharma-pratirūpaka* 於像法中 . . . .[36]

> Moreover, in the past in this Jambudvīpa there appeared a Buddha in the world. His name was called Jewel-Wisdom 實慧 Tathāgata. He was worthy of offerings, [possessing] right and universal knowledge. Fully equipped with the marks [of a great

---

[31] A possible reconstruction of the underlying Sanskrit formula would be [*tathāgatasya*] *parinirvṛtasya saddharma-pratirūpaka-vartamāne*.

[32] T No. 160, 3.342c26-27, translated by Chao-te, Hui-hsün, et al. in the 12th century CE.

[33] T No. 202, 4.431b9-11, translated by Hui-chio in 445 CE.

[34] One of the standard Chinese translations of Skt. *arhant*, lit. "worthy one."

[35] A translation of *samyaksaṃbuddha*, "one who is truly and fully enlightened."

[36] T No. 643, 15.660b24-25, translated by Buddhabhadra in 420–423 CE.

> man], he made his appearance in the world, manifesting [himself] in three ways.[37] After his *parinirvāṇa* 般涅槃後 , during *saddharma-pratirūpaka* 於像法中 . . . .[38]
>
> Then, an incalculable number of generations in the past, there was a Buddha named Great Bright Light 大光明 Tathāgata. He was worthy of offerings, [possessing] right and universal knowledge, his clarity and conduct perfect,[39] well gone,[40] understanding the world,[41] an unexcelled worthy,[42] a regulator of men of stature,[43] teacher of gods and men, a Buddha, a world-honored one.[44] That Buddha appeared in the world and manifested himself in three ways.[45] He taught and converted sentient beings and liberated people everywhere. During *saddharma-pratirūpaka* 於像法中 . . . .[46]

What all these passages have in common, in addition to the use of a single set phrase, is the fact that they contain no reference to an intervening period of *saddharma* prior to the onset of the *saddharma-pratirūpaka*. Rather, they seem to consider the entire period of the duration of the Dharma (or more specifically, its duration following the death of a given Buddha) as constituting the era of *saddharma-pratirūpaka*.[47]

---

[37] This is presumably a reference to the three means of conversion (Skt. *prātihārya*) employed by Buddhas: magical power (*ṛddhi*), mind-reading (*ādeśanā*), and the power of instruction (*anuśāsanī*); see Edgerton, *Buddhist Hybrid Sanskrit Dictionary*, p. 392a. Cf. Soothill, *A Dictionary of Chinese Buddhist Terms*, p. 73b, where these are given as the attributes of bodhisattvas rather than Buddhas.

[38] T No. 176, 3.445a5-6, translated in 350–431 CE by a translator whose name has not been preserved.

[39] Skt. *vidyācaraṇa-sampanna*, lit. "endowed with insight and conduct" (i.e., the insight and conduct appropriate to a Buddha).

[40] Skt. *sugata* (id.).

[41] Skt. *lokavid*, "knower of the world."

[42] Skt. *anuttara*, "unexcelled."

[43] Skt. *puruṣadamyasārathi*, "a tamer of men." The masculine gender is explicit in both the Chinese and the Sanskrit.

[44] A Chinese translation of Skt. *bhagavān* ("blessed one") in standard use at least since the time of Kumārajīva. The Chinese, however, is a closer approximation of the Sanskrit epithet *lokajyeṣṭa* ("honored by the world") than of *bhagavān*. Cf. *Mahāvyutpatti*, no. 13.

[45] See above, n. 37.

[46] T No. 613, 15.263b11-15, translated by Kumārajīva in 402–412 CE. Here the explicit reference to the Buddha's death has apparently been omitted.

[47] It may be significant that a substantial number of such passages occur in reference to Vipaśyin, Śākyamuni's sixth predecessor and the first of the so-called

It could be argued, of course, that the authors of these passages *did* have in mind a period of *saddharma*, but simply did not find it necessary to mention it explicitly in this context.[48] And though this seems highly unlikely, it is impossible to prove that this is not the case by an argument from silence alone. Fortunately, however, we have an example from another source in which it is clear that the author intended no distinction to be made between periods of *saddharma* and *saddharma-pratirūpaka*—that is, that the entire duration of the Dharma after the death of a given Buddha was considered an undifferentiated period of *saddharma-pratirūpaka*.

This clear-cut example occurs in the text that will be a central focus of Part Two of this study, the Tibetan version of the *Candragarbha-sūtra*. Here the bodhisattva Candragarbha, concerned about the fate of the Buddhist teachings after Śākyamuni's death, asks the Buddha the following question:

> If, after the nirvāṇa of the previous Buddha, the reflection of the True Dharma (*saddharma-pratirūpaka*)[49] disappeared after [just] seven years had passed, how long will the True Dharma (*saddharma*)[50] endure after the Lord Śākyamuni has attained nirvāṇa?[51]

At first glance this passage looks somewhat peculiar, for Candragarbha seems to be asking the Buddha to compare two dissimilar things: the duration of the *saddharma-pratirūpaka* (following the death of a past Buddha), on the one hand, and the duration of the *saddharma* (after Śākyamuni's death) on the other. Yet the Buddha's response makes it clear what is meant:

> After I have attained nirvāṇa, the reflection of the True Dharma (*saddharma-pratirūpaka*)[52] will endure for two thousand years.[53]

"Seven Buddhas of the Past" (see above, pp. 19-20).

[48] In particular, one might suspect that these authors had in mind an equivalence between the lifetime of a given Buddha and the period of *saddharma*, on the one hand, and between the duration of the Dharma after his death and the period of *saddharma-pratirūpaka* on the other. While these equations seem intuitively satisfying to modern scholars, I do not know of a single canonical text that proposes this equivalence.

[49] Tib. *dam-pa'i chos-kyi gzugs-brnyan*.

[50] Tib. *dam-pa'i chos*.

[51] See the Tibetan text given in chapter 9 below, §4, lines 4-8.

[52] Tib. *dam-pa'i chos-kyi gzugs-brnyan*.

[53] §4, lines 10-11.

Asked about the duration of the *saddharma*, the Buddha replies with a pronouncement on the *saddharma-pratirūpaka*. The implication seems clear: in this text the two terms are, for all practical purposes, interchangeable. As we have seen, the figure of two thousand years represents the total duration of the Dharma after Śākyamuni's death as envisioned in this sūtra. Thus there is no ambiguity at all in the interpretation of this passage.

In occurrences of this type, then, the term *saddharma-pratirūpaka* has a clearly chronological meaning, namely, the period of time during which the True Dharma will survive. It is not, however, contrasted with a separate period of *saddharma*; rather, it is an indication of its very presence.

For the use of *saddharma-pratirūpaka* in reference to a second and distinct period in the history of the Dharma, we will have to turn to a second group of passages in which the term has undergone a noticeable shift in meaning.

Type 2: Exclusive Uses

To understand the process by which *saddharma-pratirūpaka* came to be used as the name of a second period in the history of the Dharma it would be ideal if we could observe this concept in the process of evolution. And one sūtra, preserved only in Chinese translation, offers us just such an opportunity. Here we find several versions of a single story, identical in format but differing significantly in their treatments of the duration of *saddharma-pratirūpaka*.[54] (In the following examples the portions of the text most relevant to understanding the evolution of the concept of *saddharma-pratirūpaka* are printed in boldface type.) The first version reads as follows:

Version 1

Moreover, in the past, inconceivable *asaṃkhyeya* kalpas ago

---

[54] The passages are found in T No. 156, *Ta feng-pien fo pao-en ching* 大方便佛報恩經, listed as the work of an unknown translator of the latter Han dynasty. This attribution, however—which was accepted by the editors of the Taishō canon but questioned by the publishers of the *Hōbōgirin* catalogue—is certainly incorrect. The language of the sūtra does not correspond to that of other Han-period works, and bears a close resemblance to texts translated during the late 4th or early 5th century (in particular, to the works of Kumārajīva). It seems likely, therefore, that this translation dates from the late 4th century or after.

> there appeared a Buddha in the world called Vipaśyin Tathāgata. He was worthy of offerings, of right and universal knowledge, his clarity and conduct perfect, well gone, understanding the world, an unexcelled worthy, a regulator of men of stature, a teacher of gods and men, a Buddha, a world-honored one. That Buddha appeared in the world and taught and converted an immeasurable hundreds of thousands of myriads of tens of millions of *asaṃkhyeyas* of sentient beings, and established them all in *anuttarasamyaksambodhi*. **After that Buddha's extinction** 其佛滅後, **during** ***saddharma-pratirūpaka*** 於像法中, there was a country named Vārāṇasī. The great king of that Vārāṇasī country was astute and shrewd, humane and upright. He ruled the country according to the True Dharma (*saddharma*) and did not oppress the people.[55]

In this example we have an exact parallel of the formula found in the texts cited above: the term *saddharma-pratirūpaka* refers to the undifferentiated lifetime of the Dharma following the death of the Buddha. And it is clear that the authors of this text were not assuming that the *saddharma* had expired prior to the onset of *saddharma-pratirūpaka*, for we are told that after the death of the Buddha Vipaśyin the king of Vārāṇasī "ruled the country according to the *saddharma*." Thus the *saddharma* is still seen as accessible, even though the era known as *saddharma-pratirūpaka* has begun.

In the next example this familiar formula is modified by the addition of an explicit figure for the duration of the *saddharma*:

> **Version 2**
>
> At a time in the past, uncountable thousands of years ago, there was a country named Vārāṇasī. In it there appeared a Buddha in the world called Vipaśyin Tathāgata. He was worthy of offerings, of right and universal knowledge, his clarity and conduct perfect, well gone, understanding the world, an unexcelled worthy, a regulator of men of stature, a teacher of gods and men, a Buddha, a world-honored one. In the world he taught and converted [sentient beings] for a full 10,000 years.

---

[55] T 3.137c18-24. The story of Vipaśyin, linked with a reference to a period of *saddharma-pratirūpaka* and associated with the city of Vārāṇasī, seems to have circulated as an independent pericope. The connection of Vipaśyin with Vārāṇasī is unexpected, and may represent a conflation of his legend with that of the Buddha Kāśyapa, who is ordinarily associated with this location. For references to these and the rest of the "Seven Buddhas of the Past" see above, pp. 19–20.

> **After his extinction 滅度之後 , the *saddharma* remained in the world for 12,000 years. After the extinction of the *saddharma-pratirūpaka*** 像法滅後 , there was a king of Vārāṇasī named Mahārāja 摩訶羅闍 .[56] He was astute and shrewd, humane and upright. He ruled the country according to the True Dharma (*saddharma*) and did not oppress the people.[57]

Here we are given specific figures both for the duration of the teaching career of Buddha Vipaśyin and for the survival of the Dharma after his death. But the latter, totalling 12,000 years, is not described as the period of the *saddharma-pratirūpaka*; rather, it is labeled simply as the life span of the *saddharma* itself. Even as this version of the story seems to introduce a distinction between *saddharma* and *saddharma-pratirūpaka*, then, we still do not find the two terms used in reference to two separate periods after the Buddha's death.

In a noticeable divergence from Version 1 of the story, Version 2 then tells us that the king of Vārāṇasī will appear not during the *saddharma-pratirūpaka*, but after it has expired.[58] Once again, however, he will "rule the country according to the *saddharma*," a clear indication that the True Dharma is not yet out of reach.

The time spans given in Version 2 are admittedly enormous, framed in terms of tens of thousands of years. Yet they are dwarfed in turn by the figures given in Version 3:

Version 3

> Moreover, in the past, uncountable *asaṃkhyeya* kalpas ago, at that time there was a country called Vārāṇasī. In it there appeared a Buddha in the world called Vipaśyin Tathāgata. He was worthy of offerings, of right and universal knowledge, his clarity and conduct perfect, well gone, understanding the world, an unexcelled worthy, a regulator of men of stature, a

---

[56] *Mahārāja* is, of course, simply the Sanskrit term for "great king." The Chinese translator evidently misconstrued the word as a personal name.

[57] T 3.142c9-15.

[58] It is tempting to conclude that the text is corrupt here, and that the phrase "after the extinction of the *saddharma-pratirūpaka*" originally read something like "after that Buddha's extinction, during *saddharma-pratirūpaka*," as in Version 1. The awkwardness caused by the interpolation of specific figures for the Buddha's lifetime and the duration of the *saddharma* is evident, and the redactor must have had some difficulty in making the transition from these chronological statements back to the original train of the story.

> teacher of gods and men, a Buddha, a world-honored one. That Buddha's life span was 12 small kalpas. **His *saddharma* remained in the world for 20 small kalpas. His *saddharma-pratirūpaka* also remained in the world for 20 small kalpas.**[59] During *saddharma-pratirūpaka* (於像法中) a king appeared in the world. He was called Rāja-king,[60] the king of Vārāṇasī country. He had 20,000 wives, 4,000 ministers, and 500 bull-elephants. He was the master of 60 small countries and 800 villages. The king had three sons, and he made them all rulers of small border kingdoms. At that time the king of Vārāṇasī was astute and shrewd, humane and upright. He ruled the country according to the True Dharma (*saddharma*) and did not oppress the people.[61]

Here we finally encounter the division that is so familiar in the East Asian commentaries: the treatment of *saddharma* and *saddharma-pratirūpaka* as separate and sequential periods of time.

What we are seeing in these three versions of this story, I would suggest, is the progressive editing of this passage to conform with advances in the Indian understanding of *saddharma-pratirūpaka*. And as the distinction between *saddharma* and *saddharma-pratirūpaka* became ever more explicit, the editors of this text had increasing difficulty in fitting this new understanding into the original framework of the story.[62] The pattern we can observe in these passages,

---

[59] It is interesting that the figures given here for the Buddha's life span, the duration of his *saddharma* and the duration of his *saddharma-pratirūpaka*, respectively, are identical with those given in chapters 3 and 6 of the *Lotus Sūtra* in connection with the prediction to future Buddhahood of several disciples of Śākyamuni. In Dharmarakṣa's translation (T No. 263) see 9.74b18-23, 86b25-27 and c27-29, 87b1-3 and 24-26, and 87c13-14, with variants at 74c14-17 (*cheng-fa* and *hsiang-fa* of 22 kalpas each) and 87c13 (life span of 10 kalpas), of which the former is presumably a deliberate expansion and the latter a copying error. In Kumārajīva's version (T No. 262) the same figures are given at 9.20c3-4 and 25-26 and 21a26-27, b15-16, and c1-3, with variants at 11c4-12 and 11c27-12a2 (*cheng-fa* and *hsiang-fa* of 32 kalpas each). For the Sanskrit version see P. L. Vaidya, ed., *Saddharmapuṇḍarīka-sūtra*, p. 97, lines 8-9; p. 99, lines 19-21; and p. 101, lines 8-10. The variant reading of 32 kalpas each for the *saddharma* and *saddharma-pratirūpaka* (found on p. 48, lines 19-20, 27-29, and p. 49, line 23–p. 50, line 2) is presumably a copyist's error for an earlier reading of 22 kalpas each (i.e., *dvātriṃśatī* for earlier *dvāviṃśatī*), as represented in the Chinese translation of Dharmarakṣa.

[60] Once again the Chinese translator has apparently misconstrued the Sanskrit term "king" (*rāja*) as a personal name. Cf. above, n. 56.

[61] T 3.128b1-12.

[62] There is yet a fourth version of this story in the same sūtra (3.162c5-11),

then, is that of a gradual transition from a simple formulaic statement matching the passages of Type 1 above ("after the Buddha's extinction, during *saddharma-pratirūpaka*"), to a phase in which both *saddharma* and *saddharma-pratirūpaka* are mentioned but only a single figure for the duration of the Dharma is given, and finally to a third phase in which a two-period system appears with separate (albeit identical) durations for the *saddharma* and the *saddharma-pratirūpaka*, respectively.[63]

In the review of sources concerning *saddharma-pratirūpaka* given above it may have struck the reader as peculiar that so few of these passages make any mention of the career of Śākyamuni. But in fact only a tiny minority of the sūtras containing the term *saddharma-pratirūpaka* associate this expression with the career of the historical Buddha. There are, however, a small number of such instances, which may conveniently be summarized here.

The earliest extant text containing a reference to such a subdivision within the Dharma of Śākyamuni is yet another translation by Dharmarakṣa, the *Hsien-chieh ching* 賢劫經 (Skt. *Bhadrakalpika-sūtra*), in which the careers of the "thousand Buddhas of the Good Eon" are outlined.[64] For each of these Buddhas the sūtra provides information concerning the duration of his *saddharma* in the world. When we come to the section dealing with the Buddha Śākyamuni, however, the sūtra states:

> [His] *saddharma* will remain in the world until five hundred years [have passed], and [his] *saddharma-pratirūpaka* the same.[65]

It is only for Śākyamuni, in other words, that the sūtra offers separate figures for periods of *saddharma* and *saddharma-pratirūpaka*, respectively. The fact that this feature appears only in connection

---

which seems even more garbled than the one we have cited as Version 2. In this version we are told that the king of Vārāṇasī will appear after Vipaśyin's nirvāṇa, "when his *saddharma* [and] *saddharma-pratirūpaka* have disappeared already" (c9). Once again, however, this king "will rule the country according to the *saddharma*" (c10-11).

[63] The fact that the *saddharma* and the *saddharma-pratirūpaka* are said to be of equal length in the vast majority of such passages may serve as evidence that the two-phase system was formed via reduplication.

[64] On the concept of the *bhadrakalpa* and its evolution in Indian Buddhism see above, pp. 21–24.

[65] T No. 425, 14.21a25. For the Tibetan text see above, p. 46, n. 50.

with the career of Śākyamuni, and that this apparent discrepancy is never explained in the text, raises the strong possibility that the reference to a separate period of *saddharma-pratirūpaka* represents a later emendation.

But if we can only suspect that textual tampering has occurred in this case, in both of the two remaining texts in the sūtra section of the Chinese canon in which two separate periods are mentioned in connection with the career of Śākyamuni we have concrete evidence that such tampering has taken place.[66] The first of these texts, the *Fo pen-hsing chi ching* 佛本行集經 ("Sūtra on the Compendium of the Former Deeds of the Buddhas"), offers a rather chaotic list of some sixteen former Buddhas, including the so-called "Seven Buddhas of the Past" (Vipaśyin through Śākyamuni) and eight of their predecessors.[67] In language reminiscent of the *Mahāpadāna-suttanta*,[68] this sūtra lists the name, period of existence, caste, life span, number of disciples, and duration of the *saddharma* for each of these figures. For Śākyamuni alone, however, a second (and separate) period of *saddharma-pratirūpaka* is included, with each of the two periods lasting for five hundred years:

> After my extinction, the True Dharma (*saddharma*) will remain in the world 正法往世. There will be five hundred years 有五百歲. [Then] the *saddharma-pratirūpaka* will remain in the world, likewise for five hundred years.[69]

What is particularly telling in this case, however, is that the list of Buddhas given in this sūtra—like that in the *Mahāvastu*—includes another Buddha named Śākyamuni among the Buddhas of the past.[70] And though to do so breaks the general format of this section

---

[66] One additional example is found in a sūtra containing a Mahāyāna repentance ritual, classified in the vinaya section of the Taishō canon (T No. 1493, 24.1094a16-18).

[67] T No. 190, 3.671a–672a (translated by Jñānagupta in 587–591 CE.

[68] See above, pp. 19–20.

[69] T 3.672a5-6.

[70] In fact this entire list of sixteen Buddhas also appears in the *Mahāvastu* (III, 240–49; see Jones, trans., *The Mahāvastu*, vol. 3, 230-39) with a slight difference in the sequence of nos. 7 through 9. (The *Mahāvastu* does not, however, predict the duration of each Buddha's teachings, nor does it employ the term *saddharma-pratirūpaka* in this context.) The close match between this unusual list of names in the *Mahāvastu* and its counterpart in the *Fo pen-hsing chi ching* suggests a common ancestry for the two texts, and the fact that many of the chapter titles in the two

(which contains only one figure for the duration of the Dharma per Buddha), a consistent copy editor has nonetheless inserted a reference to "five hundred years of *cheng-fa* and five hundred years of *hsiang-fa*" in reference to this earlier Śākyamuni as well:

> After the extinction of the Tathāgata [Śākyamuni], the True Dharma (*saddharma*) will remain in the world 正法住世. The scriptures [will remain] for five hundred years 經五百歲.[71] The *saddharma-pratirūpaka* will remain in the world, also for five hundred years 像法住世亦五百歲.[72]

There is, however, another distinctive feature of this sūtra that merits our attention, for in this text the duration of the Dharma is explicitly equated with the survival of the Buddhist scriptures. For each of the Buddhas of the past (with the exception of the two Śākyamunis), we find the following formula:

> After the extinction of Tathāgata [So-and-so], the True Dharma will remain in the world 正法住世. The scriptures 經 [will remain] for [such-and-such a number] of years.[73]

Neither the *saddharma* nor the *saddharma-pratirūpaka* is mentioned explicitly in this formula, and a chronological figure is assigned only to the duration of the scriptures.

A third example of the application of this two-part timetable to the career of Śākyamuni Buddha can be found in the *Karuṇāpuṇḍarīka-sūtra*, a text that has survived in a number of Sanskrit manuscripts and in Tibetan translation as well as in two Chinese renditions. Here a bodhisattva named Samudrareṇu (who is to become Śākyamuni Buddha in the future) makes the following vow in the presence of the Buddha Ratnagarbha:

> After my *parinirvāṇa* may my *saddharma* stand for a thousand years, and may my *saddharma-pratirūpaka* stand for five hundred years.[74]

---

are identical reinforces this impression. A comparative study of these two texts would no doubt be rewarding.

[71] T 3.671c11-12.

[72] T 3.671c12-13.

[73] T 3.671b25-26.

[74] Based on the Sanskrit text given in Yamada, ed., *Karuṇāpuṇḍarīka-sūtra*, vol. 2, p. 262, lines 9-11. The Tibetan and Chinese translations offer the same figures; for the Chinese see T No. 157, 3.211b26-27 and T No. 158, 3.270a3-4. The Tibetan text is given in chapter 3 above (see p. 49, n. 59).

Later in the same chapter, however, when Ratnagarbha praises Samudrareṇu for his vow, he predicts only that his *saddharma* will last for a thousand years. In an apparent interpolation (not found in the Sanskrit or Tibetan versions), however, the two Chinese translations then go on to say that his *saddharma-pratirūpaka* will likewise last for a thousand years:

> After that Buddha's [i.e., your] *parinirvāṇa*, the *saddharma* will remain in the world for a full one thousand years. When the *saddharma* has already become extinct, the *saddharma-pratirūpaka* will remain in the world for another one thousand years.[75]

Once again we have evidence that the text has been tampered with: an original figure of one thousand years has been supplemented in the two Chinese translations, but not in the Sanskrit or Tibetan texts, by an additional one thousand years of *saddharma-pratirūpaka*. Here the editor of the text has not been thorough enough, however, for the earlier passage (in which the second period was assigned a total of only five hundred years) has been left unchanged.

A final reference to a two-part timetable associated with the career of Śākyamuni is found in the Chinese version of the *Candragarbha-sūtra*:

> After my nirvāṇa the True Dharma (*saddharma*) will remain in the world for five hundred years. . . . The *saddharma-pratirūpaka* will remain in the world for a full one thousand years.[76]

As we have seen, however, this twofold division does not appear in either the Tibetan or the Khotanese version of this sūtra. Thus we are justified in suspecting that, once again, the text has been "adjusted" to conform with new developments in the understanding of *saddharma-pratirūpaka*.

In sum, the division of the duration of the Dharma into two distinct and sequential periods is found in only a small number of canonical sūtras. And of these, only a tiny minority associate such a division with the career of Śākyamuni Buddha. It is particularly

---

[75] T No. 157, 3.219c20-22. Virtually the same wording is given in T No. 158, 3.277b12-14.

[76] T No. 397[15], 13.379c5-9.

noteworthy that several of the sūtras that in East Asia became most closely identified with the division of the Buddha's Dharma into sequential periods – in particular, the *Pure Land* and *Lotus* sūtras – do not apply a distinction between *saddharma* and *saddharma-pratirūpaka* to the teachings of Śākyamuni Buddha himself. The reading of these texts as if they contained such a distinction (supplemented by a third period of *mo-fa*, to be discussed below) is thus a contribution of later commentators, who in interpreting these texts through such a lens gave them an entirely new meaning.

We can distinguish, then, between two distinctive (though not entirely separate) uses of the term *saddharma-pratirūpaka*, which seem to have emerged in roughly the following sequence:

- a first phase, during which the term refers to the total duration of the Dharma after a given Buddha's death; and
- a second phase, during which *saddharma-pratirūpaka* is restricted in meaning to only the latter part of this period, the second of two sub-periods in the lifetime of the Dharma.

In neither case, however, is the *saddharma-pratirūpaka* referred to in explicitly pejorative terms. Rather, it refers to the real and ongoing presence of the *saddharma*, whether it is used to refer to part or all of the period when this will be the case.

SADDHARMA-PRATIRŪPAKA: TOWARD A USABLE TRANSLATION

In light of the analysis given above it now seems quite peculiar that the translation of *saddharma-pratirūpaka* (and of its Chinese counterpart *hsiang-fa*) most frequently encountered in English-language studies is "counterfeit Dharma."[77] For in none of the passages cited above would such a translation make sense. In none of these texts is there any implication that the *saddharma-pratirūpaka* is a fake or a forgery of the True Dharma; rather, it refers to the presence of the True Dharma itself, in all or part of its duration. Even when a clear-cut distinction between periods of *saddharma* and *saddharma-pratirūpaka* begins to emerge, the latter period is still viewed as pos-

[77] See for example the translations of the *Lotus Sūtra* from the Sanskrit by H. Kern (p. 68 and *passim*) and from the Chinese by Leon Hurvitz (p. 54 and *passim*). I am not aware of any translation from the Tibetan in which *dam-pa'i chos-kyi gzugs-brnyan* is rendered into English as "counterfeit Dharma."

itive (if slightly less so than that in the preceding versions), and is credited to the account, so to speak, of a given Buddha as part of the total duration of his teachings.

In none of the sources we have reviewed, then, is the *saddharma-pratirūpaka* portrayed as in any way opposed to the *saddharma*. Two questions are therefore in order: first, how did the convention of translating this expression as "counterfeit Dharma" come about? And second, are there any cases at all in which such a translation might not only be permissible, but required?

These two questions are best answered together, for the practice of translating *saddharma-pratirūpaka* as "counterfeit Dharma" appears to stem from the sole occurrence of this term in the Theravāda canon. As translated by C. A. F. Rhys Davids, this passage reads as follows:

> There is no disappearing of the true doctrine (*saddhamma*), Kassapa, till a counterfeit doctrine (*saddhamma-paṭirūpaka*) arises in the world; but when a counterfeit doctrine does arise, then there is a disappearance of the true doctrine. Just as there is no disappearing of gold so long as there is no counterfeit gold arisen in the world.[78]

Here there can be no question that Rhys Davids' translation is correct: the context requires that the Pāli term *saddhamma-paṭirūpaka* be understood as "counterfeit." But the term "counterfeit" would simply not be appropriate in any of the passages containing this expression cited above. How, then, can this discrepancy be explained?

We may begin with the observation that there are two virtually identical Sanskrit terms, differing only in the length of the vowel in the first syllable, of which one carries the primary meaning of

[78] Pāli *na tāva Kassapa saddhammassa antaradhānaṃ hoti yāva na saddhamma-paṭirūpakaṃ loke uppajjati, yato ca kho Kassapa saddhammapaṭirūpakaṃ loke uppajjati atha saddhammassa antaradhānaṃ hoti. Seyyathāpi Kassapa na tāva jātarūpassa antaradhānaṃ hoti yāva na jātarūpapaṭirūpakaṃ loke uppajjati. yato ca kho Kassapa jātarūpapaṭirūpakaṃ loke uppajjati atha jātarūpassa antaradhānaṃ hoti.* See *Saṃyutta-nikāya*, Part II: *Nidāna-varga* (London: Luzac & Co., 1960), p. 224, 5-6; English translation in C. A. F. Rhys Davids, trans., *The Book of Kindred Sayings* (*Saṃyutta-nikāya*) (1917-30; repr. London: Pali Text Society, 1972), Part II, 152. For the Chinese parallels (found in two separate translations of the *Saṃyukta-āgama*) see T No. 99, 2.226c7 and No. 100, 2.419b25. In T No. 99 the term used is *hsiang-ssu hsiang-fa* 相似像法 ; in T. No. 100 *hsiang-fa* 像法 alone is used.

"counterfeit" (*prātirūpaka*) while the other can in certain instances have that meaning, but carries the primary sense of "semblance, likeness, reflection" (*pratirūpaka*).[79] Where the Sanskrit version of the texts cited above has survived, it is uniformly the second of these spellings that is employed.

Yet it was the Pāli form *saddhamma-paṭirūpaka* (of which the second component can serve as the equivalent of either of these Sanskrit terms), in the clearly negative context cited above, that was the first to come to the attention of Western scholars. It is thus not surprising that when H. Kern, for example, encountered the corresponding Sanskrit term in the *Lotus Sūtra*, he would have had the usage found in this Pāli text in mind. In translating Sanskrit *saddharma-pratirūpaka* into English as "counterfeit Dharma" Kern was thus reading the Sanskrit text in light of the Pāli, and in so doing set a precedent that has yet to be overcome.[80]

What we can state with complete certainty, however, is that neither the Chinese nor the Tibetans understood the term in this sense. The usual Tibetan translation of *saddharma-pratirūpaka*, *dam-pa'i chos-kyi gzugs-brnyan*, cannot be construed as meaning "counterfeit Dharma." Rather, the element representing Skt. *pratirūpaka*, Tib. *gzugs-brnyan* (lit. "borrowed form"), carries the connotations of "reflection," "image," or "shadow."[81] Likewise, the Chinese term *hsiang-fa* cannot (in itself) be interpreted as "counterfeit"; the element *hsiang* 像 means simply "semblance," "likeness," or "image."[82]

How, then, are we to translate the expression *saddharma-pratirūpaka* (and its Chinese and Tibetan counterparts) into English?

---

[79] See Monier-Williams, *Sanskrit-English Dictionary*, 706c; Macdonnell, *Sanskrit Dictionary*, 175a and 185c; and Apte, *Practical Sanskrit English Dictionary*, 1069b.

[80] Kern's knowledge of the Pāli canon often influenced his readings of the Sanskrit text of the *Lotus*, as for example in his rendition of one of the ten standard epithets of the Buddha as "unsurpassed tamer of men" (65 and *passim*). This is indeed the way the term is understood in the Pāli (where it is generally written as *anuttarapurisadammasārathi*); in the Sanskrit text of the *Lotus*, however, the term *anuttara* "unexceeded" is written separately (Skt. *anuttaraḥ*) rather than as part of a compound, and is clearly intended to be construed as a separate epithet. Chinese and Tibetan authorities have generally followed the latter usage, treating Skt. *anuttara* in this context as a free-standing epithet (Ch. 無上 , Tib. *bla-na-med-pa*; see Soothill, p. 52b, and *Mahāvyutpatti*, no. 9).

[81] See Das, *Tibetan-English Dictionary*, p. 1106a, and Rerikh, *Tibetsko-russko-angliiskii slovar'*, vyp. 8, p. 179b.

[82] See Mathews, *Chinese-English Dictionary*, no. 2569 (p. 381b).

Clearly the context must dictate its significance, and it is likely that no single equivalent will be appropriate in all instances. Yet the following may be offered as general guidelines.

First of all, we must distinguish between the Indian and Tibetan renditions of the term, on the one hand, and the Chinese on the other, for these two groups are structured very differently. For the Sanskrit and Tibetan, both of which have a word for "True Dharma" embedded within a longer expression (Skt. *saddharma-pratirūpaka*, Tib. *dam-pa'i chos-kyi gzugs-brnyan*), such renditions as "semblance of the True Dharma" or "reflection of the True Dharma" are to be preferred. Such expressions convey both the literal meaning of the term and the sense that the *saddharma-pratirūpaka* is indeed in conformity with the genuine teachings of the Buddha.

The Chinese is somewhat more problematic, since *hsiang-fa* is not a full translation of *saddharma-pratirūpaka* but an abbreviation — that is, it lacks any equivalent of the component "true" (Skt. *sad-*). Moreover, the Chinese word order allows this expression to be interpreted as a type of Dharma, namely a "Semblance-Dharma," as well as a "semblance *of* the Dharma." In the case of the Chinese, then, a suitable translation would be "Semblance Dharma," which follows the word order of the original. As we shall see, it was the choice of this simplified expression — in all probability the legacy of the translator Dharmarakṣa — that paved the way for the development of the idea of a third and final period in the history of the Dharma, a period unknown in South or Central Asian Buddhism but fundamental to much of East Asian Buddhist thought.

The term "semblance," then, serves as a suitable equivalent of the Sanskrit term *pratirūpaka*, and conforms in meaning to Chinese *hsiang* and Tibetan *gzugs-brnyan* as well. The term "counterfeit" should clearly be abandoned, as it represents a radical misunderstanding of the significance of this expression in Mahāyāna usage.[83]

---

[83] It should be retained, of course, in translating the passage from the Pāli *Saṃyutta-nikāya* (and its Chinese parallels) and perhaps also in the sole Vinaya text in which it occurs, with its discussion of the five "non-Dharmas" 非法 that will appear during that time (T No. 1435, 23.358c). That the use of the term *saddharma-pratirūpaka* in the sense of "counterfeit" is restricted to Nikāya Buddhist (i.e., non-Mahāyāna) texts is intriguing in light of the fact that some of the Mahāyāna texts we have examined use the term in reference to specific (Mahāyāna) Buddhist scriptures. From the perspective of the Nikāya Buddhists, of course, such Mahāyāna scriptures did indeed represent a "counterfeit of the True Dharma."

MO-FA: THE AGE OF THE FINAL DHARMA

If we have had little difficulty in locating examples of the use of the term *saddharma-pratirūpaka* (and of the two-part timetable with which it eventually came to be associated) in Buddhist scriptures composed in India, matters are altogether different when we come to the third dispensation in the history of the Buddhist religion, known in East Asian sources as *mo-fa* 末法 (Jpn. *mappō*). Though the term itself appears in a number of sūtras translated into Chinese from Indian originals, it is not at all clear what Sanskrit Buddhist term—if any—can properly be described as its antecedent. Moreover, though the idea of a three-part timetable of *cheng-fa*, *hsiang-fa*, and *mo-fa* is so ubiquitous in East Asian Buddhist writings that much of the history of Buddhism in this region would be incomprehensible without it, it has proved singularly difficult to find examples of such a three-part scenario in any Buddhist source of certifiably Indian origin. We may begin, therefore, by evaluating some of the prevailing views concerning the ancestry and significance of *mo-fa*. Among the most influential of these assumptions are the following:

- that the term *mo-fa* is a Chinese translation of the Sanskrit Buddhist technical term *saddharma-vipralopa*;
- that *mo-fa*, wherever it occurs in Chinese Buddhist texts, refers to the third of these three periods in the history of the Dharma; and
- that Chinese Buddhists adopted this three-part scenario from their Indian coreligionists.

We will consider each of these assumptions in turn, beginning with the antecedents of *mo-fa* itself.

SANSKRIT COUNTERPARTS OF *MO-FA*

It is frequently assumed, by both Japanese and Western scholars, that the Chinese term *mo-fa* is a translation of Sanskrit *saddharma-vipralopa* (destruction of the True Dharma).[84] Yet this equivalence

---

[84] See for example *Mochizuki Bukkyō daijiten*, vol. 5, 4747a. The same equivalence

has long since been called into question by Étienne Lamotte, who contended that the proper Sanskrit equivalent of *mo-fa* would be not *saddharma-vipralopa*, but *paścima-dharma* ("after-Dharma" or "latter Dharma").[85] Strangely, however, the latter expression seems not to occur in Indian Buddhist literature.[86] This brings us, then, back to our original question: what is the real Sanskrit antecedent of *mo-fa*?

We may begin with the handful of Chinese sūtras—only three texts in all—that contain the term *mo-fa* and have surviving Sanskrit counterparts. By comparing these uses of *mo-fa* with the corresponding passages in the Sanskrit we may be able to evaluate the assertion that *mo-fa* is a translation of *saddharma-vipralopa*.

By far the earliest and most influential of the three (and the text most frequently cited by modern scholars in this connection) is Kumārajīva's translation of the *Lotus Sūtra* (Skt. *Saddharma-puṇḍarīka-sūtra*, 妙法蓮華經). In light of the close association between the general concept of a "latter age" and the text of the *Lotus Sūtra* in much of East Asian (especially Japanese) exegesis, it is somewhat surprising that the term *mo-fa* occurs only once in the recension of the text given in the Taishō canon. The passage in question is the following:

Chinese:[87] after the Tathāgata's extinction, during *mo-fa* (如來滅後於末法中)

Sanskrit:[88] after the Tathāgata's *parinirvāṇa*, in the latter time, in the latter period, in the latter fifty [years],[89] when the

is given in Nakamura, *Bukkyōgo daijiten*, vol. 2, 1284b, and has found its way into numerous secondary sources, both Japanese and Western.

85 Lamotte, *Histoire du bouddhisme indien*, 211. Conversely, one might point out (though Lamotte does not do so) that the proper Chinese equivalent of *(sad)dharma-vipralopa* is not *mo-fa* but *fa-mieh* 法滅 (Jpn. *hōmetsu*), an expression that occurs with some frequency in the Chinese Buddhist translation literature.

86 The term is not registered, at any rate, in any of the Sanskrit or Pāli texts or concordances consulted by this writer. Nor does Lamotte himself cite any instances of its occurrence, which—as readers familiar with Lamotte's scholarship will realize—constitutes a rather strong argument from silence.

87 T No. 262, 9.37c29. The term *mo-fa* does not occur in the earlier translation of the same text by Dharmarakṣa (T No. 263).

88 H. Kern and B. Nanjio, eds., *Saddharmapuṇḍarīka*, Bibliotheca Buddhica, vol. X (1912; repr. Osnabrück: Biblio Verlag, 1970), 282, lines 9-10.

89 The Sanskrit text clearly reads *paścimāyām pañcāśatyām* "in the latter fifty [years]." Kern, however, translates "the last five hundred years" (268). The confu-

> True Dharma is in the process of destruction (*tathāgatasya parinirvṛtasya paścime kāle paścime samaye paścimāyāṃ pañcāśatyāṃ saddharma-vipralope vartamāna*)

It is immediately evident even to the casual reader that the correspondence between these two passages is far from exact. And since the Sanskrit text in its present form clearly postdates Kumārajīva's translation by several centuries,[90] it is quite possible that substantial portions of this Sanskrit passage were added well after Kumārajīva made his translation. We cannot be sure, in other words, that the expression *saddharma-vipralopa* was found in the Sanskrit original used by Kumārajīva at all, let alone that he intended the term *mo-fa* as its translation.[91]

---

sion between "fifty" and "five hundred" in this and other such passages (frequently reflected in Dharmarakṣa's Chinese translation, which often reads 餘五十歲 "in the remaining fifty years" where Kumārajīva has 後五百歲 "in the latter five hundred years"), first drawn to my attention by Michel Strickmann in a lecture given at Harvard University in 1979, is easily explained if we postulate the transmission of texts containing this expression in the Kharoṣṭhī script used in northwest India and Central Asia, in which long vowels are generally not indicated. In such a script the distinction between "fifty" (*pañcāśatyām*, fem. loc. sing. < *pañcāśatī*) and "five hundred" (*pañcaśatyām*, fem. loc. sing. < *pañcaśatī*) would have been entirely invisible.

In the passage quoted here the expression *paścimāyām pañcāśatyām* is absent from a number of the Sanskrit manuscript copies, and no counterpart of the phrase is found in the Tibetan translation (Pek. No. 781, *mdo-sna-tshogs chu*, 121a7–8) or in the Chinese translations of Dharmarakṣa (T 9.108b16), Kumārajīva (T 9.37c29), or Jñānagupta and Dharmagupta (T 9.172b4), respectively. For the Sanskrit version see P. L. Vaidya, ed., *Saddharma-puṇḍarīka-sūtra*, Buddhist Sanskrit Texts No. 6 (Dharbanga: Mithila Institute, 1960), 169, lines 23-24 and n. 7. For a complete listing of references to the "latter age" in Kumārajīva's translation of the *Lotus Sūtra* and their parallels in the Sanskrit and in the Chinese translations of Dharmarakṣa and of Jñānagupta and Dharmagupta see Jan Nattier, "The *Candragarbha-sūtra* in Central and East Asia: Studies in a Buddhist Prophecy of Decline," Ph.D. thesis, Harvard University (1988), 340–47.

[90] The Nepalese manuscript copies of the Sanskrit *Lotus Sūtra*, on which published editions of the text are based, all date from the 11th c. CE or later. The relation between the Nepalese texts and the Gilgit manuscripts (which are perhaps three or four centuries earlier) is quite close, though complex; See Oskar von Hinüber, *A New Fragmentary Gilgit Manuscript* (Tokyo: Reiyukai, 1982), pp. x–xvi. A number of fragments of the Sanskrit text, dating from as early as the 6th c. CE, have also been discovered in Central Asia (modern Xinjiang); concerning these manuscripts see Akira YUYAMA, *A Bibliography of the Sanskrit Texts of the Saddharmapuṇḍarīkasūtra* (Canberra: Australian National University Press, 1970), 20–34.

[91] The earlier translation of the same passage made by Dharmarakṣa (286 CE)

The two other Chinese texts containing the term *mo-fa* for which corresponding Sanskrit versions are extant both date from several centuries after Kumārajīva's time, a fact that considerably diminishes their value, since the term *mo-fa* was by then well established in Chinese Buddhist discourse and thus might be "read into" the text by a Chinese translator in a way that earlier translators would not have done. Nonetheless it is useful to note that in neither of these cases does the Chinese term *mo-fa* correspond to Skt. *saddharma-vipralopa*. In the *Rāṣṭrapāla-paripṛcchā-sūtra* (護國尊者所問大乘經 , translated by Dānapāla in 994 CE) *mo-fa* corresponds to Skt. *paścimakāle* ("in the latter time"),[92] while in the *Gaṇḍavyūha-sūtra* (大方廣佛華嚴經 , translated by Prajñā in 798 CE) the corresponding expression is Skt. *śāsanāntardhāna-kāla-samaye* ("in the period of the time of the final destruction of the teaching").[93] There is, then, no single Sanskrit term that exhibits a regular, demonstrable correspondence to Chinese *mo-fa*. Rather, a variety of Sanskrit phrases appear in passages paralleling this Chinese expression, of which the most common (that is, the only one that occurs in more than one instance) is the phrase *paścimakāle,* "in the latter time."

This impression is seconded when we consult the Tibetan translation literature, which (due to its almost mechanical fidelity to the Sanskrit) can serve as a highly reliable guide to the contents of the underlying Sanskrit originals. By making use of materials preserved in the Tibetan canon we are able to consult an additional six sūtra texts, none extant in the original Sanskrit, whose Chinese counterparts contain the expression *mo-fa*. In two of these texts Ch. *mo-fa* has no Tibetan counterpart at all,[94] in one case the

---

is considerably more abbreviated, and does not contain the expression *mo-fa*. It reads simply "after the Tathāgata's passage into extinction (如來滅度之後)"; see T No. 263, 9.108b16.

92 T No. 321, 12.4b12; Sanskrit text in Jacob Ensink, *The Question of Rāṣṭrapāla*, 17, line 14. The term *mo-fa* does not appear in the earlier Chinese translation of the same work, done by Jñānagupta during the period 585–604 CE (T No. 310[18]).

93 T No. 293, 10.762a12–14. For the corresponding Sanskrit text see P. L. Vaidya, ed., *Gaṇḍavyūhasūtra* (Darbhanga: Mithila Institute, 1960), 236, lines 20-21.

94 No counterpart for the term *mo-fa* found in the Chinese translation of the *Sūryagarbha* chapter of the *Mahāsaṃnipāta-sūtra* (T No. 397[14],13.267a22–26) occurs in the corresponding Tibetan version (Pek. No. 923, *mdo-sna-tshogs zhu*, 191b–192a). In the case of another work belonging to the *Mahāsaṃnipāta* corpus, the *Daśacakra-kṣitigarbha-sūtra*, where the term *mo-fa* is found in the Chinese (T No.

corresponding Tibetan passage has simply "at that time" (Tib. *de'i tshe*),[95] and in another two cases the Tibetan texts read "in the latter time, in the latter age" (*slad-ma'i tshe slad-ma'i dus*),[96] a phrase that almost certainly goes back to an original Skt. *paścimakāle paścimasamaye*. The final text in this group reads "as to the [future] destruction of this teaching" (*bstan-pa 'di rab-tu 'jig-par 'gyur-ba ni*),[97] which may reflect an underlying Sanskrit expression such as **śāsanāntardhāna* or **śāsana-vipralopa*. (It cannot, however, be construed as a translation of Skt. *saddharma-vipralopa*, since in classical Tibetan *saddharma* is consistently translated as *dam-pa'i chos* while *bstan-pa* serves as the regular equivalent of *śāsana*.) The Tibetan texts thus reinforce the pattern we have observed in the three extant Sanskrit works discussed above: that there is no single expression, either in the Tibetan or in the underlying Sanskrit, that occurs consistently as the counterpart of *mo-fa*. Instead we find a variety of equivalents (when we find any at all) in passages paralleling the Chinese uses of *mo-fa*, of which the most frequent—with two occurrences in the Sanskrit and two in the Tibetan, for a total of four occurrences out of nine texts in all—is the expression *paścimakāle paścimasamaye* "in the latter time, in the latter age" (Tib. *slad-ma'i tshe slad-ma'i dus*).

Given the weight of this evidence we must discard the idea that the expression *mo-fa* was coined to serve as the Chinese translation of Skt. *saddharma-vipralopa*. Indeed, if there is any Sanskrit expression that exhibits some regularity of correspondence to *mo-fa* it is not *saddharma-vipralopa* but *paścimakāle*, a term whose significance will be considered in detail below.

410, 13.700b17–18), the Tibetan version can tell us little, for it is itself a translation from the Chinese, though from a different version of the text (T No. 411) in which the term *mo-fa* does not appear.

[95] In the Chinese translation of the **Trisaṃvara-nirdeśa-sūtra* (T No. 310[1], 11.6a10–14), corresponding to the Tibetan Pek. No. 760[1], *dkon-brtsegs tshi*, 14a2.

[96] See the *Gaganagañja-paripṛcchā-sūtra* (Pek. No. 815, *mdo-sna-tshogs nu*, 290a8), corresponding to the Chinese T No. 402, 13.582b25, and the **Saptatathāgata-pūrvapraṇidhāna-viśeṣa-vistara-sūtra* (Pek. No. 135, *rgyud da*, 246a6), corresponding to T No. 451, 14.414c22–24 in the Chinese.

[97] See the Tibetan translation of the **Ratnarāśi-sūtra* (Pek. No. 760[45], *dkon-brtsegs 'i*, 148a7), corresponding to T No. 310[44], 11.639a21–27.

MO-FA AND THE THREE-PERIOD SYSTEM

If *mo-fa* cannot be viewed simply as a translation of a well-known Sanskrit technical term, we must turn directly to the Chinese Buddhist literature in our attempt to determine its significance. Restricting our inquiry at this point to those texts translated from Indian originals (both in order to focus on the point of entry of the term into Chinese Buddhist usage and to continue our attempt to establish its proper Indian antecedent, if any), we will begin by tabulating the occurrences of the term in the first seventeen volumes of the Taishō canon—that is, in the āgama, *avadāna*, and Mahāyāna sūtra literature. Once again we will rely on the occurrences of the term registered in the index to the Taishō canon, a work whose usefulness and limitations have been discussed above.[98]

Based on the understanding of the term that was to become standard in East Asian Buddhist exegesis—that it refers to the third of three periods in Buddhist history—we would expect that in at least some instances *mo-fa* would occur in conjunction with its two "sister expressions," *cheng-fa* (Skt. *saddharma*) and *hsiang-fa* (Skt. *saddharma-pratirūpaka*). What we find in the actual Chinese translations, however, is a quite different pattern. The term *cheng-fa* "True Dharma" is of course ubiquitous in the Chinese canon, so much so that its occurrences could not be registered separately in the index. If we restrict our inquiry to tabulating the registered occurrences of *hsiang-fa* and *mo-fa*, however, we obtain the following results:

hsiang-fa	***mo-fa***
T No. 99	—
156	—
157	—
158	—
—	159
160	—
176	—
190	—
202	202*
221	—
262	262*
263	—

[98] See above, p. 69, note 10.

264	264*
——	267
272	——
273	——
291	——
——	293
294	——
——	310[1]
310[12]	——
——	310[44]
316	——
320	——
——	321
329	——
345	——
——	397[14]
397[15]	——
398	——
——	402
——	404
——	410
——	411
——	412
414	——
415	——
425	——
426	——
450	——
451	451*
456	——
461	——
485	——
495	——
565	——
587	——
613	——
——	617
639	——
643	643*
663	——
664	——
665	——
670	——
673	673*
674	——
——	697
738	——

—	748
783	—
839	839*

In sharp contrast to what we might expect, the above list shows not a multitude of texts in which *hsiang-fa* and *mo-fa* appear in conjunction, but quite the opposite. With only a handful of exceptions—those texts marked with an asterisk in the list above—either *hsiang-fa* or *mo-fa* may appear in a given text, *but not both*. The two terms do not, in other words, appear to operate in tandem; rather, each seems to be a strong counterindicator for the appearance of the other.

The impression that the terms *hsiang-fa* and *mo-fa* are operating on separate wavelengths, rather than as integral parts of a single system, is heightened when we examine more closely those few texts in which both of these expressions occur. For even in these cases the two expressions generally occur in entirely independent contexts, often separated from one another by several pages (or even entire chapters) of intervening material.[99] The overall pattern in the usage of these two terms, then, is clear: we may expect to meet with either *hsiang-fa* or *mo-fa* in a given text (or more precisely, in a given context), but not both.

Two possible explanations of this disjunction may be suggested. On the one hand, the two terms may be incompatible; that is, they may be elements in competing conceptual systems, which could ordinarily occur together only in an explicitly competitive or contrastive fashion. On the other, they may be functional equiva-

---

[99] This pattern is most noticeable in the *Sūtra on the Wise and the Foolish* (T No. 202, where *hsiang-fa* appears at 4.431b and *mo-fa* at 4.376a) and in the two later translations of the *Lotus Sūtra* by Kumārajīva (T No. 262, where *hsiang-fa* occurs at 9.11c, 20c, 28c, and 50c, while *mo-fa* occurs only at 37c) and the team of Jñānagupta and Dharmagupta (T No. 264, where *hsiang-fa* occurs at 9.144b, 155b, 163b, and 184c, with *mo-fa* appearingly only at 172b), respectively. In two other texts the terms occur in somewhat greater proximity, yet a close reading of the contexts demonstrates no discernible connection between them. See the **Saptatathāgata-pūrvapraṇidhāna-viśeṣa-vistara-sūtra* translated in 707 CE by I-ching (T No. 451), where *hsiang-fa* appears at 14.415b27 and *mo-fa* at 414c22–25, and the *Sūtra on the Samādhi-Sea of Buddha-Remembrance* (T No. 643) translated by Buddhabhadra in 420–423 CE, where *hsiang-fa* appears at 15.660b24–25 and *mo-fa* at 661a14–16. In both cases, despite the apparent proximity of the two terms (which are never, however, separated by fewer than 850 Chinese characters), these two expressions occur in entirely separate stories, and no explicit connection is ever made between them.

lents of one another, such that the use of both terms in a single context would simply be redundant. In the former case, a given text (or its translator) might belong to one camp or the other (if indeed he did not fall outside both, and use neither of these terms); in the latter, the translator might simply have a stylistic preference for, or familiarity with, only one of the two terms, and accordingly would not have used the other in his translation. A third explanation—that this either/or pattern is simply a coincidence—seems extremely unlikely, given the overwhelming regularity of its occurrence.

Before examining the two texts in which *hsiang-fa* and *mo-fa* do occur in close proximity, we should also take note of another important fact: that is, that in the entirety of the first seventeen volumes of the Taishō canon, comprising 847 separate scriptures and totalling over 16,000 pages of printed text (that is, approximately 25,296,000 Chinese characters), only 22 individual works containing the term *mo-fa* are registered in the Taishō index. Moreover, in virtually all of these cases the term appears only once in a given text, rather than being used repeatedly and serving as a major topic of discussion in its own right. While there are undoubtedly other occurrences of the term that have escaped the notice of the indexers, the overall trend is quite clear: this expression is as rare in the canonical sūtra literature as it is ubiquitous in the East Asian commentaries.

Only in two translated texts do the terms *hsiang-fa* and *mo-fa* occur in the same context, in a setting that might allow the reader—at least, the reader already predisposed to do so—to construe them as parts of a single sequential system. In the first of these, the *Chan-ch'a shan-e yeh-pao ching* 占察善惡業報經 (T No. 839, "Sūtra on Determining the Retribution of Good and Evil Conduct") the bodhisattva Firm Pure Faith 堅浄信 asks the Buddha what kind of skillful means should be used to convert and lead sentient beings in the Way, to cause them to give rise to the mind of faith (信心) and to successfully get rid of the *kleśa*s,

> on behalf of this future evil age, **when the *hsiang-fa* is about to be destroyed** (像法向盡), **and in the midst of *mo-fa*** (及末法中).[100]

[100] T 17.901c25.

Just a few lines earlier, however, the same speaker referred to a time

> after the True Dharma (*cheng-fa*) has become extinct (正法滅後), **when the *hsiang-fa* is about to be destroyed** (像法向盡), **and when [the world is] entering *mo-shih*** (及入末世).[101]

The critical portions of these two passages, printed in boldface type, are virtually identical, except that the expression "in the midst of *mo-fa*" used in the first instance is replaced by "when [the world is] entering *mo-shih*" in the second. This raises the possibility that, according to this text at least, the time of *mo-fa* and that of entering *mo-shih* (末世 "final age") are to be viewed as identical.

Whatever the intention of the author of this text, however, these passages will not provide us with evidence for the existence of a system of three sequential time-periods in Indian Buddhism. For the *Chan-ch'a shan-e yeh-pao ching* has been considered to be of suspicious origins since its initial appearance on the Chinese scene, and it is now considered by modern scholars not to be of Indian authorship at all, but an apocryphal text composed in China during the late 6th century CE.[102]

The sole remaining canonical sūtra in which we have some hope of finding a prototype for the Chinese three-period time scheme is the *Ta-sheng t'ung-hsing ching* 大乘同性經 (T No. 673, Skt. **Mahāyāna-abhisamaya-sūtra*, translated by Jñānayaśas in 570 CE), in which we find the following passage:

> The Tathāgata manifests himself and descends from the Tuṣita Heaven to uphold the entire True Dharma (*cheng-fa*), the entire Semblance Dharma (*hsiang-fa*), and the entire Final Dharma (*mo-fa*).[103]

This brief listing comprises the sole passage identified thus far in the entire body of Chinese Buddhist translation literature in which all three components of the East Asian tripartite system occur together. Yet the text tells us nothing about how they are to be understood; there is neither a description of the circumstances pertaining to each nor a discussion (if indeed they are to be construed as sequential periods) of their duration. Moreover, the date

---

[101] T 17.901c13–14.

[102] See Whalen Lai, "The *Chan-ch'a ching*: Religion and Magic in Medieval China," in Buswell, *Chinese Buddhist Apocrypha*, 175–206.

[103] T 16.651c12–13.

of translation of this sūtra postdates by several years the first detailed discussion of the periods of *cheng-fa*, *hsiang-fa*, and *mo-fa* in a Chinese scholastic text.[104] Thus it could hardly have served as the inspiration for the Chinese formulation of this system, even if it had provided a more explicit discussion of the meanings of these three terms. Finally, it is important to note that in four of the recensions consulted by the Taishō editors (the Old Sung, Sung, Yüan, and Ming editions) the term *mo-fa* does not appear in this passage at all. Rather, the expression *mieh-fa* 滅法 "destruction of the Dharma" is used instead, thus lending a quite different connotation to this passage.

This very minimal listing, then—and one not even found in all the editions of the Chinese canon itself—is the sole sūtra passage in which all three elements of the Chinese tripartite system are mentioned together. And though this sūtra has not (so far as I know) been suspected of being apocryphal, it may be significant that it has neither a surviving Sanskrit original nor a counterpart in Tibetan translation.[105] Whatever its ancestry, however, it could hardly be described as providing an explicit discussion of this three-part system or a chronological listing of its three components. Such information, in fact, is to be found nowhere in the Chinese Buddhist canonical literature—nowhere, that is, but in the works of Chinese and other East Asian writers themselves.

An obvious question arises at this point: If no explicit discussion of a sequential system of three ages in the history of Buddhism can be identified in any Chinese text known to be translated from an Indian original, then what is the source of this East Asian idea? To answer this question we must begin by examining the uses of a term that appears to be closely related to *mo-fa* and occurs, in at least some instances, in precisely the same contexts: the expression *mo-shih* or "final age."

---

[104] The three-period time system is first mentioned in the *Nan-yüeh Ssu ta ch'an-shih li shih-yüan wen*, traditionally attributed to Hui-ssu and said to have been completed in the year 558 CE. For further discussion see below, pp. 111.

[105] In fact, a substantial proportion of the earliest texts in which the term *mo-fa* appears lack such evidence of an Indian pedigree. Of the eight earliest occurrences of the term *mo-fa* (all dating from the first half of the 5th century CE or slightly earlier), only two have either an extant Sanskrit version (T No 262, the *Lotus Sūtra* of Kumārajīva) or a Tibetan counterpart not translated from the Chinese (T No. 310[44], the *Ratnarāśi-sūtra* of the Ratnakuṭa division). Of the remain-

MO-SHIH AND *MO-FA*: THE EMERGENCE OF THE "FINAL AGE"

We have seen that, while no Sanskrit (or translated Tibetan) expression serves as the regular equivalent of *mo-fa*, in a plurality—if not a majority—of instances Ch. *mo-fa* corresponds to Skt. *paścimakāle* or its reduplicated equivalent, *paścimakāle paścimasamaye*. There is, however, another Chinese expression that occurs both more frequently and more consistently as the counterpart of this Sanskrit expression, namely *mo-shih* 末世 or "final age." Moreover, *mo-shih* not only enters the realm of Chinese Buddhist discourse more than a century before the first recorded usage of *mo-fa*,[106] but it appears in the Chinese Buddhist translation literature well over twice as often.[107] In our quest for an understanding of the sources of the

---

ing six texts, three have long been suspected of being composed (or at least edited) in China—the anonymous translation of the *Daśacakra-kṣitigarbha-sūtra* (T No. 410), the *Sūtra on the Wise and the Foolish* attributed to Hui-chio (T No. 202), and the *Buddha-Visualization Samādhi-Sea Sūtra* (*Kuan-fo san-mei hai ching*) translated by Buddhabhadra (T No. 643)—and though Tibetan translations of the first of these two do exist, both are translated not from Sanskrit, but from Chinese. As to the ancestry of the three remaining texts in this category—T Nos. 267, 617, and 748—no corroborating evidence is available.

[106] The first occurrences of the term *mo-fa* are in texts translated by Kumārajīva at the beginning of the 5th century CE (T No. 262, translated in 405–406 CE and T No. 617, produced in 402–412 CE), or perhaps slightly earlier, depending on the exact date of the anonymous translation of T No. 748, assigned to the period 317–420 CE by the *K'ai-yüan shih-chiao lu* (T No. 2154, 50.617c9). The term *mo-shih*, by contrast, occurs already in the translations of Dharmarakṣa (fl. 265–313), and also appears in T No. 373, an anonymous verse translation assigned to the Latter Han. Given the difficulty of establishing the reliability of such Han-period attributions, however, together with the fact that no other use of the term is attested between the time of this extremely brief text and the time of Dharmarakṣa, we are probably justified in reserving judgment on whether this work should be considered the first occurrence of the term. In any event, credit for the popularization of the expression *mo-shih* clearly goes to Dharmarakṣa, in whose translations the following occurrences of the term are registered in the Taishō index: T No. 263 (9.99c, 104c,106c, 107a, 107b, 110b, 123c, and 134a), T No. 274 (9.375a), T No. 310[3] (11.74a, 76c), T No. 398 (13.450c), T No. 403 (13.612a), T No. 433 (14.80c, 81a), T No. 481 (14.640b, 641a–c), T No. 585 (15.30a), T No. 738 (17.542a), T No. 769 (17.705b), T No. 810 (17.769c), and T No. 815 (17.794c).

[107] While the term *mo-fa* is registered in the Taishō index as appearing only 22 times in the first seventeen volumes of the canon (comprising the āgama, *avadāna*, and Mahāyāna sūtra literature), *mo-shih* appears well over twice as often, occurring in no fewer than 56 such texts, with multiple occurrences in many of them. Moreover, it is likely that the real ratio of relative frequency is even greater, given the alertness of the Japanese indexers to the expression *mo-fa* (Jpn. *mappō*), which

Chinese Buddhist understanding of *mo-fa* as the "final age" in the history of the Dharma it is therefore vital to consider the uses of this related expression as well.

The fact that the term *mo-shih* occurs with such relative frequency in the Chinese translation literature makes it a fairly straightforward task to establish both its underlying Sanskrit antecedent and the contexts in which it is used. As to the first, a comparison of passages containing this expression with their surviving Sanskrit or Tibetan counterparts demonstrates clearly that *mo-shih* corresponds, in virtually every case, to Skt. *paścimakāle* "in the latter time" or its reduplicated equivalent, *paścimakāle paścimasamaye* "in the latter time, in the latter period."[108] But this is precisely the phrase that corresponds, in a plurality of instances, to the expression *mo-fa* as well. What are we to make of this apparent coincidence?

To answer this question we must begin with the issue of chronology: that is, the dates at which the terms *mo-shih* and *mo-fa*, as well as the name of the second era (Ch. *hsiang-fa*) in the basic two-period system, were first introduced. The results of a survey of the occurrences of these terms registered in the Taishō index are quite straightforward: while both *hsiang-fa* and *mo-shih* appear to have been introduced into Chinese Buddhist usage by the Yüeh-chih translator Dharmarakṣa, the term *mo-fa* appears around a century later, in the works of Kumārajīva or one of his immediate predecessors.[109] The term *mo-fa*, then, was first employed in an atmosphere in which *cheng-fa, hsiang-fa*, and *mo-shih* were already well established as Buddhist technical terms.

When we combine this chronological information with the fact that in a significant number of cases Ch. *mo-fa* corresponds to Skt.

---

plays such a central role in their own religious traditions, in contrast to their presumably lower alertness to *mo-shih* (Jpn. *masse*), which has no such prominence.

[108] Variant Sanskrit readings are the uncompounded forms *paścime kāle paścime samaye* (which occur frequently in the *Lotus Sūtra* and may reflect an early—that is, pre-technical—usage of these terms) and *paścātkāle*, an expression whose meaning is identical. By far the most common corresponding forms in Tibetan forms are *phyi-ma'i dus* or its reduplicated equivalent, *phyi-ma'i dus phyi-ma'i tshe*. Other translations are occasionally encountered as well, including *ma-'ongs dus-kyi tshe* "in the future time," *tha-ma'i dus-kyi tshe* "in the final time," and, in one text, *zad-pa'i dus* "in the exhausted time" (Pek. No. 406, *mdo-sna-tshogs du*, 237b1 and 300a2).

[109] See above, note 106.

paścimakāle (i.e., to an expression that is more regularly translated into Chinese as *mo-shih*), we may find the key to our puzzle: namely, that *mo-fa* originated simply as a variant of *mo-shih*, introduced by a Chinese writer already familiar with the periodization scheme built on sequential eras of *cheng-fa* and *hsiang-fa*, respectively. Viewed in this context it would have required only a small leap of inference to conclude that *mo-shih* (which implies, unlike its Sanskrit counterpart, not merely a "latter" but a *final* period) was meant as a reference to a discrete third period in the history of the Dharma, which could be expressed more clearly (or at least more symmetrically) by the term *mo-fa*. Once *mo-fa* had gained some currency—a process that must have been stimulated by the use of the term in some of the translations of Kumārajīva, whose works are among the most influential ever produced in China—the die was cast, and it fell to the lot of Chinese Buddhist scholastic writers to expound on the nature and duration of this supposed third period. In light of this scenario it should no longer surprise us that the first extended discussion of the three-period time scheme appears well after the introduction of the term *mo-fa* in the works of Kumārajīva and others, and that such discussions appear not in translated sūtras, but in the works of Chinese commentators themselves.

If this line of reasoning is correct we should no longer view the term *mo-fa* as a Chinese translation of an Indian Buddhist term, but rather as a stylistic variant of *mo-shih* (itself a genuine translation of Skt. *paścimakāle*, a term whose original meaning will be discussed below). The term *mo-fa* subsequently took on a life of its own, stimulating seemingly endless commentarial reflections in East Asia. *Mo-fa* is thus a Chinese "apocryphal word": a term created in China, with no identifiable Indian antecedent.[110]

THE "LATTER AGE" IN INDIAN SOURCES

But if the Indian Buddhist texts themselves show no sign of any familiarity with a three-period time scheme, how is the term

---

[110] The term "apocryphal word" is taken from an unpublished paper presented by Lewis Lancaster at the annual meeting of the American Academy of Religion in Atlanta, Georgia, in November 1986, in which he described the term "original enlightenment" (Ch. *pen-chüeh*, Jpn. *hongaku* 本覺) as an example of such an expression, created in China without an Indian basis.

paścimakāle (or, in its undeclined form, *paścimakāla* "the latter age") to be understood? Since the term appears fairly frequently (as reflected both in the original Sanskrit texts and in their Chinese and Tibetan translations), it is relatively straightforward to examine the contexts in which it occurs. We may begin with a clear-cut negative observation: just as *hsiang-fa* and *mo-fa* exhibit a pattern of complementary distribution rather than of occurrence in conjunction, so *hsiang-fa* and *mo-shih* only rarely occur in a single scripture. If we compare the occurrences of *hsiang-fa* with those of *mo-shih* as registered in the Taishō index, we obtain the following table:

hsiang-fa	***mo-shih***
T No. 99	—
156	—
157	—
158	—
160	—
176	—
190	—
202	—
221	—
—	228
—	235
—	236
262	262*
263	263*
264	264*
272	272*
273	—
—	274
—	279
291	—
294	—
—	310[3]
—	310[7]
—	310[8]
—	310[11]
310[12]	—
—	310[17]
—	310[24]
—	310[36]
—	311
—	312
316	—
320	—

—	328
329	—
—	341
345	—
—	346
—	373
397[15]	—
398	398*
—	400
—	402
—	404
—	410
—	411
414	—
415	—
—	416
425	—
426	—
—	433
450	—
451	451*
456	—
461	—
—	481
485	—
495	—
—	512
565	—
—	585
587	—
613	—
—	634
639	639*
643	—
—	649
—	657
—	659
663	—
664	—
665	—
670	—
—	671
673	—
674	—
—	698
738	738*
—	744

—	757
—	769
783	—
—	810
—	815
—	838
839	—
—	842
—	843
—	844

Here the asterisk is used to mark texts containing the expression *mo-shih* in which the term *hsiang-fa* also appears. Once again, the overall pattern is clearly one of disjunction rather than coexistence. Whatever *mo-shih* (that is, *paścimakāle*) may have meant in these texts, it was clearly not a third period occurring after an era of *hsiang-fa*.

We must return, therefore, to the contexts in which this expression is used to determine its original meaning. Here our task is made easier by the fact that, in the overwhelming majority of cases, the context is quite consistent: the term occurs in the context of a discussion of the merit to be derived from the acceptance, maintenance, and distribution of a given sūtra—that is, the sūtra in which the passage in question appears.[111] A typical example is found in one of the earliest Mahāyāna scriptures, the *Lotus Sūtra*:

---

[111] A partial exception is the Sanskrit version of the *Diamond Sūtra* (*Vajracchedikā-prajñāpāramitā-sūtra*), which uses a plural rather than a singular form in ascribing tremendous merit to those who "in the latter time, in the latter age, in the latter five hundred years, at the time of the destruction of the True Dharma, will take up *these very sūtras*, bear them in mind, recite them, and study them. . ." (Skt. *paścimakāle paścimasamaye paścimāyāṃ pañcaśatyāṃ saddharmavipralopa-kāle vartamāa imā evaṃrūpān sūtrāntān udrahīṣyanti dhārayiṣyanti vācayiṣyanti paryavāpsyanti* . . .; see Conze, SOR 13, p. 45, §16b). The plural also appears in at least three instances in the *Pratyutpanna-Buddha-Saṃmukhāvasthita-Samādhi-Sūtra*; see Paul Harrison, *The Samādhi of Direct Encounter with the Buddhas of the Present, An Annotated English Translation of the Tibetan Version of the Pratyutpanna-Buddha-Saṃmukhāvasthita-Samādhi-Sūtra,* Studia Philologica Buddhica Monograph Series, V (Tokyo: International Institute for Buddhist Studies, 1990), pp. 99 (§13D) and 100 (§§13F,H), "such sūtras as these" (Tib. *mdo-sde 'di-lta-bu 'di-dag*). For the Tibetan text see Harrison, *The Tibetan Text of the Pratyutpanna-Buddha-Saṃmukhāvasthita-Samādhi-Sūtra,* Studia Philologica Buddhica Monograph Series, I (Tokyo: The Reiyukai Library, 1978), pp. 104 (§13D), 105 (§13F) and 107 (§13H). Elsewhere in the text, however, the concern is clearly with this sūtra alone.

> One should always reverentially salute him with joined hands, as if he were the Chief of Jinas or the Self-born, he who in the fearful latter time (Skt. *paścimakāli* [sic]) upholds this sūtra [i.e., the *Lotus Sūtra*] of the Extinct [Buddha].[112]

Those who accept the legitimacy of the *Lotus Sūtra* and uphold its teachings after the death of the Buddha, in other words, are worthy of the reverence of the world.

Similar sentiments are reflected in other early Mahāyāna texts, for example in this passage from the *Pratyutpanna-buddha-saṃmukhāvasthita-samādhi-sūtra*:

> In the latter time, in the latter age, and in the final five hundred years, when they hear this *samādhi* [i.e., the *Pratyutpanna-samādhi-sūtra*] they will not reject it. Far from it, when they hear it they will rejoice at it, applaud it, keep, read, instruct, expound, and exert themselves in the endeavour to cultivate it. . . . [If they] rejoice when they hear it, have faith in, believe, become convinced of, and applaud it; if they also accept it when they hear it, master, keep, read, copy, cause to be copied, teach, and exert themselves in the endeavour to cultivate it, even if only for a day and a night, then, Bhadrapāla, those ladies and gentlemen will on that basis engender considerable merit. They will engender an immeasurable, incalculable mass of merit.[113]

Once again, it is the acceptance of the sūtra in which this passage occurs—in this case, the *Pratyutpanna-samādhi-sūtra*—during the "latter age" that guarantees the accruing of this merit.

But how was the term *paścimakāla* understood by the Indian authors of such passages? We may remind ourselves, first of all, of the literal meaning of the Sanskrit term *paścima*: it refers to that which comes after, or behind, something else, and thus can indicate both direction (in which case it means "west") and time (in which case it is ordinarily translated as "later," "latter," or "final").[114] The meaning of "last" or "final" (i.e., the superlative sense), which is explicit in the Chinese expression *mo-shih*, is thus

---

[112] *Saddharmapuṇḍarīka-sūtra*, ch. 10, vs. 7 (Kern and Nanjio ed., 229). English translation adapted from Kern, *Saddharmapuṇḍarīka or the Lotus of the True Law*, 218.

[113] English translation adapted from Harrison, *The Samādhi of Direct Encounter*, 62-63. For the Tibetan text see Harrison, *The Tibetan Text*, 61-62.

[114] See Monier-Williams, *Sanskrit-English Dictionary*, 612b.

not required by the underlying Sanskrit expression, which can be (and most often is) used in a merely comparative sense.[115]

An examination of the contexts in which Skt. *paścimakāle* and its Tibetan and Chinese counterparts are found in the Buddhist sūtra literature provides further evidence that this phrase was originally intended to be read in the sense of a "latter" or "future" age, not as a "final age" in the superlative sense. Most telling is the fact that this "latter age" is never contrasted with any earlier period other than the lifetime of the Buddha himself, where such a contrast regularly takes the form *tathāgatasya parinirvṛtasya paścime kāle paścime samaye paścimāyām pañcaśatyām* ("after the death of the Tathāgata, in the latter time, in the latter period, in the latter five hundred years").[116] Just as the expression *saddharma-pratirūpaka* regularly refers simply to the duration of the Dharma after the *parinirvāṇa* of the Buddha, so in these instances *paścimakāle* (and its more extended equivalent) seems to refer simply to the period following the Buddha's death.

Most interesting from the point of view of the historian of Buddhism, however, is the evident agenda that seems to have led to the use of this expression in sūtras produced by Mahāyāna writers. For the expression is used, in the vast majority of cases, in contexts where the Buddha is described as recommending "this sūtra" (i.e., the Mahāyāna sūtra in which the expression appears) for circulation among Buddhist believers after his death. The expression *paścimakāle* serves, in other words, as a kind of "Good Housekeeping Seal of Approval," certifying the sūtra in question for acceptance and dissemination in the latter (i.e., the post-Śākyamuni) age.

---

[115] Most Tibetan translators of this expression clearly took it in the comparative sense, for the most common Tibetan equivalent of *paścimakāle paścimasamaye* is *phyi-ma'i dus phyi-ma'i tshe*, in which *phyi-ma* means "later, subsequent, following" and *dus* and *tshe* are both words for "time" (Das, *Tibetan-English Dictionary*, 835a, where the phrase *phyi-ma'i dus* is also translated as "future" or "after-time"). In translating the same Sanskrit term in the expression *paścimāyāṃ pañcaśatyāṃ* "in the latter five hundred [years]," however, the Tibetans regularly chose to draw on the superlative sense, and regularly rendered this phrase as *lnga-brgya tha-ma-la* "in the final five hundred [years]." The latter translation no doubt reflects the fact that by the time the Tibetans began to translate works containing this expression they had already become familiar with the idea that the Dharma would endure well beyond its originally allotted time span of five hundred years.

[116] Kern and Nanjio, *Saddharmapuṇḍarīka*, 475, line 10.

In light of this evidence it is particularly interesting to recall where the expression *mo-shih* does, and does not, appear in the Chinese translation literature. It does not appear (according to the Taishō index) anywhere in the āgamas (i.e., the non-Mahāyāna sūtras) or in the abhidharma literature, and only two occurrences are registered in the vinaya texts.[117] The overwhelming majority of appearances of the term are found in the Mahāyāna sūtras, with another sizeable group of occurrences in the *mi-chiao* (tantric) literature.[118] The term seems to have been most popular, in other words, in the Mahāyāna sūtras, where—by stating explicitly that the Buddha promised vast merits to those who would accept and transmit the sūtra in question after his death—it served as a certification of their legitimacy.

This evidence concerning the motive for the use of the term, together with the fact that this "latter age" is never explicitly contrasted with any earlier period in the history of Buddhism (other than the lifetime of the Buddha himself), brings us to a rather unexpected conclusion: that the expression "in the latter age" (Skt. *paścimakāle*) was originally introduced into Buddhist discourse simply as a reference to the time after the death of the Buddha. Just as in the case of *saddharma-pratirūpaka* discussed above, it would seem that the idea of a "latter time" originally implied no periodization whatsoever within the lifetime of the Dharma after the Buddha's *parinirvāṇa*, but simply referred to this era as a whole.

We are now in a position to offer at least a provisional reply to the question posed earlier in our discussion: whether *hsiang-fa* and *mo-fa* almost never occur together because they are functional equivalents of one another or because they represent competing

---

[117] See T No. 1425 (a vinaya text thought to belong to the Mahāsaṃghika school), 22.243b4 and T No. 1483 (a separate text dealing with the questions of Maudgalyāyana concerning the results of violating various vinaya rules), 24.983c25.

[118] That is, the literature contained in vols. 18–21 of the Taishō canon. In fact, the term *mo-fa* occurs more frequently than *mo-shih* in this literature (with 14 occurrences in contrast to 20), no doubt reflecting the fact that *mo-fa* had become firmly established as the Chinese name of the "third period" in the history of the Dharma, and thus as an acceptable Chinese translation of the expression *paścimakāle* and its variants, by the time significant numbers of tantric texts began to be translated into Chinese (8th c. CE ff.). Interestingly, the term *hsiang-fa* is considerably less prominent here than in the Mahāyāna sūtras, occurring in only 9 out of 573 *mi-chiao* texts.

systems of thought. Since, as we have seen, *mo-fa* is not itself a translation of an Indian technical term but rather a Chinese stylistic variant of the translation term *mo-shih*, it makes better sense to rephrase our question to focus on the usage of the latter term. Why, then (as our second table above illustrates clearly), do *hsiang-fa* (Skt. *saddharma-pratirūpaka*) and *mo-shih* (Skt. *paścimakāla*) almost never occur in conjunction? The answer seems to be that both of the above propositions hold: on the one hand, both *saddharma-pratirūpaka* and *paścimakāla* (in their earliest senses) referred to the entire and undifferentiated time after the death of the Buddha; thus the two may be viewed as functional equivalents. On the other hand, in a substantial number of instances *saddharma-pratirūpaka* seems to suggest a positive vision of the duration of the Dharma, while *paścimakāla* is used to refer to the same period in a more negative light. While the former term seems to emphasize the ongoing presence of the *saddharma* in a form (*rūpa*) in which it can be apprehended and practiced, the latter portrays this same period from a different perspective, emphasizing the absence of the Buddha's guiding hand. While the two terms thus may be said to share a common referent, their affective tones are quite opposite.

THE BACKGROUND OF *MO-FA* THOUGHT: THE HEPHTHALITE HYPOTHESIS

In light of the scenario outlined above it is no longer surprising that explicit references to a three-period system first appear not in sūtra and śāstra literature translated from Indian originals, but in 6th-century Chinese scholastic texts. For if the developed notion of three periods in the history of the Dharma indeed arose in the context of reflection on the meaning of the term *mo-fa*—itself a Chinese "apocryphal word"—we should expect this notion to have emerged well after the first appearances of this expression in Chinese Buddhist literature, which took place around the beginning of the 5th century CE.[119] And this is precisely what we find, for it is Nan-yüeh Hui-ssu (515–577), best known as the teacher of T'ien-t'ai Chih-i, who is credited with having been the first to set forth

[119] See above, n.106.

in writing a three-period system based on eras of *cheng-fa*, *hsiang-fa*, and *mo-fa*, respectively, in a work completed in 558 CE.[120]

But the absence of any direct evidence for the existence of a three-period system in the literature of Indian Buddhism has not stifled attempts by modern scholars (in particular, by modern Japanese scholars, in whose own religious traditions this system continues to hold a central place) to find evidence for its origins in India. Of such attempts perhaps the most ingenious—and the one most often cited by Japanese and Western researchers—is that of YAMADA Ryūjō, who has attempted to link the appearance of the three-period system in China with the invasion of India by the Hephthalite Huns. Since Yamada's theories on this subject have been so influential, we will consider them here in some detail.[121]

Toward the end of the 5th century CE a people known in Indian sources as the *Hūṇa* swept into northwest India and Kashmir. These new invaders, generally identified by modern scholars as a branch of the Iranian-speaking Hephthalites then ruling in Bactria,[122] combined conquest with cruelty in proportions that would not be seen again until the Mongol period. The second *Hūṇa* ruler to hold power in northwest India, Mihirakula, was especially

---

[120] See his *Nan-yüeh Ssu ta ch'an-shih li shih-yüan wen* (T No. 1933), 46.786c. There is some dispute concerning the authenticity of the attribution of this work to Hui-ssu. ETANI Ryūkai argues against such an attribution in "Nangaku Eshi no Rissei ganmon wa gisaku ka," *Indogaku Bukkyōgaku kenkyū* 6/2 (1958), 524–27. Paul Magnin counters these arguments, concluding that the bulk of the text is indeed Hui-ssu's; see his *La vie et l'oeuvre de Huisi* 慧思 *(515–577)* (Paris: EFEO, 1979), especially pages 104–16. Those who question Hui-ssu's authorship place the composition of this text at a later date, however, rather than an earlier one, thus leaving intact our contention that the three-period system was not mentioned in Chinese Buddhist writings prior to the second half of the 6th century CE. There is no disagreement, at any rate, that the *Li shih-yüan wen*—whoever its author really was—contains the earliest description of this system.

[121] See especially his articles "Mappō shisō ni tsuite," *Indogaku Bukkyōgaku kenkyū* 4/2 (1956), 361–70; "Rengemen-gyō ni tsuite," in *Yamaguchi Hakase kanreki kinen* (Kyoto: Hōzōkan, 1955), 110–123; and Chapter 8 ("Kōki kyōten no haikei") of his *Daijō bukkyō seiritsu ron josetsu* (Kyoto: Heirakuji Shoten, 1959). For an English abstract of his views see "The Logic of Crisis: The Mappō Theory in India, China and Japan," in *Proceedings of the IXth International Congress of the History of Religions, Tokyo and Kyoto 1958* (Tokyo: Maruzen, 1960), 459–62.

[122] For a review of current scholarship on the Hephthalites see Frye, *History of Ancient Iran*, 346–51.

notorious in this regard, and his reputation seems to have stretched from China to Byzantium even within his own lifetime.[123]

Despite (or perhaps due to) its ferocity, however, *Hūṇa* rule in India proved to be short-lived. After invading Gandhāra in the late 5th or early 6th century, Mihirakula's forces were defeated by a Hindu confederacy (c. 530) and were forced back to Kashmir. Hephthalite rule continued in this region under two or three shadowy figures about whom little is known, and appears to have come to an end sometime in the second half of the 6th century. Meanwhile the Turks and the Sasanians combined forces to crush the Hephthalites in Central Asia, defeating them in fierce fighting in the late 550s and dividing their lands among themselves.

Though the geographical extent of *Hūṇa* control in the northwest, like its duration, seems to have been relatively limited, the violence of their rule was not easily forgotten. When the Kashmiri historian Kalhaṇa set out to record the tale of Mihirakula's atrocities some five centuries later, he found some of the details too appalling to relate: "As the touch of wicked men defiles the body, so the relation [of their deeds] defiles the speech. Therefore yet other inhuman acts of his are not narrated [by me]."[124] Similar tales of cruelty and violence were recorded by Hsüan-tsang in the mid-7th century,[125] and though there is no reason to think that the king (apparently a Hephthalite vassal) met by Sung-yün in 520 in Gandhāra was Mihirakula himself, his description of the ruler as cruel and vindictive (as well as boorish and uncultured) accords well with other descriptions of the style of Hephthalite rule.[126]

As in the Muslim conquests several centuries later, Buddhist monasteries proved to be especially easy targets for the Hephthalite armies. And according to the reports of Chinese Buddhist travelers, the Hephthalites showed active hostility toward the Buddhist religion. Yet it is important to point out a crucial difference in the results of these two invasions. While the Muslim conquest resulted in the eventual conversion of large segments of the local popula-

---

123 Yamada, "Mappō shisō," 363.

124 Sir M. Aurel Stein, trans., *Rājataraṅgiṇī* (repr. New Delhi: Motilal Banarsidass, 1975), 45.

125 Beal, *Buddhist Records*, vol. 1, 167–68.

126 Édouard Chavannes, "Voyage de Song Yun dans l'Udyāna et le Gandhāra," *BEFEO*, 3 (1903), 379–441 (esp. 408, 416–17).

tion to Islam (and weakened the surviving Buddhist community sufficiently to enable its eventual absorption into Hinduism), the results of the *Hūṇa* invasion were much more limited. As the travel records of Sung-yün and Hsüan-tsang make clear, the area still remained largely Buddhist, and though Buddhist establishments clearly suffered extensive material damages, the major religious change during the century following the invasions seems to have been the conversion of a part of the local population to the Mahāyāna.[127]

It is certain that Buddhist believers underwent considerable suffering at the hands of Mihirakula and his legions, and that their eventual liberation from the Hephthalite yoke took place not through their own military endeavors but through the efforts of a coalition of Hindu kings. Yet the Buddhists had recourse to a literary, and long-lasting, means of revenge. They recorded the story of Mihirakula in a *jātaka*-style text in which the Hephthalite ruler is portrayed as a devotee of the *purāṇas*—that is, as a Hindu[128] — who vows to destroy the Buddhist religion in a future lifetime. He is reborn as an Indian king, and succeeds in overturning the Buddha-Dharma and in smashing the Buddha's begging bowl. Karmic justice must be done, however, and Mihirakula is reborn in the Avīci hell in recompense for his actions. Though the text has not been preserved in an Indian original, it survives in a Chinese translation executed by Narendrayaśas, the same translator who produced the Chinese version of the *Candragarbha-sūtra*.[129]

---

[127] Contrast the report of Fa-hsien, who visited Udyāna around 400 CE and found a flourishing community of some five hundred monasteries in which the monks were "all students of the Hīnayāna" (Legge, *A Record of Buddhistic Kingdoms*, 28–29) with that of Hsüan-tsang (mid-7th c.), who remarks on the number of devastated monasteries but reports that the population was still largely Buddhist, and that the people were "believers in the Great Vehicle" (Beal, *Buddhist Records of the Western World*, vol. 1, 120). Sung-yün specifies that Udyāna had a Buddhist ruler when he visited (c. 520 CE), though in Gandhāra an anti-Buddhist puppet of the Hephthalites held sway (Chavannes, "Voyage de Song Yun," 408, 416–17). Even in Gandhāra, however, the population remained largely Buddhist some two generations after the Hephthalite conquest (417). For an overview of the effects of the *Hūṇa* and Muslim invasions see S. Dutt, *Buddhist Monks and Monasteries*, 206–10.

[128] The *Rājataraṅgiṇī* describes Mihirakula as a devotee of Śiva, the god of destruction—an altogether appropriate choice.

[129] *Lien-hua-mien ching* 蓮華面經, T No. 386 (12.1070–77).

As we have seen, it was in 558 CE—soon after the death of Mihirakula—that the system of the three periods of True Dharma, Semblance Dharma, and Final Dharma was first formulated (if we accept the attribution to Hui-ssu). And via an intriguing chain of arguments Yamada has suggested that it was precisely the suffering experienced by the Buddhist community under Mihirakula's rule that stimulated a sense of the Dharma's decline and led to the formulation of the concept of the "three periods" (including the notion of a period of *mo-fa*) by Indian Buddhist thinkers. One of the key figures in the transmission of these ideas to China, Yamada argues, was the translator Narendrayaśas, who himself must have lived through the *Hūṇa* devastation.

Yamada's reasoning runs as follows. The *Mahāsaṃnipāta-sūtra* (or more specifically, the *Yüeh-tsang fen* or *Candragarbha* section of that sūtra) was the most influential "decline of the Dharma" scripture in China. Thus we should expect it to have played a role in triggering the rapid spread of *mo-fa* thought in late 6th-century China. This sūtra was not translated into Chinese, however, until 566, and thus Hui-ssu's formulation in 558 of three periods in the history of the Dharma could not have been based on this scripture. Hui-ssu could, however—Yamada continues—have learned of the Indian theory of *mo-fa* directly from Narendrayaśas, who had arrived in the Northern Ch'i capital of Yeh approximately two years before the completion of Hui-ssu's *Li shih-yüan wen*. Indeed, Narendrayaśas would have been the ideal carrier for such a tradition, since he was a native of the Udyāna region of northwest India, the very area invaded by Mihirakula, and thus must himself have been a victim of this great disaster. Finally, Yamada asserts, the Hephthalite invasions served as the background not only for the formulation of the concept of *mo-fa* in India, but for the composition of the *Sūryagarbha* and *Candragarbha* sūtras (in addition, of course, to the *Lien-hua-mien ching*) as well.

Yamada's theories are intriguing, and his proposals deserve careful scrutiny. Yet there are difficulties at every stage of his argument. Most problematic is his assumption that Narendrayaśas could have brought from India the concept of a period of *mo-fa* as the third and final period in the history of the Dharma. For, as we have already seen, there is no evidence that such a system was ever known in India, and in fact there is considerable evidence that it was not.[130] Thus any role of Narendrayaśas in the "transmission" of this unattested Indian concept to China must remain entirely hypothetical.

Second, the idea of a meeting between Hui-ssu and Narendrayaśas, resulting in the transmission of *any* current Indian ideas concerning the decline of the Dharma, is likewise hypothetical. That such a meeting could have occurred may be, as Yamada suggests, "entirely natural," yet there is no concrete evidence to prove that such an encounter ever took place.

Third, though Narendrayaśas was indeed from northwest India, this does not necessarily mean that he had experienced Mihirakula's tyranny firsthand. Mihirakula's dates are uncertain, and though it is quite possible that Narendrayaśas (born in 516 CE) might have lived under his rule, we should also note that Hephthalite control seems to have been quite limited in geographical range. Thus, during the travels of Sung-yün the Hephthalites controlled Gandhāra, while the adjoining region of Udyāna (the native place of Narendrayaśas) was ruled by an independent and pro-Buddhist king. In order to establish with certainty that Narendrayaśas had personally experienced Mihirakula's atrocities we would need to know not only the specific territory in which he lived, but the exact range of Hephthalite control at the time, and—most evasive of all—the precise dates of Mihirakula's rule. All these items are elusive, however, and thus the idea of any direct contact between Narendrayaśas and Mihirakula must remain speculative.

Fourth, Yamada asserts that Mihirakula's activities served as the background for several of the texts translated into Chinese by Narendrayaśas. That Mihirakula was the prototype of the *Lien-hua-mien ching* is indisputable; the connection between Mihirakula and the *Candragarbha-sūtra*, however, is far more problematic. The Chinese *Candragarbha* text does indeed contain a prophecy of decline, and—as Yamada suggests—one might well expect such a pessimistic outlook to emerge during a period of persecution and conquest. Yet Yamada's suggestion implies that Mihirakula's actions contributed directly to the composition of the *Candragarbha* itself. There are considerable difficulties with this hypothesis, not the least of

---

[130] The fact that Buddhist texts (from the Gupta period and after) occasionally refer to the the Hindu four-*yuga* system strongly suggests that the Buddhists had no multi-era system of their own. See below, p. 280, n. 3.

which is the fact that the central motif of the chapter on the destruction of the Dharma (*Fa mieh-chin p'in*, T 13.374c27–381c11)—i.e., the story of the destruction of the Dharma at Kauśāmbī—was already circulating in India centuries before the beginning of the Hephthalite period.[131] And the version of this story given in the *Candragarbha* text (as we shall see in Part Two of this study) exhibits few divergences from these earlier recensions. Indeed, the only respect in which the *Candragarbha* differs appreciably from its predecessors is when it moves *away* from the prophecy of decline—that is, when it offers *dhāraṇīs* for the preservation of the Dharma and suggests that the Buddha's extraordinary efforts (in combination with those of ordinary believers) may be able to prolong the life span of the Dharma beyond its originally allotted time. To describe the Hephthalite incursions as the "background" of the *Candragarbha-sūtra*, then, clearly requires supporting evidence beyond that provided by Yamada.

Fifth, Yamada's contention that the East Asian understanding of the decline of the Dharma was inspired largely by the *Candragarbha-sūtra* (or by the oral account of its contents that Yamada suggests was obtained from Narendrayaśas by Hui-ssu) loses most of its impact when we recall that nowhere in this sūtra do we find any discussion of the three-period system—nor, for that matter, does the expression *mo-fa* occur anywhere in the text. Thus, while Narendrayaśas may well have been concerned with the "decline of the Dharma" in a general sense, and may even have stimulated some of his Chinese coreligionists (possibly, but not necessarily, including Hui-ssu) to reflect more deeply on this issue, there is absolutely no evidence that he, or the scriptures he translated, played a key role in the formulation of the East Asian three-period system. On the contrary, it seems more reasonable to assume the reverse: that it was the growing popularity of the concept of *mo-fa*—which by the time of Narendrayaśas' arrival was already well established in Chinese Buddhist circles—that contributed to the high level of Chinese interest in the scriptures he subsequently translated, with their more general discussions of decline.

Finally, even the basic assumption underlying Yamada's argument—that scriptures predicting the demise of the Dharma must

---

131 See below, pp. 224–25.

have been composed during a period of persecution—should not be accepted without question. For while the experience of persecution has frequently led to the reappropriation of such prophecies, above all in China, it is more often the experience of excessive ease and comfort (as we shall see in the following chapters) that has led to their initial composition.[132]

SUMMARY: THE EAST ASIAN ORIGINS OF THE THREE-PERIOD SYSTEM

Our search for the origins of the three-period system has brought us, then, to the following conclusions. The notions of *saddharma* and *saddharma-pratirūpaka* were well established in Indian Mahāyāna literature by the middle of the 2nd century CE at the latest. Meanwhile, the term *paścimakāla* ("latter age") had also entered Indian Buddhist literature, likewise in a Mahāyāna context, as a reference to the period following the death of the historical Buddha. Most often the latter term was used in contexts in which the Buddha was described as recommending the acceptance, preservation, dissemination, and so forth of the sūtra in question during the time after his death, sometimes in conjunction with a discussion of the difficulties that might attend those who do so. By the latter half of the 3rd century CE Buddhist scriptures containing all of these terms were being translated into Chinese by Dharmarakṣa, who appears to have introduced the two vital terms *hsiang-fa* (as a translation of *saddharma-pratirūpaka*) and *mo-shih* (as a translation of *paścimakāla*) into Chinese Buddhist discourse.[133]

---

[132] See below, pp. 226–27. For a discussion of some of the circumstances that have given rise to the composition of Buddhist decline texts see below, pp. 224–27 and 284–87.

[133] Unlike *hsiang-fa*, which appears to have been introduced by Dharmarakṣa as a Buddhist neologism, the term *mo-shih* already had a long history in Chinese usage (dating back to at least the 2nd cent. BCE) before it was appropriated by Dharmarakṣa as a translation for *paścimakāla*; for examples of this pre-Buddhist usage see Morohashi, *Dai kanwa jiten*, vol. 6, p. 5736b, no. 14420.81. The fact that the term *mo-shih* had both a superlative sense (meaning "final age," not simply "latter age") and that it was quite negative in tone (having been used in pre-Buddhist writings to refer to an evil and decadent age) meant that the Chinese expression *mo-shih* would have a more negative tone to a Chinese audience than would *paścimakāla* to an Indian one—a fact that was to have important implications for subsequent understandings of this "final age" in Chinese Buddhism.

Around the same time the notion of two periods in the history of the Buddhist religion (found in such Indian texts as the *Lotus Sūtra*) was becoming well established in Chinese Buddhist circles. In light of this twofold time system some Chinese Buddhists began to interpret the term *mo-shih*, which would naturally be understood in Chinese as "final age," as the name of a third such period. Based on this understanding, certain Buddhist translators (of whom the most influential, and probably the earliest, was Kumārajīva) began to use the term *mo-fa* as an occasional substitute for *mo-shih*, thus bringing the latter into greater symmetry with its "predecessors," the periods of *cheng-fa* and *hsiang-fa*, respectively. Having thus entered the scriptural corpus, the term *mo-fa* took on a life of its own, and Chinese commentators undertook with enthusiasm the task of describing the nature and duration of this anticipated third period. That they chose for its duration the quintessentially Chinese figure of 10,000 years (with its underlying implication of "an eternity") demonstrates that they were free from any constraints encountered in Indian documents, for while *mo-shih* (Skt. *paścimakāla*) is often described as comprising the "latter five hundred years," the newly coined term *mo-fa* was subject to no such restrictions. Likewise it reveals their profound sense of optimism (or, at the very least, of wishful thinking), for in assigning to this newly created period of *mo-fa* a duration of 10,000 years these Chinese commentators expressed the hope that Śākyamuni's teachings would last forever, albeit in a reduced and less accessible form.

Chapter Five

Within and Without: The Causes of Decline

UNTIL NOW we have dealt only with the duration of the Dharma, and with the various periodization schemes used to track the course of its decline. In this chapter we will consider what Buddhist writers have understood as the causes of this decline, and of the ultimate disappearance of the Dharma.

Not all scriptures dealing with the decline and demise of Buddhism, however, discuss the cause of these events. In the scholastic texts, in particular, there is a tendency to treat the decline and disappearance of the Dharma as part of an inexorable process, with few if any human actors involved in the process. In the narrative accounts, by contrast, we are often told that the decline and demise of Buddhism are due to human failings, which (it would seem) could be prevented, and thus the lifetime of the Dharma could, at least in theory, be prolonged.

The division between these two perspectives, however, is not as sharp as it would seem. In a number of narrative texts, where the effects of human actions are the center of attention, we find specific timetables for the duration of the Dharma. Yet the very existence of these timetables suggests that the life span of the Dharma is fixed, and thus not subject to human intervention. Though the scriptures reviewed below are limited to those that have something to say about the causes of decline, and therefore emphasize the human contribution to the process, we will see that even in these texts the idea that the decline of Buddhism is somehow inexorable is often present at least as part of the background.

Within those texts that adopt the human-centered perspective—that is, those that view the demise of the Dharma as due at least in part to specific human actions—we find a second set of polarities, which will be the focus of our attention in this chapter. Here the question is, to put it simply, who is to blame: is the extinction of the Buddhist religion due to the activities (or inactivity) of those within the Buddhist sangha, or to the activities of those whose deeds impinge upon it from without? There are examples of both perspectives in the Buddhist scriptures, and we will consider each in detail below.[1] Once again, however, we will find that this apparent distinction is not always maintained. In the Kauśāmbī story, in particular, the themes of internal and external causes—as well as those of human responsibility and cosmic inevitability—are interwoven with a high degree of complexity.

INTERNAL CAUSES: LAXITY WITHIN THE SANGHA

The earliest surviving sources that predict the disappearance of Buddhism are unanimous in attributing this catastrophe to failings on the part of Buddhists themselves. A number of such factors are singled out for attention in the canonical sources. For convenience, we may divide them into the following categories:[2]

1. the admission of women into the monastic community;
2. lack of respect toward various elements of the Buddhist tradition;
3. lack of diligence in meditation practice;
4. carelessness in the transmission of the teachings;
5. the emergence of divisions within the sangha;
6. the emergence of a false or "counterfeit" Dharma; and
7. excessive association with secular society.

---

[1] The distinction between internal and external causes of the death of the Dharma was introduced by KUMOI Shōzen in his article "Hōmetsu shisō."

[2] The first four of these seven categories are drawn from the discussion given in Kumoi, "Hōmetsu shisō," especially section 1, "Shoki butten ni mieru hōmetsu shisō" (289–92).

All these represent shortcomings (whether sins of omission or commission) on the part of Buddhists themselves. Thus all of them can be assigned to what we will refer to here as the category of internal causes.

The first of these categories, consisting of those passages that blame the shortened life span of the Buddhist Dharma on the creation of the order of nuns, has already been discussed above.[3] Here we may note only that this account has the peculiar feature of attributing the early demise of the Dharma not only to members of the Buddhist community (of whom Ānanda is regularly singled out for criticism), but ultimately to a decision made by the Buddha himself. This peculiarity alone suggests that this tradition was the product of a somewhat convoluted attempt by the early Buddhist community to resolve a complex and pressing set of issues related to the presence of women in the sangha.[4]

The activities described in the remaining six categories, by contrast, do not attribute the demise of the Dharma to the actions of any specific individuals. Rather, they speak in more generic terms of the *types* of actions conducive to the disappearance of the Dharma. Moreover, in contrast to the other six categories, where the offenses in question are largely ascribed to the monks, this first passage shows a concern with the conduct of all Buddhist believers, whether lay or monastic, male or female.

The second category, the lack of proper reverence toward the Buddhist tradition, is represented by a passage from the *Saṃyutta-nikāya*:

> There are five fallings (lit. "five lowering dharmas," *pañca okkamaniyā dhammā*) that are conducive to the corruption (*sammosa*)[5] and disappearance (*antaradhāna*) of the True Dharma (*saddhamma*). Which five? It is when monks, nuns, laymen, and laywomen are irreverent and unruly toward the teacher (*satthar*, i.e., the Buddha), are irreverent and unruly toward the Dharma, are irreverent and unruly toward the sangha, are ir-

---

[3] See above, pp. 28–33.

[4] See Sponberg, "Attitudes toward Women and the Feminine in Early Buddhism."

[5] The reference here is to corruption in the textual, not the moral, sense. A loose (and rather colloquial) translation of the Pāli term *sammosa* would be "muddying"; the implication of the term is that the Dharma is being mixed up, confused, and altered in transmission.

> reverent and unruly toward the training (*sikkhā*), and are irreverent and unruly toward meditational absorption (*samādhi*).[6]

The central issue here is thus not any specific action on the part of a specific individual, but a general attitude of disrespect toward the Buddhist tradition.

The third category is considerably more specific, for it addresses the issue of laxity with respect to a particular set of meditation practices:

> [Bhadda:] What, friend Ānanda, is the reason, what is the cause, due to which, when the Tathāgata has finally passed away, the True Dharma (*saddhamma*) will not last for a long time? And what, friend Ānanda, is the reason, what is the cause, why—when the Tathāgata has finally passed away—the True Dharma will last for a long time? . . .
>
> [Ānanda:] Well, friend, it is owing to not cultivating and not practicing the four foundations of mindfulness (*satipaṭṭhāna*).[7]

Ānanda then goes on to discuss each of these four meditational practices in detail, as set forth in the *Dīgha* and *Majjhima* nikāyas.[8]

The fourth category, like the third, is addressed specifically to the (male) monastic community. Here the issue is the importance of properly transmitting the Buddha's teachings:

> Monks, these five things lead to the corruption (*sammosa*) and disappearance (*antaradhāna*) of the True Dharma. What five? Monks carelessly listen to the Dharma; they carelessly master it; they carelessly bear it in mind; they carelessly test the good

---

[6] *Saṃyutta-nikāya* III, 225; English translation adapted from that given by F. L. Woodward, *The Book of Kindred Sayings* (1934; repr. London: Pali Text Society, 1973), vol. 2, 152. For the parallel passages in the two translations of the *Samyukta-āgama* preserved in Chinese see T 2.226b–c and 2.419b–c. Variants of this account occur in several places in the *Aṅguttara-nikāya*; see III, 246, III, 339–40, and IV, 84. For an English translation of these passages see E. M. Hare, trans., *The Book of the Gradual Sayings* (1935; repr. London: Pali Text Society, 1978), vol. 3, 180–81 and 239–40, and vol. 4, 49–50.

[7] *Saṃyutta-nikāya*, V, 172; English translation adapted from that given in Woodward, *Kindred Sayings*, vol. 5, 151–52. The same conversation is repeated in the following sutta (V, 173), substituting a question about the decay and non-decay (*parihāna* and *aparihāna*) of the True Dharma for the previous question concerning its lasting, or not lasting, for a long time.

[8] See the *Mahāsatipaṭṭhāna-sutta* in the *Dīgha-nikāya* (sutta no. 22, II, 290–315) and the *Satipaṭṭhāna-sutta* in the *Majjhima-nikāya* (sutta no. 10, I, 55–63).

> of the things they have borne in mind; and, knowing the good and knowing the Dharma, they carelessly go their way in the Dharma and by the Dharma.[9]

Far from being fatalistic about these events, however, the sūtra points out that if the monks act with care in connection with these five issues, this will lead to the stability, non-corruption, and non-disappearance of the True Dharma.

The same issue is taken up again in the following two sections of the *Aṅguttara-nikāya*, with comparable lists of six and seven items, respectively, that contribute to the demise of the Dharma.[10] In both sections the emphasis is on the repetition of the Dharma-texts one has learned; the first includes a complete listing of the nine sections (*aṅga*s) of the Pāli canon, while the second makes a specific reference to the reciters of the sūtra, vinaya, and abhidharma sections of the canon.[11]

One of the central preoccupations of the early Buddhist community was the danger of divisions within the sangha. The fifth category contains a passage that addresses this issue:

> Moreover, monks, the sangha is broken; then [monks] revile one another, accuse one another, quarrel with one another, and repudiate one another; those of no faith do not find faith there and the faithful fall away. This, monks, is the fifth thing that leads to the corruption and disappearance of the True Dharma.[12]

More specifically, the issue in this passage seems to be the hostility and argumentation that can emerge in sectarian rivalries, and not the simple fact of difference of opinion itself. In fact, the early monastic community developed a set of formal procedures

---

[9] *Aṅguttara-nikāya* III, 176–77; English translation adapted from E. M. Hare, *Gradual Sayings*, vol. 3, 132. The same material is recapitulated with various elaborations in the following two suttas.

[10] See *Aṅguttara-nikāya* III, 339–40 and IV, 84.

[11] In Pāli, the *dhamma-dharā* (lit. "Dharma-holders," who maintained the *sūtra-piṭaka*), the *vinaya-dharā* ("Vinaya-holders," who maintained the *vinaya-piṭaka*), and the *matikā-dharā* ("Matrix-holders," who maintained the lists known as *matikā*, Skt. *matṛkā*, that were to become the core of the *abhidhamma-piṭaka*).

[12] *Aṅguttara-nikāya*, III, 180; English translation adapted from Hare, *Gradual Sayings*, vol. 3, 134.

for ensuring that the inevitable schismatic movements, when they occurred, would take place peacefully.[13]

The sixth category, which is closely related to the fifth (insofar as it reflects the presence of differences of opinion within the sangha), has already been discussed in the previous chapter. Here the issue is the emergence of a false or "counterfeit" Dharma, which is seen as leading to the disappearance of its genuine counterpart. As we have seen, this passage represents the sole occurrence of the expression *saddharma-pratirūpaka* in the Nikāya Buddhist sūtra literature and an unusual interpretation of its meaning. It would be interesting to speculate as to what the authors of this passage understood as the "counterfeit" Dharma in question.[14]

With the seventh category we come to a factor that is discussed not only in the Nikāya Buddhist literature but in at least one Mahāyāna text as well. In one of the songs contained in the *Theragāthā* section of the Pāli canon, the elder Pārāpariya bemoans the disappearance of the good conduct and right attitude that had characterized the monastic community during the Buddha's lifetime:

> The behavior of the monks now seems different from when the Protector of the World, the Best of Men, was alive. . . . [At that time the monks] were not as eager for the necessities of life, for medicines and supplies, as they were for the annihilation of the outflows (*āsava*). In the forest at the foot of trees, in caves and grottos, devoting themselves to seclusion, they lived making [the annihilation of the outflows] their aim. . . . Now these elders with all outflows completely annihilated, [those] great meditators, great benefactors, have all passed away.[15] Now there are few such men. Because of the complete annihilation of good qualities (*kusaladhammā*) and of wisdom (*paññā*), the teaching of the Jina, endowed with all excellent characteristics, is destroyed.[16]

---

[13] For a discussion of this issue from the Theravāda perspective see the Pāli *Vinaya*, II, p. 204.

[14] See above, pp. 86–88 and p. 89, n. 83.

[15] Lit. "attained *nirvāṇa*" (Pāli *nibbutā*).

[16] *Theragāthā*, verses 921, 924–25, and 928–29; English translation adapted from K. R. Norman, *The Elders' Verses: Theragāthā* (London: Luzac & Co., 1969–71), vol. 1, 86–87. I would like to thank Reginald Ray for bringing this passage to my attention.

Though the extinction of the Dharma (here referred to as *jina-sāsana*, "the teaching of the Conqueror") is blamed specifically on the disappearance of positive dharmas (or "good qualities") and wisdom, the context makes it clear that Pārāpariya associates this dismal state of affairs with the excessive involvement of monks with secular society. In the following verses he bemoans the variety of tactics used by monks to acquire worldly goods and fame (verses 936–44), and concludes this sad recital by observing that, while it may be necessary to go into the villages in order to obtain alms, the wise monk should do so with extreme caution:

> As one might go shoeless in a thorny place, if he summoned up mindfulness, so should a sage go in a village.[17]

In this instance we have a similar passage in a Mahāyāna text, for the *Raṣṭrapālaparipṛcchā-sūtra* offers the following comments:

> Of what character is the false bhikṣu? Now, Rāṣṭrapāla, the bhikṣu considers himself to be for himself. He is possessed of an imperfect body of morality. He attaches importance to robes, alms-bowls, and riches. Abandoning [the practice of] not speaking, he procures beds, seats, and great invitations, which lead to states of woe. He is acquainted with women, nuns, and soldiers. . . . Having forsaken the word of the sūtras spoken by the Tathāgata, to the effect that the words of the sūtras must not be spoken in the noisy intercourse of householders and renunciants, and disliking the way of the ascetic and the monk, he sits apart, expounding the Dharma to women. . . . Such persons, Rāṣṭrapāla, will be born [in the future]. They are neither bhikṣus nor householders, and they will destroy the teaching of the Tathāgata.[18]

Once again the eventual death of the Dharma is ascribed to the excessive involvement of monks in worldly affairs.

In all, then, seven distinct internal causes of the demise of the Dharma are mentioned in the early Nikāya Buddhist texts, of which the last is also cited in a Mahāyāna sūtra.[19] It is easy to see

---

[17] *Theragāthā*, verse 946.

[18] Adapted from Jacob Ensink, trans., *The Question of Rāṣṭrapāla* (Zwolle: J. J. Tijl, 1952), pp. 135–36. The Sanskrit original has not been preserved; for the Tibetan text (corresponding to Pek. No. 833) see Ensink, p. 128, line 25–p. 130, line 8. I would like to thank Reginald Ray for bringing this passage to my attention.

[19] It may seem strange to the reader that so few of our examples have been

why each of these factors would have been viewed as threatening the very survival of the Buddhist Dharma by the pillars of the male monastic community. What is striking about this list, however, is not what it includes, but what it omits, for nowhere is there any explicit mention of the importance of keeping the precepts.[20]

One final point of interest is the temporal setting of these passages, for of the seven types of decline traditions listed above, only the first type—that is, those attributing the premature demise of the Dharma to the admission of women to the monastic community—is ever associated with a specific timetable. In the passages belonging to the other six categories the life span of the Dharma is never definitively stated, and the decay of the Dharma appears to be reversible if Buddhist practitioners will recognize their errors and change their ways.

EXTERNAL CAUSES: INCURSIONS FROM WITHOUT

If the passages examined above have been unanimous in placing the blame for the demise of the Buddhist Dharma solely on the shoulders of Buddhists themselves, the scriptural sources to be discussed in this section take the opposite approach. For them, the fundamental factors in the extinction or survival of the Dharma are the actions of those outside the sangha—in other words, the support or persecution of the Buddhist religion by secular authorities. Such texts predict that the extinction of the Dharma will result from one of two types of action: (1) the invasion of India by foreign, non-Buddhist powers, or (2) the overregulation of the sangha by the state. In both cases the blame for the difficulties ex-

---

drawn from Mahāyāna sūtras. Yet such sūtras only rarely predict the actual termination of the Dharma. As we shall see in the following chapters, even when they contain materials that originally predicted the demise of the Dharma, Mahāyāna sūtras often betray a clear sense of discomfort with their implications.

[20] In his English summary of Kumoi's article David Chappell describes the second of the categories outlined above as consisting of "religious and moral laxity" in general (see Chappell, "Early Forebodings," 125–26). But Kumoi does not use the term "moral laxity" in this context. In fact, what is really at issue here is not breaking moral rules or offending against moral principles, but being deficient in reverence and submission toward the Buddhist tradition itself. The main offense here, in other words, is that of being unruly and irreverent toward the traditions handed down by the Buddhist community.

perienced by the Buddhist community is placed on non-Buddhist outsiders, whose actions impinge upon the life of the community and threaten the very extinction of the Buddhist teachings.[21]

Type 1: Foreign Invasions

The Kauśāmbī story. In both Mahāyāna and non-Mahāyāna Buddhist literature we find versions of the story, introduced in chapter 1, of the demise of the Dharma culminating at Kauśāmbī. There are more than a dozen extant versions of this account,[22] and they differ in numerous matters of detail. All agree, however, that the demise of the Dharma will be precipitated by the invasion of northwest India by a coalition of foreign kings—variously named but most commonly identified with the Greeks, Sakas, and Parthians—which will result in a great intra-sangha struggle at the city of Kauśāmbī. The end result will be the complete disappearance of the lineage of the Buddha's teachings, beginning with the death of the last remaining Arhat in the world. Since the Greeks, Sakas, and Parthians did indeed invade northwest India (though in sequence, not in coalition) from the 2nd century BCE through the 1st century CE, we can assume that this tradition was formulated sometime after the appearance of the last of these three.[23]

Since we will be examining the extant versions of this story in detail in Part II of this study, the specific elements of the story need not detain us here. The important thing to note at this point is that in every version of the Kauśāmbī story the precipitating cause of the events leading to the destruction of the Dharma is the invasion of northwest India by foreigners. As we shall see, there are certain

---

[21] It is noteworthy that a substantial proportion of the traditions in this category are found in Mahāyāna texts, while those in the internal causes category are found almost exclusively in Nikāya Buddhist works. It is tempting to draw doctrinal conclusions from this asymmetry; yet the more important distinction, perhaps, is that the Mahāyāna sūtras in fact almost never predict the actual demise of the Dharma, except where they have inherited (and maintained) certain pre-Mahāyāna accounts. Even in these cases the Mahāyāna texts frequently modify these accounts, indicating that the Dharma will only appear to die out, but will not actually do so.

[22] For a complete list of these versions see the discussion in Part II, chapter 7, "Versions of the Kauśāmbī Story."

[23] Evidence for the date of the original (now lost) version of the Kauśāmbī story is discussed below, pp. 224-27.

elements within this story that might also be viewed as causes internal to the sangha itself. Without the forces set in motion by these non-Buddhist invaders, however, the disappearance of the Dharma would clearly not take place.

The Mihirakula story. Even more destructive than the invasions of the Greeks, Sakas, and Parthians (all of whom would eventually count Buddhist converts among their numbers) were the incursions of another Central Asian power. When the people known in Indian sources as the *Hūṇa* swept into northwest India and Kashmir, in the 5th c. CE, they brought misery and destruction in their wake. As we have seen, the experience of the Hephthalite subjugation was engraved in Buddhist memory, and furnished the subject matter for a sūtra dealing with Mihirakula himself.[24]

What is important to note at this point is that the Mihirakula story is not (strictly speaking) a prophecy of the extinction of Buddhism. Though this text has been treated by a number of scholars as belonging to the corpus of demise-of-the-Dharma texts,[25] a careful reading of the sūtra shows that it neither predicts the demise of the Dharma nor offers any timetable for that event. The subject of the sūtra is a temporary decline of Buddhism, not its termination. In the end the Buddhists survive the onslaught, and Mihirakula receives his just deserts.

Type 2: Excessive State Control

The *Humane Kings Sūtra*. While the first category of external causes – that of foreign invasion – offers numerous examples in the canonical texts, most of which are based on variants of the Kauśāmbī story, that of excessive government control of the sangha contains only a single scriptural example: the well-known *Humane Kings Sūtra* (*Jen-wang ching* 仁王經, T Nos. 245 and 246), which blames the demise of the Dharma not on non-Buddhist intruders but on the overregulation of the sangha by the state. And it is a text of dubious ancestry, for there is compelling evidence that this work is not an Indian but a Chinese composition. A number of convincing arguments against the Indian authorship of the text have been offered, but one of the most impressive may be the con-

[24] See above, pp. 110–17.

[25] E.g., the works of Yamada and Kajiyama cited above, p. 27, n. 1.

tent of this decline prediction itself: here the declining fortunes of the Buddhist religion are attributed neither to laxity on the part of the Buddhists themselves nor to the destructiveness of non-Buddhist invaders, but to restrictions on monastic ordinations, stūpa-building, and the crafting of images, imposed on the sangha by the government. It would be difficult to identify any period in Indian history when the Buddhist community felt threatened by an encroachment of this sort; Indian governments might patronize Buddhism or not—and we should recall that both the Kushans and the Guptas, neither an ostensibly Buddhist dynasty, appear to have made considerable financial contributions to Buddhist groups—but they were hardly known for harassing the Buddhist community by overregulation. In China, by contrast, relations between church and state were an issue almost from the outset, and concern over this problem reached a peak precisely at the time of Kumārajīva's supposed translation of this text.[26]

---

[26] In addition to the unusual content of the prophecy of decline, a number of other features of the text also seem quite un-Indian. The title itself has a suspicious appearance: the term *jen* 仁 is of course a well-established Chinese (especially Confucian) term, but it is difficult to identify any Indian Buddhist term that could have served as its antecedent. Second, while the text clearly draws heavily on the Indian Prajñāpāramitā literature, those sections that do not consist of wholesale borrowings in this style betray concerns not typically seen in Indian Buddhist literature. The mention of the "hundred families" (T 8.832c20, 843a29; see Edward Conze's synopsis in *The Short Prajñāpāramitā Texts* [London: Luzac & Co., 1974], 178), the arrangement of a series of items in groups of nine (in Kumārajīva's translation 8.832c27–29, but not in Amoghavajra's version; Conze, 179), and the apparent reference to sūtras being kept in boxes (8.832c28, 843b18; Conze 179) all smack of Chinese, not Indian, conventions.

Most telling of all, however, may be the content of this decline section itself. The issue of church-state relations was as critical in north China as it was in the south, where Hui-yüan had submitted his famous memorial on the subject to the Eastern Chin ruler in 403. For Kumārajīva, however—if he in fact is to be associated with this "translation" at all—or for any Buddhist monk operating under the far more autocratic rule of the non-Chinese Northern Wei state, a direct confrontation of this kind might well have been suicidal. It is tempting, therefore, to regard this passage as a more subtle way of communicating views comparable to those of Hui-yüan to a far less receptive audience.

A study by a Japanese scholar who argues both for the Chinese composition (or rather, compilation) of this text and for a date somewhat after the time of Kumārajīva has recently been brought to my attention by Rebecca Bernen Nowakowski (personal communication, 1989). According to Nowakowski, in his *Chūgoku mikkyō no kenkyū* (Tokyo: Daitō Shuppansha, 1979) YORITOMI Motohiro maintains that the *Jen-wang ching* consists of an original (probably Indian)

WITHIN AND WITHOUT: PATRONAGE AND ITS SIDE EFFECTS

The distinction between internal and external causes of decline is a useful one; yet not all the Buddhist scriptures that predict the eventual extinction of the Dharma can easily be assigned to either category. The events narrated in the Kauśāmbī story, in particular, repeatedly cross this boundary in assigning the responsibility for the Dharma's demise.

A case in point is the role of the central figure in the story, a pious Buddhist king who is faced with the invasion of India by the Greeks, Sakas, and Parthians. According to all the variant editions of the story he succeeds in repelling the invaders, after which he invites all the Buddhist monks in his kingdom to a feast. Yet, despite his military successes, the king is left to witness the complete destruction of the Buddhist Dharma, standing by powerless to intervene in the course of this event. Most problematic in terms of the categories outlined above is the fact that this tragedy takes place well after the invaders have been driven back from Indian soil. Thus their contribution to the demise of the Dharma, while clearly a contributing factor, does not seem to be decisive.

Who, then—if anyone—is ultimately responsible for the extinction of the Dharma? A detailed account of the various recensions of the Kauśāmbī story will be offered in Part Two, and the reader may wish to draw his or her own conclusions at that time. One key point, however, may be made here: the fact that the death of all the monks in Jambudvīpa is the result of an internal battle within the Buddhist community. More specifically, the stage is set for the conflict by the patronage of the king, who by his generous invitation to a royal feast has brought together a number of formerly separate groups.

The subject of the disagreement, as we shall see in Part II, is a

---

Prajñāpāramitā text to which various Chinese interpolations have been added. Yoritomi does not accept the attribution of the text to Kumārajīva and suggests rather that it was compiled in China during the century or so after Kumārajīva's death. Nowakowski's own analysis of these issues, together with her translation of the sūtra, will be available in the near future (Ph.D. thesis, Harvard University).

dispute over the monastic rules (or more specifically, over the proper format for their recitation). Yet it is important not to reduce this story to a conflict over proper monastic conduct. For it is precisely the opportunity for interaction among various lineages, made possible by the king's own act of generosity, that sets the stage for the battle that results in the annihilation of the Buddhist sangha.

In sum, while the Kauśāmbī story offers a clear-cut example of the importance of outside forces (namely, invading armies) in precipitating the demise of the Dharma, the final blow is dealt by members of the monastic community themselves. In a sense, then, we have come full circle, returning from a scenario based on external causes to a reassertion of the Buddhist notion of karma.

NARRATIVE AND PROPHECY: THE KAUŚĀMBĪ STORY

Not all the scriptures that predict the decline and disappearance of Buddhism offer any explanation of its cause.[27] Nor do all the texts that bemoan the decline and decadence of the Buddhist tradition go on to predict its ultimate extinction. We have texts that offer timetables for the disappearance of the Dharma, but no explanation of its cause, and we find other accounts of specific deeds that will lead to the demise of the Buddhist tradition, but without any timetable for its extinction.

The Kauśāmbī story, in fact, is the only canonical tradition that combines a prophecy of the complete extinction of the Dharma with a narrative account of the actions leading up to this event. This unique scenario offers a number of intriguing questions to the historian: to what extent, for example, is the Kauśāmbī story an *ex post facto* account of events that have already taken place? And if this is the case, when and how did the narrative portion of the text come to be associated with a prediction of the complete annihilation of the Dharma?

We will take up these questions in Part Two, following an analysis of the content of the various recensions of the Kauśāmbī story

---

[27] The *Lotus Sūtra* and the smaller *Sukhāvatīvyūha-sūtra* — to cite only two of the best-known examples — are permeated by a general anticipation of decline, yet neither has anything to say about the circumstances leading to this situation.

themselves. Before turning to a detailed study of this specific prophecy, however, we must first consider the place of understandings of time and history within the Buddhist tradition as a whole.

Chapter Six

Conclusions: Time and History in Buddhist Consciousness

HISTORY—so writes Roger Corless in a recently published textbook on Buddhism—is "a Western, post-Christian, academic discipline, [which] is non-Buddhist, even anti-Buddhist."[1] After describing historical study as a method that is alien to the Buddhist tradition itself, Corless allows that such study by modern Western scholars may have its place, but with strict qualification: "It is legitimate to write a history of Buddhism, but such a book will be more history than Buddhism."[2] And in a more humorous vein, Corless offers the following assessment of the place of history in Buddhist thought:

> Change, for Buddhism, is a primary characteristic of cyclic existence (*saṃsāra*), and history is just a lot of change. All that we can say about history, Buddhistically, is that as time goes on we get more of it.[3]

Corless's contention that a concern with history can be found only among modern Western scholars is likely to elicit immediate disagreement from sinologists, who would be quick to point out that an awareness of history is hardly the monopoly of the post-Enlightenment West. Indeed, historical writings have held a place throughout most of Chinese history not unlike that of comparable

[1] Roger Corless, *The Vision of Buddhism* (New York: Paragon House, 1989), xx.
[2] *Vision*, xx.
[3] *Vision*, xix.

accounts in the ancient Hebrew world—that is, in both of these cultures historical writings have served, in a very real sense, as scripture. In both traditional China and ancient Israel historical events were viewed as the prime arena in which the way of Heaven (in the former case) or the will of God (in the latter) could be discerned. Thus, to limit a concern with history to the modern, post-Enlightenment West would need to be justified by an extended discussion of just how "history" is to be understood.

Corless's observations concerning Buddhist attitudes toward history nonetheless raise an important question for our consideration. Is "history" as such really a non-Buddhist category? And does any attempt to discern a "historical consciousness" on the part of Buddhists who lived centuries ago in a variety of Asian cultures represent merely an imposition of our modern Western worldviews onto those who would have found such attitudes entirely alien?

Such questions are far from unimportant, for one of the most difficult challenges facing scholars studying cultures and eras other than our own is to catch ourselves as we make what seem to be entirely natural assumptions concerning how other human beings must have acted or felt or thought. Is it accurate to claim that Asian Buddhists shared (in any sense) what we modern Westerners would describe as a "historical consciousness"? Or was the 19th-century stereotype of Buddhism (and, indeed, of all religions of Indian origin) as being totally unconcerned with history based on a solid, if not altogether uniform, foundation?

The answer to each of these questions, I would suggest, is both yes and no, and which side of the spectrum is predominant has varied from one Buddhist culture (and from one period of time) to another. The issue is clearly worthy of an extended study in itself, and only a few general comments can be offered here. Nonetheless, we may pause to take note of a few key elements in the Buddhist tradition that bear on this question, which may be pursued further by those who take up these issues in the future.

TIME-FRAMES AND LINEAGE CHARTS: ABSTRACT AND CONCRETE IN BUDDHIST HISTORICAL THOUGHT

Although we have contended from the outset that Buddhists are not devoid of a concern with history, much of our discussion has focused not on the importance of specific historical events but on the abstract timetables and periodization schemes constructed by Buddhist thinkers to mark the duration (and eventual extinction) of the Buddhist Dharma. But do such impersonal frames of reference, the reader might well ask, really constitute attention to "history" as such? Would the assertion that Buddhists do indeed care about historical issues not be better supported by an appeal to (for example) the lineage charts cherished by many Buddhist schools, detailing the names of their leading teachers from the time of Śākyamuni to the present?[4]

At first it would seem that such lineage traditions—which teem with historical and parahistorical names, dates, and locations—would provide far better evidence for a concern with history on the part of the Buddhist community than do the abstract chronological systems outlined above. Yet a careful examination of the uses to which such lineage traditions have been put quickly dispels this initial impression. Whether we consider the lineage traditions of Sōto Zen in Japan, Theravāda Buddhism in South and Southeast Asia, or the Sa-skya-pa school in Tibet, we discover over and over again that those schools that place the greatest emphasis on an unbroken lineage do so not in order to emphasize the historical changes that have taken place within their own traditions, but rather to assert the unchanging identity of their teachings and practices with those originally set forth by the founder. What would seem at first glance to be the most concrete evidence of a preoccupation with history thus shows itself, upon closer examination, to be evidence of precisely the opposite.[5]

---

[4] I would like to thank Bernard Faure for drawing my attention to the importance of Buddhist lineage charts in this connection.

[5] For a discussion of the function of lineage charts in Chinese Ch'an Buddhism and their tendency to result in a "flattening" of history see John R. McRae,

When we turn to the impact of the periodization schemes discussed in the previous chapters, by contrast, we find quite another dynamic in operation. Not that this dynamic has produced entirely uniform results; far from it, for the notion of a progressively eroding Buddhist tradition has resulted in quite opposite responses in different parts of Asia, as we shall see in the following section. In general, however, it seems fair to say that in those Buddhist cultures and sectarian groups that have emphasized chronological schemes delineating the lifespan of the Dharma, a far more acute sense of time (and of the individual believer's own existence in a unique and significant age) has resulted. The question of whether this constitutes a genuine historical sense is more complex, and will be reserved for consideration below. First, however, we must deal with the fact that such chronological schemes have produced quite dissimilar results in different parts of the Buddhist world.

DECLINE AND DISPENSATIONALISM IN BUDDHIST THOUGHT AND PRACTICE

In the broadest terms, Buddhist reactions to the expectation of the eventual disappearance of the Dharma may be divided into two categories: those that envision a prolonged period of *mo-fa* (or an analogous category) and those that do not. For traditions of the non-*mo-fa* type, the Dharma is still fully accessible (albeit increasingly difficult to encounter and to practice) throughout the period of its survival on earth. At the end of its allotted lifespan, however, the Buddhist Dharma will disappear from the world in a sudden and generally cataclysmic fashion. The tradition will thus slide, as it were, over a precipice, disappearing from view and remaining inaccessible for millions (if not billions) of years until the eventual appearance of the future Buddha, Maitreya.[6]

It is easy to see how such a perspective could lead to the view-

---

"Encounter Dialogue and the Transformation of the Spiritual Path in Chinese Ch'an," in Robert E. Buswell, Jr., ed., *Paths to Liberation: The Marga and its Transformations in Buddhist Thought* (Honolulu: University of Hawaii Press, 1991), 274–300, especially 285–86 and 292.

[6] For a collection of articles on this subject see Alan Sponberg and Helen Hardacre, eds., *Maitreya, the Future Buddha* (Cambridge: Cambridge University Press, 1988).

point we actually find in much of South, Southeast, and Inner Asian[7] Buddhism: namely, a fierce conservatism, devoted to the preservation for as long as possible of the Buddha's teachings in their original form. Set within the cosmological framework described above (according to which ours is an age of general decline) and anticipating the disappearance of the Dharma within a finite number of centuries, this historical outlook views change of any kind as being—by definition—change for the worse. Thus the impulse to preservation (and, accordingly, the tendency to deny any change that may actually have taken place) is both understandable and expected.

In sharp contrast to this scenario, traditions of the *mo-fa* type—which are found, as we have seen, only in East Asia—are confronted with the task of finding a way to continue to function, as Buddhists, within the prolonged but far from auspicious age of the "Final Dharma." This challenge, acutely perceived by a great many East Asian Buddhist thinkers, has in its turn evoked two quite distinct responses. In the first instance we have what might be described as the "we-try-harder" response; that is, if the present age is indeed the final age in Buddhist history, it requires additional efforts by would-be Buddhist practitioners (efforts that fall within traditional frameworks) if there is to be any hope at all of reaching the goal. Thus for Hsin-hsing (540–594), founder of the "Sect of the Three Stages" (*San-chieh-chiao* 三階教), the appropriate response was to redouble one's efforts, since the reduced capacity of those living during the time of *mo-fa* made spiritual accomplishment a far more difficult prospect.[8] In other contexts, however, the idea of *mo-fa* has

---

[7] The term "Inner Asia" is used here (as is generally done by specialists in the study of this region) to refer to the whole of the Eurasian continent less the major sedentary civilizations of Iran, India, China, and Southeast Asia. It thus includes the cultures of Tibet and Mongolia as well as the Buddhist populations (in the pre-Islamic period) of the so-called "Silk Road," consisting of the chain of oasis towns crisscrossing what is now Afghanistan, Soviet Central Asia, and Xinjiang. The term "Central Asia" (used by some non-specialists to refer to the territory of Tibet and Mongolia as well as other parts of Inner Asia) is best reserved for these oasis towns, whose distinctive social and economic patterns (and central role as cultural middlemen between China and the West) entitle them to a separate regional identity.

[8] On the function of the concept of *mo-fa* in the Sect of the Three Stages see James B. Hubbard, "Salvation in the Final Period of the Dharma: The Inexhaustible Storehouse of the San-chieh-chiao" (Ph.D. thesis, Univ. of Wisconsin, 1986), 10–48.

been used to justify precisely the opposite response: in early 9th-century Japan, for example, the author of the *Mappō-tōmyōki* argued that one could hardly expect Buddhist monks to adhere fully to the monastic rules during such a decadent age, and thus the government should not penalize those whose behavior was less than exemplary.[9] More commonly, however, this acute sense of the inability of ordinary human beings living in the Final Age to emulate their spiritual predecessors has led to what would be described, in a Christian context, as "dispensationalism": that is, the idea that while certain teachings and practices may have been appropriate in an earlier age, we now find ourselves in a completely different era (or "dispensation") in which a wholly new spiritual repertoire is called for. Thus the arguments set forth by the Japanese Buddhist teacher Hōnen (1133–1212) in favor of discarding all Buddhist scriptures other than those concerning the "original vow" of the Buddha Amitābha (Jpn. *Amida*) were based on the idea that a fundamentally new age was now in effect.[10] Likewise, while his compatriot Nichiren (1222–1282) argued that his advocacy of chanting the *daimoku* was fully in accord with the intention of the Buddha Śākyamuni, he was also well aware that this constituted a radically new practice in the eyes of his fellow Buddhists, and he argued for its legitimacy precisely on the basis of such "dispensationalism.".[11]

Thus, while in South, Southeast, and Inner Asia (including Tibet) the threat of the decline and ultimate demise of the Dharma served largely to elicit conformity with the existing tradition and to reinforce the importance of preserving whatever elements of the Dharma still remain, in East Asia a long series of Buddhist leaders—from the Pure Land teacher Tao-ch'o in 6th-century China[12]

---

[9] In the *Mappō-tōmyōki*, traditionally attributed to Saichō; see Robert Rhodes, "Saichō's *Mappō-tōmyōki*," *The Eastern Buddhist*, n.s., 13/1 (1980), 79-103.

[10] The main source for Hōnen's uses of dispensationalist arguments is his *Senchaku hongan nenbutsu shū* (Treatise on the Selection of the *Nenbutsu* of the Original Vow). No complete translation of the *Senchaku shū* is yet available in print in any Western language; an English translation by Morris Augustine is forthcoming, however, in the Bukkyō Dendō Kyōkai translation series.

[11] For Nichiren's "dispensationalist" views see Kenneth Dollarhide, *Nichiren's Senji-shō, An Essay on the Selection of the Proper Time* (New York: Edwin Mellen Press, 1982).

[12] On Tao-ch'o's understanding of *mo-fa* and its relevance to Pure Land Buddhist practice see Chappell, "Tao-ch'o," especially 144-50.

to the Kamakura reformers of 13th-century Japan[13] —found in the idea of *mo-fa* an incentive to innovation, often leading to the formulation of new religious ideas and practices of striking creativity.

The idea of decline, then, is clearly multivalent and has served a number of seemingly contradictory purposes in Buddhist religious history. Its significance in any given time and place—or for any given individual—will be influenced by a great number of factors, one of the most important of which is the presence, or absence, of a concept of *mo-fa*. The task of living within a prolonged period of the "Final Dharma" is quite different from that of facing the imminent demise of the Dharma as a whole, and it is hardly surprising that these two prospects should have evoked such different responses.

CONCLUSIONS

The question of whether history has played an important role in the Buddhist tradition depends entirely, of course, on what definition of "history" we choose to adopt. If by "history" we mean the idea that human actions are significant and have a notable impact upon our world, then we certainly face no difficulty, for Buddhist thinkers have always accepted this view. Indeed, it might be argued that Buddhists have seen human actions as *more* significant than have the members of the so-called "historical religions" of the West, for it would be difficult to find a more sweeping statement of the significance of the actions of humans, animals, and other creatures than in the opening lines of the fourth chapter of the *Abhidharmakośa*, an influential Buddhist scholastic work dating from perhaps the 4th century CE, where it is stated that the entire universe as we know it is the product of the actions of sentient (not supernatural) beings.[14] Not all such actions are of equal impact,

[13] With the exception of Dōgen, who objected to the implications for religious practice and attainment in the *mappō* thinking current in his time (see in particular the *Bendōwa* chapter of his *Shōbōgenzō*, a work whose very title may represent an oblique challenge to prevailing understandings of *mappō*), all the great Buddhist leaders of the Kamakura period appear to have formulated their teachings with the idea of *mappō* in mind. The idea is at least as central to the thought of Hōnen and Shinran as it was to their Chinese Pure Land predecessors, and Nichiren's religious system would be incomprehensible without it.

[14] See La Vallée Poussin, trans., *L'Abhidharmakośa de Vasubandhu*, vol. 3, chapter

however, and it is hardly surprising that the Buddhist tradition has generally considered the actions of the Buddha Śākyamuni to have had the most dramatic effect on our present age.[15]

If, by contrast, by "history" we mean the idea that one historical period is radically different from another, that our present age is quite distinct from the past and that the future will likewise be different in ways we can only imagine, then again we have no problem, at least in those Buddhist cultures that have emphasized the chronological frameworks described at length above. For in these contexts we hardly find either a static or a purely cyclic view of time; rather, the view of our universe as oscillating between ages of advance and decline provides a strong incentive for concern with the specifics of historical change, at least in the medium term.

If by "history," however, we mean simply the disinterested recording of events, then we will find little evidence for such a category in the Buddhist tradition. For the motive of liberating oneself and other sentient beings from suffering is a constant and underlying theme in all Buddhist schools. In such a context there can be no purely disinterested history, for the only information

---

4, p. 1: "Par qui est faite (*kṛta*) la variété du monde des êtres vivants (*sattvaloka*) et du monde-réceptacle (*bhājanaloka*) qui ont été décrits dans le chapitre précédent? Ce n'est pas Dieu (*īśvara*) qui la fait intelligemment (*buddhipūrvaka*). La variété du monde naît de l'acte." The commentary goes on to describe how the good and evil acts of ordinary sentient beings have led to the production of all that makes up our world, both pleasant and unpleasant.

[15] There are exceptions to this rule, however, the most notable being the Nichiren Shōshū school of Japan, for whom Nichiren is not simply a reincarnation of the Bodhisattva Jōgyō (as he seems to have suggested in his own writings) but the true "Original Buddha," who in the distant past was once the teacher of Śākyamuni himself. On the identity of Nichiren as understood by the Nichiren Shōshū school (one of the key features distinguishing this sect from other Nichiren schools) see Kiyoaki Murata, *Japan's New Buddhism* (New York: Weatherhill, 1969), 61–67. A similar (though less radical) departure from the centrality of Śākyamuni is the treatment of Padmasambhava as a "second Buddha" in the Nyingma school of Tibetan Buddhism; see Helmut H. Hoffmann, *The Religions of Tibet*, epecially the chapter on "Padma and Padmaism." Śākyamuni has also suffered competition from non-historical Buddhas, of whom Amitābha is the most noteworthy example. The displacement of Śākyamuni by such "celestial" figures, however, has tended to result in the negation of history as such, rather than in the shortening of history—now seen as beginning not with Śākyamuni but with a more recent Buddha figure—that takes place in the case of genuinely historical personages.

that is genuinely of value is that which leads, on an individual and a global scale, to a reduction of suffering.

The question is tossed back, then, into the court of those historians to whom Corless is apparently referring: is there ever, in any context, such a thing as a truly disinterested history? Is not the historian always arguing from some point of view—if not to show that God (or Heaven) is working through earthly events, then in order to persuade us that the Greeks are worth emulating, that Chinese civilization has embodied and expressed important values, that capitalist cultures are marching relentlessly toward an eventual classless society, or that (at the very least) the writer of such a careful historical study must be deserving of tenure? It would be difficult indeed to find a historian who is utterly devoid of agendas; but the point—so the Buddhist is likely to argue—is simply to be clear about what our own agendas are, and to evaluate their usefulness in terms of their impact on the collective suffering of sentient beings.

The agenda in the present study, then—for to raise such a question without facing it oneself would be illegitimate—has been to demonstrate that we will miss (and misunderstand) a great deal of what has gone on in Buddhist history if we assume that this tradition has been indifferent to historical change. On the contrary, it is my contention that the question of "what time it is" has mattered, and at times has mattered very much, to a substantial proportion of Buddhist believers. A major objective of this study has been to demonstrate that there is considerable evidence in the Buddhist canonical literature itself that, far from being concerned only with "timeless realities," the Buddhist tradition has often paid careful attention to the transitory realities of this earth.

An additional objective of this study has been to show that Buddhist thinkers have exhibited tremendous creativity in interpreting the traditions received from their predecessors—far more creativity, indeed, than they have often given themselves credit for. More specifically, I have tried to show that the concept of *mo-fa* and the tripartite time scheme with which it is associated are purely East Asian innovations, based (to be sure) on ideas found in the Indian Buddhist scriptures but uniquely adapted to East Asian religious concerns. Finally, I have attempted to show that even a single religious concept—in this case, the central Buddhist concept of transitoriness, applied to the Buddhist tradition itself to predict its eventual destruction—can have radically different implications in different cultural environments, and that before generalizing about the impact of any element of Buddhist doctrine we must pay close attention to the context in which it is received.

In sum, this study has attempted to show that Buddhist attitudes toward history have undergone radical changes even as certain basic concepts and technical terminology have remained the same. The chronicle of Buddhist attempts to understand the possibilities open to us as human beings in the always-changing present age thus constitutes a record of ongoing human creativity and inventiveness, providing grist for the mill of history in the best sense of the word.

Part Two

Case Study: The Kauśāmbī Prophecy

Chapter Seven

Versions of the Kauśāmbī Prophecy

A SUBSTANTIAL NUMBER OF Buddhist texts attribute the eventual extinction of the Dharma to a dispute between two Buddhist factions at the city of Kauśāmbī, an event triggered by the invasion of northwest India by a coalition of non-Buddhist kings. Both the names and the number of these foreign invaders vary from one account to another; in fact, this version of the decline prophecy appears to have been subject to continual updating, with the names and locations of the foreign powers changed to accommodate new historical circumstances. Though the story originated in non-Mahāyāna circles, it circulated in Mahāyāna recensions as well. In sum, the prophecy of the extinction of the Dharma at Kauśāmbī appears to have enjoyed a long period of transsectarian currency.

In analyzing the content of the texts belonging to this group one of our primary concerns will be to establish a chronological stratification of these recensions, with an eye toward identifying the earliest version of the tradition and ultimately toward pinpointing the historical circumstances that may have led to its composition. Accordingly, the following discussion will begin with those texts that have some claim to chronological priority, and will conclude with those that clearly represent later adaptations of the tradition.

THE *MAHĀVIBHĀṢĀ*

Of all the surviving versions of the Kauśāmbī story—so argues Étienne Lamotte in his survey of the Buddhist decline literature—the account given in the *Mahāvibhāṣā*[1] represents "la version la plus sobre et la mieux conçue."[2] While Lamotte does not state explicitly that he considers this recension to be the oldest, he implies that this is the case both by treating this version first and by his comment (following his resumé of its contents) that "over the course of history, each time the Buddhist order felt itself to be threatened, this prophecy was re-edited and enriched with new details designed to bring it into harmony with contemporary events."[3] Lamotte's choice is perhaps somewhat surprising in view of the fact that the *Mahāvibhāṣā* survives only in a late Chinese translation. Yet the dates of the Chinese translations of Buddhist texts cannot be used to establish even a relative, let alone absolute, chronology of their actual composition. Rather, their usefulness is limited to providing a *terminus ante quem* for the existence of a given text in a language other than Chinese. Thus the *Mahāvibhāṣā* could well contain material much older than its 7th-century Chinese translation, and in fact the bulk of its content is generally assigned to around the 2nd c. CE.[4]

Lamotte's selection of the *Mahāvibhāṣā* account as the most primitive version of the Kauśāmbī story appears to be based on the relatively straightforward nature of the account, which contains few extraneous details, appeals to magical powers, or references to supernatural intervention. Moreover, the *Mahāvibhāṣā* contains the smallest number of personal names—and in fact the smallest overall cast of characters—of any extant version of the tradition. We will begin with this version of the Kauśāmbī story, then, as a possible candidate for the most primitive version of the tradition.

---

[1] *A-pi-ta-mo ta p'i-p'o-sha lun* 阿毘達磨大毘婆沙論, T No. 1545, 27.918a18–b21, translated by Hsüan-tsang in 656–659 CE. The text is available only in this Chinese translation; the Sanskrit original has not survived, and the text is not included in the Tibetan canon.

[2] Lamotte, *Histoire*, 217–18.

[3] *Histoire*, 220.

[4] *Histoire*, 424.

Since a complete French translation of the relevant passage has already been made available by Lamotte,[5] it will be sufficient to provide only a resumé of its contents here.

At an unspecified time in the future, three kings will arise in Jambudvīpa: a religious (that is, Buddhist) king in the east and two non-Buddhist kings born among the *dasyu-mleccha* ("enemy-barbarians"). These non-Buddhist kings will cause great harm to Buddhist believers and will destroy Buddhist stūpas and monasteries. The good king, hearing of this, will raise an army, and will succeed in capturing and killing the two unbelieving kings.

Subsequently the victorious king will summon all the monks of Jambudvīpa to Kauśāmbī for a great quinquennial feast (*pañcavarṣa*). Here the text offers the parenthetical comment that these monks have only left home for mercenary reasons and do not exert themselves in meditation and memorization of scriptures. At that time there will remain in Jambudvīpa only two real practitioners of the Dharma: an arhat named Sūrata[6] and a tripiṭaka-master named Śiṣyaka, the latter being the head of the sangha.

At this point five hundred pious lay people will somehow discern (the mechanism is unspecified) that the Dharma is about to disappear. In good abhidharmic fashion, these lay disciples produce a variety of theories to account for their present circumstances and to explain why their gifts to the sangha can still produce merit at this late date in the history of the Buddhist religion. On that very night—on the occasion of the recital of the *Prātimokṣa* by the monastic community—a quarrel breaks out among the monks. Śiṣyaka, it would seem, wants to recite the *Prātimokṣa* only in abbreviated fashion, arguing that there is no one alive who is able to uphold the monastic precepts in their entirety. Sūrata, however, rises to object, claiming that he does indeed adhere to all of the precepts. Śiṣyaka's disciples are outraged at seeing

---

[5] *Histoire*, 218–20.

[6] Read *Surata* by Lamotte (*Histoire*, 218, 219) and *Sorata* by Kajiyama (*Shinran*, 322), but the translation *Des-pa* ("of good nature") given in the Tibetan *Karmaśataka* and the Chinese glosses 善意 "good intention" (in the *Aśokāvadāna*) and 善 "good" (in the prose version of the Kātyāyana prophecy), as well as the Khotanese transcription of the name as *Sūratä* (~ *Sūradä*) all support the reading with the long vowel *ū* in the first syllable. (For a complete list of the renderings of this name in the texts examined in this thesis see the Appendix, "Proper Names," no. 7.)

their teacher humiliated in this fashion and, overcome by wrath, they strike and kill the arhat. At this point, the text tells us, the "absolute *saddharma*" (*paramārtha-saddharma,* Ch. 勝義正法) will disappear. Meanwhile Śiṣyaka is also killed (here the *Mahāvibhāṣā* offers a variety of theories as to the identities of the perpetrators, including a group of *devas*, *nāgas*, and *yakṣas*, the disciples of the arhat, or the king himself). At this point, we are told, the "relative *saddharma*" (*saṃvṛti-saddharma*, Ch. 世俗正法) will disappear.

For seven days and nights no one will realize that the Dharma has finally disappeared. (This is said to be the result of an obscure karmic chain of events set in motion by Śākyamuni's propensity, while he was still a bodhisattva, to hide the faults of others and to hold their secrets in confidence.) But when these seven days have expired, the end of the Dharma will be heralded by a series of earthquakes, meteor showers, and fires. The gods will beat their drums (i. e., thunder will sound), Māra and his entourage will rejoice, and an unidentified voice will proclaim: "As of today the True Dharma of Śākya, the great hermit, has disappeared."

Several features of this tale lend support to Lamotte's suggestion that it may be the oldest surviving version. First, while in other versions of the story there are three or even four unbelieving kings, here we have only two; and while other versions name each of the kings individually, in the *Mahāvibhāṣā* they—like the "good king in the east"—remain anonymous. Moreover, while other versions of the story refer not only to the good king but also to his son, here only the king himself is mentioned. Likewise, various miraculous events found in other recensions—such as the birth of sons to five hundred of the king's ministers, and of a talking foal to the king's horse, on the night that his own son is born—are lacking in this edition. The tale is, as Lamotte contends, reasonably sober and well conceived.

Despite the relative simplicity of this story, however, we should not assume that it is identical with the primitive version that served as the ultimate source for the others. Several features betray an advanced level of sophistication with respect to variants in the tradition: the offering of three different theories as to who killed Śiṣyaka certainly displays an awareness of rival versions of the tradition, while the Buddhist laity are likewise not satisfied with just one theoretical explanation of the conditions they are experiencing in the final days of the Dharma. The terminology used in the text also belies the assumption of an early date; the expression *dasyu-mleccha*, for example, is rare in Indian Buddhist texts prior to contact with the Muslims,[7] and the distinction between *paramārtha-saddharma* and *saṃvṛti-saddharma* is a rather unusual formulation that may be indebted to the terminology of the Mādhyamika school.[8]

One further point should be made with respect to the idea that simplicity itself can be used as a criterion for chronological priority. As a general rule it is certainly true that Buddhist scriptures tend to acquire extra layers through an ongoing process of accretion, and only rarely undergo a parallel process of diminution via editorial elimination. This generalization is valid primarily for the vinaya and sūtra literature, however; when we come to works of the abhidharma genre we are confronted by a very different set of literary processes. Certainly the abhidharma literature (including the *Mahāvibhāṣā*) was subject to occasional interpolations and additions. Yet during the process of the initial incorporation of existing traditions into the abhidharma literature a quite different process was in operation. This procedure might best be described as moving in two separate (even opposite) directions: first, the reduction of an existing tradition to its most essential elements, shorn of all literary flourishes, in order to cast it in a form appropriate for inclusion in an essentially scholastic work; and second, a process of expansion via the editor's attempt to catalogue all the important variants in the tradition. Thus we may expect the abhidharma version of any given story to be both more limited (in terms of plot, setting, and dialogue) and more extensive (in terms of the inclusion of variants drawn from a variety of sources) than any given example of the story found in the sūtra or vinaya literature.

It is just such a complex product that we find in the version of the Kauśāmbī story contained in the *Mahāvibhāṣā*. The account is both streamlined (with respect to the absence of ethnic names and the reduced number of characters involved in the story) and detailed (with respect to certain theoretical concerns of evident interest to

---

[7] Note that Hsüan-tsang transliterates this term (as *ta-hsu mi-li-ch'e* 達絮蔑戾車) rather than translating it into Chinese. Did he mistake this unfamiliar term for an ethnic name?

[8] The distinction also occurs, however, in Pāli; see Childers, *Dictionary of the Pali Language*, p. 334b s.v. *paramatto*.

abhidharma scholars). Thus the very simplicity of the story may serve as evidence, not of the chronological priority of this version of the story, but simply of the literary genre in which it occurs.

Finally, as a point of comparison with other versions of the Kauśāmbī story we might note that the *Mahāvibhāṣā* assumes a total duration of the Dharma of 1,000 years. No version of the Kauśāmbī story contains a shorter timetable; and if the presence of this number does not in itself confirm the priority of the *Mahāvibhāṣā* version (since numerous other recensions contain the same figure), it at least offers no evidence to the contrary.

The *Mahāvibhāṣā* recension of the Kauśāmbī story thus exhibits a number of features that we might expect to find in the most primitive version of the tale. In other respects, however, it shows clear signs of having been updated in an environment in which several versions of the tradition were already in circulation. We must reserve judgment on the priority of this recension, then, until we have first examined the rival claims of certain other versions of this story.

THE *AŚOKA-AVADĀNA* GROUP

Another nominee for the status of the most primitive recension of the Kauśāmbī story is that given in the 25th chapter of the Chinese *Saṃyukta-āgama*, described by David Chappell as "probably the oldest version of the story."[9] Chappell does not provide specific evidence for this assertion, though his reasoning may be that since the *āgamas* are among the oldest layers of the Buddhist canonical literature, this text is therefore likely to be a relatively ancient version of the tradition.[10] The version of the story given in the *Saṃyukta-āgama* cannot be considered in isolation, however, for it has close parallels in two other texts preserved in the Chinese and Tibetan Buddhist canons. The texts comprising this group (which

---

[9] Chappell, "Early Forebodings," 128.

[10] As Chappell himself notes, however ("Early Forebodings," 128), the Kauśāmbī story is absent from the corresponding section of the Pāli *Saṃyutta-nikāya*. This lack of parallel would weaken considerably any argument for the primacy of the Chinese *Saṃyukta-āgama* version of the story based solely on the section of the canon within which it occurs.

will be described here as the "*Aśoka-avadāna* group") are the following:

1. ***Saṃyukta-āgama*** (Chinese): *Tsa a-han ching* 雜阿含經, T No. 99 (2.177b12–180a5). Translated during the period 436–443 CE by Guṇabhadra.
2. ***Aśoka-avadāna*** (Chinese): *A-yu wang chuan* 阿育王傳, T No. 2042 (50.126c23–128b4).[11] Though the bulk of the text was translated in 306 CE by An Fa-ch'in, the chapters containing the Kauśāmbī story were not added until the end of the 5th century.[12] The Kauśāmbī story is not found in the other Chinese translation of the *Aśoka-avadāna* (T. No. 2043), nor does it occur in the extant Sanskrit version of the text.[13]
3. ***Karmaśataka*** (Tibetan): *Las brgya tham-pa*. Peking No. 1007 (*mdo-sna-tshogs su*, 279b2-290b4), Narthang No. 325, Derge No. 340, Lhasa No. 346. Since the text contains no colophon an exact translation date cannot be established. The title does appear, however, in the *Ldan-kar-ma*, a catalogue of the Buddhist texts that had been translated into Tibetan by the time of King Khri-srong-lde-brtsan (r. 755–797 CE).[14] Thus the Tibetan translation should be assigned to a period no later than the second half of the 8th century.[15]

These three recensions (of which the Tibetan *Karmaśataka* and the Chinese *Saṃyukta-āgama* bear the closest resemblance to one another) share a number of common features. First, in contrast to the *Mahāvibhāṣā* version (which is entirely in prose), these three recensions are all in a mixture of prose and verse. Often, but not always, the prose merely recapitulates what has already been given (or is about to be given) in verse. It would thus be possible to follow

---

[11] A complete French translation is given in Jean Przyluski, *A-yu-wang-tchouan, Chronique des premiers siècles du bouddhisme* (Paris: Paul Geuthner, 1923), chapter 9, 399–409.

[12] Lamotte, *Histoire*, 221.

[13] For an English translation of the Sanskrit *Aśoka-avadāna* see John S. Strong, *The Legend of King Aśoka: A Study and Translation of the Aśokāvadāna* (Princeton: Princeton University Press, 1983).

[14] On this catalogue see Marcelle Lalou, "Les textes bouddhiques au temps du roi Khri-sroṅ-lde-bcan," *Journal Asiatique* 241 (1953), 313–53.

[15] According to Helmut Hoffmann (*Tibet*, 127) it had been rendered into Tibetan even earlier, during the reign of Mes-'ag-tshom (r. 704–755 CE).

some, but not all, of the plot line simply by reading the verse sections alone. Second, in comparison with the *Mahāvibhāṣā* version the cast of characters is considerably expanded in these three accounts. While the *Mahāvibhāṣā* refers simply to the "king of Kauśāmbī," for example, these three texts distinguish between the king himself (named Mahendrasena) and his son Duṣprasaha, who ultimately becomes king in his turn and is the main protagonist of the story. A number of other subsidiary characters found in these three versions are also absent from the *Mahāvibhāṣā* account. Finally, while the *Mahāvibhāṣā* knows of only two foreign kings, neither of whom is named, all three texts of the *Aśoka-avadāna* group mention a triad of kings bearing the (reconstructed Sanskrit) ethnonyms *yavana* ("Greek"), *śaka* ("Saka"), and *pahlava* ("Parthian"). To this list the *Saṃyukta-āgama* alone adds a fourth king, called in Chinese *t'ou-sha-lo* 兜沙羅 (< Skt. *tuṣāra~tukhāra*?), presumably to be identified with the Kushans.[16] The presence of these ethnonyms, together with the information provided by the translation dates of the Chinese versions, allows us to determine the date of the redaction represented by the *Aśoka-avadāna* group with at least some degree of precision. Clearly this version of the story must postdate the invasions of India by the ethnic groups in question, which took place during the 2nd c. BCE–1st c. CE,[17] and it must predate the earliest attested translation of the tradition into Chinese, that of the *Saṃyukta-āgama* by Guṇabhadra in 436–443 CE. Thus the emergence of the version of the story represented by the texts of the

[16] For this derivation see Lamotte, *Histoire*, 221. Lamotte describes the reading *tuṣāra* as an error for *tukhāra*, though the term is given in MW 449c as a regular alternate for the latter. The presence of this obvious interpolation provides one piece of evidence that the *Saṃyukta-āgama* recension is not the oldest version of the story.

[17] In contrast to the statement of Lamotte (*Histoire*, 221) the addition of the Kushans or *tukhāra* to the list of evil kings in the *Saṃyukta-āgama* recension does not in itself require a later date than that of the other texts of this group (though the presence of an interpolation not shared by any of the other versions does prove that the *Saṃyukta* represents an independent branch, and not the root, of the other traditions). Recent research into the chronology of the Saka, Parthian, and Kushan invasions has demonstrated that the earliest Kushan incursions into northwest India and adjacent territories were contemporary with those of the Parthians, and presumably took place during the first century CE. For details see Richard N. Frye, *History of Ancient Iran* (München: Beck, 1983), 177–204 and the additional references given there.

Aśoka-avadāna group must have taken place during the period from the 2nd–4th c. CE.

Because the three texts in this category resemble one another so closely, their versions of the Kauśāmbī story may conveniently be summarized together. According to these texts, the story goes as follows. One thousand years after the death of the Buddha, the Dharma will be about to disappear. At that time there will arise three evil kings, "Greek" in the north, "Saka" in the south, and "Parthian" in the west.[18] (Note that in all three versions these ethnonyms are understood—or misunderstood—as personal names, a characteristic feature of all the extant versions of the Kauśāmbī story.) These kings will invade India, and will persecute Buddhist believers and destroy Buddhist monuments in their path. Meanwhile a son (named Duṣprasaha, "hard to tolerate") will be born to King Mahendrasena, ruling in the east at the city of Kauśāmbī. On the same night sons will also be born to five hundred "heads of families" (*Aśoka-avadāna*), "ministers of the king" (*Karmaśataka*), or "great ministers" (*Saṃyukta-āgama*), and a rain of blood will fall.

When the king turns to a soothsayer to learn the meaning of these mysterious omens, he is told that the young prince will grow up to conquer all of Jambudvīpa, and in so doing will kill many people. All this indeed comes to pass, and the prince conquers and kills the foreign invaders.

Meanwhile, a son has been born in Pāṭaliputra to a brahman named Agnidatta; he will grow up to be a great teacher called Śiṣyaka ("he who has disciples").[19] Likewise in Pāṭaliputra, a son will be born to an elder named Sudhana. The boy will be named Sūrata, and he will grow up to become a great arhat.

Upon the death of his father, the prince (now the king) is plunged into depression and doubt. He asks the Buddhist monks when it is that the three evil kings will destroy the Dharma,[20] and

---

[18] To this list the *Saṃyukta* version adds *tuṣāra* or "Kushan" in the east, a direction normally reserved for the "good king" of Kauśāmbī in the other versions.

[19] The reasonably accurate transcriptions and translations of proper names given in the texts of this group allow for reliable reconstructions of the underlying Indian forms, which will therefore be given without further annotation in this section. For a complete list of the proper names found in these and other versions of the Kauśāmbī story see the Appendix, "Proper Names in the Kauśāmbī Story."

[20] So the two Chinese versions (though both have previously stated that the

they reply that this will happen in twelve years. At this point the king resolves that he will hold a great *pañcavarṣa* feast during that entire twelve-year period. The quality of the monastic community, however, is not what it should be; the monks are impure and lazy, the texts tell us, due in part to their being accustomed to receiving large offerings. The gods, *nāga*s, and other non-human beings are offended, as are the laity, of whom a group of five hundred censures the monks for their misconduct and urges them to bring their quarrels to an end.

These exhortations, however, are to no avail. When the monks gather for the *poṣadha* (Pāli *uposatha*) ceremony, Śiṣyaka, the head of the sangha, wants to recite the monastic rules in abbreviated form. "If even I, who am the most learned of all, cannot keep the rules in their entirety, who else can?" he argues. But the arhat Sūrata rises to object. As in the *Mahāvibhāṣā*, Sūrata proclaims that he does indeed keep the monastic rules to the letter, and that Śiṣyaka should therefore recite the rules in their entirety. A disciple of Śiṣyaka, named Aṅgada, is outraged at this insult to his teacher, and strikes and kills the arhat. Aṅgada is in turn killed by a *yakṣa*, Dadhimukha, and one or more disciples of Sūrata then kill Śiṣyaka. Then the Buddha-Dharma, the texts tell us, gradually disappears.

When Duṣprasaha learns of these events, he flies into a blind rage and begins to kill monks and destroy stūpas and monasteries. At this point the Buddha tells the four *lokapāla*s,[21] "The Dharma that you were assigned to protect has died out." Thus relieved of their duties, the four gods return to the heavens. And with this anticlimactic finish, the story ends.

For comparative purposes, several points in this account are worthy of note. First, these three texts (like the *Mahāvibhāṣā)* give a total life-expectancy for the Dharma of 1,000 years. Among the known versions of the Kauśāmbī story, then, the texts in the *Aśoka-avadāna* group belong to the group with the shortest (and presumably earliest) timetable. Second, in all three of these texts the trio of Greeks, Sakas, and Parthians appears in the lineup of "evil, non-

---

three [or four] kings have already been killed). The Tibetan version asks simply "how long will the Dharma endure, after the destruction of the territories of the barbarian kings?"

[21] The guardians of the four directions, also known as the four *mahārāja*s.

Buddhist kings." Thus, whether the original Kauśāmbī story was formulated before or after the invasions by these groups—an issue to be considered in detail below—the recension represented by the three texts in the *Aśoka-avadāna* group must certainly postdate these events. Third, as in the *Mahāvibhāṣā* account, a group of five hundred pious lay Buddhists is explicitly singled out for favorable attention. They are even given the role of admonishing the monks, in a scene reminiscent of King Aśoka's exhortations to the sangha to bring its internecine quarrels to an end. Finally, two features of the texts in this group appear to be unknown in other versions of the story. These are (a) the death of king Mahendrasena, which in the texts of the *Aśoka-avadāna* group provokes a period of reflection and reassessment on the part of Duṣprasaha; and (b) the final actions of the king himself, who in a fit of rage turns against the Buddhist community. Since these features appear to be restricted to the texts of this group, they serve as evidence of the mutual affinity of these three translations, on the one hand, and of the separateness of this group as a whole from other recensions of the story on the other.

A peculiar element in this account, from the point of view of the Buddhist history of the region, is the portrayal of the Greeks, Sakas, and Parthians (and the Kushans as well, in the *Saṃyukta-āgama* account) as "enemies of the Dharma." The Indo-Greek ruler Menander (Pāli *Milinda*) is renowned as a friendly inquirer into, and perhaps even a convert to, the Buddhist religion, and the Kushan ruler Kanishka is widely treated in Buddhist literature as an outstanding patron of the Dharma. From Chinese sources we know that the Parthians were among the earliest Buddhist missionaries in China,[22] and from epigraphical evidence we know that many (perhaps even a majority) of the Sakas in northwest and north-central India were devoted Buddhists.[23] Why should these foreign powers, then, be treated as enemies of the faith?

There are two possible explanations for this seeming anomaly. First, all of these invaders must have caused considerable harm to

---

[22] On Parthian missionaries to China see Erik Zürcher, *The Buddhist Conquest of China* (Leiden: E. J. Brill, 1959), vol. 1, pp. 23, 25, 32, 33, 55, 70; and J. W. de Jong, "Buddha's Word in China" (reprinted in Gregory Schopen, ed., *Buddhist Studies: Selected Essays of J. W. de Jong* [Berkeley: Berkeley Buddhist Studies Series, 1979], 77–101).

[23] On Saka converts to Buddhism see Lamotte, *Histoire*, 537–43.

the Buddhist population and Buddhist monuments along their path during their initial incursions into Indian territory. And none, presumably, were Buddhists at the time of these invasions. Thus a negative initial impression among Indian Buddhists may have persisted long after many of their descendants had adopted the Buddhist faith.

There is, however, another possibility. By the 2nd century CE (if not before) the trio of Greeks, Sakas, and Parthians had become a standard *topos* for "non-brahmanic barbarians" in Indian literature.[24] Thus the appearance of all three names in this recension of the Kauśāmbī story does not necessarily imply that the invasions of all three groups (or, strictly speaking, of any of the three groups) contributed to this formulation. Rather, an invasion by any foreign power could have been described by an Indian writer as an incursion by the Greeks, Sakas, and Parthians, using this *topos* as a standard expression for foreigners.

These two possibilities have very different implications for the chronology of the text. To choose the second option requires that we date the composition of the Kauśāmbī story (or at least this recension of it) to a period well after the actual invasions, if the names had by then become formulaic and the role of each individual group only a distant memory. If we follow the former interpretation, on the other hand, we must assign the creation of this tradition to the early years of these invasions (and since the Greek incursions preceded those of the other two groups, we must opt for the early years of the Parthian invasions, which overlapped with the period of Saka control).

One additional element in the texts can help us to choose between these two options. According to all three versions in the *Aśoka-avadāna* group, the Greeks are located in the north, the Parthians in the west, and the Sakas in the south, with the king of Kauśāmbī farther to the east. This piece of information is extremely valuable, for if by *Greeks* the Hellenized population of Bactria is meant, these relative locations are quite correct. A writer

---

[24] Thus while the Śātavāhana ruler Vāsiṣṭhīputra (first half of the 2nd century CE) claimed only that his father Gautamīputra had uprooted the Sakas (a claim that is historically well founded), an inscription by Gautamīputra's mother describes her son as rooting out the "Śakas, Yavanas, and Pahlavas" (Romila Thapar, *A History of India*, vol. 1 [Baltimore: Penguin Books, 1966], 101–102) .

familiar with these three powers only by hearsay, or as a distant memory, would not be likely to have placed them so accurately.[25] So the formulation of a tradition referring to these three powers as enemies of the Buddhist religion may well date from as early as the 2nd century CE.

To say that this tradition itself may be this early, however, is not to say that the recensions belonging to the *Aśoka-avadāna* group are themselves of such ancient vintage. We can only say (on the basis of the *terminus ante quem* provided by the Chinese translations) that such recensions must have been current by the end of the 4th century CE at the latest. Nor are these the oldest surviving translations of the Kauśāmbī story. Another Chinese translation, produced no later than the beginning of the 4th century and possibly as early as the latter Han, is unquestionably the oldest extant recension of the story. Before attempting to date the recensions in the *Aśoka-avadāna* group with greater precision, then, we must examine the evidence provided by this earlier translation.

THE *PROPHECY OF KĀTYĀYANA* (VERSE TRANSLATION)

By far the oldest surviving version of the Kauśāmbī story is a little-known text whose title may conveniently be abbreviated as the *Prophecy of Kātyāyana*,[26] rendered into Chinese during or before the Western Chin dynasty (265–316 CE) by a translator whose name

[25] In later recensions these directions are sometimes scrambled (in the Chinese translation of the *Candragarbha-sūtra* and the prose recension of the *Prophecy of Kātyāyana*), or eliminated altogether (in the Tibetan and Khotanese versions of the *Candragarbha-sūtra*).

[26] Ch. *Fo-shih pi-ch'iu Chia-chan-yen shuo fa mei-chin chieh po-erh-shih chang* 佛使比丘迦旃延說法沒盡偈百二十章 (T No. 2029, 49.9c20–12c2), lit. "The Verses in 120 Sections (Concerning) the Decline and Destruction of the Dharma, Preached by the Buddha's Envoy, the Bhikṣu Kātyāyana." The title is given as the "Prediction *to* Kātyāyana" by Lamotte (*Histoire*, 220), but the prophecy is clearly spoken by the monk Kātyāyana and not by the Buddha himself. Both the form of the title and the introductory lines of the text serve to counter Lamotte's interpretation: the text is not styled a *sūtra* (*ching* 經), as one would expect if it were attributed to the Buddha, but merely a *gāthā* (*chieh* 偈), and the text begins without any trace of the expression "Thus have I heard. . ." that would serve to authenticate what follows as the word of the Buddha.

has not been preserved.[27] This text has been largely ignored by scholars interested in Buddhist decline theory,[28] yet both its chronological priority and several unusual features in its content require that we give it close attention.

The *Prophecy of Kātyāyana* relates the Kauśāmbī story as follows. At an unspecified time in the future India will be invaded by three evil kings, here associated with Rome (*ta-ch'in* 大秦),[29] Parthia (*po-lo* 撥羅),[30] and Arsacid Persia (or simply "Iran"; Ch. *an-hsi* 安息).[31] These invaders will kill monks and scholars, and destroy stūpas and monasteries. Those Buddhists who are able will flee to Madhyadeśa. The king of Madhyadeśa will then conquer and kill these invaders and will come to reside in the city of *Chien-ni* 監尼 (Skt. Kauśāmbī?).[32] The king, at the advice of his preceptor *Shih-shih* 尸師 (Skt. *Śiṣyaka*?),[33] will hold a great feast, to which he invites all the monks of Jambudvīpa. A group "numbered in the hundreds

---

[27] The early date of the translation is confirmed by its inclusion in Tao-an's catalogue (T No. 2154, 55.502a3, b25), compiled in 374 CE but including only works translated into Chinese before the end of the Western Chin dynasty.

[28] The text is discussed briefly by Lamotte in his survey of Buddhist decline literature (*Histoire*, 220) but is not mentioned except in passing in any of the other major survey articles cited above (p. 27, n. 1).

[29] The term *ta-ch'in* is used to refer to the Roman empire as early as the middle of the 2nd c. CE, when it appears in the *Hou Han shu* 後漢書 in the record of the arrival of an envoy from Rome, who arrived in China in the ninth year of Huang-ti (166 CE).

[30] The Ancient Chinese pronunciation of this term was presumably something like **pat-la* (see Bernhard Karlgren, *Analytic Dictionary of Chinese and Sino-Japanese* [1923; repr. New York: Dover, 1974], nos. 749 and 569, *pi̯ʷvt-꜀lâ*), the expected Chinese rendering of an Indian or Central Asian **pat-ra*, which in turn may be a metathesis < **par-ta* "Parthian" (cf. Greek *parthuioi*, Old Persian *parthava*). Note that Chinese texts (particularly those pre-dating the translations of Hsüan-tsang) tend to recast multisyllabic (especially three-syllable) proper names in the more acceptable format of a Chinese two-syllable name.

[31] The term *an-hsi* (A. Ch. *꜀ʼân-si̯ək*, Karlgren nos. 4, 780), though originally derived from the name of the Parthian Arsacid dynasty, continued to be used in reference to the territory of Iran as a whole long after the fall of that dynasty, much as our word "China" continues to be used more than two millennia after the demise of the Ch'in dynasty from which it was derived.

[32] A. Ch. *꜀kam'-꜀nji*, Karlgren nos. 376, 659. Since the modern Chinese pronunciations of many of the proper names in the *Kātyāyana* prophecy are quite distant from their presumed Indian originals, the Karlgren readings will be provided throughout this section.

[33] A. Ch. *꜀śi-꜀ṣi*, Karlgren nos. 878, 893.

of thousands" will assemble together, and on the 15th day (when the *Prātimokṣa* is to be recited) a quarrel will break out. A large group of *bhikṣus*, thinking themselves superior to the rest, issue a condescending statement to the effect that they understand more about the Dharma than anyone else. "If there is one *bhikṣu* who has attained enlightenment," they assert, "then he can preach about the origins and end 本末 [of the Dharma], and we will study his sūtra[s]." Much to their dismay, however, just such a *bhikṣu* happens to be present in the audience. This monk, named *Su-lai* 須賴 (Skt. *Sūrata*?),[34] rises from his seat and proclaims that he does indeed keep the precepts, has no doubts concerning the Dharma and Vinaya, has penetrated the scriptures, and truly understands the meaning of the path. He rebukes the self-righteous monks for praising themselves so much, which arouses the anger of a student of the honored teacher (= Śiṣyaka?), named *A-ssu* 阿斯 (<< Skt. *Aṅgada*?),[35] who then strikes and injures the arhat. A Dharma-loving demon (*sic*!) then seizes a vajra and strikes and kills *A-ssu*. The earth shakes in the familiar six ways, various ill omens appear, and the ultimate fate of the Dharma is described as follows: "The lamp of the Dharma is already out. The correct scriptures are already destroyed. This time is most ruined, and the drum of the Dharma will not ring out again." The text then goes on to encourage its readers (or more correctly, its listeners, since the text presumably circulated orally before eventually being recorded in writing) to strive vigorously in their Buddhist practice so that Buddhism will not yet die out, "remembering the great danger and fear to come." The text closes with a prediction that the Dharma will pass through three three-hundred-year periods: during the first three hundred years, many people will be liberated (i.e., attain nirvāṇa) by practicing Buddhism; during the second, people will still observe the precepts (*śīla*) and practice meditation, but the implication is that their level of accomplishment will be far lower

---

[34] A. Ch. *si̯u-lâi'*, K. nos. 839, 510. Karlgren notes that the syllable *lâi'* (or rather, at least one of the characters in its group) had an ancient final *-d*; the transcription of Skt. *-rat*(*a*) using this character would support this hypothesis. Note also that this text was translated at least two centuries earlier than the date of the dialectal materials (representing the spoken language of north China in the 6th c. CE) on which Karlgren's reconstructions are based.

[35] A. Ch. *˛'â-˛sie̯* (K. nos. 1, 816), but the second character may be an error for one of the characters listed under nos. 338 and 385.

than before; and during the third, they will (only) repair Buddhist temples. When a full 1,000 years have elapsed, there will be "anger and fighting"; presumably it is at this time that the Dharma will finally disappear.

The *Prophecy of Kātyāyana* differs from the texts discussed above in a number of respects. First, it is cast entirely in verse, in contrast to the prose rendition of the *Mahāvibhāṣā* and the mixed prose and verse of the *Aśoka-avadāna* texts. Second, as in two of the *Aśoka-avadāna* texts, we now have three non-Buddhist kings, not two; but their names—somewhat surprisingly—are associated with the Hellenistic world, not with India or its border regions. The names of the two leading monastic figures appear to be the same (that is, the Chinese transcriptions are arguably valid representations of the Sanskrit names Śiṣyaka and Sūrata), but their roles have been altered: now Śiṣyaka is not the self-righteous monastic leader but simply the king's loyal preceptor, who encourages him to call the feast for the monks, and the role of the arrogant revisionists is now assigned to an anonymous group of monks. Sūrata's part, however, remains unchanged: once again he opposes the idea that the level of attainment of the members of the Buddhist community (here framed in terms of the attainment of enlightenment, rather than the keeping of the precepts) is as low as the more complacent monks would imply.

This text is clearly more detailed in a number of respects than is the account given in the *Mahāvibhāṣā*. Yet more striking than the individual elaborations of detail are the numerous divergences from an Indocentric perspective. While references to identifiable Indian locations are conspicuous by their absence—the only concrete Indian geographical term, other than the city of *Chien-ni* (whose identity is obscure at best), is Madhyadeśa—the three foreign kings are clearly identifiable, and are all associated not with India, but with the greater Hellenistic world. Who, then, would have composed such a text, describing these three powers as the primary enemies of the Dharma?

Here the geographical indications given in the text provide an important clue. The three foreign powers are described as "Rome in the front, Parthia in the rear, and the Arsacids [or simply 'Iran'] in the center."[36] It is important to note, first of all, that these three

[36] T 49.11b12–13.

foreign powers have been assigned to geographically correct relative positions: if Rome is seen as in the "front," then it is correct to describe Iran as being in the center, and the territory of Parthia (comprising the easternmost segment of Iran) as in the rear. Were this not a Buddhist text, our first guess might be that the author was situated somewhere to the west of Rome, facing all three territories, with Rome in the front. The difficulties in placing a Buddhist writer to the west of Rome, however, are evident, and during much of the period with which we are concerned even the westernmost parts of Europe would have been under Roman control.

The most obvious location for the composition of a Buddhist text, of course, would be either in India properly speaking or in one of its northwestern border regions (including Gandhāra, Kashmir, and Arachosia). But the geographical indications in this text (even aside from the paucity of Indian references) do not encourage this interpretation. Surely an Indian writer would have described Parthia (his nearest neighbor of the three) as being in the front, not the rear, with Rome (a power known only at a distance) pictured as farthest in the background. Equally unlikely, perhaps, is the possibility that an Indian composer writing during or slightly before the time of the Western Chin dynasty (that is, during the 1st–3rd c. CE) would refer to Rome, Iran, and the Parthians as the "evil kings" threatening his country, choosing only the Parthians from the list of those foreign powers who had actually overrun his country in recent memory—that is, the Greeks, Sakas, and Parthians, who figure prominently in several other recensions of the Kauśāmbī story.

Who, then, would have portrayed Rome, Iran, and Parthia as the primary enemies of the Dharma, and would have arranged them with Rome in the vanguard and with the Parthians bringing up the rear? The possibilities are fairly limited: having eliminated both western Europe and India, we are left only with the possibilities of a Central Asian or a Chinese redactor. And we can eliminate the latter by virtue of distance alone: references to "barbarians" in Chinese literature abound, but there were plenty of non-Chinese antagonists much closer at hand than Rome, Iran, and the Parthians. The Central Asian possibility is thus considerably more promising. From a Central Asian perspective, however, one can picture Rome as being in the "front" only if one is standing behind the Parthians (that is, directly to their east) and is oriented toward the West. If one sees oneself as standing in the center of one's own cultural world (as both Chinese and Indian writers would surely have done), the nearest neighbor will naturally be described as being "in front." For someone with an "outpost mentality," by contrast, the world may well be perceived as oriented around a territory far away—the center, wherever that might be, of one's own cultural identity.

At least one region in western Central Asia conforms to these specifications exactly. For the ruling elite of Bactria—long the most distant outpost of Hellenistic civilization in Central Asia—the center of the cultural world was clearly located far to the west, in the homeland of their own Greek language, pre-Buddhist religion, and Hellenistic culture. And the Parthians, located immediately to the west of the Bactrians, were both their nearest neighbors and a feared and respected opponent. Thus the identification of the three evil kings with Rome, Iran, and Parthia would be perfectly logical from a Bactrian point of view.

One other feature in this text may lend additional support to the Bactrian hypothesis. In no other version of the Kauśāmbī story do we find this decline prophecy associated with a timetable consisting of three periods of three hundred years each (or for that matter, with three periods of any length). While the *Kātyāyana* prophecy does maintain a total figure of 1,000 years (a number frequently found in other versions of the Kauśāmbī story, including that of the *Mahāvibhāṣā*, and which may well have been associated with this tradition from the outset), the three-part time scheme is only tenuously associated with this figure, and gives the impression of having been superimposed upon it. What we may have here, then, is an extraneous and perhaps local time scheme, based on three symmetrical time periods, which has only with some effort been brought into conformity with the "received tradition" of a total of one thousand years.[37]

---

[37] Though the antecedents of such a time scheme are not immediately evident, other religions in the region offer some intriguing parallels. In Zoroastrian mythology we find an eschatological system based on four periods of 3,000 years each, within which the last such period (beginning from the time of Zoroaster himself) is subdivided into three equal periods of 1,000 years each (see *ERE*, vol. 5, p. 376). This is hardly an exact parallel to the scheme offered in the *Kātyāyana* prophecy, but it at least offers examples both of a chronological system based on three equal periods and of a scheme in which the number three plays an important role. In

A reasonable hypothesis, then, would treat the *Prophecy of Kātyāyana* as a Bactrian redaction of an originally Indian tradition. Such a scenario, of course, would require the presence of Buddhist Bactrians capable of producing such a text at the time with which we are concerned. But the presence of Buddhists in Bactria during this period is not at all problematic. By this time this region had already been incorporated into the Kushan empire and both cultural and religious influences from India were being rapidly assimilated.[38] Thus the idea that a Buddhist text concerning the decline of the Dharma, originally composed in India, could have found its way to Bactria and been subject to revision there is entirely reasonable.

But I have argued here only for the redaction of the text, and not its original composition, in Bactria. Could we not go farther and argue for its composition here as well? The hypothesis is attractive, but it can be entertained only with serious reservations. First, it is important to note that of all extant versions of the Kauśāmbī story only the *Prophecy of Kātyāyana* associates the "three evil kings" with Rome, Iran, and Parthia. By far the majority of the versions of this tale associate them instead with the Greeks (*yavana*), Sakas (*śaka*), and Parthians (*pahlava*)—all groups known to have invaded northwest India in historic times. Thus if we assume that the *Prophecy of Kātyāyana* is the original, we must explain why not a single one of the other surviving versions of the tale reproduces this original list of ethnic names.

The question is really a dual one: first, which group—the Bactrians or the Indians—would more likely have had a motive to produce a tale like the Kauśāmbī story in the first place? And second—since the earliest versions of this tradition containing identifiable ethnic names associate the three kings with either the

---

the Manichaean religion the idea of three ages (consisting of the age of primordial separation between light and darkness, the age of their mixture, in which partisans of the two forces battle for control, and the final age of their re-separation) played a central role (*ER*, vol. 9, p. 162). The Manichaean example is of course too late to have influenced the *Kātyāyana* prophecy directly, but it does demonstrate that such ideas were circulating in the territory of greater Iran during the 3rd c. CE, where they might have been adopted by both Mani and the Bactrian Buddhists. No appropriate analogies are found in the Hindu system, which consists of four ages (*yuga*) of generally unspecified, but unequal, length, or in any other religious system known to have existed in this region at the time.

[38] See R. N. Frye, *History of Ancient Iran*, 252–54.

Greeks, Sakas, and Parthians or with Rome, Iran, and Parthia—which side would have had the more convincing reasons to convert the other's list into its own? The origins of the Kauśāmbī story will be discussed in detail in the following chapter; here we may point out simply that the story appears to be a response to the actual experience of foreign invasions, during which numerous Buddhist believers were killed, Buddhist establishments devastated, and the validity of the Buddhist religion itself perhaps called into question. Bactrian Buddhists were certainly subjected to such events in later times, most notably during Hephthalite incursions that culminated in the conquest of Bactria and adjacent regions during the 5th century, and again during the Arab invasions of the 7th century. In the period with which we are concerned, however, there is no evidence of such events taking place. Thus a Bactrian Buddhist writer in the first centuries CE would lack any apparent motive for producing a composition of this kind.

His Indian counterparts, by contrast—at least those living in the far northwest—would have experienced some three centuries of continual invasions by just those powers described in the majority of versions of the story: the Greeks, Sakas, and Parthians. And we should note that every version of the Kauśāmbī story describes these invasions as threatening India, not Bactria (or any other region). Thus a motive for composition is easier to establish on the Indian side than on the Bactrian one.

As to a motive for the emendation of an existing tradition, however, precisely the reverse is the case. While an Indian reader might have found it convenient to change the ethnic names from Rome, Iran, and Parthia (if these were the originals) to those of actual invaders with which he was more familiar, for a Bactrian recipient of a text describing the "evil kings" as Greeks, Sakas, and Parthians, an emendation would have been a necessity, not a luxury. For among the inhabitants of Bactria were many who saw their own ethnic identity as being either Greek (dating from the time of the invasion of Alexander the Great in the mid-4th c. BCE) or Saka (dating from the Saka incursions during the late 2nd c. BCE). While the Parthians—long seen as an enemy by the Bactrians—could easily be accepted as one of the evil powers threatening the Dharma, the inclusion of the Greeks and the Sakas among their ranks would clearly have been unacceptable.

It is precisely such an emendation that we find in the *Prophecy of Kātyāyana*. While the Parthians alone are carried over from the India-oriented list, the Greeks and the Sakas (with whom much of the population of Bactria would have identified themselves) are eliminated, replaced by other foreign (and at least potentially threatening) powers—namely, Iran and Rome.

Though the *Kātyāyana* prophecy may thus be considered a secondary derivative of an originally Indian tradition, it is uniquely valuable both as evidence of the reception and adaptation of that tradition in Central Asia and as evidence of the date of the tradition. As the earliest extant translation of the Kauśāmbī story into Chinese, the *Prophecy of Kātyāyana* can provide us with an important *terminus ante quem*: it offers definitive proof that the main features of the Kauśāmbī story—the tale of a conflict within the sangha brought about by an invasion of evil kings and resulting in the final extinction of the Dharma—was already in circulation before the end of the Western Chin dynasty (316 CE). Thus the historical circumstances that first led to the formulation of this tradition must be sought in a period prior to that date—in other words, at a time well before the beginning of the Gupta period (c. 300–550 CE) in India.

THE *PROPHECY OF KĀTYĀYANA* (PROSE TRANSLATION)

Another text found in the Chinese canon carries a title similar to the one just discussed but is executed entirely in prose. This text, produced during the period 420–479 by a translator whose name has not been preserved,[39] is closer in content to the verse translation of the Kātyāyana prophecy than to any other version of the Kauśāmbī story, yet it exhibits a number of revealing divergences.

The text opens with a lengthy introduction, consisting mainly of a diatribe against Buddhist monks who become involved in worldly affairs, and then moves on to a brief and rather garbled account of the final disappearance of the Dharma. Though the text (or its antecedent) must once have contained a list of three foreign

[39] T No. 2028 (49.7a17–9c14), titled *Chia-ting pi-ch'iu shuo tang-lai pien ching* 迦丁比丘說當來變經, lit. "The Sūtra [Concerning] Future Transformations, Preached by the *Bhikṣu* Kātyāyana."

kings, only certain elements of the list have been preserved. The text refers to a group of three kings (here styled *t'ien-tzu*, "sons of heaven"): a king named *Yeh-lai-na* 耶來那 [40] (Skt. *yavana*?), in the south near Madhyadeśa; a second king, who is not named, in northern *Chin-t'u* 晉土 [41] (< Skt. *Sindhu* "Indus [River]"?); and a third, named *Chien-chiu* 揵秋 ,[42] whose location is not specified. These three will appear in *Chin* 晉 , and will kill the common people, destroy Buddhist monuments, and belittle monks. They will also lead armies into India (天竺). At this time the king of Madhyadeśa will raise an army to destroy *Chin-t'u,* and its ministers and people will return to their native place (本土). At that time the monks of *Chin-t'u* will suffer from difficulties caused by officials; some will die, some will be laicized, and some will set out towards India (天竺). The king of Madhyadeśa, who venerates the Buddhist sangha, will donate everything to the monks, and when he sees some of them breaking the precepts, he will admonish them. An elder monk named *Shih-i-chi* 尸依仇 (Skt. *Śiṣyaka*?)[43] will preach the Dharma for the king, and the king, overjoyed, will invite all the sangha to Kauśāmbī. Some 100,000 will arrive in Kauśāmbī for the final assembly.

When they assemble there, they will begin to ask one another about the fate of their teachers. When they discover that many have been killed or fallen sick along the way, they will all lament together. On the 15th day, during the reading of the 250 precepts, the monks will behave chaotically, and will be admonished by Śiṣyaka. Another monk, who had profoundly entered into meditation (and who is not named), then calls on the community to listen to his preaching. (Note that this character does not appear in any other version of the Kauśāmbī story.) A monk named *Su-t'o-liu* 須陀流 (*Sūrata*?),[44] who has become an arhat, then rises from his seat,

---

[40] A. Ch. *˛i̯a-˛lâi-'nâ'* (Karlgren nos. 226, 511, 647). The second character in this name (presumably for Sanskrit *-va-*) has not been adequately explained.

[41] A. Ch. *tsi̯ĕn'-'t'uo* (Karlgren nos. 1079, 1129).

[42] A. Ch. *'g'i̯on'-˛ts'i̯ə̯u* (Karlgren nos. 373, 1088); for the first character in this name see the Appendix, "Proper Names," n. 10.

[43] A. Ch. *˛śi-˛·e̯i-'g'i̯ə̯u* (Karlgren nos. 878, 185, 399). If the name is indeed intended to represent Sanskrit *Śiṣyaka* it has become quite garbled in transmission.

[44] A. Ch. *˛si̯u-˛d'a-˛li̯ə̯u* (Karlgren nos. 839, 1011, 564), **sutara*, metathesis **surata*, Skt. *Sūrata*? (Note that the *Aśoka-avadāna* exhibits the same feature in this name; see the Appendix, "Proper Names," no. 7.)

sounds forth the lion's roar, and proclaims that he will preach the sūtras. A disciple of the elder (the latter presumably to be identified with Śiṣyaka), whose personal name is not given but who is referred to by the epithet *shang-t'ou* 上頭,[45] rises from his seat and contends with the arhat; he then takes a metal implement and kills Sūrata. *Shang-t'ou*, in turn, is killed by a Buddha-believing *yakṣa*, who takes an iron vajra and strikes him. The earth shakes in six ways, various evil omens appear, and all sentient beings realize that the Dharma is about to disappear. Various classes of sentient beings bewail the loss of the Dharma, while the assembly of demons and the followers of heterodox teachings will rejoice.

The monk Kātyāyana then tells his followers: "Thus will be the future evil transformations. Because the Buddha-Dharma continues today, as of old, you should be diligent and practice in it." The teaching is sincerely received by his listeners, and the sūtra comes to a close.

Several things are noteworthy about this account. First is simply the garbled state in which it has reached us: some personal names are missing, others are only faintly recognizable, while still others appear in forms that are quite incomprehensible. Indeed, the most coherent portion of this sūtra is not the Kauśāmbī story itself, but the long introduction (comprising over 50% of the text) decrying the evil practices of the monks. A second notable feature is the dominance of distinctively Chinese terminology: here the three evil kings are not styled *wang* 王, or simply "king," as is usual in other versions of the story, but *t'ien-tzu* 天子, or "son of Heaven." The reference (apparently) to northwest India as *Chin-t'u* 晉土, with the first character representing the name of a Chinese dynasty and the second capable of being translated simply as "territory," raises the question of contamination by (or transference to) a Chinese geographical outlook.[46] Third, the reference to the reading of the "250 precepts" (which occurs twice in the text)[47] enables us to

---

[45] Lit. "upper head," i.e., "the best": perhaps a translation of a monastic title.

[46] Note that in one instance (9.8c27) the character *chin* is used alone, without the character *t'u* "earth," suggesting that the word *chin* was understood as a place name in and of itself. Likewise, the use of the same character *chin* in the gloss of Sūrata's name (晉言曰善, "in the *Chin* language, 'good'," T 49.9a23) suggests that these geographic references may have been understood as referring to China, not India.

[47] T 49.9a15, b11.

identify the sectarian affiliation of this recension: while the extant versions of the Buddhist monastic code (preserved in Pāli, Sanskrit, Chinese, and Tibetan) contain anywhere from 215 to 263 rules of conduct, the Chinese Dharmaguptaka version alone consists of 250 rules.[48] Since this version was the one most commonly used in China,[49] this again points to the possibility of a Chinese locus for the final recension of this version of the story.

A final anomalous feature of this translation is the absence of any reference at all to the overall duration of the Dharma. While, as we have already noted, the Kauśāmbī story is not bound to any specific timetable, it is virtually always associated with some chronological figure. In fact, in every other version of the story examined here (with the exception of what we will refer to as "late Khotanese adaptations") the Kauśāmbī story occurs in conjunction with a specific figure for the total duration of the Dharma. The absence of such a figure from the prose translation of the *Kātyāyana* prophecy thus constitutes a notable divergence from the usual format, and serves to reinforce the general impression that the Kauśāmbī story given here is only a residual version of the original tale.

Finally, it is important to note that the prose version of the *Prophecy of Kātyāyana* – though it represents a garbled version of the tradition and thus may be considered a rather distant derivative of the "original" Kauśāmbī story – still preserves the version of the plot found in the verse translation of the same text, a factor that will be of some importance in reconstructing the chain of textual transmission.[50]

THE *MAHĀMĀYĀ-SŪTRA*

Not mentioned in Lamotte's survey of versions of the Kauśāmbī story, but cited in this connection by both Przyluski and Kajiyama,

---

[48] See W. Pachow, *A Comparative Study of the Prātimokṣa* (Santiniketan: Sino-Indian Cultural Society, 1955), p. 11.

[49] See TAKASAKI Jikido, *Introduction to Buddhism*, trans. Rolf W. Giebel (Tokyo: Tōhō Gakkai, 1987), 288. The Dharmaguptaka Vinaya (T No. 1430, *Ssu-fen lü* 四分律 (was translated into Chinese only a few years before the prose version of the *Prophecy of Kātyāyana*.

[50] See below, chapter 8.

is another brief summary version, this time spoken by Ānanda in reply to a request by the Buddha's mother, Mahāmāyā.[51] This text is best known not for its rendering of the Kauśāmbī story but for its 1,500-year timetable for the total duration of the Dharma, which includes predictions of the appearances of such famous figures as Aśvaghoṣa (six centuries after the death of the Buddha) and Nāgārjuna (a century later).

The *Mahāmāyā-sūtra* is peculiar in that its version of the Kauśāmbī story includes no proper names at all; only the titles or official roles of its main characters are indicated. The story is given as follows. Fifteen hundred years after the death of the Buddha, there will be a tripiṭaka-master in Kauśāmbī (presumably to be identified with Śiṣyaka) who will preach the essentials of the Dharma; he will have five hundred followers. Likewise there will be an arhat-monk (again not named, but playing the role held by Sūrata in the other texts) who will maintain the practice of the precepts and will also have five hundred followers. At the *poṣadha* ceremony on the 15th day of the month, the arhat-monk will ascend a high seat and preach the pure Dharma, saying "This you should do, this you should not." A disciple of the tripiṭaka-master will take offense at this, and will ask the arhat why he preaches "such coarse words." The arhat replies that he does indeed maintain purity of body, speech, and mind without error. At this the disciple becomes even more outraged, and ascends the platform and kills the arhat. A disciple of the arhat rises to defend his teacher's reputation, takes a sharp knife and kills the tripiṭaka-master (*sic*; one would have expected him rather to have attacked the murderer of the arhat). The eight categories of sentient beings (gods, *nāga*s and the rest) will be troubled, but the demons and heretics will be overjoyed and will compete with one another to destroy stūpas and monasteries and kill monks. The scriptures will all flow to Kuśinagara, and a *nāga* king will carry them into the ocean. And at this, the Buddha-Dharma will become extinct.

This brief account is clearly only a residual version of the tradition; the dynamics of the interaction between Śiṣyaka and Sūrata (as they are called in the other versions) are not at all clear, and the killing of the tripiṭaka-master (rather than his disciple) appears

---

[51] *Mo-ho-mo-yeh ching* 摩訶摩耶經, T No. 383 (12.1013b14–1014a20), translated by T'an-ching during the period 479–502 CE.

senseless without sufficient background information. So little detail is contained in this recension of the story, in fact, that it is not even possible to determine with any certainty its relation to the other Kauśāmbī accounts. Only one feature of the story is at all distinctive: the events at Kauśāmbī are now expected to occur 1,500 years—not 1,000 years, as in all the versions discussed above except the prose version of the *Prophecy of Kātyāyana*, which gives no date—after the death of the Buddha. We have now moved beyond the 1,000-year time span for the first time,[52] and it is probably significant that this text was translated into Chinese nearly 1,000 years after the death of the Buddha.

Finally, in the *Mahāmāyā-sūtra* we have also encountered for the first time a Mahāyāna recension of the Kauśāmbī story. Though no Mahāyāna themes have been introduced into the plotline of the Kauśāmbī story itself, the references in the preceding section to figures such as Aśvaghoṣa and Nāgārjuna[53] make it clear that we have here to do with a Mahāyāna version of the Kauśāmbī tradition.

THE *CANDRAGARBHA-SŪTRA* GROUP

We now come to the group of texts that will form the main subject of this study. Though the *Candragarbha-sūtra* was translated into Chinese later than any of the texts discussed above except the *Mahāvibhāṣā*, it was to become by far the most influential decline prophecy in East Asia, cited at length and in passing by countless commentators in China, Korea, and Japan.[54] Likewise in Tibet this

---

[52] For a discussion of the significance of the transition from 1,000 years to more extended figures see above, pp. 62–63.

[53] T 12.1013c7–8.

[54] In China the *Candragarbha-sūtra* was used by the Pure Land patriarch Tao-ch'o to bolster his arguments that in an age of decline only devotion to the Buddha Amitābha could offer any hope of salvation (e.g. T 47.13c8–11); see David W. Chappell, "Tao-ch'o (562–645), A Pioneer of Chinese Pure Land Buddhism" (Ph.D. thesis Yale University, 1976). Likewise, his contemporary Hsin-hsing (540–594) relied on the *Candragarbha-sūtra* in his exposition of the general concept of decline and made this concept the basis of his "Sect of the Three Stages" (see YABUKI Keiki, *Sangaikyō no kenkyū* [Tokyo: Iwanami Shoten, 1927], and James B. Hubbard, "Salvation in the Final Period of the Dharma: The Inexhaustible Storehouse of the San-chieh-chiao" (Ph.D. thesis, Univ. of Wisconsin, 1986). The sūtra was also important (though perhaps less central) to a number of commentators in

text was considered to be a major source of information on the ultimate fate of Buddhism, and was quoted almost in full by the great 14th-century historian, Bu-ston, in his *History of Buddhism*.[55] Finally, its popularity in the Tarim Basin area is attested by its inclusion in the so-called *Book of Zambasta*, a poetic anthology (recast in the Khotanese vernacular) of some of the most popular Buddhist scriptures in early 8th-century Khotan.[56] Unlike some of the other decline prophecies discussed above, which were preserved but largely ignored by Chinese and Tibetan Buddhists (and whose value is thus largely restricted to helping us reconstruct the ancestry and development of the Kauśāmbī story), the *Candragarbha-sūtra* enjoyed considerable popularity in its own right in both Central and East Asia, and helped to shape the worldview of scholars and ordinary Buddhists alike.

Three versions of the decline prophecy from the *Candragarbha-sūtra* have survived down to the present (four if we count the Mongolian version,[57] which is a verbatim translation of the Tibetan and will not be dealt with separately here). As with the texts of the *Aśoka-avadāna* group, these three versions clearly share a common heritage and are best understood when studied together. The texts in this group are the following:

1. ***Candragarbha-sūtra*** (Chinese): the 20th chapter (*Fa mieh-chin p'in* 法滅盡品, "Chapter [on the] Complete Destruction of the Dharma") of the 15th (Candragarbha) section (*Yüeh-tsang fen* 月藏分) of the *Mahāsaṃnipāta-sūtra* (*Ta-chi ching* 大集經); see T No. 397[15], 13.374c–381c. The entire *Mahāsaṃnipāta-sūtra* is sometimes listed as having been translated during the Northern Liang dynasty (414–426 CE).[58] The *Candragarbha-sūtra* section, however—together with a companion work titled the *Sūryagarbha-sūtra* (Ch. *Jih-tsang*

the T'ien-t'ai and San-lun schools. In Japan references to the *Candragarbha-sūtra* appear frequently in the works of the Pure Land teachers Hōnen and Shinran and are central to the reasoning of Nichiren as well.

55 See E. Obermiller, trans., *History of Buddhism (Chos-hbyung) by Bu-ston* (Heidelberg: Harrassowitz, 1931–3), Part 2, 171–77.

56 Emmerick, *Zambasta*, 368–423.

57 For a critical edition of the Mongolian text, together with an annotated English translation and glossary, see Nattier, "The *Candragarbha-sūtra* in Central and East Asia," 220–331.

58 See for example Lewis R. Lancaster, ed., *The Korean Buddhist Canon: A Descriptive Catalogue* (Berkeley: University of California Press, 1979), p. 35b, text K 56.

fen 日藏分) and two other short texts—was translated in the middle of the 6th century by Narendrayaśas,[59] and only subsequently (in 586 CE according to Tao-hsüan[60]) incorporated into the preexisting Chinese translation of the *Mahāsaṃnipāta-sūtra*. It seems likely that the text of the *Candragarbha-sūtra* brought to China by Narendrayaśas—like the much shorter Tibetan version of its "decline of the Dharma" section alone—originally circulated as an independent work.[61]

2. ***Book of Zambasta*** (Khotanese): The so-called *Book of Zambasta*,[62] of which the Khotanese version of the Kauśāmbī story comprises a portion of the 24th chapter,[63] carries no colophon as such (aside from various remarks by the composer interspersed between certain of its chapters). A rough estimate of the date of its composition can be made, however, on internal grounds: the language and orthography of the *Book of Zambasta* clearly belong to the oldest layer of Khotanese literature,[64] which would point to a

---

[59] See the colophon to the text, T 13.298ff.

[60] T 50.434b.

[61] No integral translation of the *Mahāsaṃnipāta-sūtra* is included in the Tibetan Kanjur. At least four separate texts, however (in addition to the *Candragarbha-sūtra* itself), are identified as excerpts from that collection: the *Arya-mahāsaṃnipāta-ratna-ketu-dhāraṇī-nāma-mahāyāna-sūtra* (Pek. No. 806; cf. T 397[9]); the *Tathāgata-śrī-samaya-nāma-mahāyāna-sūtra* (Pek. No. 896; cf. T 397[16]); the *Daśacakra-kṣitigarbha-nāma-mahāyāna-sūtra* (Pek. No. 905); and the *Arya-sūrya-garbha-nāma-vaipulya-sūtra* (Pek. No. 923; cf. T 397 [13] and [14], and note that the chapter titles of the Tibetan indicate a closer parallel with [14]). Of these only the *Daśacakra-kṣitigarbha*, translated by Ho-zhang zab-mo, Rnam-par mi-rtog et al., is identified in its colophon as having been translated into Tibetan from the Chinese; strangely, however, it does not seem to parallel any of the material in the extant Chinese *Mahāsaṃnipāta-sūtra*, but is rather the proper equivalent of T Nos. 410 and 411 (of which No. 411, translated in 651 CE by Hsüan-tsang, offers the closer parallel to the Tibetan).

[62] The text itself carries no title, but was assigned this name by Sir H. W. Bailey on the basis of the name of the official who commissioned the text, a certain *Ysaṃbasta* (Emmerick, *Zambasta*, vii).

[63] According to Emmerick (*Zambasta*, 369) only about half of the chapter is extant. Much of the missing material belonged to the first part of the chapter, which contained an account of the early life of the Buddha (unrelated to the Candragarbha tale); a significant gap toward the end of the chapter (folios 429–38, containing verses 522–641), however, may well have contained a continuation of the *Candragarbha-sūtra*.

[64] Emmerick, *Zambasta*, vii.

date of composition around the beginning of the 8th century.[65] It is important to note that this work is technically an original Khotanese composition and not a translation as such; the entire *Book of Zambasta*, in fact, consists of a poetic recasting in the Khotanese vernacular of a number of Indian Buddhist works. According to a precious bit of information contained in a remark by its composer, the *Book of Zambasta* may well represent the first serious attempt to render the Buddhist literary heritage into the everyday spoken language of Khotan.[66]

3. ***Candragarbha-paripṛcchā-sūtra*** (Tibetan): titled *Byang-chub sems-dpa' Zla-ba'i snying-pos zhus-pa-las lung bstan-pa* ("The Prophecy from the *Question of the Bodhisattva Candragarbha*") in the Narthang xylograph, with variant readings in other versions. A translation entirely in prose, lacking a colophon but preserved in a manuscript found at Tun-huang[67] as well as in the printed versions of the Kanjur (Peking No. 1025, Derge No. 356, Cone No. 995, Narthang No. 343, Lhasa No. 634), and thus dating to sometime prior to the sealing of the Tun-huang caves around 1000 CE. The Tibetan text has in turn been translated into

[65] R. E. Emmerick, in *The Cambridge History of Iran*, 3(2), ed. Ehsan Yarshater (London: Cambridge University Press, 1983), 964.

[66] The composer's remarks appear at the beginning of the 23rd chapter, where he states: "I intend to translate it into Khotanese for the welfare of all beings, this tale of how the *deva* Buddha descended from the *trāyastriṃsa*-gods. . . . But such are their deeds: the Khotanese do not value the Law at all in Khotanese. They understand it badly in Indian. In Khotanese it does not seem to them to be the Law. For the Chinese the Law is in Chinese. In Kashmirian it is very agreeable, but they so learn it in Kashmirian that they also understand the meaning of it. To the Khotanese that seems to be the Law whose meaning they do not understand at all. . . . In words the essential thing is the meaning. . . . The meaning being unperceived, no one would escape from woes in *saṃsāra*" (Emmerick, *Zambasta*, 343–45). The "Kashmirian" language to which the composer refers is almost certainly Sanskrit (the language from which most of the later Khotanese Buddhist works were apparently translated, the earlier tradition having been based on Prakrit texts). The composer is clearly suggesting that the Khotanese should abandon their tradition of reading Buddhist texts only in their Indian versions, and follow instead the example of the Chinese, who had long been rendering the Buddhist scriptures into their own vernacular.

[67] Louis de la Vallée Poussin, *Catalogue of the Tibetan Manuscripts from Tun-huang in the India Office Library* (London: Oxford University Press, 1962), 185 (text no. 601.1).

> Mongolian (Ligeti No. 1120).[68] Since the Mongolian text is a verbatim translation of the Tibetan (and thus adds no new conceptual content) it has not been included in the present study.[69]

In addition to these three versions, a small fragment of a Sanskrit manuscript of the *Candragarbha-sūtra* was discovered in Chinese Turkestan early in this century.[70] This fragment, however, comes from a part of the *Candragarbha-sūtra* outside the "decline-of-the-Dharma" section, and thus does not parallel any of the material to be discussed here. It does correspond to a section of the Chinese *Candragarbha-sūtra*, however, and demonstrates that at least a part of that text once existed in Sanskrit.

The justification for treating these three recensions as a group comes as much from their sharing a common title (with the exception of the Khotanese version, which carries no title at all) as from their content, for they are not nearly as close to one another as are the texts of the *Aśoka-avadāna* group. Nonetheless, there is evidence that all are descended from a common (though distant) ancestor, and part of the objective of this section will be to elucidate the nature of this relationship. The complexity of this relationship can be illustrated by even a perfunctory survey of the basic features of these three texts. Beginning with the style of composition, we may note that the Khotanese version is entirely in verse, the Chinese version almost entirely in verse, and the Tibetan entirely in prose. The bodhisattva Candragarbha is mentioned in the title and

---

[68] L. Ligeti, *Catalogue du Kanjur mongole imprimé*, vol. I, Catalogue (Budapest: Société Kőrösi Csoma, 1942–44), p. 302. For the text itself see vol. 92, *eldeb* 33, pp. 298v–305r.

[69] The text contains much that is of interest to linguists and philologists, however, and was included in the dissertation on which this study is based (see Nattier, "The *Candragarbha-sūtra* in Central and East Asia," 220–31). It is my intention to publish the Mongolian text separately in the future.

[70] See the transcription and translation in A. F. Rudolf Hoernle, *Manuscript Remains of Buddhist Literature Found in Chinese Turkestan* (London: Oxford University Press, 1916), 103–108. The fragment in question was identified by K. Watanabe as corresponding to part of the Chinese version of the *Candragarbha-sūtra*, though no information on which section was included in the material published by Hoernle. The relevant Chinese passage has been located by Judith Boltz, who found that Hoernle's Sanskrit fragment corresponds to T 13.306a15–c1 (personal communication, 1987). The passage does not parallel any of the material in the Tibetan, Mongolian, or Khotanese versions of the text.

as an interlocutor within the text in the Chinese and Tibetan versions, but not in the Khotanese. The Khotanese and Chinese versions agree in allotting a 1,500-year life span to the Dharma,[71] while the Tibetan text has a 2,000-year timetable; the Khotanese and the Tibetan share certain peculiar spellings of proper names, however, which serve as conclusive proof that these two versions are derived (albeit at a considerable remove) from a common ancestor. While the Chinese and Khotanese versions of the story contain several minor Mahāyāna elements (none, however, common to both recensions), the Tibetan version—like all the texts discussed above except the *Mahāmāyā-sūtra*—contains no Mahāyāna elements whatsoever. Finally, the Chinese alone has preserved not only the "decline of the Dharma" section of the *Candragarbha-sūtra*, but (apparently) the text as a whole. The other nineteen chapters of the Chinese *Candragarbha-sūtra* contain material on a wide variety of topics, including an enumeration of various localities in India, Central Asia, and China that first attracted the attention of Sylvain Lévi several decades ago.[72]

In general the contents of these three versions of the Kauśāmbī story are similar enough to allow them to be summarized together. The introductory sections, however, are quite distinct, and must be treated separately. In the Tibetan version[73] the text begins with the Buddha entrusting the Dharma to the four directional gods (*lokapālas*) for protection after his death. The bodhisattva Candragarbha—a character unknown in any of the versions of the Kauśāmbī story discussed above, but found also in the Chinese *Candragarbha-sūtra*—then asks the Buddha when and how his teachings will finally disappear. The Buddha responds that the Dharma will last for 2,000 years, a total subdivided into four five-hundred-year periods. During the first five hundred years after

---

[71] Note, however, that the Chinese text gives figures of 2,000 years (T 13.370b8–11) and 2,500 years (13.363a29–b5) in other sections of the text.

[72] Sylvain Lévi, "Notes chinoises sur l'Inde, V. Quelques documents sur le bouddhisme indien dans l'Asie Centrale (Première partie)," *Bulletin de l'École Française d'Extrême-Orient* 5 (1905), 262–84 (with reference to parts of chapters 17, 18, and 19 of the *Yüeh-tsang-fen* or "Candragarbha Section").

[73] The plot summary given here is based solely on the Tun-huang manuscript, since it is clearly the oldest version of the Tibetan text. Later xylograph editions deviate from this version in a number of respects. For a discussion of these differences see the notes to the Tibetan version.

the death of the Buddha, people will still be able to put the Buddha's teachings into practice, and to achieve liberation (that is, enlightenment) by doing so. During the second five hundred years, however, they will gradually become less diligent in practice and less faithful in belief, and the number of those who are able to attain the goal of final liberation will diminish. During the third five-hundred-year period, conditions will become even worse: there will be many who expound the Buddha's teachings, but people will only listen to them passively and will not take the teachings to heart. The final five-hundred-year period is subdivided into a former period of three hundred years (during which the protective deities who had previously guarded the fortunes of Buddhism will depart from this world in disgust, abandoning its inhabitants to an onslaught of illness, famine, and warfare) and a latter period of two hundred years (during which even the monks will cease to conduct themselves in accordance with the Dharma, and will begin to engage instead in a variety of worldly activities). It is at this point that the Tibetan version begins to relate the familiar Kauśāmbī story. The Chinese version contains an entirely different introduction. The bodhisattva Candragarbha first recites a verse in which the Buddha commissions a group of *yakṣa*s (not, as in the Tibetan version, the *lokapāla*s) to protect his teachings after his death. Thereupon another bodhisattva, named "Moon-Lamp" 月燈 (**Candrapradīpa* ?), asks the Buddha not how long the Dharma will endure, but how people can use skillful means to prolong its existence. In reply the Buddha states that one hundred years after his death the Dharma will gradually decline and disappear.[74] He then delivers a long discourse on the evil actions of future sentient beings, aimed mainly at the misconduct of Buddhist monks (who are more concerned with worldly success than with religious achievement), *kṣatriya* rulers (who are accused both of cooperating with these decadent monks and of interfering with them by imposing

---

[74] T 13.375c4. No similar statement occurs at this point in the Tibetan or Khotanese version, but cf. the texts of the *Aśoka-avadāna* group, which state that the events at Kauśāmbī will take place one thousand years after the death of the Buddha (for the Chinese versions see T 2.179a.24 and 50.126b26; for the Tibetan see Pek. No. 1007, *mdo-sna-tshogs su,* 281a1–2). It is possible that the one-hundred-year figure given in the Chinese *Candragarbha-sūtra* is the result of a copying error (in Sanskrit or Prakrit, where one of the terms for "thousand" is *daśaśataṃ* "ten hundreds" [Apte 468a]) for an original figure of one thousand years.

punishment on those who do not maintain the precepts), and *caṇḍala* rulers (who will conspire with evil monks to turn out their own version of the Buddhist teachings). Only at this point does the Chinese text turn to its own version of the Kauśāmbī story.[75]

The virtually total dissimilarity between the introductions to the Tibetan and Chinese texts suggests that these portions of the texts, at least, are the products of entirely separate processes of redaction—an impression that is heightened by the fact that the Khotanese text (which shares numerous similarities with these two versions in other respects) contains no such introductory section whatsoever.[76] Likewise, in the closing sections we find similar divergences among the three versions in this group. The core of the text, however—that is, the Kauśāmbī story itself—is reasonably constant in all three recensions. We may therefore review these three versions together, noting important divergences when they arise.

As in all the versions of the story discussed above except the *Mahāvibhāṣā*, the story begins with the appearance of three evil kings. The Tibetan and Khotanese versions agree in calling them Greeks (Tib. *ya-bha-na*, Khot. *yavanä*), Sakas (Tib. *shag-ku-na*, Khot. *śśakaunä*),[77] and Parthians (Tib. *pa-la-ba*, Khot. *palvalä*), while the Chinese text labels them Parthians (波羅),[78] Persians (百祀),[79] and

[75] T 13.377bff.

[76] The Khotanese text is, however, defective at this point, and may once have contained such an introduction. Approximately seven folios (or eight, if Emmerick's placement here of the Leningrad folio [for which no folio number is available] should be incorrect) are missing just prior to the beginning of the Kauśāmbī story. Previous folios in the sequence, however, contain an account of the activities of the historical Buddha Śākyamuni, and this account may well have continued into the missing section.

[77] The ethnonym **śakuna* occurs only in these two versions of the text, and has not yet been satisfactorily explained. Lamotte's conjecture (*Histoire*, p. 222) that the term represents a conflation of the names *śaka* and *hūṇa* is intriguing, but has not been substantiated. A full examination of this issue should take into consideration both the possibility that the term is a deliberate alteration of the word *śaka* (see below, n. 97) and that it might be the result of a copying error. In the latter case the corresponding Chinese rendition "good thought Saka" (善意釋迦) and the Tibetan reading *sha-ka'i mi*, lit. "man of the Sakas," found in the *Karmaśataka* (Pek. No. 1007, *mdo-sna-tshogs su*, 281a5) might supply useful data for reconstructing the underlying Indian text.

[78] For this derivation see the Appendix, "Proper Names," no. 1 and note 12.

[79] This interpretation is rather uncertain, but to my knowledge no better reading has yet been suggested. For this derivation see the Appendix, "Proper Names," no. 1 and note 13.

"good thought Saka" (善意釋迦),[80] a form that has yet to be explained. In the Chinese the three kings are assigned to the southern, western, and northern directions, respectively, with the king of Kauśāmbī located in the east; in the Tibetan and Khotanese versions, by contrast, no directions are associated with the three kings at all, and the king of Kauśāmbī is placed in the south.[81] Meanwhile, a son named Duṣprasaha (Ch. 難看 , Khot. *Duṣprasavä*)[82] is

[80] Certainly a variant of the ethnic name Saka, though I have not seen (or been able to develop) an adequate explanation of the component "good thought."

[81] The Tibetan text states, more specifically, that Kauśāmbī is located "on the other, southern side" of the Ganges (in the Tun-huang ms., *'Ga'-'ga'i pha-rol lho-phyogs-na*; see Tibetan text, §11, line 1), and that the countries of Gandhāra, Madhyadeśa, and so on are on "this side" of the river (*'Ga'-'ga'i tshu-rol*, §10, lines 11-12). This description is geographically problematic, but can provide a valuable clue to the location of the recension of the text on which the Tibetan translation is based. The city of Kauśāmbī is indeed located on the southern bank of the Ganges river; the problem, however, is that west of this area the river runs in a north-south direction, not west to east. Thus a person living in this region (that is, in north-central India) would hardly describe the "other" side of the river as being located to the south. Moreover, by stating that both Gandhāra and Madhyadeśa are on "this side" of the river the text creates further problems, since most of the territory traditionally described as comprising Madhyadeśa is in fact to the south of the Ganges. The only vantage point from which this description would make sense (that is, from which a geographical error of this type would likely have been made) is in the far northwest, where one might know from hearsay that Kauśāmbī is on the southern bank of the Ganges, but not be close enough to that river to realize that a large segment of it runs from north to south. The reference to Gandhāra as being on "this side" of the river in itself suggests a location in the far northwest.

[82] The Chinese translation of this name (lit. "hard to look at") agrees with the Tibetan transcription of the Sanskrit *Duṣprasaha* ("hard to tolerate, hard to bear"). The Khotanese form, however, requires explanation. Clearly the form in final *-ha* is the original one; **Duṣprasava* would be meaningless in Sanskrit (or Prakrit), and all the translated or transliterated forms of the name in versions of the story other than the Khotanese can be derived from Skt. (or Pkt.) *Duṣprasaha* (see the Appendix, "Proper Names," no. 3). What must be explained, then, is how an original final *-ha* could have become *-va* in the Khotanese version (or its ancestor). A sound shift, or aural error, resulting in conversion of *-ha* to *-va* would be highly unlikely; if we look instead for a possible visual error, however, the answer may be readily apparent. In the Brāhmī script (or in the variant of that script used to write Khotanese) the letters *ha* and *va* do not resemble one another at all; in the Kharoṣṭhī script, however—long employed in the Tarim Basin for Prakrit documents of both religious and secular character—the two letters are written in the forms 2 and Z, respectively (see the chart by Rapson in A. M. Boyer et al., *Kharoṣṭhī Inscriptions Discovered by Sir Aurel Stein in Chinese Turkestan*, Part II (Oxford: Clarendon Press, 1929), Plate XIV. This clearly suggests a period of transmission of the Kauśāmbī story in the Kharoṣṭhī script, prior to its eventual recording in Khotanese.

born to King Mahendrasena, and on the same night sons are also born to five hundred ministers of the king (according to the Tibetan version), merchants (according to the Khotanese), or elders (according to the Chinese). The Tibetan alone mentions that a talking horse will be born on the same night; all three versions agree that a rain of blood will fall. In the Tibetan and Khotanese versions the king then receives a prophecy that, according to these omens, his son will conquer all of Jambudvīpa and become its sole ruler; the Chinese text states simply that the children will be brought up.

When the young prince reaches the age of twelve (according to the Tibetan version; the Chinese reads "seven," and no age is specified in the Khotanese version) the three evil kings will invade his father's territory. The Khotanese and Chinese versions have the father abdicate in favor of his son, who then takes on the invaders, and the Khotanese compiler—here clearly improvising, to good literary effect—offers considerable detail on the battle scene. (In the Tibetan version the father turns over the throne shortly thereafter, when he sees that his son has defeated the enemy.) In all three versions Duṣprasaha now becomes the ruler of all Jambudvīpa.

The young king, however, now becomes concerned about the karmic effects of his military campaigns, and he turns to a tripiṭaka-master named Śiṣyaka (here, however, written in all three versions in a form that must go back to Sanskrit or Prakrit **Śirṣaka*[83]) for advice. Śiṣyaka preaches the Dharma for the king, and in the Tibetan and Khotanese versions urges the king to "take refuge in the three jewels for twelve years" (Tib.), or to "give to the *bhikṣu-saṃgha*" (Khot.). At this point the Khotanese version alone notes that

---

[83] See the Appendix, "Proper Names," no. 5. Of all the versions of the Kauśāmbī story identified to date only the three members of the *Candragarbha-sūtra* group and the Chinese *Mahāvibhāṣā* translation contain forms of this name that clearly go back to an original **Śirṣaka*. The spelling *Śiṣyaka* (which corresponds to all the translated versions and to earliest transliterated versions) is clearly the original. Again this can be explained if we postulate a Kharoṣṭhī-script antecedent: in this syllabary system the combination *-rṣa-* is written (see Rapson's chart in Boyer, *Kharoṣṭhī Inscriptions*) while *-ṣya-* appears as (Rapson) or (A. H. Dani, *Indian Paleography* [Oxford: Clarendon Press, 1963], Plate XIIIb, line 13). Once again the possibilities for such a misreading are evident.

"fifteen hundred years are now fulfilled," and that the Dharma is about to die out.

The king then invites all the monks in Jambudvīpa to come to Kauśambī, but many are killed along the way; only 100,000 manage to arrive in the capital. At this point (in the Tibetan and Chinese versions) the king develops the desire to see an arhat and is informed in a dream about the whereabouts of Sūrata. (The Khotanese version does not mention this incident, but simply has Sūrata appear with the rest at the assembly.) On the day of the *poṣadha* ceremony the familiar conflict between Śiṣyaka and Sūrata breaks out. A disciple of Śiṣyaka, named Aṅgada, kills Sūrata—with a door-bolt according to the Tibetan and Khotanese versions, with an ordinary stick according to the Chinese—and in turn is killed by a vajra-wielding *yakṣa*, Dadhimukha. A monk named **Kedāra* (or **Kirāta*)[84] then kills Śiṣyaka. A general brawl then breaks out, and all the monks in the assembly are killed. Bad omens appear, the gods weep, and the *yakṣa*s (according to the Khotanese and Chinese versions) fall to the ground and writhe. The Tibetan version

---

[84] Written *Ge-rad* in the Tibetan, *Chi-duo-lo* 鶏多羅 in the Chinese; no name is given in the Khotanese version. Since this name appears only in these two versions of the story (and subsequently in the *Dgra-bcom-pa Dge-'dun phel-gyis lung-bstan-pa*, one of the "late Khotanese adaptations" in which proper names are quite distorted), it is difficult to reconstruct its original Indian form with certainty. The Chinese transcription suggests an original final *-a* in the Indian form (which is straightforward to reconstruct in the Tibetan, since the omission of this vowel is a frequent result of a copyist's overlooking of the dot (Tib. *tsheg*) used to divide syllables in a Tibetan text. There are very few Sanskrit (or Prakrit) terms beginning with *ge-* or *gi-*, and none corresponds to either the Chinese or the Tibetan transcription. We are thus left with the task of identifying a probable antecedent in *ki-* or *ke-*, of which *Kedāra* "name of Śiva as worshipped in Himālaya" (MW 309a) and *Kirāta* "a degraded border tribe" (MW 283c) seem the most likely. Since the transcription of *i* as *e* (and vice versa) is extremely common, our task is to decide whether the last two syllables are to be read as *-da-ra* or *-ra-ta*. Ordinarily one would suspect the Chinese rather than the Tibetan of having undergone syllabic metathesis, since in Chinese the inadvertent transposition of characters (especially in unfamiliar foreign names) is quite common. Here, however, the Tibetan offers an equally plausible solution, since *ra* and *da* are frequently confused in the Tibetan script (for examples in our text see the P1 version of the Tibetan, lines 174 [n. 2] and 179 [n. 1]). I would therefore suggest an original Indian form *Kedāra*→ Tib. * གེ་ད་ར་ → * གེ་དར་ → གེ་རད་, the form attested in the Tibetan *Candragarbha* text. This would provide an exact parallel to the Chinese spelling *Chi-duo-lo* 鶏多羅 (A. Ch. *ˌkiei-ˌtâ-ˌlâ*, Karlgren nos. 126, 1006, 569).

alone notes that the Buddha's mother, Māyādevī, and a contingent of gods then gather up the robes of the monks and carry them off.

King Duṣprasaha now comes upon the scene (accompanied by a group of merchants, according to the Khotanese text), and finds all the monks dead. The king bewails the fate of the Dharma, and at this point the Khotanese account ends.[85] In the Chinese version the king then proceeds to cremate the remains of Śiṣyaka and Sūrata (an event that occurs somewhat later in the Tibetan). At this point the Tibetan version states that the ministers will feel great pity for the king and will disguise five hundred men as monks (Tib. *ban-de*),[86] clothing them in red and black animal hides (since the colored dyes used for making monastic robes have now disappeared). The king then proceeds to question these impostors concerning the Buddhist teachings and finds, to his dismay, that they are unable to answer his questions. The king realizes that the Dharma has indeed disappeared. He then cremates the dead monks, and (in the late Tibetan xylograph editions only) himself dies of grief. The Chinese text is less coherent at this point: without mentioning any disguise on the part of loyal ministers, the Chinese text suddenly has a contingent of monks appear out of nowhere, even though the text has previously stated that all of them have been killed. The result is the same, however: when the king asks them to preach the Dharma they are unable to do so, and the king realizes that the teachings have indeed disappeared.

The Tibetan text now closes with a brief description of the general decline that will ensue:

> Then gold will turn to bad silver and stone, silver will turn to

---

[85] Or more accurately, the Khotanese text breaks off. After stating in line 521 "So greatly is this age corrupted in the end. Strive now so that even the Śāsana. . ." (Emmerick, *Zambasta*, p. 419), the text breaks off, and the following 11 folios (comprising 121 lines, according to Emmerick's calculations) are missing. It is possible that further material directly related to the Kauśāmbī story would have been contained in the missing folios; on the other hand, the story itself has been finished, and the exhortation to the reader or listener to "strive. . ." would seem to be a fitting concluding statement. When the text resumes at line 642 (folio 439, *Zambasta*, 421), it is with material that does not parallel either the Tibetan or the Chinese version of the *Candragarbha* text.

[86] On this term (which I would derive from Skt. or Pkt. *bhadante*, voc. < *bhadanta* "a term of respect applied to a Buddhist, a Buddhist mendicant" [MW 745c], rather than from the *vandya* "praiseworthy, very venerable" [MW 919b] as most authorities have done) see p. 254, note 24 to the English translation of the Tibetan.

> brass, brass will turn to copper, and jewels and pearls will turn to horn. And of the six flavors of food, four of them—sweet and so on—will disappear. And only two—the bitter and the pungent—will remain.[87]

The Chinese, by contrast, continues with a long concluding section that has no parallel in any other version of the Kauśāmbī story and is worthy of attention in its own right. After a general description of the decline to be suffered by the natural world, human beings themselves, and the Dharma, the Buddha goes on to say that he will renounce one-third of his life span for the benefit of sentient beings, thus prolonging the life span of the Dharma. It is at this point that this section of the Chinese *Candragarbha-sūtra* offers its own timetable for decline: the True Dharma (正法) will last five hundred years, the Buddha states, and the Semblance Dharma (像法) will last for 1,000 years. Interestingly, the Buddha here emphasizes the importance of giving to the monastic community, even if the monks are breaking the precepts. If someone gives offerings to them, the Buddha says, "It is like making offerings to me." The Buddha goes on to describe various austerities he performed in many previous lifetimes in order "to make the Dharma long bright" (a refrain frequently repeated in this section). The Buddha then offers a *dhāraṇī* to his followers for the purpose of making the Dharma long endure in the world—an element not found in any other version of the Kauśāmbī story. At this point various good omens appear, sentient beings of various types attain new levels of insight, and the Buddha increases the three "essential life-forces" (三精氣).[88]

The Chinese *Candragarbha* prophecy closes with the statement that the merits resulting from the Buddha's offerings to previous Buddhas during his former lives can be divided into three parts:

---

[87] See the Tibetan text given in chapter 9, §28, lines 2-6. The above translation is based solely on the Tun-huang version; the xylograph editions exhibit considerable variations in this passage.

[88] This curious term has no parallel in either the Tibetan or the Khotanese text and is not defined at this point in the Chinese. In a previous passage, however (T 13.324a13–14), these three are described as being "the essential life-force of the earth" (地精氣), "the essential life-force of all living beings" (衆生精氣), and the "wondrous essential life-force of the True Dharma" (妙正法精氣). (I would like to thank Judith Boltz for locating this passage, and for passing on this information to me.) Whatever the origin of these terms—which may well represent Chinese input into the text—they are certainly not standard Buddhist expressions.

(1) one part for himself; (2) one part for those *śrāvakas* who are firm in *samādhi*, leading to liberation; and (3) one part for *śrāvakas* who break the precepts, but recite the sūtras and put on monastic robes in the times of the True and Semblance Dharma. The Buddha asks the future Buddha Maitreya to protect these *śrāvakas* "so they will not be poor," and to prevent *caṇḍāla*-kings from harming those *śrāvakas* who break the precepts. The section closes with the joyful reception of this message by all human and non-human sentient beings.

Several elements in these three accounts are worthy of note. First, the very presence of the interlocutor, the bodhisattva Candragarbha (in the Tibetan and Chinese versions), suggests a certain degree of Mahāyāna input into this version of the tradition. It is important to note, however, that this is the only Mahāyāna element in the Tibetan text; the rest of the story, like the other versions discussed above (with the exception of the *Mahāmāyā-sūtra*), is entirely devoid of Mahāyāna content. In the Khotanese version, too, there is only a single Mahāyāna element: when the monks assemble at Kauśāmbī, we are told, they realize that "the Mahāyāna is then completely ruined."[89] In the Chinese version we find a far greater number of Mahāyāna elements, including mentions of the six *pāramitās* (375b, 377a, and 379c, the last two in conjunction with references to the arising of bodhisattvas), the bodhisattva Mañjuśrī (377a, 380b), the appearance of bodhisattvas in general (380a), and the coming of bodhisattvas to greet the believer at his or her death (381b). In the closing passages of this section the text also refers to the generation of *bodhicitta* by various sentient beings in the audience (380b). Most striking of all is the presence in the Chinese version of a *dhāraṇī* offered by the Buddha to his followers "in order to make the Dharma long endure" (380b), a feature with no counterpart in any other version of the text. All of these, however, occur outside the body of the Kauśāmbī story itself (377b–379b), in what might best be described as a "framing" section that has no close parallel in any other version of the text.

Does the addition of these Mahāyāna elements, then, constitute a genuine "Mahāyānization" of the account? Certainly this is not the case in the Tibetan and the Khotanese versions, where Mahāyāna elements are minimal and could easily be removed

---

[89] Emmerick, *Zambasta*, 411.

without noticeably altering the plot. In the Chinese version, however, the issue is more complex. The main lines of the Kauśāmbī story are still quite devoid of Mahāyāna content.[90] In the closing passages of the chapter (summarized above), however, we can discern a distinct attempt to withdraw from the conclusion implied in the other versions of the story: now the emphasis is not on the fact that the demise of the Dharma is inevitable and will take place (despite the best efforts of Buddhists to the contrary) after a fixed period of time, but on the Buddha's heroic efforts to stave off that decline.

Since both the closing section and the introduction (that is, the "framing" sections) found in the Chinese text have no parallel in any other version of the Kauśāmbī story, it is reasonable to conclude that they were not part of the early tradition but were added at some specific point in the transmission of the text. That this took place in a Mahāyāna environment is quite certain, since both segments of the "frame" contain a high concentration of Mahāyāna ideas. Since the Chinese version was not translated until 566 CE, these sections could have been added as late as the first half of the 6th century. It would be extremely interesting if we could determine whether this addition took place in India, in Central Asia, or in China. In this regard we may consider the following. First, the *dhāraṇī* given in the concluding section of the Chinese (380b5–9) does not appear, at first glance, to be a genuine transcription of Indian words (with the exception of the last three syllables, *su-p'o-ho*, which we can assume to be a transcription of Skt. *svāhā*).[91] Second, the reference to people looking upon their parents as "field deer" (379b21) is derived from Chinese, not Indian, imagery.[92] Third, in its description of the various disastrous consequences of the decline of the Dharma the Chinese version states that among these are a decrease in sexual power and pleasure (379b22); one would expect

---

[90] The same is true of the other Mahāyāna-influenced version of the Kauśāmbī story discussed above (pp. 168–70), the *Mahāmāyā-sūtra*.

[91] The evaluation of the "authenticity" of a *dhāraṇī* is always tentative, of course, since *dhāraṇī*s found in Indian texts can likewise consist of apparently meaningless terms.

[92] The expression is used at least as early as the Former Han dynasty; see Wm. T. de Bary, ed., *Sources of Chinese Tradition* (New York: Columbia University Press, 1960), vol. 1, 162, for the use of this expression in the *Ch'un-ch'iu fan-lu* 春秋繁露 of Tung Chung-shu 董仲舒 (2nd c. BCE).

an Indian Buddhist source to see this as a positive value, not a negative one. Fourth, as already noted, the repeated reference to the "three essential life-forces" does not seem to reflect any term in the Indian Buddhist repertoire.[93] Fifth, the reference to the "white Dharma" and "black Dharma" (376b25, 376c10) does not seem to correspond to Indian Buddhist terminology. Sixth, though the expression of devotion to one's parents is not absent (as Gregory Schopen has recently demonstrated) from the worldview of Indian Buddhism,[94] the direct reference to people being "unfilial to their parents" (不孝於父母 , 377b17) sounds suspiciously Chinese. Seventh, the unabashed advertising of "long life, fame, and wealth" and "never being poor" as among the benefits obtained by listening to the sūtra (381b21–22) reflects a level of concern with issues of wealth and poverty that would be unusual in an Indian Buddhist text, but very much at home in the Chinese context. Finally, throughout both the introductory and concluding sections the Chinese text exhibits a major concern with the financial support of the Buddhist community, and with exhortations to rulers not to punish those monks who do not faithfully adhere to the monastic rules. As we have seen, these are concerns that are frequently expressed in Chinese Buddhist texts but are almost unknown in Indian ones.[95] Thus we may tentatively suggest that the "frame" of the story (which is found only in the Chinese version) was added in a Chinese context, in response to Chinese conditions.

Another important task is to determine the degree of relationship among the texts in the *Candragarbha-sūtra* group, on the one hand, and of the group as a whole with other versions of the Kauśāmbī story. Beginning with the latter, in referring to the king of Kauśāmbī by name as Mahendrasena and in including his son Duṣprasaha in the story the three *Candragarbha* texts agree with the *Aśoka-avadāna* group and diverge from the other texts discussed above. The *Candragarbha* texts again agree with the *Aśoka-avadāna* group (but here also with the *Mahāvibhāṣā* and the *Mahāmāyā-sūtra*) in portraying the conflict at Kauśāmbī as a direct confrontation

---

[93] See for example 376a8 and a12; 376c25; and 379b10 and b29. For the expression "three essential life-forces" cf. above, n. 88.

[94] Gregory Schopen, "Filial Piety and the Monk in the Practice of Indian Buddhism: A Question of 'Sinicization' Viewed from the Other Side," *T'oung Pao* 70 (1984), 110–26.

[95] See above, pp. 128–29.

between the tripiṭaka-master and the arhat Sūrata, rather than between the arhat and an unnamed group of monks (as in the two *Kātyāyana* prophecies).

In other respects, however, the *Candragarbha* texts differ from the *Aśoka-avadāna* group and conform with other versions instead. First, while the *Aśoka-avadāna* texts all refer to the death of King Mahendrasena, and to Duṣprasaha's turning against the Buddhist community in the wake of the altercation at Kauśāmbī, these elements do not appear in the *Candragarbha* texts. Nor does the *Candragarbha* group include any mention of the group of five hundred pious lay disciples who criticize the monks' bad behavior, a feature found both in the *Aśoka-avadāna* texts and in the *Mahāvibhāṣā*.

In two respects the *Candragarbha* texts all agree with one another, while differing from the other texts described above. First, the *Candragarbha* texts are alone in stating that all the monks assembled at Kauśāmbī—not just a portion of the group—are killed in the intra-sangha struggle. (This shift may be seen as evidence of an ongoing process of editorial rationalization, since the survival of any monks at all might conflict with the overall premise of the account that the Dharma has completely and totally disappeared.) And second, all three texts in the *Candragarbha* group agree in transcribing the name "Śiṣyaka" with an internal *r* (< Skt./Pkt. **Śirṣaka*?), which (as discussed above) may betray the influence of a Kharoṣṭhī-script ancestor.[96] All in all, however, it is in general the continuities between the core of the Kauśāmbī story as related in the three *Candragarbha* texts and with those of other versions, rather than any striking innovations in plot, that are most striking.

Despite these important continuities, however, we can still make certain distinctions even within the *Candragarbha* group, and these can help us in determining the degree of common ancestry

---

[96] See above, note 83. This feature is not in fact restricted to the *Candragarbha* group, though this is the only group in which it occurs with complete consistency. The Chinese translation of the *Mahāvibhāṣā* also contains a form of the name "Śiṣyaka" that goes back to an underlying **Śirṣaka*, and it is possible (though in my view not probable) that the *Saṃyukta-āgama* reflects such a form as well. The *Mahāvibhāṣa*, however, is based on a large number of sources, one of which (in the late recension that served as the basis for Hsüan-tsang's translation) may well have been the *Candragarbha-sūtra* itself. For a list of all the variant forms in which this name appears see the Appendix, no. 5.

among the texts in this group. At first glance it would seem that the Khotanese and Chinese versions of the *Candragarbha* resemble each other more closely than either version does the Tibetan; both contain a 1,500-year timetable for the duration of the Dharma (in contrast to the 2,000-year timetable of the Tibetan), and both are cast either entirely (Khotanese) or predominantly (Chinese) in verse. Yet a closer look reveals that these seemingly common features do not indicate a close genetic relationship between the two. The stylistic similarity, first of all, cannot be used as evidence, for the selections contained in the Khotanese *Book of Zambasta* are all cast entirely in verse, regardless of the literary style of their Indian originals. As to the 1,500-year timetable, the Khotanese and Chinese versions insert this figure at different points in the story, and the Chinese goes on to divide this total time period into two subperiods of five hundred years (*cheng-fa*) and one thousand years (*hsiang-fa*), a distinction not made in the Khotanese version. One's overall impression, then, is that the 1,500-year timetable has been added to these two texts quite independently, just as a 2,000-year time scheme has been added to the Tibetan.

A better case can in fact be constructed for a close connection between the Tibetan and Khotanese versions, which agree in a number of key respects. In both of these recensions the directional locations of the three evil kings have been omitted, and the king of Kauśāmbī is located in the south; this is in contrast to the Chinese version, which preserves a vestige of the original locations of the three evil kings and places Kauśāmbī—as is standard in most of the sources discussed above—in the east. Again the Tibetan and Khotanese agree on the implement used to kill the arhat: both versions state that Aṅgada employs a door-bolt, a rather unusual weapon (cf. the Chinese, which says simply that he is killed with a stick). Most striking of all, however, is a seeming aberration in the name of one of the three foreign powers: both the Tibetan and the Khotanese versions replace the ethnonym "Saka" (Sanskrit *śaka*) with an otherwise unattested ethnonym, Skt./Pkt. **śakuna*. That this form does not appear in any other version of the Kauśāmbī story in itself suggests a common ancestry for the Tibetan and Khotanese versions of this text.[97]

---

[97] It is entirely possible that this change was made in the Tarim Basin region, with the intention of removing any association with the Sakas (i.e., the people of

All in all, then, there is little significant innovation (that is, little change that is doctrinally significant) in the versions of the Kauśāmbī story contained in the *Candragarbha* texts. Despite the peripheral Mahāyāna accretions that begin to appear in these texts, they represent a continuation of a long-established tradition, not a radical innovation in the understanding of the decline myth.

LATE KHOTANESE ADAPTATIONS

All of the texts discussed above, despite numerous variations in detail and an ever-increasing layer of accretions, can fairly be described as versions of a single story. All place the scene of the disappearance of the Dharma at the city of Kauśāmbī, and locate the invasions by the three foreign kings in the northwestern part of India. And with the exception of the verse translation of the *Prophecy of Kātyāyana*, which alters the names of the three foreign kings to read "Rome, Iran, and Parthia" (and to a lesser extent the Chinese *Candragarbha-sūtra*, which apparently replaces the word "Greek" with "Persian"), all the versions of the story in which the names can be deciphered describe the invaders as the Greeks, Sakas, and Parthians. The story itself, the main characters, and the geographical references within it all make sense in terms of the experience of Buddhists living in and around the northwestern part of the Indian subcontinent in the early centuries of the common era.

The texts we are about to examine, by contrast, do not fit this description at all. All three were almost certainly composed in Khotan, but are preserved only in Tibetan translations. Though they can tell us little about the origins of the Kauśāmbī story in India, they provide considerable information about the ways in which the story was updated and altered to fit the requirements of new historical circumstances. They are referred to as "late" because they all refer to historical events that took place in the first half of the 8th century CE; I have styled them "Khotanese" because there is every indication that these traditions were first formulated,

---

Khotan). (On the ethnonym *saka* and related forms see H. W. Bailey, *Khotanese Texts*, vol. 7 [London: Cambridge University Press, 1985], 63–75.) We should also note, however, the occurrence of the form *śakuni* in the Sanskrit epic *Mahābhārata*, V 196.7 (cited in Bailey, *Khotanese Texts*, vol. 6, 335).

and subsequently set down in writing, in or around the city of Khotan.[98]

The three texts included in this category are the following:

1. ***Li'i yul-[gyi dgra-bcom-pas] lung-bstan-pa*** ("The Prophecy of [the Arhat of] Khotan"): Peking No. 5699, Derge No. 4202; also in the Narthang edition (vol. 94 [*mdo nge*], 420b3–424b1). Three Tun-huang manuscript copies have also been preserved,[99] as well as a Chinese translation based on the Tibetan.[100] In this case, however—in contrast to that of the Tibetan *Candragarbha-sūtra* editions discussed above—the xylograph editions clearly represent a separate translation, as they contain numerous differences in vocabulary, phrasing, and content from that of the Tun-huang copies.[101] None of the manuscript or xylograph copies contains an indication of translation date, but for reasons discussed below the Khotanese original cannot have been composed earlier than the second half of the 8th century CE.

Of the three texts in this group the *Prophecy of Khotan* (called in some but not all recensions the *Prophecy of the Arhat of Khotan*)[102]

---

[98] Here I differ with F. W. Thomas, who viewed at least the first two of these works as original Tibetan compositions, and suggested that the three might have been produced in Tun-huang, Tibet, and Sha-chou, respectively (see his *Tibetan Literary Texts and Documents Concerning Chinese Turkestan* [London: Royal Asiatic Society, 1935], vol. 1, pp. 42, 50, 51, and 307, n. 3). R. E. Emmerick, who has published an edition of the third of these works (in *Tibetan Texts Concerning Khotan* [London: Oxford University Press, 1967]), does not commit himself on this issue, stating only that the text demonstrates a "close association with Khotan" (xi) and uses terms that "could only have been known to someone familiar with Khotanese usage" (xi–xii).

[99] Tun-huang text nos. J597, J598, J601.2 (kept in the India Office Library division of the British Museum). Critical editions and English translations of the Tibetan and Chinese versions of this text are currently in preparation by Christopher I. Beckwith and TAKEUCHI Tsuguhito. In the meantime see the pioneering but now outdated translation by Thomas in his *Tibetan Literary Texts*, vol. 1, 77–87.

[100] Pelliot no. 2139 (Tun-huang ms.), translated from the Tibetan by Chos-grub (Ch. Fa-ch'eng 法成). See the discussion by Pelliot in *Journal Asiatique*, vol. 1 (1914), 144–45.

[101] Here too I differ with the opinion of Thomas, who saw the xylograph editions as mere revisions of an original similar to the surviving Tun-huang texts (*Tibetan Literary Texts*, vol. 1, 41). Thomas's reasoning was of course swayed by his assumption that the text was not a translation at all, but an original Tibetan composition (41–42).

[102] See Thomas, *Tibetan Literary Texts*, vol. 1, p. 77, n. 1 and p. 87. This text

contains the shortest version of the Kauśāmbī story, which is simply summarized in a paragraph at the end of the text. The bulk of the account is devoted not to events in India at all, but to the fate of a group of monks and nuns from Khotan.

The story, in brief, goes as follows. During the reign of the seventh ruler of Khotan, King Vijayakīrti, there was an arhat named Saṃghavardhana (Tib. *San-gha-bardha-na*).[103] A student of the arhat, who had seen the *Prophecy of Candragarbha*, asks the arhat how long the Dharma will endure in the three countries of *Li* (Khotan),[104] *Shu-lig* (Kashgar),[105] and *'An-se* (Kucha).[106] The arhat replies that the Dharma will endure for 2,000 years after the Buddha's nirvāṇa.[107] At that time these three countries will suffer from disturbances brought about by a variety of enemies, among

---

should not be confused with another work, titled "Prophey of the Li Country" by Emmerick (see the edition and translation in his *Tibetan Texts*, pp. 2–75) and "Annals of the Li Country" by Thomas (translation in *Tibetan Literary Texts*, vol. 1, 89–136). The latter does not include a version of the Kauśāmbī story and will not be considered here.

[103] The same figure reappears in the following text.

[104] No satisfactory explanation for the regular Tibetan rendering of the name of the kingdom of Khotan as "Li country" (Tib. *li-yul*)—a name that does not appear in the Khotanese sources themselves, or for that matter in any other language—has yet been offered. The suggestion by R. A. Stein (*Recherches sur l'épopée et le barde au Tibet* [Paris: Presses Universitaires de France, 1959], 284 and 313, n. 126) that *Li* represents a Tibetan transcription of the Chinese family name *Li* 李, adopted by the Khotanese ruling family around the beginning of the 10th century, is not in my view persuasive, especially since the Tibetan sources began to employ this name considerably before that date.

[105] Not *from* Chinese *Shu-lo* 疏勒, as stated by Emmerick (*Tibetan Texts*, 105a, s.v. *śu-lig*), but a transcription of a local name of Kashgar, of which the Chinese (A. Ch. *˛ṣi̯ʷo'-lək*, K. nos. 904, 523) is also a representation.

[106] Presumably a transcription of Chinese *an-hsi* 安西 ("pacified west"), the name of the Chinese protectorate established in the Tarim Basin region during the T'ang period, with its main headquarters located at Kucha during part of this period. C. I. Beckwith (*The Tibetan Empire* [Princeton: Princeton University Press, 1987], 198) is correct in asserting that this term should not in general be confused with the name of Kucha, but in the present instance the context requires the identification of *'an-se* with the kingdom of Kucha itself, and not with a broader administrative unit.

[107] So the Tun-huang mss; the xylograph editions, however, read "1,000 years" (see Thomas, *Tibetan Literary Texts*, vol. 1, p. 78 and n. 4). Thomas states that the number 1,000 is "doubtless the more original figure" (n. 4); I would argue, however, that its presence here—in the xylograph editions alone—is not the result of its antiquity, but of a copying error.

them the Chinese (*rgya*), Tibetans (*gdong-dmar*, lit. "red faces"),[108] Supīyas (*so-byi*),[109] Turks (*drug-gu*), and Uighurs (*hor*).[110] The countries of Kucha and Kashgar will be particularly disturbed by these upheavals, and most of the monks residing there will flee to Khotan. At that time a bodhisattva will take birth as king of Tibet,[111] and the practice of Buddhism will flourish in Tibet. During the time that Khotan is under the sway of Tibet the Buddhist sangha in both countries will flourish. Afterwards, in the seventh generation,[112] there will (again) be a bodhisattva ruling Tibet; his consort will be the Chinese princess Kong-co, who will have great faith in Buddhism.[113] Meanwhile, in Khotan a non-Buddhist king will

---

[108] The listing of the Tibetans among the hostile forces, as well as the use of this term (which occurs throughout the text) in place of the ordinary Tibetan self-designating ethnonym *bod*, is sufficient evidence in itself, in my view, that the text is not a Tibetan composition. The epithet "red faces" is a reference to the Tibetan custom, current during the imperial period, of smearing their faces with red pigment. Note that the same expression is attested as a name for the Tibetans in the Khotanese *Book of Zambasta*, 15.9 (Khot. *heinā-khoca*, for which see Bailey, *Khotanese Texts*, vol. 7, pp. 12, 87). Bailey describes this term as a Khotanese rendering of a Tibetan self-designation, but in my view the reverse—that *gdong-dmar* represents a Tibetan translation of Khot. *heinā-khoca*—is more likely.

[109] The Supīyas, who inhabited the northern slopes of the Kun-lun mountains and were a constant threat to the inhabitants of the oasis towns in the southern Tarim Basin throughout most of the first millennium CE, are mentioned already in the Kharoṣṭhī documents from the Niya region (3rd c. CE); see the index to A. M. Boyer et al., *Kharoṣṭhī Inscriptions*, s.v. *supiya*. The transcription of their name here as *So-byi* (in contrast to the usual Tibetan spelling *Sum-pa*) is again an indication that this text was translated into Tibetan from another language. In this connection we should note the spelling of the name in Khotanese as *Supīya* (see Bailey, *Khotanese Texts*, vol. 7, 79–81), as well as Bailey's suggestion (80) that the Tibetan *so-byi* is derived from a Chinese form.

[110] Eventually this term comes to mean "Mongol," but in the imperial period it was still used to refer to the Uighurs. The corresponding Chinese text has *hui-ho* 回紇, "Uighur."

[111] Here the reference is presumably to Srong-btsan sgam-po, founder of the Tibetan empire, whose Buddhist sympathies are, however, only legendary (see Hoffmann, *Tibet*, 126–27).

[112] The chronological problem that concerned Thomas (see *Tibetan Literary Texts*, vol. 1, p. 79, n. 6) has vanished with improved knowledge of the history of this period. For a chart of the Tibetan rulers in this era see Beckwith, *The Tibetan Empire*, 215.

[113] On the events in question, which took place during the reign of the Tibetan ruler Mes-'ag-tshoms (r. 704–755 CE), see Hoffmann, *Tibet*, 44, 128. The Buddhist cause was supported by the king's Chinese wife, Chin-ch'eng Kung-chu 金城公主 (known as *Kong-co* in Tibetan sources), herself a fervent Buddhist. The queen

come to the throne and will command the monks to either become householders or leave the country. Having assembled at Tsar-ma, the oldest monastery in Khotan, the monks and nuns will decide to go to Tibet in hopes of receiving better treatment. With supernatural assistance from Vaiśramaṇa[114] and from a goddess named Śrī-mahādevī[115] they will survive the rigors of the journey and arrive in Tibet. For three years they are well received. Subsequently, however, an epidemic breaks out, taking the life of the Chinese queen herself. After her death a group of ministers succeed in persuading the king that the epidemic is due to the presence of so many foreign monks,[116] and that they should all be expelled. The Tibetan monks cast in their lot with their foreign compatriots (who now include a large contingent of Chinese monks, who have left China and come to Tibet due to the ruler's pro-Taoist policies[117]) and join them on a long and arduous journey to Gandhāra. Due to supernatural assistance—in this case offered by a *nāga* king, who turns his body into a bridge to provide a shortcut across a lake—most of them are able to arrive at their destination.

For two years the Khotanese and Tibetan monks will prosper in Gandhāra. Then, however, the king of the country will die, and

---

died, however, during a smallpox epidemic that swept through Tibet in 740–741, some three years after the arrival of the Khotanese monks, and opponents of Buddhism (including many of the ministers of state) took advantage of the situation to argue that the Tibetan gods were angry with the presence of these foreign religious figures. Their arguments were successful, and the Khotanese monks were again sent on their way.

[114] Note that this name is transliterated as *Bai-shra-ma-ṇa* (a form derived from the Buddhist Hybrid Sanskrit (or Prakrit) spelling *Vaiśramaṇa*, not Skt. *Vaiśravaṇa*; see Edgerton, BHSD, 513a), and not translated (as *Rnam-thos-kyi bu*) as is usually done in Tibetan. On the forms of this name in Khotanese and other Central Asian languages see H. W. Bailey in *Bulletin of the School of Oriental and African Studies* 10 (1942), 912.

[115] Not a standard figure in the Indian pantheon; possibly a local goddess in Buddhistic garb.

[116] The *Prophecy of Khotan* specifies that the epidemic was spread by monks from Nepal, a fact not mentioned in other versions of the story (see Thomas, *Tibetan Literary Texts*, vol. 1, p. 49).

[117] The reference to Taoism appears only in this version of the Kauśambī story. The ruler in question is presumably emperor Hsüan-tsung (r. 712–756), whose pro-Taoist sentiments are well known (see Stanley Weinstein, *Buddhism Under the T'ang* [Cambridge: Cambridge University Press, 1987], 51–57 and 168, n. 26). The Tibetan text specifies that the pro-Taoist policies went into effect some time after the arrival of Kong-co in Tibet in 710.

a succession struggle between his two sons—one a follower of Buddhism (*lha-chos*), the other a partisan of "heretical religion" (*mu-stegs-kyi chos*, almost certainly a reference to Islam)—will ensue. The monks of course support the Buddhist candidate, who (with their assistance) is successful in gaining the throne. After only six months, however, an unnamed monk will assassinate the king and take the throne for himself. At this point the people of Gandhāra rise in revolt, kill the usurper-monk, and expel the other monks from the kingdom. Now the reflection of the True Dharma (*saddharma-pratirūpaka*, Tib. *dam-pa'i chos-kyi gzugs-brnyan*) will perish in Gandhāra, and the monks will again begin their wanderings.

Finally we come to the brief passage that parallels the Kauśāmbī story itself. Here the three foreign kings have not yet been subjected to the wholesale changes of name that occur in the other two versions, but are referred to simply as "king[s] of the west and king[s] of the north, 'Greek' and so on."[118] Though the story is told in condensed form, it has undergone no visible changes in plot:

> . . . increasing in power, those three kings will seize the western and northern country. The three kings, each accompanied by an army of a hundred thousand men, having marched into the country of Kauśāmbī, the king of Kauśāmbī will annihilate the armies of three hundred thousand men, along with the kings, leaving not a single man. Then the king of Kauśāmbī, in order to purge the sin of slaying so many armies, will invite all the monks resident in Jambudvīpa; after arriving in the country of Kauśāmbī the sanghas will quarrel and slay each other, and the reflection of the True Dharma (*saddharma-pratirūpaka*) in Jambudvīpa will perish completely.[119]

Of particular interest for our purposes is the following line, which reads "but the details may be known as stated in the *Sūtra of the Prophecy Made to the Bodhisattva Candragarbha*."[120] Thus in the closing

---

[118] Tib. *nub-phyogs-kyi rgyal-po dang / byang-phyogs-kyi rgyal-po ya-na-ba* [*sic*, for *ya-ba-na*] *la-sogs-pa* (Pek. No. 5699, *mdo-'grel nge*, 447b6).

[119] Following the translation of F. W. Thomas (*Tibetan Literary Texts*, vol. 1, p. 86, which he based on the Tun-huang manuscripts rather than on the noticeably different xylograph editions), with certain emendations.

[120] Thomas, *Literary Texts*, vol. 1, p. 86. This sentence is omitted in the xylograph editions, which, however, contain a final sentence (not found in the Tun-huang mss.) reading "accords with the *Prophecy of Candragarbha*" (in the Peking edition, *Tsan-dra-gar-bha'i lung-bstan-pa dang mthun-no* [448b3]).

of the text, as in the opening, the *Prophecy of Candragarbha* is described as a standard source of information on the ultimate disappearance of the Dharma. In general, then, it is fair to say that the description of the decline and disappearance of the Dharma given in the *Prophecy of Khotan* follows the main lines of the *Candragarbha* account. The 2,000-year timetable found in the Tun-huang manuscripts matches that of the Tibetan *Candragarbha* translation, and though the proper names cannot be used as a major point of comparison (since in this brief resumé virtually all proper names have been eliminated), the preservation of the name of one of the evil kings, *ya-ba-na* or "Greek," demonstrates that the author of this text must have had in mind the original trio of Greeks, Sakas, and Parthians. What is strikingly new in this account, however, is its association with the fate of the monastic community of Khotan, and this change paved the way for much more sweeping emendations of the Kauśāmbī tale in other Khotanese texts.

2. ***Dgra-bcom-pa Dge-'dun 'phel-gyis lung-bstan-pa*** ("The Prophecy of the Arhat Saṃghavardhana"): Peking No. 5698, Derge No. 4201; Narthang vol. 94 (*mdo nge*), folios 412–20. The text contains no colophon, and thus cannot be dated with precision; as in the case of the *Prophecy of Khotan*, however, this work refers to historical events of the mid-8th century, and thus the original composition must be assigned to the second half of the 8th century at the earliest. Thomas considered this text to be older "by far" than the *Prophecy of Khotan* just discussed, but I am unable to go along with his reasoning.[121] In my view the *Prophecy of the Arhat Saṃghavardhana* represents not the antecedent of the *Prophecy of Khotan*, as Thomas would have it, but rather an adaptation and amplification of its content. In any case it is clearly the most detailed of the three Khotanese adaptations, and offers a number of interesting divergences from earlier versions of the Kauśāmbī story.

---

[121] Thomas, *Tibetan Literary Texts*, vol. 1, 43. More specifically, he assumes that a shorter version of a prophecy attributed to an arhat Saṃghavardhana, composed in "some form of Buddhist Sanskrit or Prakrit" (50), once circulated in the Tarim Basin region. This ancient version was then recast in expanded form in Sanskrit, or possibly Khotanese or Tibetan (51). Thomas dismisses the statement of a Tanjur catalogue (presumably the Narthang edition, though he provides no reference) that this text and the *Prophecy of Khotan* "seem to be translations from Khotan" as "a conjecture of no weight" (51).

As in the *Prophecy of Khotan*, the text opens with a question by a pupil to his teacher, the arhat Saṃghavardhana,[122] concerning the duration and ultimate fate of the Dharma in Khotan.[123] This time we find no direct mention of the *Prophecy of Candragarbha* (nor does such a reference occur anywhere in this text); the text states only that the pupil had heard that, "with the passing of two thousand years from the nirvāṇa of Buddha, Buddha's doctrine would decline in the Indian country Kauśāmbī."[124] The arhat replies that 1,500 years after the death of the Buddha unbelievers (i.e., non-Buddhists) will arise in these countries, and the Dharma will suffer from fighting. Moreover, an unbelieving king will arise in Khotan,[125] and the fortunes of the Buddhist monastic community will decline. Accordingly, many monks and nuns will become extremely concerned with making a living and will support themselves by carrying on various secular activities. As a result, the fortunes of the country will decline.

Then those monks and nuns of Khotan who are still devoted to Buddhism will gather in the Tshar-ma monastery and decide to go to Tibet. With assistance from Vaiśravaṇa and Śrī-mahādevī,[126] most of the group will arrive safely.

At that time a Chinese princess, "born of a bodhisattva family," will be the chief queen of the king of Tibet. She will argue the cause of the Khotanese monks and nuns before the king, and he will allow her to furnish them with supplies. Meanwhile, a group of monks from a variety of Central Asian countries[127] who have taken

---

[122] Here the name is translated (as *Dge-'dun 'phel*), rather than transliterated as in the *Prophecy of Khotan*. Note also that the arhat is described as residing in the Phru-ña monastery "in this country"; since the monastery in question was located in the kingdom of Khotan (Thomas, vol. I, 118–20) this would indicate that the text was a Khotanese composition.

[123] More specifically, the inquiry concerns the fate of the Dharma "in the countries of Khotan and so on" (*Li-yul la-sogs-pa*, Pek. No. 5698, *mdo-'grel nge*, 435b4 and *passim*). Presumably more or less the same area described in the *Prophecy of Khotan*—that is, the countries of Khotan, Kashgar, and Kucha—is meant.

[124] Thomas, *Tibetan Literary Texts*, vol. I, 52. Note that the timetable is again the same as that of the Tibetan *Candragarbha-sūtra*.

[125] More literally, "in this country of Khotan" (*Li-yul 'dir*), again an indication that the text was composed in Khotan.

[126] See above, n. 115.

[127] The countries listed are *'An-tse* (~ *An-rtse*), *Gus-tig*, *Par-mkhan* (~ *Bar-wan*), and *Shu-lig* (~ *Shu-lag*) (see Thomas, *Tibetan Literary Texts*, vol. 1, 61 and the Peking

refuge in Gilgit (Tib. *Bru-sha*) will hear of the good reception Buddhism is receiving in Tibet, and they too will arrive in that country. For three years all will be well. After that time, however, an epidemic will spread in Tibet, and the queen herself will die of the disease. The ministers of the king, blaming the epidemic on the presence of the foreign monks, will insist that they all be expelled from the country. The king apparently agrees (though this is not stated explicitly in the text), and the Tibetan monks, together with their foreign compatriots (including a contingent from China[128]) set out for Gandhāra. As in the *Prophecy of Khotan*, however, the new arrivals will enjoy peace in Gandhāra for only two years. During the third year of their sojourn there the king of Gandhāra will die, triggering a succession dispute between his two (one Buddhist and one non-Buddhist) sons. The immigrant monks support the Buddhist candidate,[129] who is successful in his claims. After just five months, however, he will be assassinated by a group of "upland" monks,[130] who will put one of their number on the throne. The latter will rule for two years, after which the people of Gandhāra will revolt and will assassinate the king and kill all the foreign monks they can find. Only a few will succeed in fleeing into Madhyadeśa.

At this point the text launches into the familiar Kauśāmbī story, but here with a striking difference: now the three evil kings are not the Greeks, Sakas, and Parthians, but the Persians (*stag-gzig ~ta-zig*), Turks (*drug-gu~dru-gu*), and Tibetans (*bod*)![131] The story follows the account given in the Tibetan *Prophecy of Candragabha* quite closely, though with somewhat less detail. King Mahendra-

---

edition, 439b6). Of these, *Shu-lig* is the usual Tibetan name for Kashgar (see above, n. 105) and *Gus-tig* is an unidentified city along the northern Silk Road through the Tarim Basin (see Beckwith, *The Tibetan Empire*, 131). The identification of the other two is uncertain.

[128] Cf. above, n. 117. Here we have no reference to Taoism, however, but only to the general strife and suffering experienced by Buddhist monks in China (Tib. *skye-bo dang rtsod-pa'i dus de'i tshe rgya-yul-gyi dge-slong-rnams kyang shin-tu sdug-bsngal-bas gzir-nas yul Gan-dha-rar 'gro-bar 'gyur-ro*, Pek. 440b1–2).

[129] Here the text stresses that among their ranks are a number of young monks, who prove to be excellent fighters.

[130] Tib. *stod-po*; the corresponding Chinese text has *hsi* 西 , "western." On the meaning of the terms *stod* and *stod-phyogs* in Old Tibetan texts see Beckwith, *The Tibetan Empire*, 203–205.

[131] The inclusion of the Tibetans among the three "evil powers" should be sufficient evidence in itself to demonstrate that this work is not a Tibetan composition.

sena is not mentioned, but the circumstances surrounding the birth of his son Duṣprasaha[132] are the same, as are the results of his campaigns against the three invading kings—their complete and total annihilation. Once again the king regrets the suffering he has caused and is advised to invite Śiṣyaka (here, as in the *Candragarbha* group, spelled with an internal *r*, Tib. *Shir-sha-ka*) to come from Pāṭaliputra. The preceptor urges him to atone for his deeds by inviting all the monks of Jambudvīpa to come to Kauśāmbī, and the king follows his advice. The text notes that 100,000 monks will arrive in Kauśāmbī (there is no mention here, however, of the harm suffered by some of them along the way). Then, on the evening of the fifteenth day, the *poṣadha* ceremony is held, and the familiar conflict between Śiṣyaka and Sūrata[133] breaks out. Sūrata is killed by Śiṣyaka's student, Aṅgada (Derge *A-kan-bi*, Peking and Narthang *A-gna-bi*[134]), who again wields a door-bolt as a weapon; Aṅgada in turn is killed by Sūrata's disciple **Kedāra*.[135] The monks all become enraged and kill one another, and when the battle is over the *trāyastriṃśa* gods will bemoan their deaths and will carry off their monastic robes, hair, and nails. And various ill omens will appear.

In the morning the king, seeing all the monks lying dead, will weep and lament their deaths, calling out to the arhat and the tripiṭaka-master by name. "Now that you are both dead," he will cry, "this world is become desolate." Then the gods will flee, "defeated by the *asuras*," and various plants, types of cloth, and precious metals will disappear. Fine colors and flavors will also perish, and the images of the Buddha will be carried off by the *nāgas*.

The text then closes with an intriguing chronological note:

---

132 Here translated as *Bzod-dka'*, "hard to tolerate."

133 Spelled *Su-ta-ra* [*sic*] in the Derge edition (167b5).

134 For the reference to the Narthang spelling see Thomas, *Tibetan Literary Texts*, vol. 1, p. 68 and n. 1; Thomas reconstructs an original Indian form "Agnāvī." For the Peking see 443a4. The name has suffered serious deformation in transmission; cf., however, Khot. *Aṃ-ggadī* found in the *Book of Zambasta* (see the Appendix, no. 8).

135 Spelled *Ka-ra-ta* in the Peking, Derge, and Narthang editions. The Narthang edition reads *ngag-slong ka-ra-ta*, "the grammarian Karata" according to Thomas (*Tibetan Literary Texts*, vol. 1, p. 68, n. 3). The term *ngag-slong* ངག་སློང་ is clearly a carving error for *dge-slong* དགེ་སློང་ "monk," which appears correctly in the Peking (443a5) and Derge (167b7) editions. For the reconstruction of this name see above, note 84.

"from the time that calculations were made by an assembly of Pandits during the reign of King Rje-btsan-legs of Khotan until the disappearance of the Dharma, there will be 102 years."[136]

In broad terms, then, it is fair to describe the *Prophecy of the Arhat Saṃghavardhana* as a faithful representation of the plot of the original Kauśāmbī story, but with an important shift in the cast of characters. By naming the three evil kings as the Persians,[137] Turks, and Tibetans, the text has introduced a wholesale shift in perspective to the point of view of an inhabitant of the Tarim Basin during the period of contention among these three powers, i.e., during the late 7th–early 8th centuries CE.[138] Moreover, the text agrees with the *Prophecy of Khotan* (and with the *Religious Annals of Khotan*, to be discussed immediately below) in associating the Kauśāmbī story with the fate of a group of monks and nuns from Khotan. In one important respect, however, both the *Prophecy of Khotan* and the *Prophecy of the Arhat Saṃghavardhana* agree with earlier versions of the story: both texts treat the events at Kauśāmbī as the final disappearance of Buddhism on earth, and end their accounts on this clearly pessimistic note. The chronological calculations that conclude the *Saṃghavardhana* account serve only to reinforce the general sense that the ultimate disappearance of the Dharma, and the timetable according to which it will occur, are unalterable.

In the following account, however, the Kauśāmbī story does not serve as the conclusion of the text. Rather, we find (as in the Chinese version of the *Candragarbha-sūtra*) that it is followed by an additional section, in which its authors stress not the eventual disappearance of the Dharma, but various measures that can be taken for its preservation. In this text—which I believe represents the latest of this group—we see the complete adjustment of the tradition to fit the Khotanese context, an adjustment that involves a withdrawal from the finality of decline (as presented in earlier versions

---

[136] Tib. *Li yul-gyi mkhan-po-rnams 'dus-nas li rje-btsun legs-kyi ring-la yos-bu'i lo-la brtsis-nas de-nas lo brgya-rtsa-gnyis-na dam-pa'i chos nub-par 'gyur-ro* (Pek. 443b8–44a1; the Narthang and Derge texts are identical).

[137] By "Persians" (Tib. *stag-gzig* ~*ta-zig*) we may assume that the Arab Umayyad dynasty, which included the territory of Persia, is meant.

[138] For a detailed and up-to-date study of the interactions of these three powers, based on extensive use of primary sources (including those written in Tibetan) see Beckwith, *The Tibetan Empire*, especially 27–146.

of the story) toward a more Mahāyānistic, and relativistic, attitude toward history.

3. ***Li-yul chos-kyi lo-rgyus*** ("The Religious Annals of Khotan"). Not included in the Tibetan canon; the text is known from a single manuscript copy from Tun-huang.[139] Like the *Saṃghavardhana* prophecy, the *Religious Annals of Khotan* relates the Kauśāmbī story in considerable detail; but like the *Prophecy of Khotan*, it mentions explicitly that the *Prophecy of Candragarbha* is one of its sources. The text concludes, in fact, with a colophon stating that the work is "a mere epitome, newly translated by the preceptor *Mo-rgu-bde-shil*,[140] from the texts of the Dharma-sūtras *Sūryagarbha*, *Candragarbha*, and *Vimala[prabhā-pari]pṛcchā*."[141] (Note that this is the only one of the texts treated in this section that states explicitly that it is a translation.) As with all the texts in this category, the manuscript gives no indication of the date of its composition or translation. Since the text again deals with events known to have taken place during the reign of Mes-'ag-tshoms, however, we may again assume that the

---

[139] Pelliot no. 960. An edition of the text and glossary of vocabulary is given in Emmerick, *Tibetan Texts*, 78–91 (text) and 93–160 (glossary). The only available English translation is the by now quite outdated version given by Thomas in *Tibetan Literary Texts*, vol. 1, 305–23.

[140] The term *mo-rgu-bde-shil* (more frequently *mo-rgu-de-shi* or *mo-rgu-bde-shi*) is not in fact a personal name, but a Tibetan transcription of the Khotanese religious title *mārgaupadeśai* (for which see H. W. Bailey, *Khotanese Texts*, vol. 4, 87–88) <Skt. **mārgopadeśaka* (according to Emmerick, *Tibetan Texts*, 102b). The term is defined as *lam ston-pa*, "way-shower," in another text translated by Emmerick (*Tibetan Texts*, 30, folio 178b1–2). The form in *-l*, which seems to occur only in the *Religious Annals of Khotan*, has not yet been satisfactorily explained, though Emmerick's suggestion that the final *-l* is due to a false association with BHS *śīla*-"moral restraint" (*Tibetan Texts*, 102b) is at least plausible (cf. Thomas, *Tibetan Literary Texts*, vol. 1, p. 307, n. 3 for the suggestion that this spelling reflects a local Chinese pronunciation). The fact that the translator of our text held this title (not, as Emmerick suggests on page 102b, a personal name) strongly suggests that the translation in question was made from a Khotanese original.

[141] Tib. *dar-ma mdo-sde su-rya-ga-rba dang / tsan-dra-ga-rba dang / bye-ma-la-pri-tsa'i gzhung-las mdo-tsam-zhig / mkhan-po mo-rgu-bde-shil-gyis / gsar-du bsgyuro* (see Emmerick, *Tibetan Texts*, p. 91, lines 113–14). For an English translation of the *Vimalaprabhāparipṛcchā-sūtra* see Thomas, *Tibetan Literary Texts*, vol. 1, 179–258; as Thomas points out (139) the text is certainly a Khotanese composition, though no Khotanese original survives. The *Sūryagarbha-sūtra* (Peking No. 923, Derge No. 257, Narthang No. 242, Lhasa No. 258; cf. T No. 397[13] and [14]) has not yet been translated into English.

original was composed no earlier than the second half of the 8th century CE.

The text begins at a much earlier point in the history of Khotan than do the other two works discussed above—in fact, the opening section deals with the initial appearance of Buddhism in Khotan. The introduction of an alphabet, followed by the Buddhist religion, is described; the text then narrates the construction of various stūpas and monasteries. At this point the text shifts backwards in time, describing the foundation of the land of Khotan itself, which is said to be due to the drying up of a lake that resulted from its penetration by the staffs of Śāriputra and Vaiśravaṇa during the time of the historical Buddha, Śākyamuni.

The account then moves forward again, relating the arrival of the first king of Khotan, a son of king Aśoka of India, and his temporary adoption by the emperor of China.[142] This is followed by a list of the eight major tutelary deities of Khotan, the eight "self-originated bodhisattvas" said to be resident in Khotan, and a brief description of the principles followed by adherents of the Mahāyāna, on the one hand, and the *śrāvaka*s on the other.[143] (The account here emphasizes the predominance of the Mahāyāna contingent over the "Hīnayānists.")

Once again the time frame shifts dramatically, as the text now looks into the distant future when Khotan will again become a lake. This is expected to happen, we are told, when the ten *karmapatha*s (i.e., the basic moral precepts)[144] are no longer practiced. In the even more distant future, when the future Buddha Maitreya appears in the world, the lake will again dry up and will offer a place for the worship of Maitreya and his retinue. Then the text interposes a peculiar line: "This *Prophecy of the Li Country* (*yul li-yul-gyi lung-bstan 'di*)," we are told, "is not even to be handled by

---

[142] As Sir Aurel Stein has pointed out in *Ancient Khotan* (Oxford: Clarendon Press, 1907), p. 158, this legendary account (and the similar story that occurs in Hsüan-tsang's travel account) correctly reflects the combination of Indian and Chinese elements in early Khotanese culture.

[143] The Mahāyānists are said to follow the principles (lit. "enter the door," *sgor 'jug*) of non-conceptualization (*rnam-par myi-rtog-pa*) and *śūraṃgama-samādhi* (lines 39–40), while the *śrāvaka*s adhere to the four [noble] truths (line 40).

[144] The ten are: three pertaining to the body (not killing, not stealing, not indulging in sexual misconduct), four to the power of speech (not lying, not slandering, not using harsh speech, and not indulging in frivolous talk), and three to the mind (not falling prey to envy, hatred, or false views).

common people." The text goes on to extol the merits that come from even hearing, let alone reading, the text. In fact, the extant version of the *Prophecy of* [*the Arhat of*] *Khotan* does end with a prediction of Maitreya's advent; it is possible that at least one recension of that text also added a few lines extolling its own merits, and that those lines were copied directly into the "epitome" recorded here. In any case, the *Religious Annals* then turns to what has served as the main subject matter of the other two texts examined above: the decline of Buddhism in Khotan, and the flight of a group of Khotanese monks to Tibet. As in the accounts we have already examined, a group of monks from other cities in the Tarim Basin[145] arrive in Khotan, only to find that the people of Khotan at that time are "without faith in the True Dharma," and show contempt (and in particular, a lack of financial support) toward the sangha. After the usual meeting at Tsar-ma monastery, the assembled monks decide to set out for Tibet, where the emperor is said to have great faith in Buddhism. Vaiśravaṇa and Śrī-Mahādevī once again appear to offer assistance to the wanderers, and the majority of the group arrives safely in Tibet.

The immigrant monks enjoy a period of asylum in Tibet for twelve years, according to this version (cf. the three-year period cited in the other texts). After the death of the Chinese consort, however, the popular mood shifts to an anti-Buddhist position, and the monks are expelled from the country. They then set out for Gandhāra, and at this point the text turns to the narration of

145 The text actually reads "all the sanghas of the four fortified cities of *stod*" (Tib. *stod-kyi mkhar bzhi'i dge-'dun-rnams ril-kyis*). According to Beckwith *stod-kyi mkhar bzhi* is to be understood as a reference to the Four Garrisons (*ssu chen* 四鎮) established by T'ang China in the Tarim Basin region (Beckwith, *The Tibetan Empire*, p. 204, 3d; note that the page reference given there is a misprint, and should be corrected to read "R. Emmerick, 1967:84 [lines 49–50]"). Beckwith's assessment may well be correct; it is also possible, however, that *stod-kyi mkhar bzhi* is the result of a transmission error for an earlier *thod-dkar bzhi* (for Tib. *thod-dkar* see P. Kvaerne, *Acta Orientalia* (Budapest) 34 [1980], 101, and J. Bacot et al., *Documents de Touen-houang* [Paris: Paul Geuthner, 1940], p. 83). This expression would parallel exactly the phrase "the four *tokhri*" still preserved in 9th-century Sogdian texts as *ctβ'r twγr'k* (in Sogdian script) and *ch'r twγryst'*[*n*] "country of the four *tokhri*" (in Manichaean script); see W. B. Henning, *Bulletin of the School of Oriental Studies* 9 [1938], 550–51. The same expression has been identified by Henning (551) in an Uighur text as well (*twγrt twγry*). In either case, it is certain that in the present instance the territory of the Tarim Basin is meant.

the Kauśāmbī story. Two things are immediately striking about the account of the events at Kauśāmbī found in the *Religious Annals of Khotan*: first, the high degree of deformation in virtually all the proper names (a feature indicative of the story's transmission through at least three separate languages), and second, the new set of ethnonyms associated with the three evil kings. As in the *Saṃghavardhana* prophecy, we have here a list that has been reformulated to reflect the concerns of an inhabitant of Khotan, but at a slightly later time period than the one just considered. Now the kings are identified with the Chinese (*rgya*), the Tibetans (*bod*) and the Uighurs (*hor*),[146] a list that would suggest a date of composition not earlier than the late 8th–early 9th century.[147]

The story resembles that given in the *Saṃghavardhana* prophecy quite closely, so much so that it is not necessary to recapitulate the story here. We should note, however, that each of these two texts contains certain details not found in the other, and thus neither work (as it stands) can be directly derived from the other. Of particular interest are the forms of the names and the epithets of the major characters given in the *Religious Annals*. The king of Kauśāmbī is here named *'Dre-spe-sad* (*sic*, for Skt. *Duṣprasaha*), and is described as the son of *Man-'dre-seng-ge* (< *Mahendrasena*). Śiṣyaka's name again appears with the intrusive *r* typical of the *Candragarbha* group in general (Tib. *Shir-zhag* ~ *Zhir-shag*), and it is of particular interest that he is given the title *dri-bi-le* (~ *dir-bi-le*), a Tibetan transcription of the Khotanese title *ttṛvīlei* "tripiṭaka-master," which serves as yet another indication that the text is a translation from the Khotanese.[148] Śiṣyaka's pupil Aṅgada has become *Ang-ghan*, the *yakṣa* Dadhimukha has been transformed into *'Dra-dha-mu-ka*, and Sūrata's name is unexpectedly spelled with a final *-g* (Tib. *Su-rag*).[149] Clearly this recension is the end-product of a long chain of

---

[146] For the term *hor* used in a reference to the Uighurs see above, note 110.

[147] The Uighurs first become a factor in the struggle for control of the Tarim Basin in the 760s. For a detailed account of the Uighur, Chinese, and Tibetan roles in this contest see Beckwith, *The Tibetan Empire*, especially 146–72.

[148] On this term see Emmerick, *Tibetan Texts*, 132a.

[149] Not *Ra-su-rag*, as read by Thomas (*Tibetan Literary Texts*, vol. 1, 316); apparently (judging from Emmerick's edition of the text) Thomas mistook the last character of the previous word as part of the name of Sūrata. Once again this spelling offers evidence of transmission of its antecedent in the Kharoṣṭhī script: the Tibetan letters *ta* ཏ་ and *ga* ག་ do not resemble one another at all, but it is easy to see

copying (and miscopying) of the text. The variation in the name of Śiṣyaka—which appears as both *Shir-zhag* and *Zhir-shag*, spellings that are more similar in sound than in appearance—suggests further that at least some of this transmission may have been via dictation.

The account does not end, however, with the death of the monks at Kauśāmbī. Rather, the text goes on to consider other issues as well: first an enumeration of the various guardian spirits and images appointed by the Buddha to preserve the Dharma in Khotan, then a prescription for dealing with threats of war, invasion, and strife (the believer is instructed to read the the *dhāraṇīs* from the *Lotus Sūtra* and the *Vimalaprabhā-paripṛcchā*). The text then turns to a very different topic: the story of *Shi-ri-dan*, treasurer to an Indian king, who meets a group of Sogdian[150] merchants looking for a victim for a human sacrifice and offers his own body to spare other potential victims. *Shi-ri-dan* is saved from his fate by divine intervention and goes on to become in future incarnations a *nāga* king, then an arhat, then (one wonders at the spiritual trajectory implied here) a *nāga* king again. Finally he receives a prediction to future Buddhahood from Śākyamuni, an event that demonstrates the underlying Mahāyāna perspective behind the story. The text concludes on what would seem (in light of the dire predictions contained in the Kauśāmbī story) to be an inordinately optimistic note: having enumerated the population of the various monasteries in the country of Khotan, the text concludes by saying that "even now there are dwelling among those monks [lit. 'sanghas'] many bodhisattvas, who manifest themselves acting in various ways to bring about the benefit of sentient beings."[151] The Kauśāmbī story has now been relegated to the background: it is still perhaps an important element of the received Buddhist tradition, but is no longer viewed as having the last word on the fate of Buddhism in Khotan.

---

how a Kharoṣṭhī-script final *-ta* 𐨟 could have been misread as *-ga* 𐨒 (see the chart by Rapson in A. M. Boyer et al., eds., *Kharoṣṭhī Inscriptions*). From here it is straightforward to reconstruct an original final *-a* in the Tibetan, omitted in copying through the inadvertent omission of the single dot used to separate syllables in Tibetan.

[150] Tib. *sog-dag*.

[151] Tib. *da-ltar yang dge-'dun de-dag-gi nang-na yang // byang-cub-sems-pa* [*sic*] *thabs-kyis rol-cing sems-shan*[*sic*]*-gyi don mdzad-cing sprul-pa yang mang-du bzhugs-so*.

It is not altogether clear, in fact, whether the Kauśāmbī story is here being treated as a prophecy at all. The text styles itself not a prophecy (Tib. *lung-bstan-pa*) but a "religious annals" (*chos-kyi lo-rgyus*), and the story is consistently related in the past tense. It is striking, in fact—and I believe significant—that this text is the only version of the Kauśāmbī story (with the exception of the prose *Prophecy of Kātyāyana*, which may well be defective in this regard) that offers no timetable at all for the decline of the Dharma. It is possible, though not certain, that the composer of this text believed that the Dharma had in fact already died out in the city of Kauśāmbī, but not yet in his own homeland of Khotan.

In summary, the Khotanese adaptations of the Kauśāmbī story all exhibit a clear reliance (made explicit in two of the three texts) on a version of the *Candragarbha-sūtra* current in the Tarim Basin at the time. They all go beyond the content of that text (or at least of any extant version of it), however, in associating the Kauśāmbī story with the fortunes of Buddhism in the Khotan. In so doing, two of the three texts alter the names of the three evil kings to reflect the names of foreign powers threatening Khotan during the late 7th–early 9th centuries, and in relating the flight of a group of Khotanese monks and nuns into Tibet offer information that allows us to date all three works to a period no earlier than the second half of the 8th century. Finally, though only one of the three (the *Religious Annals of Khotan*) explicitly states that it is a translation from some other (unspecified) language, all three texts offer considerable internal evidence that they are translations based on Khotanese originals. Though they are preserved only in Tibetan,[152] these texts offer us a unique window into some of the religious (and political) concerns of the inhabitants of the Tarim Basin during the 8th and 9th centuries.

SUMMARY: VARIETIES OF THE KAUŚĀMBĪ PROPHECY

We have reviewed a total of thirteen versions of the Kauśāmbī prophecy, representing all the extant versions of the story

[152] The two canonical texts presumably exist in Mongolian translations as well, though the relevant volumes of the catalogue to the Mongolian Tanjur have not yet appeared. For the first three volumes see Rintchen, *Catalogue du tanjur mongol imprimé* (New Delhi: International Academy of Indian Culture, 1964–).

identified to date. Though no Sanskrit or Prakrit original has come down to us, these versions (preserved in Chinese, Tibetan, and Khotanese translations) can still be used to reconstruct the nature of the underlying Indian original. One of our main objectives in the remainder of this study will be to try to identify the context, both spatial and temporal, in which this prophecy was first produced, with an eye toward gaining a greater understanding of the forces that have led to the production of Buddhist decline literature in general.

The nature of the texts reviewed above may be summarized as follows. The earliest extant translation of the Kauśāmbī story is the *Prophecy of Kātyāyana* (verse recension), which has come down to us in a Chinese translation dating from the late 3rd or early 4th century CE. Not only is this an early translation, but it represents an early stage of the Indian tradition as well, for in this recension the prophecy is not yet attributed to the Buddha but to a monk named Kātyāyana. This version is also peculiar in that the names of the three invading kings are given as Rome, Iran, and Parthia—an aberration (with respect to most other versions) that suggests, if the reasoning outlined above is correct, that this recension was produced in Bactria. Nothing in the text allows us to determine with certainty its sectarian affiliation, though the absence of any specifically Mahāyāna elements makes it clear that it must have belonged to one of the Nikāya Buddhist schools. Its prose counterpart, translated into Chinese slightly later (420–479 CE), appears quite garbled, and may tell us more about the inadequate transmission of the story than about the circumstances of its origins. Its reference to "250 monastic rules," however—if not a Chinese interpolation—may point to a period of circulation in a Dharmaguptaka milieu.

A different sectarian orientation is represented by the members of the *Aśoka-avadāna* group, comprised of three texts all of which are products of Sarvāstivādin redaction. Of these, the two Chinese translations were both produced in the 5th c. CE (the *Aśoka-avadāna* toward the end of that century, and the *Saṃyukta-āgama* during the period from 436-443), while the Tibetan member of this group is naturally much later (the *Karmaśataka*, translated in all probability during the first half of the 8th century). In all three of these texts we find the standard list of three invading kings, namely the Greeks, Sakas, and Parthians, though the *Saṃyukta-āgama* adds a fourth king (Skt. **tuṣāra*, presumably a reference to the Kushans) to the lineup. Likewise, in all three of these texts the prophecy is treated as *buddhavacana*, classified as an *avadāna* in two cases and as a sūtra in the third.

Yet another Sarvāstivādin version of the story is found in the scholastic compendium known as the *Mahāvibhāṣā* — or perhaps we should say "versions," for this is actually an epitome based on several versions of the story. Though the *Mahāvibhāṣā* is preserved only in a late Chinese translation (7th century CE), it is clearly based on an Indian text of some centuries earlier. The peculiar character of this version of the Kauśāmbī story is thus due to the fact that it is contained in a scholastic text whose author drew on a number of different sources, and not to a late date of composition.

With the *Mahāmāyā-sūtra* we come to the earliest extant Mahāyāna translation of the story, rendered into Chinese in 479-502 CE. Here the tale is retold only in summary fashion, providing us with little to go on in determining its relationship to other recensions of the prophecy. That it is a Mahāyāna recension is quite clear, however, since it makes reference to Nāgārjuna and Aśvaghoṣa.

Far more detailed are the texts belonging to the *Candragarbha-sūtra* group, which are likewise Mahāyāna recensions. Though Mahāyāna emendations have been introduced in only the most superficial fashion in the Tibetan and Khotanese versions of the text (both dating from around the 8th century CE), the Chinese version (translated during the second half of the 6th century) is far more thoroughly Mahāyānist in character. Once again the three kings are the Greeks, Sakas, and Parthians, though in the Chinese version the word "Greek" has apparently been emended to read "Persian." No major changes have been made in the plot line or in the setting of the story, and it seems fair to say that there is a general continuity throughout all ten of the recensions described above.

When we come to the "late Khotanese adaptations," by contrast, such continuity disappears, for although certain elements have been carried over from earlier versions of the prophecy the setting of the story has been subjected to wholesale alteration, now reflecting the fortunes of Buddhism not in India, but in Khotan. It is hardly surprising that in these versions — all dating from the second half of the 8th century or after, and all representing Mahāyāna recensions of the story — we find major changes in the names of the invading forces, now updated to include such powers as China, the Uighurs, and Tibet. These texts are of particular importance for reconstructing the religious and political concerns of the inhabitants of Khotan during this period, but they add nothing to our knowledge of the circumstances that led to the original production of the tale.

The extant versions of the Kauśāmbī prophecy thus span a period from the 3rd to 8th century CE. And since the dates of translation of these texts provide only a *terminus ante quem* for their original composition, it is likely that the core of the Kauśāmbī story goes back to an Indian original that is even older. Our task in the following chapter, therefore, will be to determine the approximate time and place of the original formulation of this story, and to offer some preliminary suggestions concerning the circumstances that led to its composition.

Chapter Eight

Origins and Transmission of the Kauśāmbī Prophecy

AS WE HAVE SEEN, the Kauśāmbī prophecy appears in a wide variety of sources, and has been told in a number of different ways. Though the prophecy has not been preserved in its original Sanskrit (or far more likely, Prakrit) version, no fewer than thirteen extant versions of the tale have been preserved in the Chinese, Khotanese, and Tibetan languages.[1] A comparative analysis of the contents of these thirteen recensions will enable us to make considerable progress toward identifying both the environment within which the text was first produced and the motives that led to its composition. Such an analysis should provide data that is useful not only for reconstructing the history of the Kauśāmbī story itself, but also for gaining a clearer understanding of the circumstances that have led to the composition of other Buddhist prophecies of the decline and disappearance of the Dharma. Our primary concern in this chapter, therefore, will be to attempt to determine where, when, and under what conditions the prophecy of the demise of the Dharma at Kauśāmbī was initially composed.

In order to locate this environment it is vital to determine, first of all, which of the extant editions of the Kauśāmbī story is the oldest, and thus might bear the closest resemblance to the original. To

[1] A fourteenth version, a Mongolian translation based directly on the Tibetan and exhibiting no variations in content other than those introduced through translation or copying errors, has been dealt with separately and will not be included here. See Nattier, "The *Candragarbha-sūtra* in Central and East Asia," 220–331.

do so we will focus our attention on two types of information contained in the extant recensions of the story: first, the individual components of the plot itself, which vary considerably from one recension to another; and second, the transcriptions (or in other cases, translations) of ten selected proper names. Taken together, these two types of information can provide us with sufficient evidence to construct a lineage chart, or stemma, depicting the relationships among the extant recensions.

Beginning with the first category, we may sort the thirteen versions of the Kauśāmbī prophecy according to the presence or absence of the following elements of the plot: a king named Mahendrasena; a son of the king, named Duṣprasaha; a group of "evil kings" (with special attention to the names, if any, given to their members, and to the total number of kings mentioned); a preceptor of the king, named Śiṣyaka; an arhat named Sūrata; a disciple of Śiṣyaka named Aṅgada; a *yakṣa* named Dadhimukha; the death of king Mahendrasena; the killing of the arhat; the killing of the king's preceptor; the killing of Aṅgada; the death of all monks in the assembly at Kauśāmbī; the presence or absence of Mahāyāna elements in the story; and the specification of the total duration of the Dharma (with special attention to the chronological figures given). By tracking the presence or absence of these fourteen key elements in the story we will be able to identify some of the telltale signs of editorial emendation and expansion in the text, which will provide us with valuable evidence concerning the relationship among the various recensions in this group.

A second body of evidence can be derived from the spellings of proper names themselves (whether in translation or transliteration) found in the various recensions of the Kauśāmbī story. If a certain peculiar spelling is found, for instance, in three texts in this group but not in the other ten, this commonality may serve as evidence that the three texts in question share a particularly close relationship. As we shall see, the evidence provided by the analysis of individual components of the plot is generally corroborated by the forms of these proper names, which fall into similar textual "families."

Beginning with the plot components listed above, if we correlate these with each of the versions of the Kauśāmbī prophecy in the order of discussion given at the end of the previous chapter, we obtain the following chart:

	king named Mahendrasena	prince named Duṣprasaha	number of "evil kings"	preceptor named Śiṣyaka	arhat named Sūrata	disciple named Aṅgada	*yakṣa* named Dadhimukha	Mahendrasena dies	arhat killed	preceptor killed	Aṅgada killed	all monks killed	Mahāyāna elements	duration of Dharma
Kātyāyana (verse)	*	N	3	Y	Y	?	*	N	Y	N	N	N	N	1,000
Kātyāyana (prose)	*	N	3	Y	Y	N	*	N	Y	Y	N	N	N	—
Saṃyukta-āgama	Y	Y	4	Y	Y	Y	Y	Y	Y	Y	N	?	N	1,000
Aśoka-avadāna	Y	Y	3	Y	Y	Y	Y	Y	Y	Y	N	?	N	1,000
Karmaśataka	Y	Y	3	Y	Y	Y	Y	Y	Y	Y	N	?	N	1,000
Mahāvibhāṣā	N	N	2	Y	Y	N	N	?	Y	Y	N	?	N	1,000
Mahāmāyā-sūtra	N	N	0	*	*	*	N	N	Y	Y	*	N	Y	1,500
Ch. *Candragarbha*	Y	Y	3	Y	Y	Y	Y	N	Y	Y	Y	Y	Y	1,500[2]
Book of Zambasta	Y	Y	3	Y	Y	Y	Y	N	Y	Y	Y	Y	Y	1,500
Tib. *Candragarbha*	Y	Y	3	Y	Y	Y	Y	N	Y	Y	Y	Y	Y	2,000
Prophecy of Khotan	*	N	?	N	N	N	N	N	N	N	N	N	Y	2,000[3]
Saṃghavardhana	N	Y	3	Y	Y	Y	N	N	Y	N	Y	Y	Y	2,000
Religious Annals	Y	Y	3	Y	Y	Y	Y	N	N	N	N	N	Y	—

Here the letter Y indicates that a given element is present, N that it is absent, and an asterisk that the character in question appears in the story but is not named. Where it is impossible to determine the presence or absence of an element in the story as we have it, I have simply written a question mark.

It is immediately evident that there are certain patterns in the evolution of the Kauśāmbī story. First, the vast majority of recensions of the story speak of three evil kings (although their names,

---

[2] Figures of 2,000 years and 2,500 years also appear, however, elsewhere in the text (see above, pp. 52–56).

[3] The number 2,000 is replaced by 1,000 in the xylograph editions. See above, p. 190, n. 107.

as we have seen, have varied considerably). Second, the timetables for the life span of the Dharma associated with this story range from 1,000 to 2,000 years, with a clear progression from the earliest recensions (with a figure of 1,000) to the latest ones (with more extended figures). Moreover, the non-Mahāyāna (Nikāya Buddhist) scriptures are unanimous in assigning a figure of 1,000 to the total duration of the Dharma, while in all the Mahāyāna recensions this number has been expanded to either 1,500 or 2,000 years. Third, the preceptor Śiṣyaka and the arhat Sūrata are apparently original elements in the story, for they are present (and so named) in all recensions with the exception of the two texts that only summarize the tale (the *Mahāmāyā-sūtra* and the *Prophecy of Khotan*). The distinction between a father (Mahendrasena) and a son (Duṣprasaha), however, may not be part of the earliest story, since it is absent from the two oldest extant recensions (the two *Kātyāyana* texts). Fourth, the death of King Mahendrasena is apparently restricted to the *Aśoka-avadāna* group and serves as one indicator of the distinctive character of this textual family. Fifth, while in the majority of accounts both Śiṣyaka and Sūrata are killed, the death of Śiṣyaka is not mentioned in the verse translation of the Kātyāyana text and thus may not be an original element of the story. Finally, both the death of Aṅgada and the explicit statement that "all the monks of Jambudvīpa" are killed in the battle at Kauśāmbī must have been added quite late, as these elements are restricted to the *Candragarbha* corpus (in addition to one Khotanese text, the *Saṃghavardhana* prophecy, that drew on that sūtra as one of its sources).

These individual elements in the Kauśāmbī prophecy can thus help us to establish the family relationships within this group. But a second body of data—the renderings of proper names in these texts—provides vital corroborating information. These names (which occur in both translated and transliterated forms) reveal not only the relationships among the surviving texts, but often provide valuable information concerning the languages and/or scripts in which these texts were transmitted. These names have been collected in the Appendix for reference and will not be discussed individually here.[4]

---

4 The main issue in tracking the transmission of proper names is not whether

CONSTRUCTING A STEMMA: METHODOLOGY

In devising the textual lineage chart given below I have followed the methodology used by scholars in Greek and Latin studies to establish the critical edition of a text, as outlined in the standard discussion by Paul Maas.[5] This approach is intended primarily for use in reconstructing the original version of a single text of which multiple copies exist, each exhibiting minor variants, additions, and deletions. In the present case, however, we have not multiple copies of a single work, but widely differing recensions of a given story. With some adjustments, however, the same methodology can still be applied, and this procedure will allow us to determine with reasonable certainty the relationships among the extant versions of the story. The methodology employed here is the following. Any element found in one or more versions of the text, but not in all versions, can be used to sort the texts into family groups. For example, if two versions of the text (which we may call A and B) share a peculiar feature – e. g., the spelling of a proper name – that is not found in any other recension of the story, we may assume (unless other evidence argues to the contrary) that A and B are descended from a common ancestor. If these texts further share another feature (e. g., a distinctive element in the plot) with a third text (C), and this element is not found in any other version of the story, we may assume that these three recensions are related as follows:

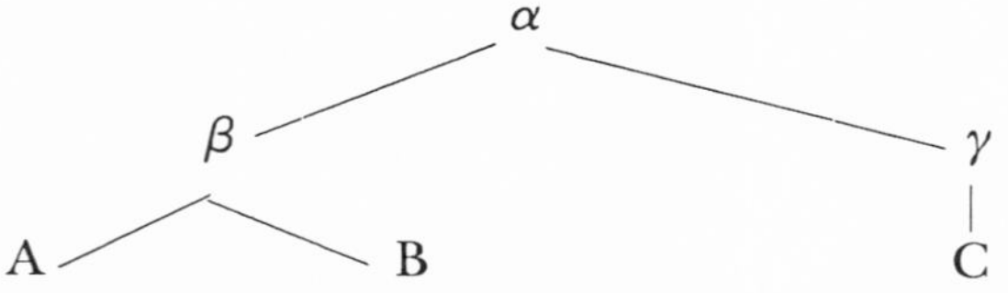

(Following the procedure used by Maas, I have used lower-case Greek letters to indicate versions of the text that have not survived.) By extending this approach to the other texts in the group,

they are translated or transliterated – for within a given group of closely related recensions we may find examples of both – but what original Indian form, or intermediary spelling, underlies a given text. As is usual in such detective work it is the aberrations (misspellings, mispronunciations, and faulty copying of Chinese characters) that can provide the most valuable clues.

[5] Paul Maas, *Textual Criticism*, trans. Barbara Flower (Oxford: Clarendon Press, 1958).

we can derive a diagram depicting the chain of textual transmission of the group as a whole.

In deciding which of any two given variants is to be preferred (that is, is closer to the original), classical textual criticism applies two basic principles: first, when deciding between a shorter and a longer rendition, the shorter is generally the better; and second, the more difficult of any two readings is to be preferred. The first of these principles is based on the assumption that a scribe is more likely to embellish a text (in particular, to add what he sees as helpful explanatory material) than to omit a portion of the text. The second follows a similar line of reasoning; here it is assumed that a scribe may try to clarify an obscure or seemingly corrupt expression by "correcting" it, resulting in a more accessible (but less original) formulation.

There are, of course, certain exceptions to these general rules, and in particular to the first one. In certain cases a scribe may consciously or unconsciously omit material from the text: where a text contains repetitive expressions, for example, the scribe's eye may jump from one occurrence of a common phrase to the next, resulting in the omission of all the material between the two. Such omissions can also be deliberate: in some instances the requirements of new political, geographical, or doctrinal circumstances, differing from those under which the text was first composed, may lead the scribe to make conscious changes in the text. To say that these are conscious, of course, need not imply that the scribe is being deliberately deceptive; he may only see his emendations as restoring what the text must originally have said. Whatever his motives, however, the net result is the same: the removal of offending material from the text, and in some cases its replacement by an alternative passage.[6]

In establishing a family tree of versions of the Kauśāmbī story I have applied these principles as follows: (1) a shorter rendition of the story is presumed to be older than a longer one, *unless* it can be shown that the author (or editor) of the shorter version would have had a reasonable motive for deleting material found in previous versions of the text; and (2) a complex but coherent version

[6] For a useful discussion of the types of errors that can occur in textual transmission see Bruce M. Metzger, *The Text of the New Testament* (New York: Oxford University Press, 1964), 186–206.

of the plot is presumed to be older than one in which the story has been overly, and artificially, rationalized (via extraneous explanations, symmetrical or standardized numbers, and relentless parallelism); a genuinely chaotic account, by contrast, is assumed to represent a degenerate version of an earlier and more coherent text.

There are, however, a few cases in which the application of these principles will not enable us to fit a given version of the Kauśāmbī story within the stemma constructed below. First, an author may deliberately condense a text in order to fit it within the parameters of a specific literary form, in the process omitting material that would have allowed us to determine the ancestry of his version of the text. Second, an author (or editor) may make use of more than one version of the story in preparing his own recension. And finally—since we are dealing not merely with the copying of manuscripts, but with much more extensive developments in a literary tradition—we must also take into consideration the possibility that oral versions of the story may have influenced written ones, and vice versa. In such cases the trajectory of a given version of the story will be extremely difficult to trace, and much of its ancestry may be impossible to reconstruct.

Of the thirteen versions of the Kauśāmbī story discussed above, only two have proved impossible to place within the stemma given below. The first of these, the account preserved in the *Mahāvibhāṣā*, has apparently suffered from two of the three types of alteration just described: the author has clearly consulted a number of different versions of the story in the process of compiling his synopsis, and has further reduced the scope of the story to fit within the stylistic requirements of abhidharma literature.[7] The resulting recension lacks important elements found in all other versions of the text, while simultaneously including other items that occur nowhere else. It is thus impossible to reconstruct the precise connection between the *Mahāvibhāṣā* account and the other extant versions of the story.

The other case for which we have insufficient data is the story contained in the *Mahāmāyā-sūtra*. Here the plot is so brief and contains so few details and proper names that we simply do not have

[7] For a discussion of the stylistic exigencies of the abhidharma genre see above, pp. 149–50.

enough evidence to determine its precise connection with the other texts. This may well be an example of the re-recording of the story in written form after a period of oral circulation, during which many of the more complex elements of the story would have been omitted.[8]

Having eliminated the *Mahāmāyā-sūtra* and the *Mahāvibhāṣā* from consideration, however, the remaining sources can be sorted into textual families with little difficulty. In the chart given on the following page I have provided the names of the extant texts themselves (rather than Roman letters, as in the examples given by Maas) in order to minimize cross-referencing. The Greek letters, by contrast, indicate versions of the text that have not survived, but whose content can be reconstructed with some certainty on the basis of the extant exemplars. For each of these I have given a synopsis of its distinctive content (i.e., those variants of which it is the carrier), literary style, and—where these can be determined—its probable language and sectarian affiliation.

DESCRIPTION OF THE RECONSTRUCTED ARCHETYPE AND HYPARCHETYPES[9]

χ = The original (presumably oral) version of the Kauśāmbī story, for which no independent evidence is available.

α = The reconstructed archetype to which all other versions of the text can be traced. Three foreign kings (the Greeks, Sakas, and Parthians) are named as the cause of disruption within the Indian Buddhist community. A pious Buddhist king (unnamed),

[8] The one text with which the Kauśāmbī story found in the *Mahāmāyā-sūtra* can plausibly be connected is the brief synopsis of the story found in one of the Chinese translations of the (Mahāyāna) *Mahāparinirvāṇa-sūtra* (T No. 374, 12.473c14–474a5). In both of these versions the tripiṭaka-master (i.e., Śiṣyaka) is described as having five hundred followers, a feature found in no other version of the text.

[9] In the terminology used by Maas "archetype" refers only to that exemplar (lost or surviving) from which the first split in textual transmission originated. This exemplar is free from all errors (including accretions and editorial amplifications) arising after the split. The term "hyparchetype," by contrast, is used to refer to all intermediary exemplars, or "variant carriers," to which one or more descendants can be assigned. The letter χ is assigned to the assumed original text, the archetype itself is designated by the letter α, and all subsequent hyparchetypes are designated by β, γ, etc. For further details see Maas, *Textual Criticism*, 2–5.

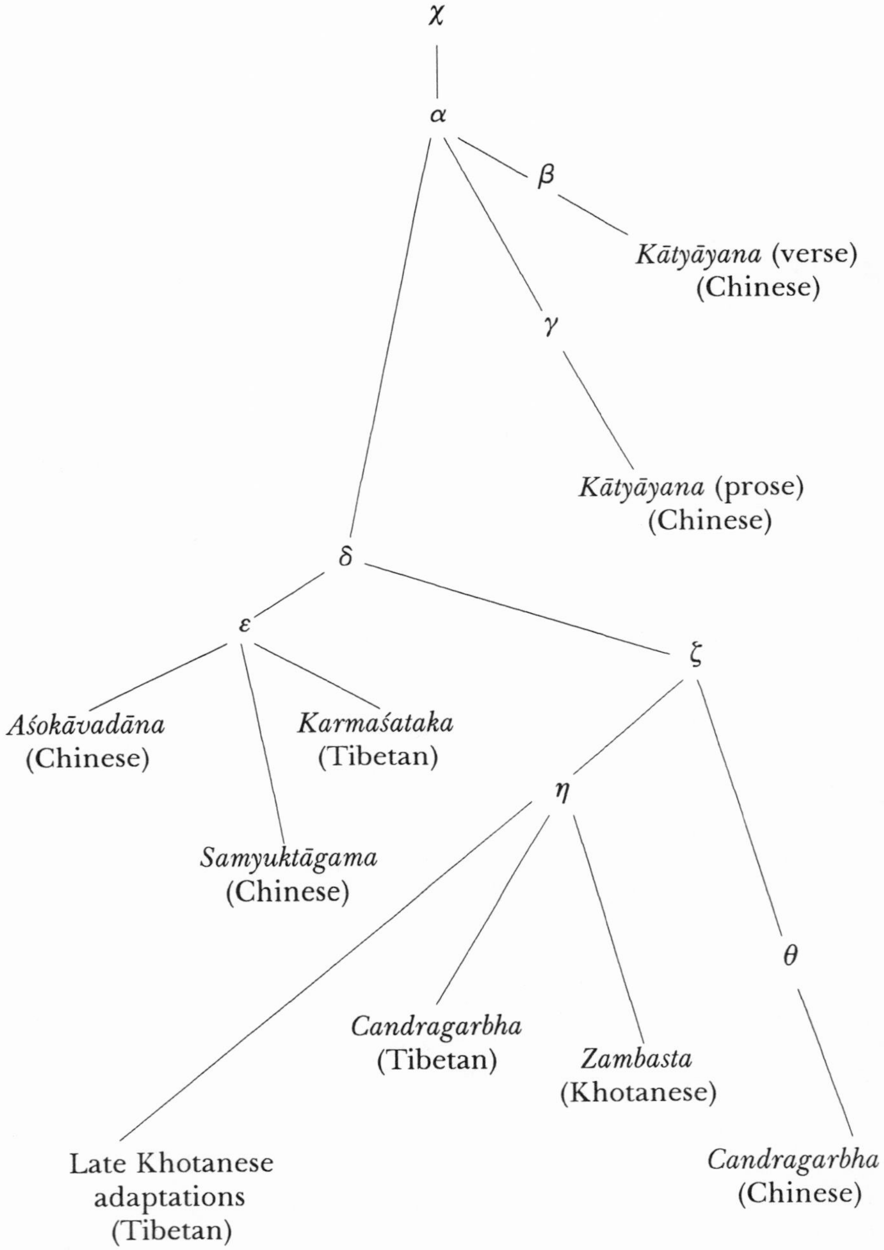
χ
α
β
Kātyāyana (verse)
(Chinese)
γ
Kātyāyana (prose)
(Chinese)
δ
ε
ζ
Aśokāvadāna
(Chinese)
Karmaśataka
(Tibetan)
η
Samyuktāgama
(Chinese)
θ
Candragarbha
(Tibetan)
Zambasta
(Khotanese)
Late Khotanese
adaptations
(Tibetan)
Candragarbha
(Chinese)

ruling at Kauśāmbī, invites all the monks of Jambudvīpa to a *mahādāna* feast at the suggestion of his advisor, the monk Śiṣyaka. A dispute then breaks out between an arhat, Sūrata, who insists on strict observance of all monastic rules, and a group of more complacent monks; Sūrata is killed by a disciple of Śiṣyaka, who in turn is killed by a *yakṣa*.
Not considered a canonical text (that is, *buddhavacana*); attributed to the monk Kātyāyana.
Style: probably entirely in verse.
Language: probably a northwest (e.g., Gāndhārī) Prākrit, in the Kharoṣṭhī script.
Sectarian affinity: uncertain.

β = A Bactrian recension (not, however, in the Bactrian language[10]), similar to α but with the names "Greeks, Sakas, and Parthians" changed to read "Rome, Iran, and Parthians."
Style: entirely in verse.
Language: presumably northwest Prakrit, in the Kharoṣṭhī script.
Sectarian affinity: uncertain.

γ = A somewhat garbled recension of α with a few additional details, including the mention of 250 monastic rules.
Style: either entirely in prose or entirely in verse.[11]

---

[10] Despite ample evidence of the presence of Buddhism in Bactria over a period of several centuries, there is no indication that any Buddhist scriptures were ever set down in writing in the Bactrian language (or for that matter in any of the vernacular langauges of western [now Soviet] Central Asia). It appears, rather, that during the first four or five centuries CE Buddhist scriptures were transmitted across Central Asia to China only in Indian languages (Sanskrit and Prakrit), and that only subsequently—from the second half of the millennium onwards—such scriptures were rendered into the local Central Asian vernaculars, and then only in eastern Central Asia (modern Sinkiang). For a detailed discussion see Jan Nattier, "Church Language and Vernacular Language in Central Asian Buddhism," *Numen* 37/2 (1990), 195–219.

[11] The complex style of much of Indian poetry, together with the common practice of giving no indication of the end of each line (or verse) in written texts, sometimes led to the inadvertent rendering of Indian poetry into prose translations in other languages. This happens less frequently, however, when the Indian original consists of a mixture of prose and verse, since it is a common practice in these texts to set the verse off from the prose in a recognizable fashion.

Language: presumably northwest Prakrit, in the Kharoṣṭhī script.
Sectarian affinity: possibly Dharmaguptaka.

δ = An amplified version of α. The king of Kauśāmbī is now given the name Mahendrasena, and an additional character, his son Duṣprasaha, is introduced. The intra-sangha conflict is now portrayed as a dispute between Sūrata and Śiṣyaka; in the ensuing melée not only are Sūrata and his assailant (here, and possibly in α , named "Aṅgada") killed, but Śiṣyaka is killed as well. Kātyāyana's name is removed as the text moves toward acceptance as a canonical work, and the entire discourse is placed in the mouth of the Buddha.
Style: entirely in verse.
Language: presumably northwest Prakrit, in the Kharoṣṭhī script.
Sectarian affinity: uncertain.

ε = Similar to δ, but with several new elements: a group of five hundred lay disciples is portrayed as criticizing monastic laxity; king Mahendrasena dies, causing a period of depression on the part of his son Duṣprasaha; and following the conflict between Śiṣyaka and Sūrata, Duṣprasaha himself turns against the sangha, killing monks and destroying Buddhist monuments.
Style: mixed prose and verse.
Language: Sanskrit (or Buddhist Hybrid Sanskrit).
Sectarian affinity: Sarvāstivāda.

ζ = Another adaptation of δ, but here all the monks of Jambudvīpa are portrayed as being killed in the conflict at Kauśāmbī. Śiṣyaka's name has been altered (or misunderstood) as *Śirṣaka (or *Śīrṣaka), and an interlocutor named Candragarbha is added.
Style: entirely in verse.
Language: northwest Prakrit (in the Kharoṣṭhī script).
Sectarian affinity: uncertain. Possibly transmitted in Mahāyāna circles.

η = Similar to ζ, but the word Śaka has been altered (deliberately?)

to read Śakuna. Directional locations of the three foreign kings are omitted, and Kauśāmbī is placed in the south, not the east.
Style: uncertain; possibly entirely in prose.
Language: northwest Prakrit (in the Kharoṣṭhī script).
Sectarian affinity: uncertain, but circulating in Mahāyāna circles in Khotan.

θ = A Mahāyāna adaptation of ζ, with additional proto-tantric elements (*dhāraṇī*). The entire story is now incorporated into a Mahāyāna text titled the *Candragarbha-sūtra*, and additional (Mahāyāna-oriented) materials are introduced as a frame for the Kauśāmbī story itself.
Style: in verse, with a brief prose introduction and an extended prose conclusion.
Language: Buddhist Hybrid Sanskrit.
Sectarian affinity: Mahāyāna.

FROM STEMMA TO STORY: RECONSTRUCTING THE ORIGINAL KAUŚĀMBĪ TALE

What, then, can we learn from the construction of such a stemma? In classical textual scholarship the objective is to restore a given text to a form as close to that of the original as possible. Given the far-flung nature of our sources, however—preserved in Chinese, Tibetan, and Khotanese, but not in the original Indian languages—our objective must be much more modest. What we can attempt to do on the basis of the data compiled above is the following: (1) determine with a reasonable degree of accuracy the form of the original (no doubt oral) version of the story; (2) identify the sectarian environment within which the story first arose, or at the very least eliminate certain environments from consideration; and (3) discover whether any important shifts in the content and context of the story have taken place during the course of its transmission.

Beginning with the first of these issues, the stemma constructed above allows us to reconstruct the original tale as a rather simple story, and one not very flattering to the Buddhist community. Eliminating those elements that we can be reasonably sure were added at a later date, we are left with the story of an unnamed king ruling at Kauśāmbī who successfully repels a foreign invasion. At the suggestion of his Buddhist advisor, the preceptor Śiṣyaka, the king then invites the monks from surrounding regions to Kauśāmbī for a religious feast. When these monks come together, however, certain differences in their traditions—more specifically, in the degree of their adherence to the monastic rules—begin to surface. Ultimately this leads to an open and violent conflict, in the course of which a monk named Sūrata—widely acknowledged as an arhat—is killed by Śiṣyaka's student Aṅgada, who believes that the honor of his teacher has been impugned. Since the crime of killing an arhat cannot go unpunished, a *yakṣa* appears to avenge the arhat's death, killing Aṅgada on the spot. This would appear to be the end of the story in its original version. No other monks, in this primitive version, are killed, and the response of the king to this debacle is not revealed. The focus of the story is on Aṅgada's heinous crime of killing an arhat, and on the immediate retribution he receives.

The story is, of course, associated with a prediction of the end of the Dharma even in its earliest surviving recensions. But was this a part of the original tale? Or might the original story simply have been the narration of an actual historical event, which—despite its manifestly uninspiring content—was simply too vivid a memory to be forgetten?

In favor of the latter hypothesis is the fact that the proper names of the main characters—the king's preceptor Śiṣyaka, the arhat Sūrata, and his assailant Aṅgada—are all quite specific (and remain consistent, allowing for a certain amount of deformation in transmission, throughout all extant recensions of the story), as we might expect in an account dealing with actual historical characters. Moreover, with the exception of the name "Śiṣyaka" (which is really more an epithet than a proper name) these names are rather unusual. Were this an entirely fanciful account concocted to illustrate a point, one might expect its creator to have chosen names that were either more common (and thus more accessible) or more explicitly didactic in their content. And if the story had originated as a general prediction of the demise of the Dharma, one wonders if it would have contained any such proper names at all. Would not a straightforward account of a battle in which all the monks of Jambudvīpa are killed, rather than an ambiguous story of the assassination of a single arhat (following which the rest of the monastic community, with the exception of his assailant, is still left alive), have served the purpose better?

In this connection a point well worth our attention is the stance of the narrator himself, which is implicit but quite identifiable in both the early and later versions of the story. Of the two factions—the supporters of Sūrata, on the one hand, and of Śiṣyaka on the other—it seems clear that the narrator exhibits a preference for the former. No criticism of the arhat (or his followers) appears in any extant recension of the story, while in even the earliest versions it is suggested that the preceptor Śiṣyaka (or an anonymous group of monks, in the verse *Prophecy of Kātyāyana*) can be faulted for a lack of rigorous adherence to the teachings. Most revealing, however, is the identity of the figure who avenges the arhat's death. Aṅgada (Sūrata's murderer) is killed not by one of the arhat's own students—which might allow the reader to find fault with this faction—but by a character introduced from outside, as it were, and a non-human one at that. The killing of Aṅgada by a vajra-wielding *yakṣa*[12] thus serves the dual purpose of avenging the grievous crime of arhaticide while simultaneously diverting any guilt for that act of vengeance away from the arhat's own following.

It is possible, then—though this must remain speculative—that the origins of the Kauśāmbī story are to be sought in an actual historical event, as told by a member of the pro-Sūrata faction. Only later, perhaps, was the story shifted into the future and brought into conjunction with a prophecy of the end of the Dharma.

To return to the story as we have it, however—that is, the Kauśāmbī story in the form of a decline prophecy—what can we say about the point of origin of the tale? Beginning with the question of sectarian affiliation we can say with complete certainty that the original story was not a Mahāyāna composition. This is quite clear from the location of the Mahāyāna recensions of the story (which constitute a distinct minority) in the diagram: these are all found toward the bottom of the stemma, and thus are the farthest removed from the original text. Turning to the non-Mahāyāna

---

[12] Or are we to take the term *vajra* here simply in its original sense of "thunderbolt," and to understand that Aṅgada was struck dead by lightning on the spot? In either case, we clearly have here a *yakṣa ex machina*.

candidates, the fact that several extant versions of the story can be attributed with confidence to the Sarvāstivāda school[13] might suggest that the tradition originated in a Sarvāstivādin environment. Here again, however, the results of the stemma would suggest caution, for these versions are clustered suspiciously close to one another in a single branch of the stemma. Thus it is possible that the adoption of the story by the Sarvāstivādins took place only at the level of hyparchetype ε (from which all extant Sarvāstivāda versions are derived), and not at a point closer to its origins.

Other possibilities are rather limited. The Kauśāmbī story is conspicuous by its absence from the voluminous Theravādin literature; thus this school is certainly not a candidate. Aside from the Sarvāstivāda, the only school for which we have a known recension of the story is the Dharmaguptaka school (to which the prose *Prophecy of Kātyāyana* can probably be attributed).[14] And the evidence cited above for the transmission of the story across Central Asia in the Kharoṣṭhī script suggests that we should pay particular attention to this possibility, since the Dharmaguptaka is one of the two schools (the other being the Mahāsāṃghika) known to have used the Kharoṣṭhī script by preference in that region.[15]

[13] Known Sarvāstivāda recensions are those found in the *Saṃyukta-āgama* (Chinese), the *Aśoka-avadāna* (Chinese), and the *Karmaśataka* (Tibetan).

[14] This information must be used with caution, however, since the mention of 250 monastic rules (which is the clue that allows us to establish the Dharmaguptaka affinity of the text) could have been added in China.

[15] The well-known Gāndhārī *Dharmapāda* found near Khotan, written in northwest (Gāndhārī) Prakrit in the Kharoṣṭhī script and dated to around the 2nd c. CE, is most commonly assigned to the Dharmaguptaka school (though, as John Brough has pointed out, other possibilities cannot be excluded; see Brough, *The Gāndhārī Dharmapāda* [London: Oxford University Press, 1962], 44). And in fact use of the Gāndhārī language (which in turn is closely associated with the use of the Kharoṣṭhī script) has been taken by some scholars as sufficient evidence of the Dharmaguptaka origins of the text in question, though Oskar von Hinüber has recently advised greater caution in this regard ("Die Bestimmung der Schulzgehörigkeit buddhistischer Texte nach sprachlichen Kritirien," in Heinz Bechert, ed., *Zur Schulzgehörigkeit von Werken der Hīnayāna-Literatur,* Part I [Göttingen: Vandenhoeck & Ruprecht, 1985], 57–75). As to the Mahāsāṃghika use of the Kharoṣṭhī script (and a Prakrit language), recent excavations at Kara Tepe (old Termez, in Bactria) have shown that an earlier layer of Mahāsāṃghika inscriptions, in the Kharoṣṭhī script, preceded a later group of Sarvāstivādin dedications written in Brāhmī (see J. Harmatta [Ya. Kharmatta], "K interpretatsii indiĭskikh nadpiseĭ na keramike iz Kara-tepe," in B. Ya. Staviskiĭ, gen. ed., *Buddiĭskie peshchery Kara-Tepe v starom Termeze* [= *Kara Tepe*, 2] [Moscow: Nauka, 1969], 32–39). Evidence

It is not possible, then, to establish with certainty the precise sectarian environment within which the Kauśāmbī prophecy first arose. A Dharmaguptaka context seems as likely as any other alternative; yet this hypothesis must remain provisional, and we should also keep in mind that the story may have been the exclusive property of a single school only for a very brief period of time.

What we can say with certainty, however, is that the original Kauśāmbī story was utterly devoid of Mahāyāna content.[16] And indeed when the story finally begins to appear in Mahāyāna contexts the authors seem rather uncomfortable with its pessimistic conclusions, and show signs of attempting to step back from the finality of the extinction of the Dharma that it portrays.[17]

---

from the Chinese canon likewise points to a the use of a Prakrit language (and thus possibly, though not necessarily, the Kharoṣṭhī script) by the Dharmaguptaka and Mahāsāṃghika schools, in contrast to the use of Sanskrit by the Sarvāstivādins (see Ernst Waldschmidt, "Central Asian Sūtra Fragments and their Relation to the Chinese Agamas," in Heinz Bechert, ed., *Die Sprache der ältesten buddhistischen Überlieferung,* Abhandlungen der Akademie der Wissenschaften in Göttingen, Phil.-Hist. Klasse, Dritte Folge, No. 117, 1980, 136–74). In summary, then, while the Sarvāstivādins did make use of the Kharoṣṭhī script (and a Prakrit language) for inscriptions in India itself, by the time they became active in transmitting Buddhism across Central Asia they appear to have shifted to the use of the Sanskrit language and the Brāhmī script.

[16] That a non-Mahāyāna story should be set at Kauśāmbī sometime during the early centuries of the first millennium CE is not surprising. Both Fa-hsien (who visited the area at the beginning of the 5th century CE) and Hsüan-tsang (who passed through the region in the mid-7th century) report that the Buddhist community at Kauśāmbī was composed mostly (according to Fa-hsien) or entirely (in Hsüan-tsang's time) of non-Mahāyānists. (See James Legge, trans., *A Record of Buddhistic Kingdoms* [1886; repr. New York: Dover, 1965], 96, and Samuel Beal, *Buddhist Records of the Western World* [1884; repr. New York: Paragon, 1968], vol. 1, 235.) Fa-hsien does not mention the Kauśāmbī story, and was perhaps unaware of it; he relates a different version of the decline of the Dharma, based on the migration and ultimate disappearance of the Buddha's alms-bowl (Legge, *Record,* 109–10). Hsüan-tsang, however, appears to be familiar with the story, for he states in connection with his visit to Kauśāmbī that "The law of Śākya becoming extinct, this will be the very last country in which it will survive" (Beal, *Buddhist Records*, vol. 1, 237).

[17] A classic example of such editorial emendation is found in the Mahāyāna *Mahāparinirvāṇa-sūtra*, where a brief retelling of the Kauśāmbī story (12.473c14–474a5) is framed by the statements that "the Three Jewels manifest disappearance, but this also is not permanent extinction" (473c), and "My True Dharma is not really extinct! At that time [Kauśāmbī] will have 120,000 bodhisattvas who will righteously uphold my teaching" (474a).

Finally, we come to the third question posed above: whether there have been any identifiable shifts in the content or context of the story over time. Certainly we do find a clear-cut shift in the context of the story in the three texts in the "late Khotanese adaptations" category, where the events at Kauśāmbī are framed by an account of the fate of Buddhism in Khotan. And in one of these texts, the *Religious Annals of Khotan*, we even find a movement away from the prophecy genre toward a historical narrative, and the possible treatment of the story as an event that has already taken place in the past.

As to the content of the story, however, what we find throughout the recensions we have surveyed is a rather striking continuity over the centuries. The main characters, the plot, even the uses to which the story is put remain largely consistent in all the versions surveyed. Only in two of the texts examined above—the Chinese *Candragarbha-sūtra* and the Tibetan translation of the *Religious Annals of Khotan*—do the editors seem uncomfortable with the outcome of the story, and attempt to tone down the pessimistic conclusions it implies.

In summary, the Kauśāmbī story does not exhibit any major deformations in plot due to changing historical circumstances. And it is only when the story reaches Khotan—and then only in texts dating from the 8th–9th centuries—that we find an identifiable shift in the historical context of the story. Likewise, it is only when the story enters a Mahāyāna milieu that we find its editors beginning to tamper with its conclusions—but then for reasons that appear to stem from philosophical, not historical, discontent. Having reconstructed the form and content of the original story as best we can, we may now pause to consider those most elusive issues in Indian Buddhist history: the date and provenance of the tradition.

SOURCES OF THE STORY: THE HISTORICAL SETTING

In establishing the date of the Kauśāmbī story the Chinese sources, as always, are of primary importance, since they can offer at least a *terminus ante quem* for the existence of the story in India. Since the verse translation of the *Prophecy of Kātyāyana* was rendered into Chinese no later than 316 CE,[18] we must assume that its Indian an-

[18] See above, pp. 157–58.

cestor had taken shape no later than the second half of the 3rd century. Moreover, since the verse translation of the *Prophecy of Kātyāyana* appears to represent a Bactrian recension of the story (and is thus one step removed from its Indian ancestor), a conservative approach would suggest that the Indian text must have been in existence no later than the first half of the 3rd century CE.

On the Indian side, a *terminus post quem* is provided by the names of the Greeks, Sakas, and Parthians, who seem to have been mentioned already in archetype α. Though the chronology of this period in Indian history is still extremely problematic, the best current estimate is that the Parthians—the last of these three groups to arrive on the scene—invaded northwest India sometime during the first half of the first century CE.[19] Thus the composition of a decline prophecy containing their names should date from no earlier than the second half of that century. Allowing for a sufficient interval for these historical events to be converted into the stylized myth found in the Kauśāmbī story, we may offer the conservative estimate that the story took shape during the period 100–250 CE.[20]

As to the provenance of the original story, there is no persuasive reason to question the assumption that the events it narrates—that is, the conflict within the sangha and the death of the arhat Sūrata—did indeed take place at Kauśāmbī. To say that the decline prophecy itself was formulated there, however, is another matter altogether. For if the story does indeed relate an actual historical event, a minimum requirement for the conversion of that event into a prophecy is that this historical grounding be forgotten. While it is possible that this process took place at Kauśāmbī, it is more likely that this took place at a considerable distance in both time and space.

Of the extant versions of the Kauśāmbī story, only the version of the *Candragarbha-sūtra* preserved in Tibetan translation offers specific geographical clues as to the area where it was recorded. As we have seen, this text describes Kauśāmbī as being located on the "other, southern side of the Ganges River," while Gandhāra and

---

[19] On the Parthian invasions of northwest India see Frye, *History of Ancient Iran*, 197–204.

[20] This time period, incidentally, would correlate well with the fact that the earliest versions of the story are all associated with a timetable for the duration of the Dharma of 1,000 years, a timetable that appears to have been most popular during the first five centuries CE (see above, pp. 62–63).

Madhyadeśa are said to be located on "this side." This suggests that the Indian recension upon which the Tibetan translation was based stems from the far northwest of India, and possibly from Gandhāra itself.[21]

In addition to this explicit clue, we have also the implicit information offered by the evidence for the transmission of the story in the Kharoṣṭhī script. For this script—a descendant of the Aramaic script used by the Achaemenids when they controlled Gandhāra and parts of the Punjab (c. 550–330 BCE)—never gained widespread currency outside its homeland in the far northwest, and in those Central Asian regions to which it was exported.[22]

If the Kauśāmbī decline prophecy appears to have emerged in northwest India sometime between the beginning of the 2nd century CE and the middle of the 3rd, what can this tell us about the context in which it was formulated? Once again precise chronologies evade us, but throughout most or all of this period northwest India was a part of the powerful Kushan empire.[23] One might wonder, however, at the suggestion that such a prophecy could have emerged out of this setting. Artistic remains from the Kushan period provide ample evidence of a cultural golden age, and available sources strongly suggest that the Buddhist community—though legends of the conversion of King Kaniṣka himself appear to be a pious fiction[24] —flourished under Kushan rule. What, then,

---

[21] See above, p. 178, n. 81.

[22] The well-known lion capital inscription (dating from the Saka period) found at Mathura is the exception rather the rule, and the use of the Kharoṣṭhī script in this instance is an indication of the importation of this script to the region by the Sakas, not of its general local use. For the inscription in question see Sten Konow, ed., *Kharoṣṭhī Inscriptions with the Exception of Those of Aśoka,* Corpus Inscriptionum Indicarum 2, 1 (Calcutta: Government of India, 1929), 30–49.

[23] On some of the vexing problems of Kushan chronology see A. L. Basham, ed., *Papers on the Date of Kaniṣka* (Leiden: E.J. Brill, 1968). Despite a number of international conferences on the topic, no consensus has yet been reached on the dates of Kushan rule. For a wealth of bibliographic references on chronology and other aspects of Kushan studies see Frye, *History of Ancient Iran*, 249–69.

[24] On the supposed conversion of Kaniṣka see John M. Rosenfield, *Dynastic Arts of the Kushans* (Berkeley: University of California Press, 1967), 29–30. Despite the great amount of attention that has been paid to one of Kaniṣka's coins, which portrays a standing Buddha (the earliest known Buddha-image) and the Bactrian legend BOΔΔO (see Rosenfield, pp. 76–77 and Plate V, coin no. 88), it is important to emphasize—as Rosenfield does—that this image is the exception rather than the rule, and that the occasional Buddha images on Kushan coins are far outnumbered by

could have led the Buddhist subjects of such a cosmopolitan realm, presumably enjoying all the material and spiritual benefits afforded by the long-lasting *pax kushanica*, to produce such a prophecy of decline?

Here a close examination of the plot of the story reveals certain details relevant to this question. For it is not the invasions themselves that are portrayed as bringing an end to the Dharma. The events at Kauśāmbī take place after King Duṣprasaha has succeeded in subduing the foreign invaders and has himself become king (and a Buddhist king at that) of all of Jambudvīpa. Likewise, the monks who converge on Kauśāmbī do not do so in flight from invading forces, but at the express invitation of the king, who invites them to an opulent Dharma-feast.

It is not the upheavals of war, then, that lead to the death of the Dharma in this account, but the munificence of a well-intentioned Buddhist king. Moreover, it is the Buddhist community itself—or more specifically, some of its more complacent and self-satisfied members—whose actions result in the death of an arhat, and ultimately in the disappearance of the Dharma from the world. In a sense, then, we have come full circle, finding ourselves in the presence of yet another account attributing the demise of the Dharma to causes internal to the sangha itself.

Viewed in this light, the Kauśāmbī prophecy makes good sense as the product of a Kushan environment. As a tale of events set in a period of post-invasion prosperity, the account portrays quite well the circumstances that must have obtained during the two or three centuries of Kushan rule. And though once again (given the less than adequate nature of our sources) this hypothesis must remain provisional, there is no significant evidence to contradict the Kushan provenance of the prophecy,[25] and a considerable amount to support it.

---

deities drawn from other (especially Iranian) religious traditions.

[25] The reference to the *t'ou-sha-lo*—i.e., the Tokharians or Kushans—as a fourth "evil king" (found in the Chinese translation of the *Saṃyukta-āgama*; see above, p. 153 and note 18) need not contradict this hypothesis, since it is an isolated occurrence found only in a Chinese translation dating from the mid-5th century. The archetype α—which is the only version I am suggesting was produced under Kushan rule—clearly contained a list of only three kings.

Chapter Nine

The Tibetan *Candragarbha-sūtra*: Text and Translation

THIS CHAPTER CONTAINS a critical edition of the Tibetan version of the *Candragarbha-sūtra*, together with an annotated English translation. Because of the large number of Tibetan recensions used in preparing this edition and because of the substantial divergences among them, I have followed certain special procedures outlined below.

THE TIBETAN TEXTS

The critical edition given here has been prepared on the basis of five xylograph copies (belonging to the Narthang, Peking 1, Peking 3, Derge, and Lhasa editions of the Kanjur) and one manuscript copy (found at Tun-huang) of the Tibetan *Candragarbha-sūtra* in its entirety. In addition I have consulted the *History of Buddhism* (Tib. *Chos-'byung*) composed by the great 14th-century scholar Buston, in which more than 80% of the sūtra is quoted verbatim.[1]

Ordinarily the procedure used in producing a critical edition of a Tibetan text would be to simply collate all the available ver-

[1] For an English translation see Obermiller, *History of Buddhism (Chos-hbyung)*, Part 2, 171-77. The Tibetan text itself has been published in Lokesh Chandra, ed., *Bu-ston's History of Buddhism. Tibetan Text from the Collection of Prof. Dr. Raghu Vira* (New Delhi: International Academy of India Culture, 1971). For the Kauśāmbi story see folios 867 (118a according to the Tibetan pagination), line 4, through 873 (Tib. 121a), line 7.

sions, noting the variant readings in the critical apparatus. In the present case, however, the divergences among the various manuscript and xylograph copies proved too substantial to make this practical. In fact, the texts fall into three distinct groups, reflecting the continual elaboration and editing of the text in Tibet.

THE TUN-HUANG MANUSCRIPT

By far the oldest of the extant versions of the text is the Tun-huang manuscript, which I have transcribed from the original kept in the India Office Library division of the British Museum in London.[2] It is probably to be assigned to a date not later than the mid-9th century CE., the last period of effective Tibetan control in the Tun-huang area. In any case it is not later than around 1000 CE., the date at which the cave containing this and thousands of other manuscripts was sealed. The text is a manuscript copy on coarse paper in palm-leaf format, with a string-hole at the center of each page. With the exception of the first page (where the text is written on one side only, with seven lines on the page), the text is written on both sides of each folio, with nine lines per page.

The orthography of the text is typical of Old Tibetan of the imperial period. The letter *m* is regularly written with a subscribed *ya* when followed by the vowel *i* or *e* (e.g., *myes* for classical Tibetan *mes*, *myi* for classical *mi*, and so on). The *'a-chung* (འ་) is applied in positions where classical orthography does not require it, in particular following the nominal suffix *-pa* (e.g., *bka'-stsal-pa'* for classical *bka'-stsal-pa*). The letter *i* is almost invariably written in the reversed position (i.e., ྀ for classical ི), which I have indicated in the edited text by underlining the letter *i̲* when it is written in this form. Letters that are aspirated in classical orthography are sometimes unaspirated here (e.g., *c* for classical *ch* in *byang-cub-sems-dpa'*), and vice versa (e.g., *-s.ho* for classical *-so* in the final stop, as in the well-known closing formula *rdzogs-s.ho*, a reading regularly retained in the Peking xylograph Kanjur as well). Other archaisms can be observed in the spellings of various suffixes (e.g., *nub-te* for classical *nub-ste*, *gcig-du* for *gcig-tu*, *nad-gyis* for *nad-kyis*, and so on), in the reading *las-stsogs-pa* for classical *la-sogs-pa*, and in

---

[2] See La Valleé Poussin, *Catalogue*, p. 185, text no. 601.1. The current catalogue number in the India Office Library is J601.1.

the spelling *ched-po* (which occurs frequently, though not consistently) for classical *chen-po* "great." In two instances the scribe has placed an initial *nga* before a base consonant, a position in which it does not occur in the classical language. Thus we find *ng.gsol* ངགསོལ་ for classical *gsol*,[3] and *ng.ni* ངནི་ for classical *ni*.[4]

Two syntactic features are worthy of note. First is the placement, in one instance, of the word *lnga* "five" before (rather than after) the word it modifies,[5] a feature that is maintained in the xylograph editions of the *Candragarbha-sūtra* and is also attested in other Tun-huang materials.[6] Second, the plural suffix *-rnams* is frequently (though not consistently) treated as a free-standing collective noun, connected to the previous word or phrase by a genitive particle.[7]

Finally, with respect to punctuation the text exhibits the tendency (likewise common in Tun-huang texts) to place a *shad* (|) at the end of each line, regardless of whether or not this is syntactically appropriate, a procedure that produces some rather odd sentence divisions when the symbol is taken as a genuine punctuation mark.

The separate treatment of the Tun-huang manuscript in the critical edition can be justified by its antiquity alone, as well as by the numerous respects in which it diverges from the blockprint editions. I have therefore edited it separately, labeling it "T" in the critical edition.

---

[3] §15, line 11.

[4] §24, line 5.

[5] This occurs in the expression *lnga mngon-par shes-pa-zhig*, "one who possesses the five *abhijñā*s" (§12, lines 1–2).

[6] The expression ordinarily rendered *phung-po lnga-po*, "the five *skandhas*," in classical Tibetan regularly appears as *lnga phung* in the manuscript copies of the shorter *Heart Sūtra* (a version not found in the Kanjur) discovered at Tun-huang. These manuscripts, which seem to represent a Tibetan translation based on a Chinese (not a Sanskrit) original, are the subject of an article in progress by John R. McRae and myself.

[7] See, for example, the expressions *sems-can srungs-ma'i̲ rnams* (§6, line 2), *chos-la bgegs byed-pa'i̲ rnams* (§8, line 3), and *dge-'dun-gyi̲ rnams* (§18, line 1). This same usage is preserved in one instance in the Narthang version as well (*mchod-rten-gyi rnams*, §8, line 8 and n. 13).

THE NARTHANG GROUP

Of the five xylograph editions consulted in the preparation of this edition it is somewhat surprising that the Narthang and not the Peking edition is the most archaic, since the woodblocks for the Narthang edition were completed only in 1732, while the Peking 1 and 3 editions (discussed below) date from 1692 and 1720, respectively. The Narthang edition, however, maintains readings approximating those of the Tun-huang manuscript in a number of cases where the other xylograph copies, including the two Peking editions consulted, have been substantially revised. Due to typesetting considerations the Narthang edition has not been treated separately here, but is simply included as one of the xylograph versions of the text (labeled "X" in the critical edition). The version quoted in Bu-ston's *Chos-'byung* is, as one would expect, closer to the Narthang than to any of the other xylograph editions.[8] Though Bu-ston's citation from the sūtra has not been incorporated into the present critical edition, a comparison of his text with that of the Narthang xylograph is available elsewhere.[9]

The version of the Narthang edition cited here is that of the xylograph edition, printed in black ink on rough paper, kept in the Harvard-Yenching Library at Harvard University (text No. 343, *mdo-sde a*, 331a1–336b6).

OTHER XYLOGRAPH EDITIONS

The remaining xylograph editions—drawn from the Peking 1 (P1), Peking 3 (P3), Derge (D) and Lhasa (L) editions of the Kanjur, respectively—are quite close to one another in most respects, and can be thought of as variants of a single version of the text. Most of the divergences within this group are relatively minor. The Peking version (in particular, Peking 1) shows the greatest number of archaisms, as one would expect. In a number of cases P1 has

[8] On Bu-ston's involvement in the editing of the Zha-lu canon (an expanded version of the "Old Narthang" edition) see D. S. Ruegg, *The Life of Bu ston Rin po che*, Serie Orientale Roma, vol. 34 (Rome: Istituto Italiano per il Medio ed Estremo Oriente, 1966), pp. 20-35.

[9] See Nattier, "The *Candragarbha-sūtra* in Central and East Asia," pp. 146-47 and 156-95. Readers with a special interest in the Narthang edition of the text will also find it treated separately here.

maintained an approximation of the spellings of proper names found in the Tun-huang and Narthang versions, while the other xylograph editions (including P3) have been emended to bring the spellings into conformity with their presumed Sanskrit originals.

Since the P3 version is simply a newer printing from the P1 woodblocks with certain intermediate changes and corrections in carving, the catalogue and page numbers of these two versions are identical (No. 1025, *mdo sna-tshogs ke*, 225a1–229b2). For P1 (the earliest known xylograph edition of the Peking Kanjur, printed from blocks completed in 1692) I have used the blockprint edition kept in the Harvard-Yenching Library, a pale but legible version printed in now-faded red ink on thick paper of good quality. The copy of this Kanjur kept at Harvard is of particular interest in that it contains hand-made corrections that correspond, in a number of instances, to the emended carvings that appear in later Peking blockprint editions.

For P3 (a slightly later version, incorporating corrections to the woodblocks made through 1720) I have used the Ōtani University photoreproduction of the Peking Kanjur (Kyoto, 1930). Though the two versions agree in most respects, there are certain striking divergences between them, particularly in the case of proper names (e.g., P1 *Shir-sha-ka* vs. P3 *Shi-ṣya-ka* in §16, line 3 and n. 7). Where such divergences occur, P1 generally concurs with the Tun-huang and Narthang readings, while P3 corresponds with the later xylograph editions.

The Derge (No. 356, *mdo-sde a*, 216a5-220b5) and Lhasa (No. 364, *mdo-mang a*, 342a6–349a7) editions—printed from blocks completed in 1733 and 1933, respectively—represent the most recent versions consulted, and these two editions agree with one another in most respects. Certain predictable deviations do occur, most noticeably in the inveterate tendency of the Lhasa editors to place a *shad* (|) after virtually every occurrence of the word *dang*, regardless of its grammatical function, and to emend the unpleasant phrase *the-tsom zhus-pa* ("asked [concerning one's] doubts") to *chos zhus-pa* ("asked [concerning the] Dharma"). For both Derge and Lhasa editions I have used blockprint copies kept in the Harvard-Yenching Library. The Derge Kanjur is printed in red ink (still vivid as of this writing) on paper of moderate thickness and fair quality, while the Lhasa Kanjur is printed in black ink on thin, good-quality paper, and is widely renowned for its high degree of legibility. The Cone edition, in virtually all respects a derivative of the Derge, has not been consulted, as it is likely to provide little if any independent information.

RELATIONSHIP AMONG THE TEXTS

A careful analysis of the content of the Tibetan versions of the *Candragarbha-sūtra* (in particular, the spellings of proper names and the form of any material found in some but not all versions of the text) makes it possible to determine with a high degree of accuracy the relationship among the seven versions consulted. This information can then be used to produce a stemma (following the methodology outlined in chapter 8) depicting the nature of these relationships. Only the Lhasa edition must be excluded from the chart, since it represents an intra-Tibetan "critical edition" in itself; that is, the editors of the Lhasa Kanjur consulted a number of different editions of the Kanjur in preparing their own edition. Excluding the Lhasa version, then, the relationship among the various editions of the Tibetan *Candragarbha-sūtra* can be diagrammed as shown on the following page.

As the form of this stemma suggests, all seven versions can ultimately be derived from a single archetype (indicated by the letter α). There is no evidence that the text was translated into Tibetan more than once; rather, all of the extant versions are descendants of a common ancestor.

EDITORIAL EMENDATION IN THE XYLOGRAPH EDITIONS

Though the extant Tibetan versions can be traced to a single antecedent, in one respect we must look to a source beyond the *Candragarbha* itself to explain the content of the late (i. e., non-Narthang) xylograph editions. In these versions—that is, the Peking, Derge, and Lhasa editions—the proper names in the text have been subjected to emendation in two respects: the transliterated spellings found in the earlier editions are "corrected" to approximate their presumed Sanskrit originals, on the one hand, and these transliterations have been supplemented by etymological translations into Tibetan, on the other. These changes clearly represent an effort on the part of the editors toward bringing the text into conformity with the standards of classical Tibetan translation procedures: that is, the ideal of basing all Tibetan translations on a "correct"

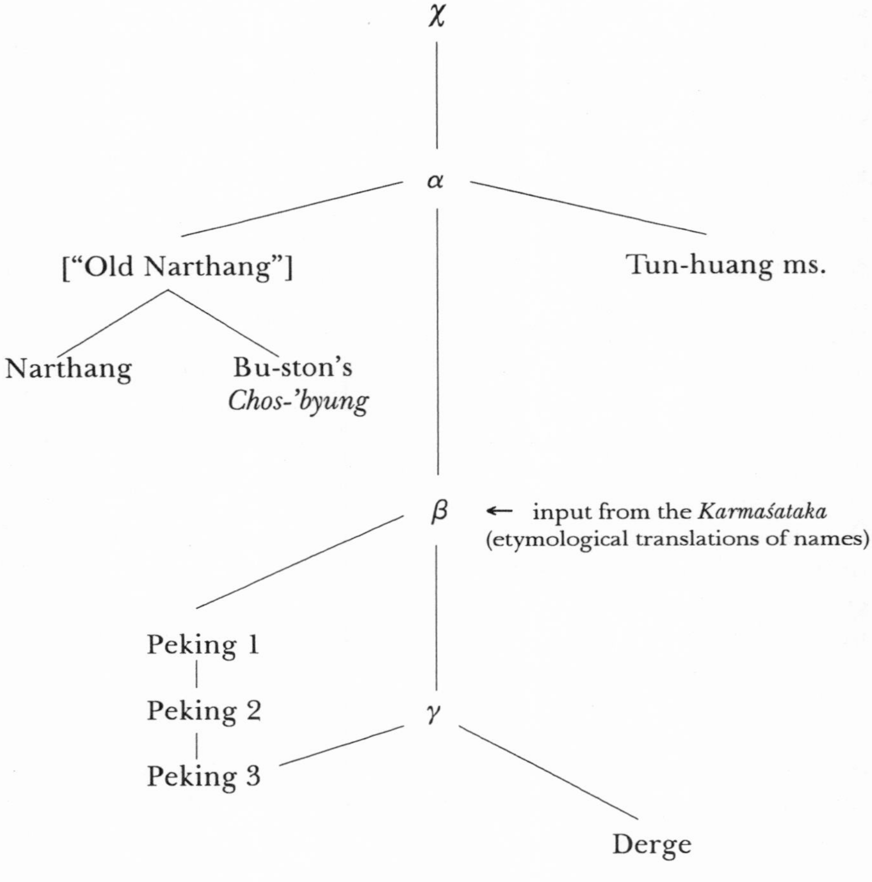

Tibetan versions of the Candragarbha-sūtra

In the diagram given above the letter χ refers to the original Tibetan translation of the text, for which no independent evidence is available; α refers to the archetype from which all extant versions can be derived; β represents an amplified version, to which certain additional explanations of the plot as well as Tibetan translations of a number of transliterated personal names have been added; and γ represents a "re-Sanskritized" version of β, in which those transliterated personal names that had suffered from deformation in transmission have been restored to their presumed original Sanskrit spellings. The "Old Narthang" edition of the Kanjur, a manuscript version whose existence is known from references in Tibetan historical sources, is no longer extant. The Peking 3 edition (or possibly Peking 2, a version I have not yet had the opportunity to examine) was revised in light of the changes introduced in γ, hence the double descent lines indicated for Peking 3.

Sanskrit text, on the one hand, and the policy of rendering all foreign (usually Sanskrit) names into Tibetan translation—not merely transliteration—on the other.

What is peculiar about the changes introduced into the Tibetan *Candragarbha* text, however, is that the insertion of etymological translations *precedes* the correction of the transliterated names. Thus we find in several cases Tibetan translations that correspond not to the transliterated names given in the text, but to the corrected transliterations added only in later editions. An example from the Peking 1 edition will suffice to illustrate this phenomenon. Here the name of the tripiṭaka-master is transliterated as *Shir-sha-ka* (a form that corresponds to the spellings found in the Tun-huang and Narthang editions); it is also translated into Tibetan, however, as *Slob-ma-can*, "he who has disciples" (Tib. *Shir-sha-ka-ste / Slob-ma-can zhes-bya-ba-zhig*, §15, lines 10–11). The transliterated name *Shir-sha-ka*, however—if it were connected with any Sanskrit or Prakrit antecedent at all—would certainly have been derived from *śīrṣaka* "one possessing a head" (< *śīrṣa* "head, skull; top," MW 1078c), not *śiṣyaka* "one possessing disciples" (< *śiṣya*, "student, disciple," MW 1077a). This nonconformity between the transliterated name and its etymological translation strongly suggests that these translations were introduced by the Tibetan editors from another source.

We need not look far to discover what this source might be. In addition to the *Candragarbha-sūtra*, a total of four other versions of the Kauśāmbī story are known to exist in Tibetan (three in the "late Khotanese adaptations" category, the fourth in the *Karmaśataka*). Of these the *Prophecy of Khotan* contains no proper names at all (with the exception of the name of one of the three evil kings), while the *Religious Annals of Khotan* and the *Prophecy of the Arhat Saṃghavardhana* give virtually all proper names in transliteration. In the *Karmaśataka*, however, all the proper names have been translated into Tibetan, and the correspondences between these translations and those introduced into the Tibetan *Candragarbha-sūtra* at the level of hyparchetype β are striking. The transliterated name *Agnidati* (not, we should note, an exact reconstruction of the Indian original, which must have been **Agnidatta*) is rendered *Mes-sbyin* in the *Karmaśataka*, and *Mes-byin* in the *Candragarbha-sūtra*. Śiṣyaka appears as *Slob-ma-can* in both versions, while Sudhana (the father of Sūrata) is translated as *Tshong-dpon nor-bzangs* in the *Karma-*

śataka, and *Tshong-dpon nor-bzang* in the *Candragarbha-sūtra* (*-bzangs* in P1). Sūrata appears as *Des-pa* in both versions, and the name of the *yakṣa* Dadhimukha is likewise identical, being rendered as *Zho-gdong* ("curd-face") in both. Most telling of all, however, is the rendering of the name of Śiṣyaka's student Aṅgada in these two texts. The word *aṅgada* means in Sanskrit "a bracelet worn on the upper arm" (see MW 7c); inexplicably, however, the late xylograph editions of the Tibetan *Candragarbha-sūtra* render this name as *Aṃ-ga-da-ste Dpung-gi tshogs 'jigs-su rung zhes-bya-ba* ("the one called Aṅgada, that is to say, 'Fearful Assembly of the Upper Arm,'" §21, line 3). The expression *Dpung-gi tshogs* is almost certainly an editor's (or copyist's) hypercorrection of an original *dpung-*[*gi*] *rgyan*, "upper-arm ornament," which the copyist must have felt to be an error for the far more common expression *dpung-gi tshogs*, "assembly of *dpung*," that is "armed forces" (in which *dpung* is understood as "army" rather than "[upper] arm"; note the similar semantic associations of the two terms in English and in Tibetan). And indeed the *Karmaśataka* renders this name as *Dpung-rgyan*, "upper-arm ornament." But where did the *Candragarbha-sūtra*'s editors get the extraneous element *'jigs-su rung*, "fearful"?

A glance at the relevant section of the *Karmaśataka* provides a ready answer. There the character Aṅgada is introduced in the following phrase: *de-nas Slob-ma-can-gyi slob-ma Dpung-brgyan zhes-bya-ba 'jigs-su rung-ba de langs-te smras-pa*, that is, "Then *Slob-ma-can*'s student—that fearful one (*'jigs-su rung-ba de*), called *Dpung-brgyan*—got up and spoke [as follows]."[10] What has happened here is obvious: the emenders of the *Candragarbha-sūtra* simply mistook Aṅgada's epithet *'jigs-su rung-*[*ba*] "fearful" for a part of the translation of his name.

There is no question, then, that it was the *Karmaśataka* that served as the source for the emendation of hyparchetype β of the *Candragarbha-sūtra*. And while this is only an isolated example, it provides an intriguing glimpse into some of the methods used by the editors of the Tibetan canon.

---

[10] Peking No. 1007, *mdo-sna-tshogs su*, 285b1. The same name is spelled *-rgyan* in the verse (line 2).

ENGLISH TRANSLATION OF THE TIBETAN TEXT: METHODOLOGY

The style of the Tibetan *Candragarbha-sūtra* poses a number of challenges to the translator. First, though the text is cast in the form of a prophecy and should thus be written uniformly in the future tense, all the Tibetan recensions occasionally lapse from future forms into the past. Ideally one would want to reproduce these lapses in the English translation to give the reader a clear idea of the nature of the original. This degree of literalness, however, would be problematic in at least two respects. First, not all recensions exhibit these lapses in tense in the same places; thus the task of reproducing each variant would make the translation hopelessly cumbersome. Second, there is not a simple one-to-one correspondence between the English past tense and the Tibetan perfective. What is often described as a "past tense" in Tibetan is in fact simply an indication of a completed action, and that completion may as well take place in the future as in the past. I have therefore maintained the future tense throughout the translation, leaving it to the specialist to consult the critical edition for a complete record of these variants.

Another difficulty is presented by the less than elegant character of the Tibetan text itself. The Tibetan translation is repetitive, even awkward, in places. In an attempt to be as literal as possible—short of sinking into utter unreadability—I have generally repeated words unnecessarily when the Tibetan does, and have left long and convoluted sentences largely as they are. Where additional words not found in the Tibetan are necessary to save the English from total opacity, I have provided these in brackets.

Because the translation given below is based on a large number of manuscript and xylograph copies, I have employed a special set of techniques in rendering the text into English. First, I have used the symbol { } to indicate material that is found in one or more—but not all—versions of the text. Most frequently this is material that is absent from the earlier (Tun-huang and Narthang) editions, but has been added in the Peking, Derge, and Lhasa xylographs; occasionally the reverse is true. In each instance I have indicated in a footnote which versions do, and do not, contain this material. In other cases, where certain versions of the text have not simply added new material, but have substituted one word or phrase for another, I have generally translated the reading of the oldest version (that is, the Tun-huang manuscript) and have given the alternative reading(s) in a footnote. Only where the Tun-huang edition is clearly corrupt have I adopted the reading of a later version; in these cases the content of the Tun-huang version is discussed in a footnote. For those interested in comparing the Tibetan versions with translations into other languages, variants in proper names are of particular importance. I have therefore provided all variant readings of proper names in the footnotes.

While such textual variants are given in footnotes (ordered alphabetically) at the bottom of each page, more general issues of content are discussed in endnotes (identified by number rather than letter). Here the reader will find discussions of such matters as grammatical usage, etymological issues, and Buddhist technical terms. In both footnotes and endnotes the recensions consulted are abbreviated as follows: T (Tun-huang ms.), N (Narthang), D (Derge), P1 (Peking 1), P3 (Peking 3), and L (Lhasa). Other symbols used in the text and translation follow the conventions listed above (see "Special Symbols," page xvi). For convenience of reference both text and translation have been arbitrarily divided into twenty-nine sections, marked by numbers in brackets in the left margin.

The resulting translation, based as it is on a total of six original texts, is thus somewhat experimental in format. Some readers may find the inclusion of *all* the words found in *any* of the texts a bit distracting. This method, however, offers one important advantage. The synoptic presentation of the content of all six texts provides an x-ray view of the process of growth and development undergone by the *Candragarbha-sūtra* as it was continually expanded and "corrected" by its Tibetan editors. By making these layers visible within the English translation as well as within the critical edition of the Tibetan text, I hope to make this information available to all readers, whether they have access to the original Tibetan or not.

*ĀRYA-CANDRAGARBHA-PARIPṚCCHĀ-SŪTRA[1]

[1] {The Prophecy (*vyākaraṇa*) of the Way the Buddha's Teaching Will Endure and Be Destroyed, from the *Ārya-Candragarbha-paripṛcchā-sūtra*.}[a]

[2] {Formerly}[b] the Buddha, the Lord Śākyamuni, was dwelling at the top of Mt. Khadiraka,[c,2] and at that time—when the great-powered ones (the bodhisattva-mahāsattvas of the ten directions together with [their] retinues, arhats, gods, *nāga*s, *yakṣa*s, *gandharva*s, *asura*s, *kiṃnara*s, *mahoraga*s, *garuda*s, *māra*s and so on[3]) had all assembled [there]—at that time from the space between the eyebrows on the face of the Buddha, the Lord Śākyamuni, there came forth a ray of light, completely permeating [with] the ray of light the four continents: Videha in the east, Jambudvīpa in the south, Aparagodanīya in the west, and Uttarakuru in the north. At the time when the ray of light was sent forth, it shone equally on Mt. Meru[d] in the center and the rest of the great mountains, and on all the [ordinary] mountains, woods, medicinal valleys, mountain caves,[e] and ravines,[4] and all four continents were illuminated and became visible, as if [they were in] the palm of one's hand. And from those rays of light there emerged a host of Buddha-forms,[f] luminous and of various colors and shapes. And all [those] {many}[g] sentient beings—bodhisattvas, {gods,}[h] *nāga*s and so on—saw them, and were amazed.

[3] Then the four great[i] kings—Vaiśravaṇa[j,5] and so on—said to the Lord Śākyamuni, "A ray of light like this—for what reason was it produced?" And the Lord replied, "After I have attained nirvāṇa, the scriptures of the True Dharma (*saddharma*) that I have pronounced, [my] relics, and [my] images will arise like this [i.e., will

---

[a] X only.
[b] Not in P1.
[c] T *Kha-dhiṛhag*, N *Kharhi-hag*, P1 *Kha-dhi-rhag*, P3,D,L *Kha-rhi-rhag*.
[d] T *ṛi Mye-ro 'bar-ba*, N *Me-ro bar*, X *Ri-rab*.
[e] T *sla-sul*, N,X *ri-sul*.
[f] T,N *sangs-rgyas phal-po-che'i sku-gzugs*, X *sangs-rgyas-kyi sku-gzugs*
[g] X only.
[h] Not in T.
[i] N,X *chen-po*, T *ched-po* (henceforth not noted).
[j] T,P1,P3 *Be-sha-ra-ma-na*, N *Bai-shrar-ma-na*, D,L *Bai-shra-wa-na*.

appear everywhere] in the four continents. These I shall commit[6] into your hands. Protect [them]!"

[4] Then the bodhisattva Candragarbha said to the Lord, "O Lord, it is a great kindness[k] [on your part] that, out of such great kindness as this, the True Dharma will be committed to the great kings after the Lord has entered nirvāṇa. If after the nirvāṇa of the previous Buddha [i.e., Kāśyapa] the reflection of the True Dharma (*saddharma-pratirūpaka*) disappeared after [only] seven years had passed,[7] how long will the True Dharma endure after the Lord Śākyamuni has attained nirvāṇa?" Then the Lord replied, "It is good that you have asked [concerning] your doubts[m] in this way. Listen well, and I shall explain [to you]. After I have attained nirvāṇa, the reflection of the True Dharma will endure for two thousand years."

[5] The bodhisattva Candragarbha asked, "O Lord, how will this True Dharma finally[n] disappear? For what reason will it decline, and who will bring it to an end?" [The Lord] replied, "After {I}[o] have attained nirvāṇa, during a period of five hundred years there will be many sentient beings who will practice my teachings and attain liberation. Then again, during a [second] period of five hundred years, there will be many who practice contemplation (*samādhi*).[8] But even though {many}[p] kings and {ministers and ordinary}[q] sentient beings will believe in the True Dharma and practice it, afterwards they will become few. Then, during a [third] period of five hundred years, there will appear many teachers who will teach the True Dharma, lead sentient beings, and cause them to attain liberation. [But] as to *śravaka*s and arhats, they will become few. Kings, {ministers,}[r] and ordinary sentient beings[9] will be reduced to merely listening [to the teaching]; they will not take it to heart and practice it, nor will they exert themselves, and their faith (*śraddhā*) will decrease. The protectors of the True Dharma will be displeased, and the power of sentient beings who do not be-

---

[k] T,N "it is a great kindness" (*thugs-rje che'o*), X "it is very marvelous" (*shin-tu ngo-mtshar-to*).

[m] L *chos zhus-pa* ("asked [concerning] the Dharma").

[n] T *mtha'*, N,X *tha-mar*.

[o] Not in T.

[p] N only (*sems-can phal-po-che*).

[q] X only (*blon-po dang / sems-can phal-rnams*).

[r] Not in N.

lieve in the True Dharma will become greater than before. The kings of Jambudvīpa will lead armies to and fro against one another, and will do battle. {[And] the party of Māra will increase.}[s]

[6] Then at the time of the [next] five hundred year [period], as for [the first] three hundred years, the protectors of sentient beings who dwell in the True Dharma—gods, *nāga*s and so on—will not remain, {but will go [elsewhere] to spread the True Dharma.}[t] {Sentient beings will no longer believe in the Dharma.}[u] Even those sentient beings who practice the Dharma will not practice it in accordance with the basic Dharma texts. Because [their] efforts are small, their attainments will be few. The four [principal] colors[10] and those derived from the four will decline, and {smell,}[v] taste, and so forth will diminish. And human diseases, animal diseases, and famine will arise.

[7] In [the final] two hundred years, even monks will not practice in accordance with the True Dharma. They will seek worldly profit and fame; their compassion will be meagre, and they will not live according to the precepts (*śikṣā*). They will put down those who do practice in accordance with the True Dharma, and will cast aspersions upon them. They will steal [their] valuables and necessities. Relying on assassins[w] of worldly kings, they will grasp at the kingdom. Acting as the king's messengers, they will go about seeking profit. They will sow discord between kings and their subjects, and will search for ways to trade and make a profit. Even those who do practice the True Dharma will not do so having truly taken it to heart. [Rather,] they will occupy themselves with all sorts of frivolous talk, casual activities, and playful vacuities.

[8] At that time all the gods and *nāga*s who delight in the Dharma will abandon the land where the monks of the kingdom act in such a way, and will not remain, and the party of those who obstruct the Dharma—the party of Māra and so on—will arise there, and their power and strength will increase. Kings, ministers, and so on will decline in faith; they will no longer perceive the distinction between virtue and vice, and they will do harm to the True Dharma.

---

[s] Not in N.

[t] Not in N; X reads *dam-pa'i chos gang-du dar-bar 'gro-bar 'gyur* ("will go to where the True Dharma is spreading").

[u] Not in T.

[v] Not in T.

[w] reading *gsang* ("secret") as an error for *gsad* ("killer").

They will make use of the treasures of the Three Jewels and the goods of the sangha and will steal them, and they will not shrink from sin. They will gradually destroy images and stūpas,[x] and the goods [used for] worship will diminish.

[9] At that time there will remain a few monks and householders who will practice the True Dharma without error, and because of their merit (*puṇya*) there will exist[y] {a few}[z] happy countries where rain will fall in the region at the proper times, {harvests will be good,}[aa] and human and animal diseases will be few. But for the great numbers who do not live in this way,[ab] various kinds of sufferings and unhappiness will arise.

[10] At that time there will arise three great Indian and non-Indian[11] kings—the three [being] Greek,[ac] Parthian,[ad,12] and Saka[ae,13]—and these three will not practice the True Dharma. Leading armies and waging war, they will annihilate many territories in the west and north. {Then}[af] they will destroy and set fire to the stūpas, temples, and so on in those territories, and they will steal and appropriate the materials [used for] worship and the treasures belonging to the Three Jewels. These three kings will inflict various kinds of harm on one another, and the kingdoms of the three of them will become unhappy. After that, the three kings will join forces and, having united their many armies, they will seize and take over the countries of India. At that time they will seize and take over the countries on this side of the Ganges[ag] River—the countries of Gandhāra,[ah] Madhyadeśa,[ai] and so on.[14]

[11] At that time, on the other side of the Ganges, on its southern bank, in the country of Kauśāmbī[aj] a son will be born to the king

---

[x] T *gzugs-brnyan dang mchod-rten-gyi̱ khams*, presumably an error for *-gyi rnams* (as in N).

[y] T,N *yod*; X *'byung* ("will arise").

[z] X only.

[aa] Not in T.

[ab] X "in that way" (*de-lta-bu*).

[ac] T *ya-bha-na*, N *yā-ba-na-ha* [*sic*], X *ya-ba-na*.

[ad] T *pa-la-ba*, N *ba-la-bā*; X *ba-lhi-ka* ("Bactrian").

[ae] T *sheg-ku-na*, N *shi-ku-na*, X *sha-ku-na*.

[af] X only.

[ag] T,N *'Ga'-'ga'*, X *Gang-gā*.

[ah] T *'Ga'-'dha-ra*, N,P3 *'Gan-dha-ra*, P1 *Bgan-da-ra*, D,L *Gan-da-ra*.

[ai] T *Mad-dha-dhe-sha*, N *Ma-ha-de-sha*, P1,P3 *Ma-dhya-de-sha*, D,L *Ma-ddya-de-sha*.

[aj] T *Ke'u-sham-'byi̱*, N *Ko'u-sha-bi*, P1,P3 *Ke'u-sham-bhi*, D,L *Ko'u-shām-bī*.

named Mahendrasena.[ak] His name will be called Duṣprasaha,[al] and he will be born with an iron mole between his eyebrows and with his arms covered with blood from the elbows down. At the same time, to five hundred ministers {of that king}[am] there will be born five hundred sons, all born with their hands bloody from the wrists down. At that time to the king {'s horse}[an] there will be born a foal that is able to speak. And that evening {when these have been born to the king, his ministers, and [his] horse,}[ao] showers of blood will fall from the sky.

[12] Then King Mahendrasena[ap] will ask a seer-preceptor (*ṛṣyupadhyāya*) possessed of the five[15] superknowledges (*abhijñā*), "The birth of sons to our retinue and such a marvel as this to [my] horse, and the falling of a rain of blood—of what is this an omen?" And the seer will reply, "Your son will soak this territory of Jambudvīpa with blood. And afterwards, your son will become the king of [all] Jambudvīpa."

[13] When twelve years have passed from the time that prince is first born, at that time the assembled armies of 300,000 of the three kings Greek,[aq] Parthian,[ar] and Saka,[as] together with the kings [themselves], will invade the country of King Mahendrasena.[at] And because of the arrival of these vast armies in [his] country, the king will be cast down and will be in distress. His son Duṣprasaha[au] will ask his father, "Father, why are you so cast down?" And when he says this, his father will reply, "I am unhappy because the armies of the three [great?] kings have appeared in our country." When he says this the son will reply, "Father, do not be unhappy! {Do not be unhappy!}[av] I shall take on these armies." And when he says this

---

[ak] T *Mhen-dra-se-na*, N *Ma-he-na-'dra-se* [*sic*], X *Ma-hen-dra-se-na*.

[al] T *Drus-sprha-lha-hra*, N Tu-pra-sa-ha, P1,P3,D *Du-spra-sa-ha-sta*, L *Du-sbra-sa-ha-sta*.

[am] X only.

[an] X only.

[ao] X only.

[ap] T *Men-drha-se-na*, N *Ma-he-na-'dra-se-na*, P1,P3 *Ma-hen-gra-se-na*, D,L *Ma-hen-dra-se-na*.

[aq] T,X *Ya-ba-na*, N *Ya-ba* [*sic*].

[ar] T *Pa-la-ba*, N *Ba-lā-ba*, X *Ba-lhi-ka*.

[as] T *Shag-ku-na*, N,X *Sha-ku-na*.

[at] T *Men-dra-se-na*, N *Ma-he-na-'dra-se-na*, X *Ma-hen-dra-se-na*.

[au] T *Du-spra-ba-sam* [*sic*], N *Du-pras-has*, P1,P3 *Du-spra-sa-ha-sta*, D,L *Du-spra-sa-hasta*.

[av] T only.

the father will reply, "Good!"

[14] Then his son, the five hundred marvelous [sons] of the ministers, and so on will assemble an army of 200,000 and send it forth. And having done this, during the battle the iron mole between the eyebrows [of the prince] will grow prominent, and his entire body will become [like] iron; and filled with wrath, he will fight. The army of Duṣprasaha[aw] will be victorious, and upon their return his father will say, "Son, it is good that you have fought with armies like these of the three kings and have been victorious. From now on, you take over the kingdom. As for me, I shall go forth [as a monk]." [The king] having so instructed him, the son will take over the kingdom.[ay] Then, having fought with the armies of the three kings for twelve years, [Dusprasaha] will destroy all [their] many armies.[ay] And having seized the three kings, he will put them to death. And from then on, he will become the great king of Jambudvīpa.[az]

[15] Then the king will say to[ba] the ministers, "I am happy to be king of Jambudvīpa, but there is still one thing that makes me unhappy." And when he speaks thus, the ministers will say, "What is it that makes you unhappy?" When they have asked him that, the king will reply, "I am unhappy because of the great sin of having killed so many sentient beings. What can I do to purify this sin?"[bb] When he speaks thus, the ministers will reply, "In the country called Pāṭaliputra[bc] {that is to say, 'Possessing a Red Son'},[16] there lives in a hermitage-place a Dharma-master who knows the tripiṭaka, the son of the brahman Agnidatta[be] {that is to say, 'Fire-given Son'},[bf] a son named Śiṣyaka[bg,17] {that is to say, 'He Who Has

---

[aw] T,N *Du-spra-sa-ha*, P1,P3 *Du-spra-sa-ha-sta*, D,L *Du-spra-sa-hasta*.

[ax] X "he will give the kingdom to his son" (*srid kyang bu-la byin-no*).

[ay] X "he will also destroy all their military officers" (*dmag-dpon yang ril-gyis gtubs*).

[az] T "the king[s] of Jambudvīpa will be annihilated" (*'Dzam-bu-gli̲ng-gi̲ rgyal-po myed-par gyur-ro*, where *myed* is a copying error for *byed*).

[ba] N,X *smras-pa*, T "will ask" (*dris-pa*).

[bb] N replaces the last sentence with "having committed a sin like this, by whom will it be purified?" (*sdig-pa 'di-lta-bu-zhig-tu byas-nas / sus 'byang-bar 'gyur*).

[bc] T *Ba-da-li̲'i-pod-tra*, N *Bo-da-li-po-tra*, P1 *Ba-ta-li-bu-tra*, P3 *Pa-ṭa-li-phu-tra*, D,L *Pa-ṭa-li-pu-tra*.

[bd] X only.

[be] T *Ag-na-tra-ta'i̲ bu*, N *A-kan-dra-dha'i bu*, P1,P3 *Ag-ne-ta-ti-bu-tra*, D,L *Ag-ni-da-ti-pu-tra*.

[bf] X only.

[bg] T *Shi̲r-sha-ga*, N,P1 *Shir-sha-ka*, P3 *Shi-ṣu-ka* [*sic*, where *-ṣu-* is a copying error

Disciples'}.[bh] If you invite him {and do homage to him,} he will be able to purify your sin."

[16] When they say this the king will be delighted, and he will send a summons to the monk Śiṣyaka.[bi] And [Śiṣyaka] will come into the presence of the king. Then the king will bow before Śiṣyaka[bj] the preceptor and will ask, "{O preceptor,}[bk] the sins that I have committed—by what means can they be purified?" When he says this, the preceptor will reply, "O great king, if you worship the three jewels and take refuge in them for a period of twelve years, [your] sins will be purified."

[17] Then [the king] will send a summons to all the monks living in Jambudvīpa,[bl] and they all will come and assemble on the other side of the Ganges,[bm] {at the place} where {Duṣprasaha,}[bo] the king of the country of Kauśāmbī,[bp] is dwelling. And as a result, the other regions of Jambudvīpa will become devoid of practitioners of the Dharma {and of monks}.[bq] At the time when those monks assemble, many will have perished along the way, only 100,000 will arrive at the king's court. Those monks who have perished along the way, moreover, will have perished by being carried off by various wild animals, human savages, water, and so on. When many sanghas[18] [do] arrive, the king will offer them a religious feast, and will do homage to them with offerings.

[18] At that time, when the sanghas exchange news with one another—each saying "Where is your preceptor? Where have [your] students gone? Where are your companions and fellow practitioners?"—when they have given out the news that they were killed by

---

for -*ṣya*-], D,L *Shi-ṣya-ka*.

[bh] X only.

[bi] See note bg.

[bj] T *Shir-she-ka*, N,P1 *Shir-sha-ka*, P3,D,L *Shi-ṣya-ka*.

[bk] X only.

[bl] X replaces the first portion of this sentence with "Then King Duṣprasaha will send many messengers to the ten directions, and all the monks of Jambudvīpa . . ." (*de-nas rgyal-po Du-spra-sa-ha-stas pho-nya mang-po phyogs-bcur btang-ste*). P1 and P3 then add "and [they] will summon all the monks in Jambudvīpa" (*'Dzam-bu'i gling-na dge-slong 'dug-go-cog bkug-te*).

[bm] T,N *'Ga'-'ga'*, X *Gang-gā*.

[bn] X only.

[bo] X only.

[bp] T *Ke'u-sham-'byi*, N *Ko'u-sha-bi*, P1 *Ke'u-sham-ha* [*sic*], P3 *Ko'u-sham-ba'i*, D,L *Ko'u-shām-bī*.

[bq] X only.

tigers, lions, and human savages, [or] carried off by water, [or] were struck by illness and died, the monks will each be distressed, and overcome by sobs they will beat their breasts. Then at that time the king will bid them "Do not be upset! Do not weep!" [But] the sanghas will not heed him. And the king too, having become unhappy, will turn his face aside and fall asleep.

[19] While he is sleeping he will make a vow: "Now in these worldly sanghas there will be no refuge.[br] Let me see the face of an arhat!" And when he has made that vow, a god of [this] world will reveal to him in a dream: "On the mountain Mt. Gandhamādana,[bs] {that is to say, the mountain called 'Having the Smell of Incense'}[bt] there is dwelling {an arhat,} Sudhana's son[bv,19] {that is to say, 'Son of the Merchant "Good Wealth",' a renunciant named}[bw] Sūrata[bx] {that is to say, whose name is called 'Of Good Nature,' who has attained the fruit of arhat[ship].}[by] If you invite him, {honor him, and confess [your] sin to him,} [your] sin will be purified, and your doubts will also be removed," thus he will reveal. And having dreamed [this], when the king awakens he will again send out a messenger. And having invited {the arhat Sūrata from Having-the-Smell-of-Incense Mountain},[ca] [the arhat] will come {to the king's palace}.[cb] And the king will do homage and bow to the arhat.[cc]

[20] At that time, at the time of the evening of the fourteenth day,[20] from among all the assembled sanghas [some] newly arrived

---

[br] X replaces this sentence with "Although I have taken refuge in and done homage to the sangha of [ordinary] people, I have not seen the face of an arhat" (*gang-zag-gi dge-'dun-la ni skyabs-su song-nas mchod-pa byas-na | bdag-gis dgra-bcom-pa'i zhal ma-mthong-ste*).

[bs] T *K.han-dha-ma-ha-ya-na'i̱ ri*, N *Gan-dha-ma-ha-na'i ri*, P1 *Gan-da-ma-ya*, P3,D,L *Gandha-māda-na*.

[bt] X only.

[bu] T,N only.

[bv] T *S.hu-dha-ra-sh.ha-na'i̱ bu*, N *Su-rad-sha-na'i bu*, P1 *Su-dha-rha-sha-na*, P3 *Su-dha-na-pu-tra-ra-tna-sha* [*sic*], D,L *Su-dhana-pu-tra-ra-tna-sa*.

[bw] X only.

[bx] T *Su-rad*, N *Su-ra-da*, P1 *Su-dha-dha*, P3 *Surat*, D,L *Su-ra-ta*.

[by] X only.

[bz] X only.

[ca] X only.

[cb] X only.

[cc] X replaces this sentence with "And the king, bowing to him in the [proper] manner, will honor and do homage to him."

monks will ask the tripiṭaka-knower Śiṣyaka,[cd] the preceptor, to explain the Vinaya.[ce] [But] Śiṣyaka[cf] will say, "To a man who is blind, and has no nose or ears, what need is there for a mirror? What will he [be able to] see? Even if I explain the Vinaya, you will not act according to the Vinaya. To those who do not keep the Buddhist precepts (*dharma-śikṣā*), what is the use of explaining the Vinaya?" And when he speaks thus, at that time the arhat will speak with the voice of a lion: "From the time when I first took the Buddhist precepts until now, I have not harmed so much as [a blade of] *kuśa* grass. Do not say such words. Explain the Vinaya!"[cg]

1] And when he says this, Śiṣyaka[ch] the preceptor—having realized that [Sūrata] is an arhat—will be deeply ashamed, and will not say a word. The monk named Aṅgada[ci] {that is, "Fearful Assembly of the Upper Arm" [sic]},[cj,21] who is Śiṣyaka's[ck] disciple, will arise from among those assembled together and will [shout] angrily at that arhat named Sūrata,[cl] "How can you say these words to my preceptor? You don't keep [lit. 'have'] the precepts,[cm] and you don't know the Vinaya! So why do you despise my preceptor, who possesses[cn] the tripiṭaka?" he will rage [at him]. And seizing a door-bolt, he will strike the arhat and kill him.

2] At that time a Dharma-loving *yakṣa* named Dadhimukha,[co] {[that is,] "Curd-face Dīrghamukha"}[cp] will appear grasping a vajra in [his] hand, and will say to the monk Aṅgada,[cq] "Why did you kill an arhat?" And bringing out the vajra, he will kill him. At

---

[cd] T *Shi̱r-sha-ka*, N,P1 *Shir-sha-ka*, P3 *Shi-ṣu-ka*, D,L *Shi-ṣya-ka*.

[ce] X replaces "explain the Vinaya" with "recite the *Prātimokṣa*" (*prā-ti-mo-kṣa gden-pa*).

[cf] T *Sher-sha-ka*, N,P1 *Shir-sha-ka*, P3 *Shi-ṣu-ka*, D,L *Shi-ṣya-ka*.

[cg] X replaces this sentence with "Recite the *Prātimokṣa*!" (*prā-ti-mo-kṣa thon-cig*).

[ch] T *Shi̱r-she-kya*, N,P1 *Shir-sha-ka*, P3 *She-ṣu-ka*, D,L *Shi-ṣya-ka*.

[ci] T *A-gandhe'i̱* [*sic*], N *A-ka-de*, P1 *A-gan-ti*, P3 *Aṃ-ga-ta*, D,L *Aṃ-ga-da*.

[cj] X only.

[ck] T *Shi̱r-she-ka*, N,P1 *Shir-sha-ka*, P3 *Shi-ṣu-ka*, D,L *Shi-ṣya-ka*.

[cl] T,N,P1 *Su-rad*, P3 *Su-rat*, D,L *Su-ra-ta*.

[cm] Following N and X, which read *khyod khrims kyang med* "you do not have the precepts," vs. T *khyod khri̱ms-zla yang myed* "you do not have fellow practitioners."

[cn] N,X read "who knows the tripiṭaka" (*sde-snod gsum-ka mkhas-pa*).

[co] T *'Dhi̱d-dha-mu-kha*, N *Di-ta-mu-kha*, P1 *Dir-rga-mu-kha*, P3,D,L *Da-dhi-mu-kha*.

[cp] P3,D,L only. Note that P3 reads *Dir-nam-kha'* [*sic*] for the *Dir-rga-mu-kha* of the other two versions.

[cq] T *A-gan-la*, N *A-ga-di*, P1 *A-gan-ti*, P3 *A-gad*, D,L *Aṃ-ga-da*.

that time a monk named Kedāra[cr,22] will strike Śiṣyaka[cs] the preceptor and kill him. Then after that[ct] the sanghas will all fight and kill one another; and not a single one will remain [alive].

[23] At that time {from}[cu] the sky the tears of the gods, *nāgas* and the rest of the host of *dharmapālas* who will be unhappy and weep will fall {to the ground}[cv] as a rain of blood and fire. The skies will become yellow and black, and there will be lightning and thunder. From the body [of] a star named Dhūmaketu[cw] what looks like black smoke will come forth, and then[cx] the moon, stars, and so on will be deprived of their light, and not a single one [of them] will be visible. At that time the gods of the *trayastriṃśa* heaven—mother Mahāmāyā[cy] and the rest—together with [their] numerous retinues will arrive there, gather up all the colored robes of the sangha, and carry them off.

[24] At that time the king will say, "What is the cause of such a great hue and cry as this?" And [his retinue] will tell him, "the sanghas have fought and killed one another." And the king will be unhappy and will get up and go at dawn to the temple outside the castle. Some of the monks will have their heads cut off, some their hands and feet cut off,[cz] some their eyes plucked out. And when he sees that they have died in those various ways, having found the bodies[da] of the arhat and of Śiṣyaka[db] the preceptor, who knew the tripiṭaka, [the king] will place one under each arm[dc] and say, "The arhat was my mother;[dd,23] Śiṣyaka[de] was my Dharma-treasury. [Now that] these two have passed away, from now on I do not care even

[cr] T,N,D *Ge-rad*, P1 *Gi-rang*, P3 *Ge-rang*, L *Gi-rad*.

[cs] T *Shi̱r-she-ka*, N,P1 *Shir-sha-ka*, P3 *Shi-shuka*, D,L *Shi-ṣya-ka*.

[ct] N,X *de'i rjes-la*, T *rdo-rje'i̱ rjes-la*, "after the vajra" [*sic*].

[cu] N only; accidentally omitted in T, changed to *-la* ("in") in X.

[cv] T,N only.

[cw] T *'Du-mu-ge-ta*, N,P1 *Du-ma-ke-du*, P3 *Du-ma-ke-du*, D,L *Dhū-ma-ke-tu*.

[cx] T,N *de-nas*, X "by that" (*des*).

[cy] T illegible; N *Māhāmaya*, P1 *Ma-ya-dem-bi*, P3 *Ma-ya-de-ba'i*, D,L *Mā-yā-de-bi*.

[cz] Following the reading of N and X; T has *rkang-po bcag* ("their legs were injured").

[da] N,X "having searched for the bodies of the arhat and of Śiṣyaka the preceptor, who knew the tripiṭaka, and finding the bodies of the two of them."

[db] T *Sher-sha-ka*, N,P1 *Shir-sha-ka*, P3 *Shi-shu-ka*, D,L *Shi-ṣya-ka*.

[dc] Lit "placing them at his right and left armpits."

[dd] T,N *ma* "mother"; X *pha* "father."

[de] T *Shi̱r-she-kha*, N *Shir-shā-ka*, P1 *Shir-sha-ka*, P3 *Shi-ṣu-ka*, D,L *Shi-ṣya-ka*.

for my [own] body and soul (*jīva*). As to [the] kingdom, I shall give it to whoever wants it." And when he has spoken thus, his eyes will become dark, and he will be unable to see.

25] At that time the ministers will take pity upon the king, and in order to relieve his suffering they will disguise five hundred men as [Buddhist] mendicants (*bande*).[24] Not cutting [their] hair and beards with a razor, they will burn their hair and beards with fire. Since the one hundred and ten[df] kinds of dyes will also have disappeared at that time, the five hundred *bande* will be unable to obtain monastic robes and will put on black[dg] and red animal hides.[25] And having disguised themselves as *bande*, they will go before the king.

26] The ministers will say to the king, "Five hundred *bande* have arrived." The king will be delighted. His eyes will open, and when he looks at[dh] the *bande*, he will not see that they are all dressed in animal skins, and that their hair and beards have not been shaved, but are burned with fire.[di] The king will be delighted, and will order [his retinue] "Bring me the materials to do homage to the three jewels!" {And he will do homage to the *bande*.}[dj]{When the king examines the *bande* closely, he will see clearly that they are dressed in monastic robes [made of] animal skins, and that their hair and beards have not been shaved, but burned with fire. Then the king will grow doubtful. "These are surely not monks," he will think [to himself], "let me question them a bit."}[dk]

7] When the king asks {the *bande*}[dl] concerning his doubts,[dm] {they will not know a single thing about the Dharma.}[dn] {Not one of them will know even a little bit about monks' views, precepts, and religious practices, so they will not answer the king, but will sit saying nothing. And the king will think [to himself]: "Now look

---

[df] X "one hundred" (*brgyas*).

[dg] Bu-ston changes this unexpected color to read "yellow" (*ser*). For further discussion of this passage see endnote 25 to this chapter.

[dh] X "when he examines" (*brtags-na*).

[di] The Tun-huang ms. is totally corrupt here; it reads *myes ma-btab-bar mthong-nas*, "seeing that they are not struck by fire."

[dj] Not in T.

[dk] X only.

[dl] T only.

[dm] N "when the king asks [concerning] the Dharma" (*rgyal-pos chos dris-pa-dang*), X "when he asks what the monks' views and precepts are" (*dge-slong-gi lta-ba dang tshul-khrims gang yin zhes dris-na*).

[dn] T,N only.

how the Buddha's teaching has disappeared, and the way of the three jewels is completely cut off!"}[do] And the king will be overcome by {great}[dp] suffering and will weep. {Then the king}[dq] will take all the many dead bodies of the many *bande*[dr] and will cremate them and do homage to them. {And after that the king himself, his heart pained by the fact of the disappearance of the teaching, will pass away.}[ds,26]

[28] At that time, on that occasion, the True Dharma (*saddharma*) in Jambudvīpa will completely disappear. {And even the letters of the scriptures will become invisible, as if one erased a conch shell.}[dt,27]

[Then] gold will become bad silver and stone.[du] As to silver, it will become brass.[dv] Brass will become copper {and iron will become stone.}[dw] Jewels and pearls will turn to horn. Of the six flavors of food,[28] four—sweet,[dx] {sour, and salty flavors}[dy] and so on—will disappear. [And only] two—the bitter and the pungent[dz]—will remain.

[29] The {occasion of the}[ea] prophecy {[concerning] the way in which the teaching will endure and be destroyed after the nirvāṇa of the Buddha},[eb] from the {sūtra}[ec] requested {of}[ed] the Buddha Śākyamuni by the bodhisattva-{mahāsattva}[ee] {Ārya-}[ef] Candragarbha is ended.[eg]

[do] X only.

[dp] X only.

[dq] X only.

[dr] N "having collected all the dead bodies of the *bande*" (*ban-de shi-ba'i ro ril-gyis bsdus-nas*); X "having taken the corpses of the many *bande* who had been killed and died" (*ban-de phal-po-che btungs-te shi-ba'i ro-rnams blangs-te*).

[ds] X only; P1,P3 replace "pass away" (*'das-so*) with "come away" (*'ongs-so*).

[dt] X only.

[du] X "gold will become silver" (*gser ni dngul-du 'gyur-ro*).

[dv] N "will become bad brass and stone" (*ra-gan ngan-pa dang rdor 'gyur*); X "will become copper and iron" (*zangs dang lcags-su 'gyur-ro*).

[dw] X only.

[dx] T *dngar-zhi̱ng zhi̱m-ba*, N *mngar-zhing zhim-pa*, X *mngar-ba*.

[dy] X only.

[dz] T *cub-pan*, N *rtsub-pa*; X "astringent" (*bska-ba*).

[ea] X only.

[eb] X only.

[ec] X only.

[ed] Not in T.

[ee] T only.

[ef] X only.

[eg] T,P1,P3 *rdzogs-s.ho*, N *rdzogso*, D,L *rdzogs-so*.

NOTES TO THE TRANSLATION

[1] This Sanskrit title is a reconstruction based on the Tibetan and does not occur in any extant version of the text. Its absence may be due simply to the fact that this text is an excerpt from a longer work, which presumably would have carried such a Sanskrit title only at the beginning. We should note, however, that during the imperial period such Indian titles were apparently not used, and those that appear in the much later Kanjur editions may well be later reconstructions based on the Tibetan (see Marcelle Lalou, "Les textes bouddhiques au temps du roi Khri-sroṅ-lde-bcan," *Journal Asiatique* CCXLI [1953], 313–53 [p. 315]).

[2] Mt. Khadiraka, one of the seven mythical "great mountains" said to surround Mt. Meru (La Vallée Poussin, trans., *Abhidharmakośa*, ch. 3, §48b–49c [p. 141]), is a highly unusual locale for the preaching of a Buddhist sūtra. Generally the preaching of a sūtra by the Buddha is localized at a known historical site on the Indian subcontinent; indeed, such historical specificity served to confirm the authenticity of the scriptures during the formative stages of the tradition (see Étienne Lamotte, "La critique de l'authenticité dans le bouddhisme," in *India Antiqua: A Volume of Oriental Studies Presented to Jean Philippe Vogel* [Leiden: E. J. Brill, 1947], 213–22). The same mountain is the site of the preaching of two other sūtras found in the Tibetan Kanjur: the *Daśacakra-kṣitigarbha-sūtra* (Pek. No. 905) and the *Sūryagarbha-sūtra* (Pek. No. 923). Note that both of these works form part of the *Mahāsaṃnipāta-sūtra* cycle, which may suggest a special association between Mt. Khadiraka and the *Mahāsaṃnipāta* literature.

[3] The expression "and so on" is written *la-sogs-pa* in the newer xylograph editions, but note that the Peking 1 edition maintains the older *-stsogs-* for *-sogs-*. The Tun-huang manuscript provides an example of the most ancient attested form of this expression, *las-stsogs-pa'*, in which the ablative, not the dative, particle was used. The etymology of the original expression cannot be established with certainty, but cf. the forms *stsogs-pa* "neighbor" (Roerich, vyp. 7, 221b) and *rtsog-pa* "pioneer, one gone ahead or going on ahead" (Das 1014b).

[4] The expression *grag-grog* (N *grag-grogs*) is not attested in existing dictionaries, but appears to be a reduplicative formation of the type discussed by G. Uray in *Acta Orientalia* (Budapest) 4 (1954), 220–31, in which the original vowel is retained in the second syllable but reduced to *a* in the first. For a likely antecedent of this form see *grog-po* (Roerich, vyp. 2, 106b), "a deep ravine in which a torrent flows; laternal valley." The Mongolian translation of the Tibetan version renders *grag-grog* as *subaγ qaγurqal*, an expression which is somewhat problematic in itself but appears to mean something like "aqueduct-crevice." For further discussion see Nattier, "The *Candragarbha-sūtra* in Central and East Asia," 260, n. 35.

[5] For the mythology surrounding this figure see the article "Bishamon" in Paul Demiéville, et al., eds., *Hōbōgirin*, fasc. 1 (A-Bombai) (Tokyo: Maison Franco-Japonaise, 1929), 79a–83b; and more recently Phyllis Granoff, "Tobatsu Bishamon: Three Japanese Statues in the United States and an Outline of the Rise of This Cult in East Asia," *East and West* 20 (1970), 144–67. Note that the older Tibetan versions use forms of his name (T, P1, P3 *Be-sha-ra-ma-na*; N *Bai-shrar-ma-na*) derived from the Central Asian Prakrit spelling *Vaiśramaṇa* (cf. Edgerton, *BHSD*, 513a) and not from Sanskrit *Vaiśravaṇa*. In standard classical Tibetan the name is

translated, not transliterated, as *Rnam-thos-kyi bu* (e.g. *Mvy.* nos. 3146, 3367).

[6] The future form "shall commit" is written *gtad-do* in the Tun-huang manuscript and *btad-do* [*sic*] in the Narthang edition, but as *gtad-kyis* in the other xylograph editions. On the use of *-kyis* (*-gis, -gyis, -yis, -'s*) as a future particle see Helmut H. Hoffmann, "Über ein wenig beachtetes Hilfswort zur Bezeichnung der Zukunft im Tibetischen," *Corolla Linguistica: Festschrift Ferdinand Sommer* (Wiesbaden: Harrassowitz, 1955), 73–79. A later spelling (which frequently replaces the *-kyis* series in the Lhasa Kanjur) is *-kyi* (*-gi, -gyi, -yi, -'i*); for this form see Marcelle Lalou, *Manuel élementaire de tibétain classique* (Paris: Imprimerie Nationale, 1950), §26,10. It is possible to discern here a progression from *-kyis* (older literary Tibetan) → *-kyi* (later literary Tibetan) → *-kyi-yin* / *-kyi-red* (modern spoken Tibetan).

[7] This number is unexpectedly small, but cf. the *Fo pen-hsing chi ching* (T No. 190, 3.672a2–3), where the total duration of Kāśyapa's Dharma is given as only seven days. In the *Bhadrakalpika-sūtra*, by contrast, it is said that Kāśyapa's Dharma will last for seventy thousand years (T No. 425, 14.50c15).

[8] The expression *ting-nge 'dzin*, which serves as the regular Tibetan equivalent of Skt. *samādhi* "contemplation, meditative absorption" (*Mvy.* nos. 126, 145, 506–623, 736, 811 and *passim*), exhibits several anomalous features. First, while the usual Tibetan practice is to render Sanskrit technical terms into Tibetan by means of etymological translation (based on real or fictional etymologies), there is no visible connection between the literal meaning of Skt. *samādhi* ("putting together, joining or combining with" (< *sam-ā-√dhā*, MW 1159c) and Tib. *ting-nge 'dzin* (lit. "to grasp *ting-nge*," in which the element *ting-nge* is unattested separately), unless perhaps the Tibetans excerpted the elements *ā √dhā* alone and interpreted them in the fairly uncommon sense of "keep, hold, possess" (MW 138b). Second, the elements *ting* and *nge*, whether taken together or separately, have no apparent etymologies in Tibetan. Third, the initial letter *t-*, while not unknown in Tibetan, is relatively rare, occurring most commonly in loan words of Indian (or occasionally Chinese) origin or in onomatopoeic expressions (Das, 512a–19b).

Given that the majority of the Tibetan words in initial *t-* are of foreign origin, we might consider the possibility that *ting-nge* represents a loan word borrowed into Tibetan during the early stages of the formation of Buddhist vocabulary (that is, prior to the time when the convention of translating rather than transliterating foreign terms was put into effect). The word was clearly well established already during the imperial period, since it appears in numerous entries in the *Mahāvyutpatti*, a compilation dating from the early 9th century, and it occurs in at least one of the titles (no. 535) of Buddhist works translated into Tibetan by the time of King Khri-srong lde-btsan (d. 797 CE); see M. Lalou, "Les textes bouddhiques au temps du roi Khri-sroṅ-lde-bcan," *Journal Asiatique* CCXLI (1953), 313–53. No Indian antecedent for the term *ting-nge* is readily apparent. On the Chinese side, however, the word *ting* 定 ("establish, fix, settle") is used as one of the standard translations of Skt. *samādhi*. An antecedent of the component *nge* is less apparent, but perhaps we should consider the expression *ting-i* 定意, another Chinese translation of Skt. *samādhi* (see Paul Harrison, *The Samādhi of Direct Encounter*, 246).

It is also possible (though in my view considerably less likely) that the syllable *nge* is a native Tibetan suffix of the type discussed by G. Uray in "The suffix *-e* in Tibetan" (*Acta Orientalia* [Budapest] [1953] 3, 229–44). All such formations cited by

Uray, however, are based on native Tibetan words, not on loan words from other languages, and as noted above there is no Tibetan term **ting* on which such a formation could have been based.

Whatever the source of the second syllable in this expression, it seems quite clear that the first syllable of Tibetan *ting-nge* is a loan word from Chinese *ting*. In view of the still-lively debate concerning the extent of Chinese (especially Ch'an) influence on early Tibetan Buddhism, the presence of a Chinese loan word meaning "meditation" in the earliest layer of Tibetan Buddhist vocabulary is of considerable significance as evidence of the extent of Chinese input during the formative stages of that tradition.

[9] Note the use of the plural suffix *-rnams* as a free-standing collective noun in the Tun-huang and Narthang versions, where it is preceded by a genitive particle.

[10] The four principal colors are presumably black (including dark blue and dark green), yellow, red, and white (or "shining"); see Childers, *A Dictionary of the Pāli Language*, 549b, s.v. *vaṇṇo*.

[11] The phrase translated here as "Indian and non-Indian" is rendered by Obermiller as "neither of Indian, nor of Chinese descent" (Part 2, p. 173). The Tibetan text—which reads (in the Tun-huang version) *rgya-gar dang / rgya-ma-yi̱n-ba / rgyal-po ched-po gsum*—is completely ambiguous, and admits of either translation. It is relevant, though certainly not decisive, that the Mongolian translation of the Tibetan takes this phrase to mean "Indian and non-Indian" (*enedkeg kiged busu-ača*, lit. "from India and elsewhere"). No exact counterpart of this expression (which could help us to decide between these two alternatives) occurs in any other version of the Kauśāmbī story. The closest parallel is in the *Prophecy of the Arhat of Khotan* (*Li-yul-gyi dgra-bcom-pas lung-bstan-pa*, Pek. No. 5699), which reads "kings of the west and kings of the north, *Ya-ba-na* and so on" (*nub-phyogs-kyi rgyal-po dang / byang-phyogs-kyi rgyal-po ya-ba-na la-sogs-pa*). The choice of a translation of this phrase has important implications for the history of the text, since a recension referring to the three foreign kings as "neither Indian nor Chinese" could be suspected of having undergone redaction in Central (or more broadly, Inner) Asia.

[12] The later xylograph editions regularly emend the name of the long-forgotten Parthians (Tib. *pa-la-ba*) to "Bactrian" (*ba-lhi-ka*), a reading also found in the Tibetan *Karmaśataka*.

[13] For a discussion of this peculiar term (Tib. *sha-ku-na* and variants) see above, p. 177, n. 77, and p. 187, n. 97.

[14] This passage provides an important geographical clue, suggesting that the redaction of this version of the *Candragarbha-sūtra* (or rather, of the Prakrit antecedent of the Tibetan) took place in the far northwest of India, possibly in Gandhāra. For further discussion see above, p. 178, n 81.

[15] Note the unusual position of this number, which precedes (rather than following) the term it modifies.

[16] Note that these etymological translations of proper names appear only in the late xylograph editions (P1, P3, D, L) and that they appear *before* the transliterations have been sufficiently re-Sanskritized to allow for their independent derivation. For a discussion of the significance of this pattern see above, pp. 233–36.

[17] For an explanation of the probable factors underlying the transition from *Śiṣyaka* to **Śirṣaka* see above, p. 179, n. 83.

[18] Note the peculiar use of the word *saṃgha* (Tib. *dge-'dun*) in reference to individual monks, where one would rather expect the term *bhikṣu* (Tib. *dge-slong*).

This is a fairly common usage in Old Tibetan texts; for numerous examples see the translations in Thomas, *Tibetan Literary Texts*, vol. 1. The same confusion occurs in Buddhist Chinese, where the term *seng* 僧 (A. Ch. *˛səng* [K. no. 1047] < Skt./Pkt. *saṃgha*) serves as one of the usual terms for "monk."

[19] The forms of the Sanskrit name *Sudhanaputra* in the Tun-huang and Narthang versions (which read *S.hu-dha-ra-sh.ha-na'i̱ bu* and *Su-rad-sha-na'i bu*, respectively) are peculiar. Were it not for the complete agreement among all other versions of the text, which clearly go back to a Sanskrit or Prakrit original *Sudhana* (see the Appendix, no. 6), one might suspect that the original Indian form was **Sudarśana*. Given the consensus of the other versions, however, what must be explained is how an original *Sudhana* became Tib. **Su-dar-sha-na* (the form we may assume lies behind both the Tun-huang and the Narthang versions). No aural or visual error that could lead to such a shift is immediately apparent. An intriguing parallel, however, is found in the Sogdian version of the *Vessantara-jātaka*, where the name *Sudhana* appears in the form *Swδ''šn* (presumably to be read *Sudāšin*; see E. Benveniste, *Vessantara Jātaka. Texte sogdien édité, traduit et commenté* [Paris: Paul Geuthner, 1946], p. 6 and *passim.*). An appealing, if somewhat speculative, derivation is offered by N. Sims-Williams (in "Indian Elements in Parthian and Sogdian," in Klaus Röhrborn and Wolfgang Veenker, ed., *Sprachen des Buddhismus in Zentralasien* [Wiesbaden: Harrassowitz, 1983], 132–141 [p. 139]), who derives the term from Skt. *Sudāna* (a form he does not explain, but which could be derived from an original *Sudhana* via an aural error) → Parthian **Suδāšin* (< Skt. *su-* "good" + Parthian *δāšin* "gift") → Sogdian *Swδ''šn*. To get from this Sogdian form to **Swδršn* (a form that might underlie our Tibetan text) we need only note that Sogdian regularly exhibits an intrusive *r* in loan words from Sanskrit or Prakrit; cf. the Sogdian forms *kwrty* (< Skt./Pkt. *koṭi*), *brγ'r* (< Skt./Pkt. *vihāra*) and **k'rš'* (a form not attested in Sogdian texts published to date, but found in Uighur in the spelling *karša*, which is presumably a loan word from Sogdian). If such a chain of transmission is implicated in the text with which we are concerned, this would suggest that Sogdian missionaries played a role in the transmission of the Kauśāmbī prophecy along the Silk Road through Central Asia, from which it ultimately reached Tibet.

[20] The day of the full moon, one of the two occasions per month when the monastic rules are recited by the assembled community.

[21] An erroneous translation of the name Aṅgada, "upper-arm bracelet," based on a borrowing from the *Karmaśataka*. See above, p. 236.

[22] The original form of the name reconstructed here as **Kedāra* cannot be determined with certainty, but the numerous instances of confusion between *da* and *ra* in Tibetan texts would suggest that in this instance it is the Tibetan form, and not the Chinese, that has undergone metathesis. For further discussion see above, p. 180, n. 84.

[23] Note the apparently deliberate change from "mother" in the older editions to "father" in the more recent xylographs.

[24] The Tibetan term *ban-de* ~ *ban-dhe* has generally been derived by modern scholars from Skt. *vandya* "praiseworthy, very venerable" (MW 919b), a deriation apparently based on the testimony of "Hodgson's learned Nepalese authority" (Jäschke 365b; the same derivation is given in Das 865a and by Tucci in *Religions of Tibet*, 10, but without any attribution). A minority view is offered by R. A. Miller, who finds the antecedent of the term in "some form related to *paṇḍita*" (*Studies in*

the Grammatical Tradition in Tibet [Amsterdam: John Benjamins B. V., 1976], p. 4). Jäschke also states that *ban-de* is the regular equivalent of Tib. *btsun-pa*, which, however, is equated in the *Mahāvyutpatti* (nos. 8702, 9220) not with *vandya* but with Skt. *bhadanta* ("a term of respect applied to a Buddhist, a Buddhist mendicant"; see MW 745c, *BHSD* 405b). In this connection we might note the existence of the contracted Pāli form *bhante* "Sir, venerable sir," a term whose origins are controversial but which appears to be derived from either *bhavanta* or *bhadanta* (*PTSD* 498a). I am inclined to agree with the sole advocate of the derivation of Tib. *ban-de* from Skt. *bhadanta* (see Roerich, vyp. 6, 169a), though I would posit a Prakrit form resembling Pāli *bhante* as an intermediary. The term is used in Old Tibetan texts in the general sense of "monk, Buddhist cleric," and is so translated in (for example) H. E. Richardson, *A Corpus of Early Tibetan Inscriptions* (London: Royal Asiatic Society, 1985), 171.

[25] The peculiar color of these Buddhist monastic robes—here described as black and red, not saffron-colored—could help us to localize the time and place of this redaction if sufficient information on the color of monastic garments and their changes over time were available. Red robes are of course standard for Buddhist monks in Tibet, as are black robes in China, yet we may not have to look so far afield for the basis of this passage. In the *Lotus Sūtra*, for example, we find the preacher of the Dharma being instructed to put on "a clean, nice, red robe, dyed with good colours, and a black woollen garment" (Kern trans., 269 [ch. 13, vs. 27]). (These colors are not mentioned in the Chinese translation of Kumārajīva.) The reference to wool—certainly not a favored fabric on the Indian subcontinent—suggests that this portion of the *Lotus* was composed somewhere in the far northwest of India, in Gandhāra or an adjoining region. A similar reference to red and black monastic garments occurs in the *Pad-ma thang-yig*, Book II, c. 2 (fol. 962) according to Thomas, *Tibetan Literary Texts*, 265–66.

[26] Note that the king's death is mentioned only in the late xylograph editions—a clear example of editorial rationalization in progress. I have not translated the expression *zhal 'tshos-te* (P1, P3 *zhal mchos-te*), which has appeared as meaningless to my Tibetan informants as it does to me. This phrase occurs only in the late (post-P1) xylograph editions, and is not translated in the Mongolian version.

[27] The meaning of this sentence (which occurs only in the late xylograph editions) is quite obscure. In accordance with the apparent literal meaning of the Tibetan the Mongolian translation renders this sentence as *labai-yi arčiγsan metü*, "as if one erased a conch shell." What this means, however, is not at all evident.

[28] The six flavors, according to Indian tradition, are sweet (*madhura*), sour (*amla*), salty (*lavaṇa*), pungent (*kaṭuka*), bitter (*tikta*), and astringent (*kaṣaya*); see MW 869c, s.v. *rasa*.

TIBETAN TEXT

[1] T: –

X: ’Phags-pa Zla-ba’i snying-pos zhus-pa’i mdo-las / sangs-rgyas-kyi bstan-pa gnas-pa dang[1] ’jig-pa’i tshul lung-bstan-pa /[2]

[1] L inserts / [2] N omits entire title.

[2] T: sngon sangs-rgyas bcom-ldan-’das Shag-kya thub-pa’ // r[i̲] Kha-dhi̲rhag-gi̲ steng-na bzhug-ste // de’i tshe phyogs . . .u. . byang-cub-sems-dpa’sems-dpa’-chen-po ’khor dang-bcas de dang / dgra-bcom-pa dang / lha dang / klu dang gnod-sbyi̲n dang dri̲-za dang / lha dang / lha-ma-yin dang / myi̲-’am-ci̲ dang / lto-’phye-chen-po dang / nam-ka-ldi̲ng dang / bdud sdi̲g-can las-stsogs-pa’ / mthu-bo-che thams-cad tshogs-pa de’i̲ dus-na // sangs-rgyas bcom-ldan-’das Shag-kya-thub-pa’i̲ zhal-gyi̲ smyin-mtshams-nas / ’od-gzer shar-gyi̲ Lus-’phags dang / lho’i̲ ’Dzam-bu-gli̲ng dang / nub-gyi̲ Ban-lang-spyod dang / byang-gi̲ Sgra-myi̲-snyan dang / gli̲ng ’di̲ bzhi̲r ’od-gzer kun-du khyab-par bkram-ste / ’od-gzer btang-ba de’i̲ tshe / ri̲ Mye-ro ’bar-ba las-stsogs-pa’ / ri̲ chen-po dang ri̲ dang / nags-tshal dang / sman-ljongs sla-sul gragrog kun-la myi̲-snang-bar mnyam-ste // lag-mthi̲l dang ’dra-bar gli̲ng bzhi̲-char gsal-zhi̲ng snang-bar gyur // ’od-gzer de-dag-las sangs-rgyas phal-po-che’i̲ sku-gzugs kha-dog dang / dbyi̲bs sna-tshogs ’od dang bcas-pa / phal-po-che byung-ba / byang-cub sems-pa’ [*sic*] dang / klu las-stogs-pa’ / sems-can kun-gyi̲s mthong-ste ngo-mtshar-du gyur-to //

X: sngon[1] sangs-rgyas bcom-ldan-’das Shā-kya-[2]thub-pa ri Kha-rhi-rhag[3]-gi steng-na bzhugs-te / de’i tshe phyogs bcu’i byang-chub-sems-dpa’ sems-dpa’-chen-po ’khor dang-bcas-pa dang / dgra-bcom-pa dang / lha dang /[4] klu dang / gnod-sbyin dang / dri-za dang / lha-ma-yin dang / mi’am-ci[5] dang / lto-’phye-chen-po dang / nam-mkha’[6]-lding dang / bdud sdig-can la-sogs[7]-pa mthu-bo-che thams-cad tshogs-pa de’i dus-na /[8] sangs-rgyas bcom-ldan-’das[9] Shā-kya[10]-thub-pa’i[11] zhal-gyi smin-mtshams-nas ’od-zer shar-gyi Lus-’phags dang / lho’i[12] ’Dzam-bu’i[13]-gling dang / nub-kyi[14] Ban[15]-glang-spyod dang / byang-gi Sgra-mi-snyan[16] dang / gling 'di bzhir[17] 'od-zer kun-du[18] khyab-par bkram-ste / 'od-zer[19] btang-ba de'i tshe[20] Ri-rab[21] la-sogs-pa ri chen-po dang / ri dang /[22] nags-tshal dang / sman-ljongs[23] /[24] ri-sul /[25] grag-grog[26] kun-la yang[27] snang-bar mnyam[28]-ste / lag-mthil dang 'dra-bar gling bzhi-car[29] snang-bas[30] gsal-bar gyur[31] / 'od-zer[32] de-dag[33]-las sangs-rgyas-kyi[34] sku-gzugs kha-dog dang[35] dbyibs sna-tshogs 'od[36] dang-bcas-pa[37] phal-po-che byung-ba / byang-chub-sems-dpa' dang / lha dang / klu la-sogs-pa sems-can mang-po[38] kun-gyis mthong[39]-ste ngo-mtshar-du[40] gyur-to //[41]

[1] P1 omits *sngon* [2] N,P3 *Shākya-* [3] P1 *Kha-dhi-rhag*, N *Kharhi-hag* [4] P1,P3 omit / [5] P1 *mi-'am-ci* [6] N *namkha'* [7] P1 *stsogs* [8] P1,P3,D omit / [9] N adds *-kyis* [10] P3 *Shākya-* [11] N omits *Shā-kya-thub-pa'i* [12] P3 *lha'i* [13] L *-bu* [14] P3 *-gyi* [15] P1,P3,N *ba* [16] N adds *-pa* [17] N *bzhi* [18] N,L *-tu* [19] N *-gzer* [20] N inserts / [21] N replaces *Ri-rab* with *Me-ro bar* [22] P1,P3,N omit / [23] P1,P3 *-ljong* [24] N omits / [25] N omits / [26] N *-grogs* [27] L *-la'ang* [28] N *snyam* [29] P1,P3 *bzhi-bcar*, N *bzhi-gcig-car* [30] N *-bar* [31] L *'gyur* [32] N *-gzer* [33] P3 *-dak-* [*sic*] [34] N omits *-kyi* and adds *phal-po-che'i* [35] L inserts / [36] N omits *'od* [37] N omits *-pa* [38] N omits *mang-po* [39] N xyl. *mthod* [40] L omits *-du* [41] L /

3] T: de-nas bcom-ldan-'das Shag-kya-thub-pa-la / Be-sha-ra-ma-na las-stsogs-pa' / rgyal-po ched-po bzhis gs.lo [*sic*] -pa' // 'od-gzer 'di-lta-bu de'i don-du mdzad-pa gang lags shes zhus-pa-las // bcom-ldan-'das-gyis bka'-stsal-pa' // nga mya-ngan-las 'das-pa'i 'og-du // gling bzhir ngas gsungs-pa'i dam-pa'i chos-gyi gsung-rab dang / ring-bsrel dang / gzugs-brnyan 'di-lta-bu-dag 'byung-ste / 'di khyed-kyi lag-du gtad-do // srungs-shig //

X: de-nas bcom-ldan-'das Shā-kya[1]-thub-pa-la[2] Bai-shra-wa-na[3] la-sogs-pa rgyal-po chen-po bzhis gsol-pa / 'od-zer 'di[4]-lta-bu[5] de[6] ci'i don-du[7] mdzad-pa lags[8] zhes[9] zhus[10]-pa-las / bcom-ldan-'das-kyis bka'-stsal-pa / nga mya-ngan-las 'das-pa'i 'og-tu gling bzhir ngas gsungs-pa'i[11] dam-pa'i chos-kyi gsung-rab dang / ring-bsrel[12] dang / gzugs-brnyan 'di1-lta-bu-dag 'byung-ste / 'di khyed[13]-kyi lag-tu gtad-kyis[14] srungs[15]-shig //[16]

[1] P3,N *Shākya-* [2] N inserts / [3] P1,P3 *Be-sha-ra-ma-na*, N *Bai-shrar-ma-na* [4] N *de* [5] P1,P3 *-bus* [6] N omits *de* [7] P1,P3 *-tu* [8] P3 adds / [9] N *shes* [10] N omits *zhus*

[11] N omits *gsungs-pa'i* [12] P1,P3 *-srel* [13] N *khyod* [14] N *btad-do* [15] P1,P3 *bsrungs* [16] L /

[4] T: de-nas bcom-ldan-'das-la / byang-cub-sems-dpa' Zla-ba'i snyi̲ng-pos gsol-pa' // bcom-ldan-'das 'di̲-lta-bu'i̲ thugs-rje ched-pos bcom-ldan-'das / mya-ngan-las 'das-pa'i̲ 'og-du dam-pa'i̲ chos rgyal-po ched-po-la gtad-pa thugs-rje che'o // snga-ma 'das-pa'i̲ sangs-rgyas mya-ngan-las-'das-nas // lo-dgung bdun lags-nas // dam-pa'i̲ chos-gyi̲ gzugs-brnyanub [*sic*] -na / bcom-ldan-'das Shag-kya-thub-pa mya-ngan-las-'das-pa'i̲ 'og-du // dam-pa'i̲ chos ci̲-tsam-du gnas-par 'gyur // de-nas bcom-ldan-'das-gyi̲s bka' stsal-pa' // 'di̲-lta-bu the-tsom zhus-pa legs-so // legs-par nyon-ci̲g dang ngas bshad-do / nga mya-ngan-las 'das-nas / dam-pa'i̲ chos-gyi̲ gzugs-brnyan lo nyi-stong-du gnas-par 'gyur-ro //

X: de-nas bcom-ldan-'das-la byang-chub-sems-dpa' Zla-ba'i snying-pos gsol-pa[1] / bcom-ldan-'das /[2] 'di-lta-bu'i[3] thugs-rje[4] chen-pos bcom-ldan-'das mya-ngan-las 'das-pa'i 'og-tu dam-pa'i chos rgyal-po chen-po-dag-[5]la gtad[6]-pa shin-tu[7] ngo-mtshar-to[8] / snga-ma 'das-pa'i sangs-rgyas mya-ngan-las 'das[9]-nas dgung-lo bdun[10] lags-nas dam-pa'i chos-kyi gzugs-brnyan nub-na / bcom-ldan-'das Shā-kya[11]-thub-pa mya-ngan-las 'das-pa'i 'og-tu dam-pa'i chos ji-tsam-gyi bar-du gnas-par 'gyur / de-nas bcom-ldan-'das-kyis bka' stsal-pa / 'di-lta-bu'i the-tshom[12] zhus-pa legs-so[13] // legs-par[14] nyon-cig dang /[15] ngas bshad-par bya'o[16] // nga mya-ngan-las 'das-nas dam-pa'i chos-kyi gzugs-brnyan lo nyis[17]-stong-du[18] gnas-par 'gyur-ro[19] //

[1] N *zhus-pa* [2] P1,P3 omit / [3] N *-bu* [4] N *rdzu-'phrul* (xyl. *rju-*) [5] N omits *chen-po-dag* [6] P1,P3 *gtang* [7] P1,P3 *-du* [8] for *shin-tu ngo-mtshar-to* N reads *thugs-rje che-*[*ba*] [9] N adds *-pa-* [10] P1 *dun* [11] P3,N *Shākya-* [12] P1,P3 *-tsom*; L replaces *the-tshom* with *chos* [13] N inserts *legso* before *legs-so* [14] N omits *legs-par* [15] N omits / [16] N replaces *bshad-par bya'o* with *bshad-do* [17] P3 *nyi* [18] N omits *-du* [19] N *'gyuro*

[5] T: byang-cub-sems-dpa' Zla-ba'i̲ snyi̲ng-pos gsol-pa' / bcom-ldan-'das dam-pa'i̲ chos 'di̲ mtha' ci-lta-bur nub // rgyu ci-las nyams sus ma-mchi̲s-par bgyi̲s // bka' stsal-pa' // mya-ngan-las-'das-'pa'i 'og-du lo lnga-brgya-'i̲ bar-du / nga'i̲ bstan-pa spyod-pa'i̲ sems-can-rnams grol-thar-pa mang-du 'gyur-ro // de-nas yang lo lnga-

brgya’i̲ bar-du / ti̲ng-nge-’dzi̲n spyod-pa mang-du ’gyur / rgyal-po dang sems-can dam-pa’i̲ chos-la dad-ci̲ng spyod-pa yang phyi̲r-zhi̲ng nyung-bar ’gyur-ro // de-nas lo lnga-brgya’i̲ bar-du / dam-pa’i̲ / [*sic*] chos ston-ci̲ng sems-can ’dren-ci̲ng thar-par byed-pa’i̲ ’slobs-dpon mang-du ’byung // nyan-thos dang dgra-bcom-ba ni̲ nyung-bar ’gyur / rgyal-po dang blon-po dang sems-can phal-gyi̲-rnams kyang / nyan-pa-tsam-du zad-gyi̲ nyamsu len-ci̲ng spyod-pa’am / brtson-’grus ni̲ myi-byed-de / dad-pa ’bri̲-bar ’gyuro / dam-pa’i̲ chos-gyi̲ srungs-ma-rnams kyang myi̲-dga’-bar ’gyur-te // dam-pa’i̲ chos-la ma-dad-pa’i̲ sems-can-rnams ni̲ // sngon-bas mthu dang stobs skyes-par gyur-te // ’Dzam-bu gli̲ng-gi̲ myi̲’i rgyal-po-rnams kyang / phan-tshun gci̲g-la-gci̲g dmag ’dren-ci̲ng ’khrug-par ’gyur-ro // bdud-gyi̲ ris kyang ’phel-bar ’gyur-ro //

X: byang-chub-sems-dpa’ Zla-ba’i snying-pos gsol-pa / bcom-ldan-’das /[1] dam-pa’i chos ’di tha-mar ji-ltar nub-par ’gyur / rgyu ci-las nyams / sus ma-mchis-par bgyid / bka’ stsal-pa / nga mya-ngan-las ’das-pa’i ’og-tu lo lnga-brgya’i bar-du[2] nga’i bstan-pa[3]-la spyod-pa’i sems-can rnam-par[4] grol-ba mang-du ’gyur-ro[5] // de-nas lo lnga-brgya’i bar-du ting-nge[6]-’dzin-la[7] spyod-pa mang-du ’gyur-ro[8] // rgyal-po dang /[9] blon-po dang[10] / sems-can phal-rnams[11] kyang[12] dam-pa’i chos-la dad-cing[13] spyod-pa yang[14] phyir-zhing nyung-bar ’gyur-ro[15] // de-nas lo lnga-brgya’i bar-du dam-pa’i chos ston-cing[16] sems-can ’dren-pa dang / thar-par byed-pa’i slob-dpon mang-du ’byung-ngo[17] /[18] nyan-thos dgra-bcom-pa ni nyung-bar ’gyur-ro[19] / rgyal-po dang /[20] blon-po dang /[21] sems-can phal-rnams[22] kyang nyan-pa-tsam-du zad-de[23] / nyams-su[24] len-cing spyod-pa’am[25] / brtson-’grus ni mi-byed-de[26] / dad-pa ’bri-bar ’gyur-ro // dam-pa’i chos-kyi srungs[27]-ma-rnams[28] kyang mi-dga’[29]-bar ’gyur-te / dam-pa’i chos-la ma-dad-pa’i[30] sems-can[31]-rnams[32] ni sngon-pas mthu[33]-stobs skye-bar ’gyur-ro[34] // ’Dzam-bu[35]-gling-gi mi’i rgyal-po-rnams kyang phan-tshun gcig[36]-la-gcig dmag ’dren-cing[37] ’khrug-par ’gyur-ro // bdud-kyi ris kyang ’phel-bar ’gyur-ro //[38]

[1] P1,P3,D,N omit / [2] N adds / [3] N omits *-la* [4] P3 replaces *rnam-par* with *-rnams* [5] N omits *-ro* [6] N writes *tinge* in place of *ting-nge* [7] N omits *-la* [8] N omits *-ro* [9] P1,P3 omit / [10] N omits *blon-po dang* [11] N *phal-po-che* [12] N omits *kyang* [13] N adds / [14] L *spyod-pa’ang* [15] N *’gyuro* [16] N adds / [17] N omits *-ngo*

[18] P1,P3 // [19] N *'gyuro* [20] P1,P3 omit / [21] N omits *blon-po dang* / [22] N *phal-gyi rnams* [23] N *zad-kyi* [24] N *nyamsu* [25] P1,P3 *-pa-'am* [26] N omits *-de* [27] P1,P3 *bsrungs* [28] N replaces *-rnams* with *-dag* [29] D *-dgra-* [sic] [30] N *-pa* [31] N omits *sems-can* [32] L omits *-rnams* [33] N *mthus dang* [34] N writes *skyeso* for *skye-bar 'gyur-ro* [35] P1,P3,D *-bu'i* [36] P1,P3 *cig* [37] N adds / [38] N omits *bdud-kyi ris kyang 'phel-bar 'gyur-ro* //

[6] T: de-nas yang lo lnga-brgya'i̱ tshe / lo sum-brgya ni̱ dam-pa'i̱ chos-la gnas-pa'i̱ lha klu las-stsogs-pa / sems-can srungs-ma'i̱ rnams myi̱-gnas-shi̱ng // dam-pa'i̱ chos-la dar-par 'gro-bar 'gyur // — sems-can chos spyod-pa-rna°s kyang / chos-kyi̱ gzhung-bzhi̱n ma-spyad / brtson-'grus chung-bas 'grub-pa nyung-bar 'gyur // 5 kha-dog bzhi̱ dang bzhi̱-las-gyur-pa yang 'bri̱ / ro las-stsogs-pa yang chung-bar 'gyur-ro // myi̱-nad phyugs-nad dang / mu-ge yang 'byung-bar 'gyur-ro //

X: de-nas yang lo lnga-brgya'i tshe[1] lo sum-brgyar[2] ni[3] dam-pa'i chos-la[4] gnas-pa'i[5] lha klu la-sogs-pa / sems-can srungs[6]-ma-rnams mi-gnas-shing[7] dam-pa'i chos gang-du dar-bar 'gro-bar 'gyur[8] /[9] sems-can chos-la ma-dad-par 'gyur / sems-can chos spyod-pa-rnams kyang[10] chos-kyi gzhung-bzhin[11] mi-spyod /[12] 5 brtson-'grus chung-bas[13] grub[14]-pa[15] nyung-bar 'gyur /[16] kha-dog bzhi dang /[17] bzhi-las gyur-pa yang[18] 'bri /[19] dri dang /[20] ro la-sogs-pa'ang[21] chung-bar 'gyur-ro[22] // mi-nad dang /[23] phyugs-nad dang / mu-ge'ang[24] 'byung-bar 'gyur-ro[25] //

[1] P3 *che*; N adds / [2] N *-brgya* [3] P1 *na* [4] N omits *-la* [5] N *spyod-pa'i* [6] P1,P3 *bsrungs* [7] N adds / [8] N omits *dam-pa'i chos gang-du dar-bar 'gro-bar 'gyur* / [9] P1,P3 // [10] N adds / [11] L adds *-du* [12] P1,P3 // [13] P1 *tshungs-pa*; P3 *tshungs-pas*, D *chungs-pas* [14] P3 *gub* [15] N adds *yang* [16] P1,P3 // [17] P1,P3,N omit / [18] L *gyur-pa'ang* [19] N omits *'bri* / [20] N omits / [21] N omits *'ang*; L *gyur-pa'ang* [22] N *'gyuro* [23] N omits *dang* / [24] L *mu-ge'ang* [25] N *'gyuro*

[7] T: lo nyi̱s-brgya-la dge-slong yang dam-pa'i̱ chos-bzhi̱n myi̱-spyod /'ji̱g-rten-gyi̱ khe dang grags-pa tshol // snyi̱ng-rje chung / khri̱ms-la myi̱-gnas / dam-pa'i̱ chos ma-nor-par spyod-pa-la ni̱ / g .. bkr[u]n-ci̱ng skur-pa 'debs/ longs-spyod dang yo-byad 'phrog // 'ji̱g-rten-gyi̱ rgyal-po'i̱ gsang-la̱ rten-ci̱ng / rgyal-sri̱d 'dzin 5 /rgyal-po-pha 'gri̱n-pa'i̱ pho-nyar ngo-'phral tshol / [sic] -zhi̱ng' gro //rgyal-po dang 'bangs-gyi̱ srid 'khrug-pa'i̱ dbyen byed / nyo-

tshong dang khe-spogs byed // thabs tshol dam-pa'i chos spyod-pa yang snyi̲n̲g-nas nyams-su blangste / myi̲ s[py]od-gyi̲ // phal-cher kha-gsag dang 'phral-gyi̲ tshul 'chos-pa ya-ma brla byed-de /

X: lo nyis-brgyar[1] ni dge-slong yang chos-bzhin mi-spyod / 'jig-rten-gyi khe dang[2] grags-pa tshol /[3] snying-rje chung-zhing[4] khrims[5]-la mi-gnas / dam-pa'i chos tshul-bzhin[6] spyod-pa-rnams[7]-la ni glan-ka tshol-zhing[8] skur-pa[9] 'debs / longs-spyod dang[10] yo-byad 'phrog / 'jig-rten-gyi rgyal-po'i gsang-la rten[11]-cing[12] rgyal-srid 'dzin /[13] rgyal-po'i phrin-pa'i[14] pho-nyar[15] ngo[16]-phral[17] tshol-zhing 'gro[18] / rgyal-po dang / 'bangs-srid[19] 'khrugs[20]-pa'i dbyen byed / nyo-tshong dang /[21] khe-spogs[22] byed[23] thabs tshol /[24] dam-pa'i chos spyod-pa'ang[25] snying-nas[26] nyams-su[27] blangs-te[28] mi-spyod-kyī[29] phal-cher kha-gsag dang /[30] 'phral-gyi tshul 'chos-pa'i[31] ya-ma brla[32]-byed-de[33] /

[1] N *-brgya-la* [2] L inserts / [3] L omits / [4] N omits *-zhing* [5] N *tshul-khrims* [6] N *ma-nor-pa* [7] N omits *-rnams-* [8] N writes *bkrun-cing* in place of *glan-ka tshol-zhing* [9] P1,P3 *bskur-ba* [10] L adds / [11] P1,P3 *brten* [12] N adds / [13] N omits / [14] N *-par* [15] N writes *'gro-zhing* in place of *pho-nyar* [16] P1,P3 *ro* [*sic*!] [17] N *-'phral* [18] N omits *-zhing 'gro* [19] N omits *-srid* [20] P1,P3 *'khrug* [21] D,N omit / [22] P1,P3 *phogs* [23] P1,P3,N insert / [24] P1,P3 omit / [25] L *-pa'ang* [26] N adds *ni* [27] N *nyamsu* [28] N adds / [29] P1,P3 omit / [30] N omits / [31] N *-pa* [32] P1,P3,N *rla* [33] N omits *-de*

T: de'i̲ dus-na' // chos-la dga'-ba'i̲ lha klu thams-cad-gyi̲s / rgyal-khams-gyi̲ dge-slong de-ltar spyod-pa'i̲ sa-gzhi̲ bor-te // myi̲-gnas-shi̲n̲g bdud-ri̲s las-stsogs-pa chos-la bgegs byed-pa'i̲ rnams der byung-ste // mthu dang stobs sky[e]-bar 'gyur / rgyal-po dang blon-po las-stsogs-pa dad-pa 'bri̲ // dge-sdi̲g̲-gi̲ mtshams myi̲-zi̲n̲ // dam-pa'i̲ chos-la rma 'byi̲n̲ // dkon-mchog-gi̲ dkor dang / dge-'dun-gyi̲ rdzas-la spyod-ci̲n̲g rku 'phrog byed / sdi̲g̲-la myi̲-'dzem / gzugs-brnyan dang mchod-rten-gyi̲ khams khad-gyi̲s khad-gyi̲s bshi̲g̲-shi̲n̲g mchod-pa'i̲ yo-byad ni̲ bri̲ //

X: de'i dus-na[1] chos-la dga'-ba'i lha klu thams-cad-kyis rgyal[2]-khams-kyi dge-slong 'di-ltar spyod-pa'i sa-gzhi bor-te mi-gnas-shing / bdud-kyi ris la-sogs-pa[3] chos-kyi bgegs-kyi[4] ris[5]-rnams der 'byung-ste / mthu dang[6] stobs skye-bar 'gyur / rgyal-po dang /[7] blon-po la-sogs-pa dad-pa 'bri[8] / dge-sdig-gi dmigs mi-phyed[9]

/ dam-pa'i chos-la rma 'byin / dkon-mchog gsum-gyi dkor dang dge-'dun-gyi rdzas-la spyod-cing[10] rku 'phrog byed-de[11] sdig-la mi-'dzem / gzugs-brnyan dang[12] mchod-rten-[13]rnams khad-kyis[14] bshig /[15] mchod-pa'i yo-byad phri[16] /

[1] N *-nas* [2] N omits *rgyal* [3] N omits *-pa* [4] N omits *-kyi* [5] N omits *ris* [6] L adds / [7] L adds *blon-p[o] dang* / [8] N *bri* [9] N substitutes *mtshams mi-zin* for *dmigs mi-phyed* [10] N omits *spyod-cing* [11] N omits *-de* and adds / [12] L adds / [13] N adds *-gyi* [14] P1,P3 *khang-gyis* [*sic*!] [15] L omits / [16] N *bri*

[9] T: de'i tshe-na dam-pa'i chos ma-nor-par spyod-pa / dge-slong dang khyim-pa 'ga'-'ga'-tsam gnas-pa de'i bsod-nams-kyis yul-phyogs-su kha-char dus-dus-su bab-cing / myi phyugs-la nad nyung-zhing yul bde-ba-dag yod // 'di-lta-bu myi-gnas-pa der phal-cher ni sdug-bsngal myi-bde-ba sna-tshogs 'byung //

X: de'i tshe dam-pa'i chos ma-nor-bar spyod-pa[1] dge-slong dang / khyim-pa 'ga'[2]-tsam gnas-pa de'i bsod-nams-kyis yul-phyogs-su[3] char chu[4] dus-su 'bab[5]-cing lo legs / mi-rgyags-la nad[6] nyung-zhing yul bde-ba-dag kyang bar 'ga' 'byung[7] / de[8]-lta-bu mi-gnas-pa phal-cher ni sdug-bsngal mi-bde-ba sna-tshogs 'byung /[9]

[1] N adds / [2] P1,P3,D *'ga'-'ga'-* [*sic*!] [3] N *-phyogsu* [4] N writes *kha-char* in place of *char chu* [5] N *bab* [6] N writes *mi-nad phyugs-nad* in place of *mi-rgyags-la* [7] N substitutes *yod* for *bar 'ga' 'byung* [8] N *'di* [9] N omits /

[10] T: de'i dus-na / rgya-gar dang / rgya ma-yin-ba / rgyal-po ched-po gsum 'byung-ste // gsum-la Ya-bha-na dang / Pa-la-ba dang / Sheg-ku-na dang / 'di gsum dim [*sic*] -pa'i chos myi-spyod / dmag 'dren-cing 'thab-rtsod / nub-tsa dang byang-gi yul-khams mang-mo-zhig myed-par byas // yul-khams de'i mchod-rten dang gtsug-lag-khang las-stsogs-pa bshig myeds btang / mchod-pa'i yo-byad dang / dkon-mchog gsum-gyi dkor las-stogs-pa phrogs bcom / rgyal-po 'di g°su [*sic*] gcig-la-gcig gnod-pa sna-tshogs-gyis thab-mo byed // gsum-car-gyi rgyal-srid myi bde-bar 'gyur // de'i rjes-la rgyal-po 'di gsum mjal dum-ste / srid gcig-du byas // dmag mang-po 'dus-nas // rgya-gar-gyi yul 'Ga'-'ga'-'i tshu-rol 'Ga'-'dha-ra dang / Mad-dha-dhe-sha las-stsogs-pa'i yul phrogs-nas bzung //

X: de'i dus-su[1] rgya-gar dang / rgya ma-yin-pa'i[2] rgyal-po chen-po gsum 'byung-ste / gsum-la /[3] Ya[4]-ba-na dang / Ba-lhi-ka[5] dang / Sha[6]-ku-na dang /[7] 'di-dag[8] gsum dam-pa'i chos mi-spyod / dmag 'dren-cing g.yul 'gyed[9]-de[10] / nub dang[11] byang-gi yul-khams mang-po-zhig 'bebs[12]-par byed-de[13] / de-nas[14] yul-khams de'i mchod-rten dang[15] gtsug-lag-khang la-sogs-pa yang[16] bshig-cing[17] mes[18] bsregs[19]-te[20] / dge-'dun-gyi[21] yo-byad dang[22] dkon-mchog[23] gsum-gyi[24] dkor la-sogs-p yang[25] brogs[26]-shing[27] bcom-ste[28] / rgyal-po 'di gsum gcig[29]-la-gcig[30] gnod-pa sna-tshogs-kyis 'thab[31]-mo byed-de[32] / gsum-car-gyi rgyal-srid mi-bde-bar 'gyur-ro[33] // de'i rjes-la[34] rgyal-po de[35] gsum[36] nang[37]-srid gcig[38]-tu byas-nas[39] dmag mang-po 'dus-te[40] /[41] rgya-gar-gyi yul[42] chu-bo[43] Gang-gā'i[44] tshu-rol Gan[45]-dha[46]-ra dang / Ma-ddya[47]-de-sha[48] la-sogs-pa'i yul phrogs-nas bzung /

[1] N *-na* [2] N *-pa* [3] N omits / [4] N *Yā* [5] N *Ba-la-bā* [6] N *Shi* [7] N omits *dang* / [8] N omits *-dag*; P1,D read *'di-'di* [*sic*!] [9] L *'byed* [10] N substitutes *'thab-rtsod* for *g.yul 'gyed-de* [11] L inserts / [12] N *med* [13] N *byas* [14] N omits *de-nas* [15] N,L add / [16] N omits *la-sogs-pa yang* [17] N omits *-cing* [18] L *me* [19] P1,P3 *sregs* [20] N substitutes *'tang* for *bsregs-te* [21] N *mchod-pa'i* [22] N,L add / [23] N omits *-di* [24] N omits *gsum-gyi* [25] N omits *yang*; L *-pa'ang* [26] P1,P3,N *phrogs*, D *phregs* [27] N omits *-shing* [28] N omits *-ste* [29] P1,P3 *cig* [30] P1,P3 *-cig* [31] P1,P3,D *thab* [32] N omits *-de* [33] N omits *-ro* [34] N substitutes *de-nas* for *de'i rjes-la* [35] N *'di* [36] N adds *mjal dum-ste* / [37] N omits *nang* [38] P1,P3 *cig* [39] N omits *-nas* [40] N *-nas* [41] P1,P3,D omit / [42] N *yul yul* [*sic*] [43] N omits *chu-bo*; P1,P3 *chu'o* [44] N *'Ga'-'ga'i* [45] P1 *Bgan-*, P3 *'Gan-* [46] P1,P3,D,L *-da-* [47] N *-ha-* [48] P1,P3 *Ma-dhya-dhe-sha*

T: de'i dus-na 'Ga'-'ga'i pha-rol lho-phyogs-na // Ke'u-sham-'byi'i yul-na rgyal-po Mhen-dra-se-na zhes-bya-ba de-la bu-zhig byung-ba / mying ni Drus-sprha-lha-hra zhes-bya-ba-zhig byung-ste // smyin-mtsams-na lcags-gyi smye-ba-can / gru-mo m.ran-cad khrag-gis bskus-pa-zhig byung / de-dang dus gcig-du blon-po lnga-brgya bu khye'u lnga-brgya byung-ste / ril-gyis lag-pa 'khrig-ma man-cad khrag-can-du byung // de'i dus-na rgyal-po'i rte'u smra-shes-pa gcig kyang byung / de'i nub-mo — gnam-las khrag-gi char-pa-dag kyang bab-nas//

X: de'i dus-na chu-bo[1] Gang-gā'i[2] pha-rol lho-phyogs-kyi[3] rgyun[4]-na / yul[5] Ko'u-shām-bī[6] zhes-bya-ba'i[7] rgyal-po Ma-hen-dra-se-na[8] zhes-bya-ba de-la sras[9]-zhig btsas-te[10] / de'i ming ni

Du-spra[11]-sa-ha-sta[12] zhes-bya-ste[13] / smin-mtshams-na lcags-kyi sme-ba-zhig yod-pa /[14] lag-pa[15] gru-mo man-chad khrag-gis bskus[16]-pa-zhig 'byung[17]-ngo[18] // de[19]-dang dus gcig-tu[20] rgyal-po de'i[21] blon-po lnga-brgya-la yang[22] bu[23] khye'u[24] lnga-brgya[25] btsa'[26]-ste[27] / de[28] ril-gyis[29] lag-pa khrig-ma[30] man-chad khrag-can-du 'byung[31]-ste /[32] de'i dus-na[33] rgyal-po'i[34] rta[35]-la rte'u smra-shes-pa-shig[36] skyes-te[37] / rgyal-po dang / blon-po dang / rte'u smra-shes-pa skyes-pa'i[38] nub-mo'ang[39] nam-mkha'-las[40] khrag-gi char-pa[41] bab-nas /

[1] N omits *chu-bo* [2] N *'Ga'-'ga'i* [3] N omits *-kyi*, P3 *-gyi* [4] N omits *rgyun;* P1,P3,D *rgyud* [5] N omits *yul* [6] P1,P3 *Ke'u-sham-bhi*, N *Ko'u-sha-bi'i* [7] N writes *yul-na* in place of *zhes-bya-ba'i* [8] N *Ma-he-na-'dra-se* [9] N *bu* [10] N *'byung-ba* [11] L *-sbra-* [12] N *Tu-pra-sa-ha* [13] N omits *-ste* and adds *zhig 'byung-ste* [14] P1,P3 omit / [15] N omits *lag-pa* [16] L *bkus* [17] D *phyung* [18] N *-ba* [19] N *de-dag* [20] N writes *lhan-cig-tu* in place of *dus gcig-tu* [21] N omits *rgyal-po de'i* [22] N omits *yang*; L *-'ang* [23] P1,P3,L omit *bu* [24] N omits *khye'u* [25] N omits *lnga-brgya* [26] P1,P3 *btsa* [*sic*] [27] N substitutes *'byung-ba yang* for *btsa'-ste* [28] N,L omit *de* [29] P1,P3,D *ril yang* [30] P3,D *khrig-pa*, L *mkhrig-ma* [31] P1,P3 *gyur* [hand-corrected in P1] [32] N omits *-ste* / [33] N substitutes *de dang dus gcig-tu* for *de'i dus-na* [34] N *-po* [35] N *de* [36] P1,P3,N *-cig*; D *-zhig* [37] N *kyang 'byung* [38] N omits *rgyal-po dang / blon-po dang / rte'u smra-shes-pa skyes-pa'i* and substitutes *de'i* [39] N *-yang* [40] N *gnam-las* [41] N omits *-pa*

[12] T: rgyal-po Men-drha-se-nas// drang-srong-gi mkhan-po lnga mngon-bar shes-pa-zhig-la / — bdag-cag 'khor-gyi bu dang rta-la ya-mtshan 'di-lta-bu byung // khrag-gi char-pa bab-pa ci'i ltas shes brtags-pa-dang / drang-srong na-re / khyod-gyi bus 'Dzam-bu-gling-gi sa-gzhi 'di myi-khrag-gis gsher-par byas // de'i 'og-du khyod-gyi bu 'Dzam-bu-gling-gi rgyal-po byed-par 'gyur-te //

X: rgyal-po Ma-hen-dra[1]-se-nas[2] drang-srong-gi mkhan-po lnga mngon-par shes-pa-zhig-la[3] bdag-cag[4] 'khor-gyi[5] bu dang / rta-la[6] ya-mtshan 'di-lta-bu byung-ba dang[7] / khrag-gi char-pa[8] bab-pa 'di[9] ci'i ltas[10] zhes[11] smras-pa dang[12] / drang-srong na-re /[13] khyod-kyi bus 'Dzam-bu'i gling-gi sa-gzhi[14] 'di mi'i khrag-gis gsher-bar byed-par 'gyur-ro[15] // de'i 'og-tu khyod-kyi bu[16] 'Dzam-bu'i gling-gi rgyal-po chen-po byed-par 'gyur-ro[17] zhes smras-so //

[1] P1,P3 *-gra-*, N *-'dra-* [2] N adds / [3] N adds / [4] N *bdag-gi* [5] N *'khor-du* [6] N omits *-la* [7] N omits *-ba dang* [8] N omits *-pa* [9] N omits *'di* and adds / [10] P1,P3 *bltas* [11] N *shes* [12] N substitutes *brtags-pa-las* for *smras-pa-dang* [13] P1,P3,D omit / [14] P1,P3 *-bzhi* [15] N substitutes *byas-nas* for *byed-par 'gyur-ro* [16] N omits *khyod-kyi bu* [17] N omits *-ro*; P1,P3 add //

3] T: thog-ma btsas-nas lo bcu-gnyis lon-pa-dang / de'i tshe rgyal-po Ya-ba-na dang // Pa-la-ba dang / Shag-ku-na gsum 'dus-pa'i dmag sum-'bum rgyal-po dang cha-ste // rgyal-po Men-dra-se-na'i yul-du drangs-pa-las / yul-du dmag phal-po-che byung-bas / rgyal-po snying myi-dga'-ste / mya-ngan byed-cing 'dug-pa-las / bu Du-spra-ba-sam [sic] / pha-la dris-pa yab 'di-ltar thugs myi-dgyeds-pa ci-las gyur / ces zhus-pa dang / pha na-re rgyal-po byin-po-che gsum-gyi dmag bdag-cag-gi yul-du byung-bas myi-dga' zhes smras-pa-dang / bu na-re yab myi-dgyes-su ma-mdzad-cig // yab myi-dgyes-su ⌞ma⌟-mdzad-cig // dmag 'di-dag bdag-gis thub-par bgyi'o zhes-pa-dang / <ba> pha na-re legs-so zhes-smras-te /

X: rgyal-bu de thog-ma[1] btsas-nas lo bcu-gnyis lon-pa-dang / de'i tshe rgyal-po Ya-ba-na[2] dang / Ba-lhi-ka[3] dang / Sha-ku-na gsum 'dus-pa'i dmag sum-'bum rgyal-po dang-bcas-te[4] /[5] rgyal-po Ma-hen-dra-se-na'i[6] yul-du drangs-pa-las / yul-du dmag phal-mo[7]-che byung-bas rgyal-po snying mi-dga'-ste / mya-ngan byed-cing 'dug-pa-la[8] bu Du-spra-sa-hastas[9] pha-la dris-pa / yab /[10] 'di-ltar[11] thugs mi-dgyes-pa ci-las gyur ces zhus-pa-dang[12] / pha na-re /[13] rgyal-po[14] gsum-gyi dmag-byin chen-po[15] bdag-cag-gi yul-du byung-bas mi-dga' zhes smras-pa-dang[16] / bus smras-pa /[17] yab[18] mi-dgyes[19]-su[20] ma-mdzad-cig /[21] — dmag 'di bdag-gis thub-par bgyi'o[22] zhes bgyis[23]-pa-dang / pha na-re[24] legs-so[25] zhes smras-nas /

[1] N omits *de thog-ma* [2] N omits *-na* [3] N *Ba-lā-ba* [4] N *dang-chas* [5] N omits / [6] N *Ma-he-na-'dra-se-na'i* [7] N *-po-* [8] N *-las*, and adds / [9] P1,P3 *Du-spra-sa-ha-stas*, N *Du-pras-has* [10] P1,N omit / (removed by hand in P1) [11] N *'di-lta-bu* [12] N *zhus-pa-las* [13] P1,P3,D omit / [14] N adds *byin* [15] N omits *-byin chen-po* [16] N *smraso* [17] N omits / [18] L adds / [19] P3 *-bgyes-* [20] N *mi-dgyesu* [21] P1,P3 // [22] P1 adds / [23] N omits *bgyis*; P1,P3 *bgyi* [24] L adds / [25] N *legso*

[14] T: bu dang blon-po'i̲ mtshan-ma-can lnga-brgya las-stsogste [d. . . . .] btang-nas // thab-mo byas-pa'i̲ tshe / smyi̲n-mtshams-na lcags-gyi̲ smye-ba yod-pa bskyed-nas / lus ri̲l-gyi̲s lcags-su byas-nas / rab-du khros-te brgal // Du-spra-sa-ha'i̲ dmag rgyal-te / phyi̲r log-pa-dang / pha na-re bu khyod-gyi̲s rgyal-po gsum-gyi̲ dmag 'di̲-lta-bu dang / thab-mo byas-pa-las rgyal-ba legs-so // da phyi̲n-cad khyod-kyi̲s rgyal-sri̲d zung-shi̲g / nga ni 'byung-ngo zhes bsgo-nas rgyal-sri̲d kyang bus bzung-ngo // de-nas lo bcu-gnyi̲s-gyi̲ bar-du / rgyal-po gsum-gyi̲ dmag dang 'thabs-pa-las / dmag mang-po ri̲l-gyi̲s gtugs // rgyal-po gsum yang bzung-nas // myed-par byas-so / / de phyi̲n-cad 'Dzam-bu-gli̲ng-gi̲ rgyal-po byed-par gyur-ro //

X: bu dang[1] blon-po'i[2] bu ya-mtshan-can lnga-brgya la-sogs-te /[3] dmag nyis-'bum bcas-te[4] btang-nas[5] thab[6]-mo byas-pa'i tshe / smin-mtshams-na[7] lcags-kyi sme[8]-ba[9] yod-pa[10] bskyed[11]-nas[12] lus ril lcags-su[13] byas-nas[14] rab-tu khros-nas[15] brgal[16]-ba-dang / Du-spra-sa-hasta'i[17] dmag rgyal-te[18] phyir log-pa-dang / pha na-re[19] bu[20] khyod-kyis rgyal-po gsum-gyi dmag 'di-lta-bu dang[21] thab[22]-mo byas-pa-las rgyal-ba legs-so[23] // da phyin-chad khyod-kyis rgyal-srid zung-shig /[24] nga[25] ni 'byung-ngo[26] zhes bsgo-nas srid[27] kyang[28] bu-la byin-no[29] // de-nas lo bcu-gnyis-kyi bar-du[30] rgyal-po gsum-gyi dmag dang 'thabs-pa-las[31] dmag-dpon[32] yang ril-gyis gtubs[33] / rgyal-po gsum yang bzung-nas med-par byas-so // de tshun[34]-chad[35] 'Dzam-bu'i[36]-gling-gi rgyal-po chen-po[37] byas-par gyur-to //

[1] N replaces *bu dang* with *rgyal-po*; L adds / [2] P1,P3 *-po'i̲* [3] N omits / [4] N substitutes *dang-chas-nas* for *bcas-te* [5] N omits *btang-nas* [6] L *'thab* [7] N *-nas* [8] P1,P3 *rme* [9] N adds *-la* [10] N omits *yod-pa* [11] N *skyed* [12] N adds / [13] N *lcagsu* [14] L *-na*; N adds / [15] N *-te* [16] P1,P3 *brgol*, N *brgyal* [17] P1,P3 *-ha-sta'i*, N *-ha'i* [18] N adds / [19] L inserts / [20] L inserts / [21] N adds / [22] L *'thab* [23] N *legso* [24] P1,P3,D // [25] P1,P3 *da* [*sic*] [26] N *'byungo* [27] N *rgyal-srid* [28] P1,N omit *kyang* [29] N substitutes *bus bzung* for *bu-la byin-no* [30] N adds / [31] N adds / [32] N substitutes *mang-po* for *dpon* [33] P1,P3,N *btubs* [34] N *phan* [35] D *-cad* [36] N *-bu-* [37] N omits *chen-po*

[15] T: de-nas rgyal-pos blon-po-rnams-la dri̲s-pa / nga 'Dzam-bu-gli̲ng-gi̲ rgyal-po ched-po byed-pa ni̲ dga' / gud-na myi̲-dga'-ba-ci̲g kyang yod ces smras-pa-dang / blon-pos smras-pa' / ci myi̲-dgyes shes zhus-pa-dang / sems-can mang-po 'di̲ snyed-cig

bsad-pa sdi̲g che-bas myi̲-dga / [*sic*] ’-na / 1 sdi̲g ’di̲ ci-lta-bu-zhi̲g-du byas-na ’byang-bar ’gyur zhes smras-pa-dang / blon-pos gsol-pa / Yul Ba-da-li̲’i̲-pod-tra zhes-bgyi̲-ba-na // chos-gyi̲ mkhan-po sde-snod gsum shes-pa // bram-ze Ag-na-tra-ta’i̲ bu / Shi̲r-sha-ga ces-bya-ba’i̲ bu-zhi̲g dgon-ba’i̲ sa-la gnas-pa de // spyan-drangs-na sdi̲g de ’byang-bar ’bgyi̲d-pa’i̲ rngo-thog-go zhes ng.gsol [*sic*]-pa-dang /

X: de-nas rgyal-pos[1] blon-po-rnams-la smras-pa / nga ’Dzam-bu’i-gling-gi rgyal-po chen-po[2] byed-pa ni dga’-na[3] gud-na[4] mi-dga’-ba-zhig kyang[5] yod ces smras-pa-dang[6] / blon-po-rnams-kyis smras-pa[7] / ci mi-dgyes zhes zhus[8]-pa-dang / sems-can mang-po[9] ’di[10]-snyed-cig bsad-pa[11] sdig[12] che-pas[13] mi-dga’-na / sdig[14] ’di ji-[15]lta-bu-zhig-tu[16] byas-na[17] sus[18] ’byang[19]-bar ’gyur zhes smras-pa-dang / blon-po-rnams-kyis[20] gsol-pa[21] / Yul Pa-ṭa-li-pu-tra[22]-ste[23] Dmar-bu-can[24] zhes bya[25]-ba-na[26] chos-kyi mkhan-po sde-snod gsum-la mkhas-pa[27] / bram-ze Ag-ni-da-ti- pu-tra[28]-ste Mes-byin-gyi bu zhes-bya’o // ming[29] ni[30] Shi-ṣya-ka[31]-ste / Slob-ma-can[32] zhes-bya[33]-ba-zhig dgon-pa’i gnas[34]-na gnas-pa de spyan-drangs-nas[35] mchod-bkur bgyis-na[36] sdig-pa[37] ’byang[38] rngo thogs-so[39] zhes[40] gsol-pa-dang /

[1] N *-po* [2] N omits *chen-po* [3] N adds / [4] N *-nas*, L *-pa* [5] N omits *kyang* [6] N *smraso* [7] N omits *smras-pa* [8] N *dris* [9] N *-po’i* [10] N *de* [11] P1,P3 *bsang-ba*, N *bsad-pa’i* [12] P1,P3,N *sdig-pa* [13] P1,P3 *add* / [14] N *sdig-pa* [15] N omits *ji* [16] P1,P3 *-du* [17] N *-nas* [18] P1,P3 omit *sus* [19] P1,P3 *’byad* [*sic*] [20] L *-kyi* [21] N *smras-pa* [22] P1 *Ba-ta-li-bu-tra*, P3 *Pa-ṭa-li-phu-tra*, N *Bo-da-li-po-tra* [23] N omits *-ste* [24] N omits *Dmar-bu-can* [25] N *-bgyi-* [26] N adds / [27] N replaces *-la mkhas-pa* with *shes-pa* [28] P1,P3 *Ag-ne-ta-ti-bu-tra*, N *A-kan-dra-dha’i bu* [29] P1,P3 *mid* [*sic*] [30] N omits *-ste Mes-byin-gyi bu zhes-bya’o // ming ni* [31] P1,N *Shir-sha-ka*, P3 *Shi-ṣu-ka* [*sic*!] [32] N omits *-ste / Slob-ma-can* [33] N *-bgyi-* [34] N *sa* [35] N adds / [36] P1,P3 *-ni*; N omits *mchod-bkur bgyis-na* [37] N omits *-pa*; P1 hand-corrected to *-pā’i* [*sic*!] [38] N adds *-bar bgyid* [39] P1,P3 *thog-go*, N omits *-so* [40] N *ces*

6] T: rgyal-po dga’-nas // dge-slong Shi̲r-sha-ga ’gugs-pa’ btang-nas / rgyal-po’i̲ drung-du’o ’ongs-so // mkhan-po Shi̲r-she-ka-la rgyal-pos phyag-bya-ste // sdi̲g-pa byas-pa’i̲-rnams / thabs ci̲-zhi̲g-gi̲s sbyangs zhes zhus-pa-dang / dkon-mchog gsum-la lo bcu-gnyi̲s-gyi̲ bar-du / mchod-ci̲ng skyabs gsol-na / sdi̲g ’byang-bar ’gyur-ro zhes byas-so //

X: rgyal-po yang[1] dgyes[2]-nas dge-slong Shi-ṣya-ka[3] yang 'gugs-pa btang-nas[4] rgyal-po'i drung-du 'ongs-so[5] // de-nas[6] mkhan-po Shi-ṣya-ka[7]-la rgyal-pos phyag-byas-te / mkhan-po[8] bdag-gis[9] sdig byas-pa-rnams cis[10] 'byang[11]-bar 'gyur zhes gsol[12]-pa-dang / mkhan-po smras-pa / rgyal-po[13] chen-po[14] dkon-mchog gsum-la lo bcu-gnyis-kyi bar-du mchod-cing[15] skyabs-su[16] song[17]-na[18] sdig[19]-rnams[20] 'byung [*sic*]-bar 'gyur-ro[21] zhes smras-pa-dang[22] /

[1] N omits *yang* [2] N *dga'* [3] P1,N *Shir-sha-ka*; P3 *Shi-ṣu-ka* [4] N *-ste* [5] N *'ongso* [6] N omits *de-nas* [7] P1,N *Shir-sha-ka* [8] P1 *-pos* [9] N omits *mkhan-po bdag-gis* [10] N *ci-zhig-gis* [11] N *byang* [12] N *zhus* [13] P3 *-pos* [*sic*] [14] N omits *mkhan-po smras-pa / rgyal-po chen-po* [15] N adds / [16] N *skyabsu* [17] N *gsik* [18] N adds / [19] P1,P3,N *add -pa* [20] N omits *-rnams* [21] N *'gyuro* [22] N replaces *smras-pa-dang* by *byaso*

[17] T: de-nas 'Dzam-bu-gling-na dge-slong 'dug-go-cog 'gugs-pa btang-ste / ril-gyis 'Ga'-'ga'i pha-rol yul Ke'u-sham-'byi'i rgyal-po gnas-par bsdus-ste // yul-sa gzhan-du chos spyod-par myi-ster-par 'gyur-ro // dge-slong bsdus-pa de'i tshe / lam-du chud zos-pa yang mang / rgyal-po'i 'khor-du ni 'bum-tsam-zhig-gis phyin-par gyur-ro // dge-slong lam-du chud zos-pa yang / gcan-zan sna-tshogs dang / myi-rgod dang / chu las-stogs-pas khyer-te chud zos-so // dge-'dun mang-po phyin-ba dang // dge-'dun-la rgyal-pos mchod-ston gsol / yon-phul mchod-par byas-so //

X: de-nas rgyal-po Du-spra-sa-ha-stas pho-nya mang-po phyogs-bcur btang-ste /[1] 'Dzam-bu'i gling-gi dge-slong ril[2] 'ongs-te /[3] chu-bo Gang-ga'i[4] pha-rol[5] yul Ko'usām-bī'i[6] rgyal-po Du-spra-sa-ha-sta'i[7] gnas[8] ga-la-ba der[9] bsdus-pas[10] yul-khams[11] gzhan[12] chos spyod-pa dang / dge-slong-dag med-par 'gyur-ro[13] // dge-slong bsdus-pa de'i tshe-na[14] lam-du dge-slong gyag-cing[15] chud zos-pa yang mang-ste[16] / rgyal-po'i[17] pho-brang[18]-du ni 'bum-tsam-zhig[19] phyin-par 'gyur-ro[20] / dge-slong lam-du gyag-cing[21] chud zos-pa yang gcan-gzan[22] sna-tshogs dang / mi-rgod dang / chu la-sogs-pas phal khyer-te[23] chud zos-so // dge-'dun mang-po phyin-pa-dang /[24] rgyal-pos mchod-ston drangs[25] / yon phul-te mchod-pa byas-so[26] /

[1] P1,P3 *-te*; P1, P3 add *Dzam-bu'i gling-na dge-slong 'du-go-cog bkug-te* / [2] P1,P3 *ril-po* [3] N omits *rgyal-po Du-spra-sa-ha-stas pho-nya mang-po phyogs-bcur btang-ste / 'Dzam-bu'i gling-gi dge-slong ril 'ongs-te / chu-bo* and substitutes *'Dzam-bu-gling-na dge-slong 'dug-gi chog-la 'gug-pa btang-ste / ril-gyis* [4] N *'Ga'-'ga'i* [5] N adds *-tu* [6] P1 *Ke'u-sham-ha'i* [*sic*], P3 *Ko'u-sham-ba'i*, N *Ko'u-sha-bi-na* [7] N omits *Du-spra-sa-ha-sta'i* [8] N adds *-par* [9] N omits *ga-la-ba der* [10] N *-ste* [11] N omits *-khams* [12] P1,P3 add *-na*, N adds *-du* [13] P1,P3 *gyur-to*; N omits *spyod-pa dang / dge-slong-dag med-par 'gyur-ro* and substitutes *spyod-du mi-ster-bar 'gyuro* [14] N omits *-na* [15] N omits *dge-slong gyag-cing* [16] N omits *-ste* [17] P1,P3 *-po'i* [18] N substitutes *'khor* for *pho-brang* [19] N omits *-zhig* and adds *-gis* [20] P1,P3 *gyur-to*, N *'gyuro* [21] N omits *gyag-cing* [22] P1,P3 *-zan* [23] P1,P3 add / [24] N adds *dge-'dun-la* [25] N *gsol* [26] N substitutes *mchod-do* for *mchod-pa byas-so*

[8] T: de'i tshe dge-'dun-gyi-rnams gcig-la-gcig gtam-du smras-pa // khyed-gyi mkhan-po ga-re slob-ma gar-song / grogs-po khrims-zla ga-re zhes-so-so-nas gtam-du glengs-pa-las / stag dang seng-'ge dang / myi-rgod-gyis bsad-pa dang / chus khyer-ba dang / nad-gyis btabs-ste shi-ba las-stsogs-pa'i gtam byas-pa-nas dge-slong so-so-nas mya-ngan langs-nas // ngud-mos 'debs brang rtob-par 'gyur-ro // de-nas de'i tshe rgyal-pos / mya-ngan ma-bgyid ma-ngu zhes bsgo-ba-dang / dge-'dun-rnams ma-nyan-pa-dang / rgyal-po yang myi-dga'-bar gyur-nas / kha phyog-ste nyal-lo //

X: de'i tshe dge-'dun-rnams gcig-la-gcig gtam-du smras-pa / khyed-kyi mkhan-po ga-re / slob-ma gar song / grogs-po khrims-zla ga-re zhes so-sor gtam-du[1] glengs[2]-pa-dang / stag dang / seng-ge dang / mi-rgod-kyis[3] bsad-pa dang / chus khyer-pa dang / nad-kyis btab-nas[4] shi-ba la-sogs-pa'i gtam byas-nas dge-slong so-so-nas mya-ngan langs-te[5] ngud[6]-mos[7] 'debs-te[8] brang rdung-ngo[9] /[10] de-nas de'i tshe rgyal-pos mya-ngan ma-bgyid[11] ma-ngus[12] zhes bsgo-ba-dang[13] / dge-'dun-rnams[14] ma-nyan[15]-pa-dang / rgyal-po yang mi-dga'-nas[16] kha phyogs-te nyal-lo /[17]

[1] P1,P3 *-tu* [2] N *dris* [3] P1,P3 *-gyis* [4] N *-ste* [5] P1,P3,N add / [6] P1 *ngur* [7] N *-mo* [8] N omits *-te*; P1,P3 add / [9] N *rdob-par 'gyuro* [10] P1 // [11] N *ma-byed-cig* [12] P1 *-ngu*, P3 *-tus* [*sic*!], N omits *ma-ngus* [13] N omits *dang* [14] N adds *-kyis* [15] P1,P3 *mnyan* [16] N *mi-dga'-bar gyur-nas* / [17] N //

[19] T: nyal-ba’i̲ tshe smon-lam-du btab-pa // da ’ji̲g-rten-gyi̲ dge-’dun-rnams-la ni̲ skyabs kyang ma-byung-na // dgra-bcom-ba’i̲ zhal mthong-bar shog-shi̲g ces smon-lam btab-pa-las / ’ji̲g-rten-gyi̲ lhas rmyi̲-lam-du bstan-pa / ri̲ K.han-dha-ma-ha-ya-na’i̲ ri̲-la / — S.hu-dha-ra-sh.ha-na’i̲ bu — Su-rad ces-bya-ba dgra- bcom-ba-zhi̲g bzhug-ste // de spyan-drangs-na / sdi̲g kyang ’byang / the-tsom yang khrel-to zhes bstan-pa rmyi̲s-pa-dang // rgyal-po sad-nas ’phral-du pho-nya bskye-ste — — spyan-drangs-nas phyi̲n-pa-dang // dgra-bcom-ba-la rgyal-pos mchod-ci̲ng phyag-byas-so // —

X: nyal-ba’i tshe smon-lam-du btab-pa /[1] gang-zag-gi[2] dge-’dun-la ni skyabs-su song-nas mchod-pa byas-na[3] / bdag-gis[4] dgra-bcom-pa’i zhal ma-mthong-ste / bdag-gis[5] dgra-bcom-pa-zhig-gi zhal[6] mthong-bar shog-shig ces smon-lam-du btab-pa-dang / ’jig-rten-gyi lha-zhig-gis[7] rmi-ltas[8]-su[9] bstan-pa / Gandha-mā-da-na[10]-ste[11] Spos-ngad-ldan zhes-bya-ba’i ri-la[12] Su-dhana- pu-tra-ra-tna-sa[13]-ste[14] Tshong-dpon nor-bzang-gi[15] bu zhes-bya-ba rab-tu byung-ba[16] Su-ra-ta[17]-ste[18] Des-pa[19] zhes[20] bya-bar[21] ming btags[22]-pa[23] dgra-bcom-pa’i[24] ’bras-bu thob-pa[25]-zhig bzhugs[26]-te / de spyan-drangs-nas[27] bsnyen-bkur byas-te / de-la[28] sdig bshags[29]-na[30] sdig[31] kyang[32] ’byang /[33] the-tshom[34] yang bral[35]-bar ’gyur-ro[36] zhes lhas bstan-pa rmis-pa[37] dang / rgyal-po sar-pa[38]-dang ’phral-du pho-nya bkye[39]-ste / Spos-ngad-ldang-ga[40] ri-las dgra-bcom-pa Su-ra-ta[41] spyan-drangs-te[42] / rgyal-po’i pho-brang-du[43] byon[44]-pa-dang /[45] rgyal-pos kyang tshul-bzhin-du[46] phyag byas-shing[47] mchod-de bsnyen-bkur byas-so[48] //

[1] N omits / [2] N omits *gang-zag-gi* and substitutes *da ’jig-rten-gyi* [3] N replaces *skyabs-su song-nas mchod-pa byas-na* with *skyabs kyang ma-byung-na* [4] N omits *bdag-gis* [5] P3 *-gos* [*sic*] [6] N omits *ma-mthong-ste / bdag-gis dgra-bcom-pa-zhig-gi zhal* [7] N *lhas* [8] P1,P3 *-bltas-* [9] N *rmi-lam-du* [10] P1 *Gan-da-ma-ya* [*sic*!], N *Gan-dha-ma-ha-na’i* [11] N omits *-ste* and adds *ri-la* /[12] N omits *Spos-ngad-ldan zhes-bya-ba’i ri-la* [13] P1 *Su-dha-rha-sha-na*, P3 *Su-dha-na-pu-tra-ra-tna-sha*, N *Surad-sha-na’i bu* [14] N omits *-ste*; P3 substitutes *zhes-pa’ang snang ni sta* [*sic*] [15] P1 *bzangs-gyi* [16] N omits *Tshong-dpon nor-bzang-gi bu zhes-bya-ba rab-tu byung-ba* [17] P1 *Su-dha-dha*, P3 *Surat* [*sic*], N *Su-ra-da* [18] N omits *-ste* [19] N omits *Des-pa* [20] N *ces* [21] N *-ba* [22] P1,P3 *gdags* [23] N omits *ming btags-pa* [24] N *-pa-zhig* [25] N omits *’bras-bu thob-pa* [26] N *gzhugs* [27] N *-na* [28] P1 *de-las*; P3 *ngo-las* [*sic*] [29] P3 *gshegs* [30] N omits *bsnyen-bkur byas-te / de-la sdig bshags-na* [31] P1,P3 *sdig-pa* [32] P1,P3 *yang* [33] P1,P3 omit / [34] P1,P3 *tsom* [35] N *srel* [36] N *’gyuro*; P1,P3 add //

[37] N omits *lhas bstan-pa rmis-pa* [38] P1,P3 *sang-ba*, N *sad-de* [39] P1,P3 *bskye* [40] P1 *-gi*; P3 *-ge* [41] P1 *Su-dha-dha*, P3 *Su-rat*; N omits *Spos-ngad-ldang-ga ri-las dgra-bcom-pa Su-ra-ta* [42] N *-nas* [43] N omits *rgyal-po'i pho-brang-du* [44] N *phyin* [45] N adds *dgra-bcom-pa-la* [46] N omits *kyang tshul-bzhin-du* and substitutes *mchod-cing* [47] N *byaso* [48] N omits *mchod-de bsnyen-bkur byas-so*

20] T: de'i̲ dus-na tshes bcu-bzhi̲'i̲ nub-mo dge-'dun ri̲l-gyi̲s 'dus-pa'i̲ nang-nas // dge-slong gsar zhugs-rnams-gyi̲s // sde-snon [*sic*] gsum 'tshal-pa Shi̲r-sha-ka-la 'dul bshad-par gsol-ba-las / Sher-she-ka na-re / myi̲-la myi̲g zhar sna dang // rna-ba myed-na mye-long ci̲ dgos / bltar ci̲ yod / 'dul-ba bshad kyang khyod 'dul-ba ltar myi̲ spyod // chos-khri̲ms myi̲ srung-ba' / [*sic*]-la 'dul-ba bshad kyang ji'i̲ phan zhes smras-pa-dang / de'i̲ tshe So-rad ces-bya-ba dgra-bcom-bas / seng-ge'i̲ sgra bzhi̲n-du smras-pa' / sangs-rgyas bcom-ldan-'das-gyi̲ chos-khri̲ms ngas mnos-nas / da-tsam-gyi̲ bar-du rts*v*a-mchog-tsam yang ma-nyams-na // de-skad ma-zer-bar 'dul-ba shod-ci̲g ces ⌞smras⌟-pa-dang /

X: de'i dus-na tshes bcu-bzhi'i nub-mo dge-'dun ril-gyis[1] 'dus-pa'i nang-nas / dge-slong gsar zhugs-rnams-kyis sde-snod gsum shes-pa'i mkhan-po Shi-ṣya-ka[2]-la Prā-ti-mo-kṣa[3] gden[4]-par gsol-pa-las / Shi-ṣya-ka[5] na-re /[6] mi-la mig zhar / snga dang[7] rna-ba med-na[8] me-long ci dgos / bltar ci yod / 'dul-ba bshad kyang khyed 'dul-ba-ltar[9] mi-spyod / tshul[10]-khrims mi-bsrungs[11]-ba-la 'dul-ba bshad kyang[12] ci phan zhes smras-pa-dang / de'i tshe Su-ra-ta[13] zhes[14] bya-ba dgra-bcom-pas seng-ge'i sgra byung[15]-nas[16] smras-pa / sangs-rgyas bcom-ldan-'das-kyi tshul[17]-khrims ngas[18] mnos-nas[19] da[20]-tsam-gyi[21] bar-du rtsv̲a̲[22]-mchog-tsam yang ma-nyams-na / 'di[23]-skad ma-zer-bar Prā-ti-mo-kṣa[24] thon-cig-par[25] smras-pa-dang /

[1] N omits *ril-gyis* [2] P1,N *Shir-sha-ka*; P3 *Shi-ṣu-ka* [3] P1 replaces *Prā-ti-mo-kṣa* with *mo-kṣa*, P2 with *mo-kā* [*sic*], N with *'dul-ba* [4] P1,P3 *gdon*, N *bshad* [5] P1,N *Shir-sha-ka*; P3 *Shi-ṣu-ka* [6] N,D omit / [7] L adds / [8] N adds / [9] P1 *bltar* [10] N *chos* [11] N *srung* [12] N *na* [13] P1 *Su-rad*, P3 *Surat* [*sic*], N *Su-rad* (xyl. *Su-su-rad*) [14] N *ces* [15] P1,P3,D *phyung* [16] N omits *byung-nas* and adds *bzhin-du* [17] N *chos* [18] P1 *des* [19] N adds / [20] P3 *nga* [21] L *-gyis* [22] P1,P3 *rtsa* [23] N *de* [24] P1,P3 *bra-sti-mo-kṣa*, N *'dul-ba* [25] N omits *thon-cig-par* and substitutes *shod ces*

[21] T: mkhan-po Shi̲r-she-kya yang dgra-bcom-ba ngo-shes-nas / rab-du gnong-ste / myi̲-smra-'o // Shi̲r-she-ka'i̲ slob-ma dge-slong A-gan-dhe'i̲ zhes-bya-ba de'i̲ 'khor-du 'dus-pa'i̲ nang-nas langste / Su-rad ces-bya-ba dgra-bcom-ba de-la / khyod ci̲-ste nga'i̲ mkhan-po-la 'di̲-skad ces smra / khyod khri̲ms-zla yang myed 'dul-ba yang myi̲-shes // nga'i̲ mkhan-po sde-ba snon [*sic*] gsum dang / [*sic*] ldan-ba-la / ci̲'i̲ phyi̲r brnyas-te khros-nas / sgo-gtan blangste / dgra-bcom-ba-la brdegs-nas bsad-do //

X: mkhan-po Shi-ṣya-ka'ang[1] dgra-bcom-par[2] ngo[3] shes-te[4] rab-tu skyengs-nas cang[5] mi-zer-ba-dang[6] / Shi-ṣya-ka'i[7] slob-ma dge-slong Aṃ-ga-da[8]-ste Dpung-gi tshogs 'jigs-su rung[9] zhes bya-ba de 'khor 'dus[10]-pa'i nang-nas langs-te Su-ra-ta[11] zhes[12] bya-ba dgra-bcom-pa de-la khyed[13] ci-ste nga'i mkhan-po-la de-skad smra / khyod khrims kyang med / 'dul-ba'ang[14] mi-shes-na[15] / nga'i mkhan-po sde-snod gsum-la mkhas-pa de-la[16] ci'i phyir kha-zlogs[17] zhes[18] khros-nas sgo-gtan blangs-te /[19] dgra-bcom-pa brdegs[20]-nas[21] bsad[22]-do //

[1] P1,N *Shir-sha-ka yang*; P3 *Shi-ṣu-ka yang* [2] N *dgra-bcom-pa yin-par* [3] N omits *ngo* [4] N *-nas* [5] N omits *skyengs-nas cang* and reads *gnong-ste* [6] N omits *mi-zer-ba-dang* and writes *mi-smra'o* [7] P1,N *Shir-sha-ka'i*; P3 *Shi-ṣu-ka'i* [8] P1 *A-gan-ti*, P3 *Aṃ-ga-ta* (abbrev. *A°-ga-ta*), N *A-ka-de* [9] P1,P3 add *-ba*; N omits *-ste Dpung-gi tshogs 'jigs-su-rung* [10] L *'dug* [11] P1,N *Su-rad*; P3 *Su-rat* [12] N *ces* [13] N *khyod* [14] P1,P3,D *-yang* [15] P1,P3 omit *na* [16] N adds / [17] P1,P3 add /; N omits *kha-zlogs* and writes *brnyas* [18] N *ces* [19] N omits *sgo-gtan blangs-te /* [20] P1,P3 *gdegs* [21] N *-te* [22] N *gsad*

[22] T: de'i̲ tshe chos-la dga'-ba'i̲ gnod-sbyi̲n 'Dhi̲d-dha-mu-kha zhes-bya-ba lag-par rdo-rje thog-ste / mngon-du byung-nas // dge-slong A-gan-la-la [sic] ci̲-ste-ba dgra-bcom-ba bsad ces-smras-nas / rdo-rje phyungs-ste bsad-do // de'i̲ dus-na dge-slong Ge-rad ces bya-bas / mkhan-po Shi̲r-she-ka-la brdegs-ste / bsad-do // de-nas rdo-rje'i̲ rjes-la dge-'dun ri̲l-gi̲s / gci̲g-gi̲s-gcig bsad-de // gci̲g kyang ma-lus-so //

X: de'i tshe[1] chos-la dga'-ba'i gnod-sbyin Da-dhi-mu-kha[2] Zho-gdong[3] Dir-rga-mu-kha[4] zhes bya-bas[5] lag-par rdo-rje thogs-nas[6] mngon-du byung-ste[7] / dge-slong Aṃ-ga-da[8]-la /[9] ci-ste dgra-bcom-pa bsad ces zer-te[10] rdo-rje phyung-nas bsad-do // de'i dus-na dge-slong Ge-rad[11] ces bya-bas mkhan-po[12] Shi-ṣya-ka[13] brdegs-te bsad-do // de-nas de'i rjes-la dge-'dun[14] ril-gyis 'khrugs-nas[15] gcig-gis-gcig bsad-de[16] gcig[17] kyang ma- lus-so //

[1] N omits *de'i tshe* [2] N *Di-ta-mu-kha* [3] P1 omits *Da-dhi-mu-kha Zho-gdong* [4] P3 *Dir-nam-kha'* [*sic*]; N omits *Zho-gdong Dir-rga-mu-kha* [5] N adds / [6] N *-te* [7] N *-nas* [8] P1 *A-gan-ti*, P3 *A-gad*, N *A-ga-di* [9] N omits / [10] N *smras-nas* [11] P1 *Gi-rang*, P3 *Ge-rang*, L *Gi-rad* [12] N *dge-slong* [13] P1,N *Shir-sha-ka*, P3 *Shi-shuka* [*sic*] [14] N *dge-slong* [15] N omits *'khrugs-nas* [16] P3 *-da*, N *-do //* [17] P1,P3 *cig*

23] T: de'i̲ dus-na nam-ka ⌞lha klu⌟ las-stsogs-pa chos-gyi̲ srungs-ma phal-mo-che myi̲-dga'-nas / ngus-pa'i̲ mchi̲-ma ni̲ khrag dang mye'i̲ char-pas gzhi̲ der bab-bo // nam-ka yang ser-po nag-po-dag-du gyur-zhi̲ng ldog-sgra chen-po 'byung // skar-ma 'Du-mu-ge-ta [*sic*] zhes-bya-ba lus-las du-ba nag-po mthong-ba-zhi̲g byung-ste / de-nas zla-ba dang skar-ma las-stsogs-pa 'od kyang myed gci̲g kyang bltar mi . . . . de'i dus-na sum-cu-rtsa-gsum gnam-gyi̲ lha . . . . phal-mo-che dang der 'ongs-nas // dge-'dun-gyi̲ gos mtshon-can ri̲l-gyi̲ [sic] bsdus-te khye . . . .

X: de'i dus-na nam-mkha'-la[1] lha klu la-sogs-pa[2] chos-kyi srung[3]-ma phal-po-che ma[4]-dga'-nas[5] ngus-pa'i mchi-ma ni khrag dang[6] me'i char[7] bab-bo // nam-mkha'[8]-dag ni[9] ser[10] dang /[11] nag-por[12] gyur[13] / glog[14] dang /[15] sgra chen-po byung / skar-ma Dhū-ma-ke-tu[16] zhes bya-ba[17] lus-las du-ba nag-po gtong-ba[18]-zhig byung-nas[19] / des skar-ma[20] dang[21] zla-ba[22] la-sogs-pa[23] 'od kyang med / gcig kyang bltar mi-snang-bar 'ong-ngo[24] // de'i dus-na sum-cu[25]-rtsa-gsum gnam-gyi lha dang / yum Mā-yā-de-bi[26] la-sogs-pa[27] 'khor phal-mo[28]-che dang[29] der 'ongs-nas[30] dge-'dun-gyi[31] gos tshon-can ril-gyis[32] bsdus-nas[33] khyer-bar 'ong-ngo[34] //

[1] N *-las* [2] N adds / [3] P1,P3 *bsrungs* [4] N *mi* [5] P1,P3 insert / [6] N,L insert / [7] N adds *sa-gzhi der* [8] N *namkha' yang* [9] N omits *-dag ni* [10] P1,N *ser-po* [11] N omits *dang /* [12] N *-po //* [13] N *gyur-cing* [14] P1,D *glog-po* [15] N omits *dang /* [16] P1,N *Du-ma-ke-du*, P3 *Du-me-ke-du* [17] N *-ba'i* [18] N omits *gtong-ba* [19] N *-ste* [20] N *zla-ba* [21] L adds / [22] N *nyi-ma* [23] N *-pa'i* [24] P1 *'od-do* [25] P1,P3 *-bcu-* [26] P1 *Ma-ya-dem-bi*, P3 *Ma-ya-de-ba'i*, N *Mā-hā-ma-ya* [27] N adds / [28] N *-po-* [29] N omits *dang* [30] N adds / [31] D *-kyi* [32] N omits *-gyis* [33] N *-te* [34] N *'ongo*

[24] T: de'i̲ dus-na rgyal-pos 'di̲-lta-bu'i̲ ku-cho sgra chen-po byung-ba ci̲-las gyur ces smras-pa dang / dge-'dun 'khrugs-nas / gci̲g-gi̲s-gci̲g bsad-par gyur-to zhes gsol-pa-dang / rgyal-po myi̲-dga'-ste langs-nas tho-ras . . mkhar dgy . . phyi̲ . r . . gyi̲ lha-gang-du phyi̲n-ba dang / dge-'dun la-la-ni̲ . . . . . . kha-cig ng.ni̲ [*sic*] rkang-pa bcag // kha-ci̲g ni̲ dmyi̲g phyungs-ste // de-ltar sna-tshogs-su shi̲-ba mthong-nas / dgra-bcom-ba dang Sher-she-ka sde-snod gsum shes-pa'i̲ mkhan-po'i̲ ro rnyed-nas // mchan [*sic*]-khung g.yas-g.yos-su bcug-nas // dgra-bcom-ba ni̲ nga'i̲ ma yi̲n / Shi̲r-she-kha ni̲ chos-gyi̲ mdzod yi̲n-te / 'di̲ gnyi̲s 'das-par gyur-pa ni̲ / da phyi̲n-cad nga'i̲ lus dang srog-la yang gces-pa myed // rgyal-sri̲d kyang su 'edod [*sic*]-pa sbyi̲n-no zhes smras-nas // dmyi̲g kyang btsums-ste // myi̲-mthong-bar 'gyur-ro //

X: de'i dus-na rgyal-po[1] 'di-lta-bu'i ku-co[2] sgra chen-po byung-ba ci-las gyur ces smras-pa-dang / dge-'dun 'khrugs-nas gcig-gis-gcig bsad-par gyur-to zhes gsol-ba-dang / rgyal-po mi-dga'-ste[3] / langs-nas[4] tho-rangs mkhar-gyi phyi-rol-gyi lha-khang-du phyin-pa-dang / dge-'dun la-la ni mgo bcad / la-la ni mig phyung / la-la ni[5] rkang lag bcad-de[6] / de-ltar sna-tshogs-su[7] shi-ba mthong-nas / dgra-bcom-pa dang / Shi-ṣya-ka[8] sde-snod gsum shes-pa'i mkhan-po'i ro btsal[9]-nas gnyis-ka'i[10] ro snyed-pa-dang[11] / mtshan-khung g.yas-g.yon-du[12] bzhag[13]-nas[14] dgra-bcom-pa ni nga'i pha[15] yin / Shi-ṣya-ka[16] ni chos-kyi mdzod yin[17] / 'di gnyis 'das-par gyur-pa ni da-phyin-cad nga'i lus dang /[18] srog kyang gces-pa med / rgyal-srid kyang su 'dod-pa-la sbyin-no zhes smras-pa-dang[19] / mig kyang ldongs[20]-te mi-snang[21]-bar gyur-to[22] /

[1] N *-pos* [2] N *-cho* [3] N *-nas* [4] N *-ste* [5] P1 omits *ni* [6] N omits *la-la ni mgo bcad / la-la ni mig phyung / la-la ni rkang lag bcad-de / de-ltar* and substitutes *la-la ni rkang lag bcad / kha-cig ni mig phyung 'di-ltar* [7] N *-tshogsu* [8] P1,N *Shir-sha-ka*, P3 *Shi-shu-ka* [9] P1,P3 *brtsal* [10] N *gnyi-ga'i* [11] N *snyed-de* [12] N *-su* [13] P1,P3 *gzhag*, N *bcug* [14] N adds / [15] N *ma* [16] P1 *Shir-sha-ka*, P3 *Shi-shu-ka*, N *Shir-shā-ka* [17] N adds *-te* [18] N omits *dang*, L adds / [19] N *smras-nas* [20] N *btsums* [21] N *-lta-* [22] N *'gyuro*, L *gyur-te*

[25] T: de'i̲ dus-na blon-po-rnams-gyi̲s / rgyal-po-la snyi̲ng-brtse-ste / mya-ngan bsang-ba'i̲ phyi̲r / myi̲ lnga-brgya ban-de de-ltar bcos-ste / mgo dang kha-spu breg-du spu-gri̲s ma-mchod-nas // kha-spu dang skra yang myes bsregs / mtshon sna brgya-rtsa-bcu

yang de'i̲ tshe nub-pas // ban-de lnga-brgya' yang chos-gos myi̲-bdog-nas / phyugs nag-po dang dmar-po'i̲ ko-ba gyon-te ban-de ltar bcos-nas // rgyal-po'i̲ drung-du 'ongs-so //

X: de'i dus-na blon-po-rnams-kyis[1] rgyal-po-la snying-brtse[2]-ste / mya-ngan bsang-ba'i[3] phyir[4] mi lnga-brgya[5] ban-de[6] ltar bcos-te / skra[7] dang[8] kha-spu breg-tu spu-gris ma-chod[9]-nas / skra dang[10] kha-spu mes bsregs / tshon sna brgya yang de'i tshe nub-pas ban-de[11] lnga-brgya yang chos-gos mi-bdog-nas[12] phyugs nag-po dang / dmar-po'i ko-ba gyon-te / ban-de[13] ltar bcos-nas rgyal-po'i drung-du 'ongs-so //

[1] N omits *-kyis* [2] P1,P3 *-rtse-* [3] P1 *bsad-pa'i* [4] N adds / [5] P1,P3 *-brgyar* [6] L *bande* [7] N *mgo* [8] D, L insert / [9] P3 *mchod-* [10] L inserts / [11] P1,P3 *ban-dhe* (*h* added by hand in P1), L *bande* [12] N omits *skra dang kha-spu mes bsregs / tshon sna brgya yang de'i tshe nub-pas ban-de lnga-brgya yang chos-gos mi-bdog-nas* [13] P1,P3 *ban-dhe*, L *bande*

6] T: blon-pos rgyal-po-la ban-de lnga-brgya 'ongs-so zhes gsol-pa-dang / rgyal-po dga'-nas dmyi̲g phye-ste ban-de-la bltas-na / 'di̲r yang ri̲l-gyi̲s phyugs-gyi̲ phags-pas gos-su gyon-la // skra dang skha-spu las-stsogs-pa ma-bregs-par myes ma-btab-bar mthong-nas / rgyal-po dga'-nas / dkon-mchog gsu°-la mchod-pa'i̲ yo-byad 'on-ci̲g ces-bsgo-nas // ban-de-rnams-la — — — —

X: blon-pos rgyal-po-la ban-de[1] lnga-brgya 'ongs-so zhes gsol-pa[2]-dang / rgyal-po dga'-nas mig phye-ste[3] bande[4]-dag[5]-la /[6] brtags-na[7] / ban-de[8] yang ril-gyis phyugs-kyi pags-pa[9] gos-su[10] gyon-la / skra dang /[11] kha-spu ma-bregs-par[12] mes bsregs-pa[13] ni[14] ma[15]-mthong-nas rgyal-po yang[16] dga'-ste / dkon-mchog-gsum-la mchod-pa'i yo-byad 'on-cig ces[17] bsgo-nas[18] ban-de[19] de-rnams-la mchod-de[20] /[21] ban-de[22]-rnams-la rgyal-pos zhib-tu[23] brtags-na / phyugs-kyi pags-pa chos-gos-su gyon[24]-la / skra dang[25] kha[26]-spu ma-bregs-par mes bsregs-pa gsal-bar mthong-nas rgyal-po-nyid som-nyi-ru gyur-te / 'di-dag dge-slong ni ma-yin mod-kyi / bdag-gis cung-zad-cig dri'o[27] snyam-nas /ban-de[28]-rnams-la rgyal-pos zhib-tu[29] brtags-na / phyugs-kyi pags-pa chos-gos-su gyon[30]-la / skra dang[31] kha[32]-spu ma-bregs-par mes bsregs-pa gsal-bar mthong-nas rgyal-po-nyid som-nyi-ru gyur-te / 'di-dag dge-slong ni ma-yin mod-kyi / bdag-gis cung-zad-cig dri'o[33] snyam-nas /[34]

[1] P1,P3 *ban-dhe,* L *bande* [2] N *smras-pha* [3] P1,P3 *phyed-de* [4] P1,N,D *ban-de,* P3 *ban-dhe* [5] N omits *-dag-* [6] P1,P3,N omit / [7] N *bltas-pa-dang* [8] P1,P3 *ban-dhe,* L *bande* [9] N *ko-ba* [10] N *gosu* [11] D omits / [12] N omits *ma-bregs-par* [13] N *-par* [14] N omits *ni* [15] N omits *ma* [16] N omits *yang* [17] N omits *ces* and adds *-par* [18] N adds // [19] P1,P3 *ban-dhe,* L *bande* [20] N *-do* [21] N // [22] P1,P3 *ban-dhe,* L *bande* [23] P1,P3 *-du* [24] P3 *gon-,* P1 *gyon* (*y* added by hand) [25] L inserts / [26] P3 *la-,* P1 hand-corrected (from *la*?) to read *kha-* [27] P1,P3 *'dra'o* [28] P1,P3 *ban-dhe,* L *bande* [29] P1,P3 *-du* [30] P3 *gon-,* P1 *gyon* (*y* added by hand) [31] L inserts / [32] P3 *la-,* P1 hand-corrected (from *la*?) to read *kha-* [33] P1,P3 *'dra'o* [34] N omits *ban-de-rnams-la rgyal-pos zhib-tu brtags-na / phyugs-kyi pags-pa chos-gos-su gyon-la / skra dang kha-spu ma-bregs-par mes bsregs-pa gsal-bar mthong-nas rgyal-po-nyid som-nyi-ru gyur-te / 'di-dag dge-slong ni ma-yin mod-kyi / bdag-gis cung-zad-cig dri'o snyam-nas /*

[27] T: ⌞rgyal-po⌟ the-tsom dris-pa-dang // chos ci gcig kyang myi-shes-nas / — — — — rgyal-po yang mya-ngan langs-ste / ngu'o // ban-de phal-mo-che shi-ba'i ro phal-mo-che ril-gyis bsregs-ste mchod-pa byed-do // —

X: dge-slong-gi lta-ba dang / tshul-khrims gang yin zhes dris-na / de-rnams gang-gis kyang dge-slong-gi lta-ba dang / tshul-khrims dang / brtul-zhugs cung-zad kyang mi-shes-pas rgyal-po de-la[1] lan ma-btab-par cang mi-smra-bar 'khod-pa-dang / rgyal-pos bsams-pa / da ni sangs-rgyas-kyi bstan-pa nub-ste[2] / dkon-mchog gsum-gyi tshul yang-dag-par rgyun-chad-pa lta-zhig snyam-nas[3] rgyal-po yang mya-ngan chen-po[4] langs-te[5] ngu-bar 'gyur-ro[6] // de-nas rgyal-po des[7] ban-de[8] phal-po-che btungs-te[9] shi-ba'i ro-rnams[10] blangs-te[11] bsregs-nas[12] mchod-pa[13] byas-te[14] /[15] de'i 'og-tu rgyal-po-nyid kyang bstan-pa nub-pa'i thugs ngan-gyis zhal 'tshos[16]-te 'das-so[17] //[18]

[1] N omits *dge-slong-gi lta-ba dang / tshul-khrims gang yin zhes dris-na / de-rnams gang-gis kyang dge-slong-gi lta-ba dang / tshul-khrims dang / brtul-zhugs cung-zad kyang mi-shes-pas rgyal-po de-la* and substitutes *rgyal-pos chos dris-pa-dang / chos tshig-gcig kyang mi-shes-nas /* [2] P1,P3 *-te* [3] N omits *lan ma-btab-par cang mi-smra-bar 'khod-pa-dang / rgyal-pos bsams-pa / da ni sangs-rgyas-kyi bstan-pa nub-ste / dkon-mchog gsum-gyi tshul yang-dag-par rgyun-chad-pa lta-zhig snyam-nas* [4] N omits *chen-po* [5] N adds / [6] N replaces *ngu-bar 'gyur-ro* with *ngu'o* [7] N omits *de-nas rgyal-po des* [8] P1 *ban-dhe* (*h* added by hand); L *bande* [9] N omits *phal-po-che btungs-te* [10] N omits *-rnams* and adds *ril-gyis* [11] N *bsdus-nas* [12] N *-te* [13] N *-pha* [14] N *byed-do* [15] N // [16] P1,P3 *mchos-* [17] P1,P3 *'ongs-so* [18] N omits *de'i 'og-tu rgyal-po-nyid kyang bstan-pa nub-pa'i thugs ngan-gyis zhal 'tshos-te 'das-so //*

28] T: de'i̲ tshe de'i̲ dus-na / 'Dzam-bu-gli̲ng-gi̲ chos ri̲l-gyi̲s der nub-bo // — — gser ni̲ dngul ngan-pa dang rdor gyur // dngul ni̲ ra-gan-du gyur / ra-gan ni̲ zangs-su gyur / ri̲n-po-che dang mu-ti̲g ni̲ rbar gyur / kha-zas-gyi̲ ro drug yod-pa-las / dngar-zhi̲ng zhi̲m-ba las-stsogs-pi̲ [sic] ⌞bzhi̲⌟ ni̲ nub / kha-ban dang cub-pan gnyi̲s ni̲ lus-so // //

X: de'i tshe de'i dus-na 'Dzam-bu'i gling-gi dam-pa'i chos[1] ril-gyis[2] nub-ste[3] /[4] gsung-rab[5]-kyi yi-ge-rnams kyang dung[6] byi[7]-pa bzhin-du bltar mi-mngon-par gyur-to /[8] gser ni dngul-du[9] 'gyur-ro[10] // dngul ni zangs dang /[11] lcags-su 'gyur-ro //[12] zangs dang[13] lcags ni rdor 'gyur-ro //[14] rin-po-che dang[15] mu-tig ni rvar 'gyur-ro[16] //[17] kha-zas ni[18] ro drug yod-pa-la[19] mngar-ba dang / skyur-ba dang / lan-tshva'i[20] ro la-sogs-pa ni nub-bo[21] //[22] kha-ba dang /[23] bska-ba[24] gnyis ni[25] lus-so[26] //

[1] N replaces *dam-pa'i chos* with *lha-chos* [2] N omits *-gyis* [3] P1,P3 *-te,* N *-bo* [4] N // [5] P1,P3 *-rabs-* [6] P1 hand-corrected to read *rung* [7] P1,P3,D *phyis* [8] P1 //; N omits *gsung-rab-kyi yi-ge-rnams kyang dung byi-pa bzhin-du bltar mi-mngon-par gyur-to* / [9] N replaces *dngul-du* with *dngul ngan-pa dang rdor* [10] N omits *-ro* [11] P1,P3 omit / [12] N replaces *zangs dang / lcags-su 'gyur-ro //* with *ra-gan ngan-pa dang rdor 'gyur* / [13] L inserts / [14] N replaces *zangs dang lcags ni rdor 'gyur-ro //* with *ra-gan ni zangsu 'gyur* / [15] L inserts / [16] N omits *-ro* [17] N / [18] N replaces *kha-zas ni* with *zas-la* [19] P1,P3,N *-las* [20] P1,P3 *-tsha'i* [21] P1 *-pa*; N replaces *mngar-ba dang / skyur-ba dang / lan-tshva'i ro la-sogs-pa ni nub-bo* with *mngar-zhing zhim-pa la-sogs-pha bzhi ni nub* [22] N / [23] P1,P3,N omit / [24] P1 *ska-ba,* P3 *bka'-ba,* N *rtsub-pa* [25] P1,P3 omit *ni* [26] N *luso*

9] T: sangs-rgyas Shag-kya-thub-pa' / byang-cub-sems-dpa' sems-dpa'-chen-po Zla-ba'i̲ snyi̲ng-pos zhus-pa-las — lung bstan-ba rdzogs-s.ho //

X: sangs-rgyas bcom-ldan-'das[1] Shākya-thub-pa-la 'Phags-pa Zla-ba'i snying-pos zhus-pa'i mdo-las / sangs-rgyas mya-ngan-las 'das-nas bstan-pa gnas-pa dang / 'jig-pa'i tshul lung bstan-pa'i skabs[2] rdzogs-so[3] // //

[1] N omits *bcom-ldan-'das* [2] P3 inserts // // ; P1 inserts / only (other three *shad* hand-erased in P1) [3] P3 *-s.ho*; N replaces *'Phags-pa Zla-ba'i snying-pos zhus-pa'i mdo-las / sangs-rgyas mya-ngan-las 'das-nas bstan-pa gnas-pa dang / 'jig-pa'i tshul lung bstan-pa'i skabs rdzogs-so* with *byang-chub sems-da' Zla-ba'i snying-pos zhus-pa-las lung bstan-pa rdzogso*

Chapter Ten

Conclusions: The Fate of the Kauśāmbī Story

IN LIGHT OF the clearly non-Mahāyāna origins of the Kauśāmbī story it is striking that the version that was to become most influential in East and Inner Asia was one found in a Mahāyāna text. Though the Kauśāmbī story was available in Chinese translation in the form of the *Prophecy of Kātyāyana* no later than the end of the Western Chin dynasty (316 CE), it was the version contained in the *Candragarbha-sūtra*, translated only in 566 CE, that was to become a standard reference point for Chinese commentators. Likewise in Tibet there was a non-Mahāyāna version of the Kauśāmbī story—the Sarvāstivādin recension contained in the *Karmaśataka*—available at least as early as the second half of the 8th century CE. Yet this version was generally ignored (or overlooked) by commentators in favor of the *Candragarbha* prophecy.

The primacy of the *Candragarbha-sūtra* in the Chinese and Tibetan environments as a source of information on the ultimate fate of the Dharma thus requires some explanation. Beginning with the Tibetan case, which is the more straightforward of the two, we should note first of all that the Tibetans do not seem to have obtained this sūtra directly from India. Rather, all the available evidence indicates that the *Candragarbha-sūtra* reached Tibet from the Tarim Basin, where (as the frequent citations of the text in the late Khotanese adaptations make clear) it was viewed as a particularly authoritative source on the decline and disappearance of the Dharma. Thus the *Candragarbha-sūtra* would have been received by the Tibetans not simply as one Buddhist text among many, but as an especially important and frequently cited work.

The Chinese preference for the *Candragarbha-sūtra* appears to be the result of a more complex set of circumstances. First we should note simply that (unlike virtually all the earlier translations of the story) the *Candragarbha-sūtra*, at least in its extant Chinese recension, is a Mahāyāna text. And the Chinese preference for the Mahāyāna was established quite early.[1] Thus, given a variety of texts containing prophecies of the end of Buddhism, it is not at all surprising that the Chinese would select a Mahāyāna version of the story as the most authoritative.[2]

A second factor that led to the highlighting of the *Candragarbha* prophecy in the Chinese context was certainly the date of its translation. The text became available in Chinese at a particularly opportune time: Narendrayaśas, an Indian translator who had arrived in the Northern Ch'i capital in 556 CE, completed his translation of the *Candragarbha-sūtra* in 566 CE, just eight years before the onset of one of the major persecutions of Chinese Buddhist history (574–577, under the Northern Chou dynasty). In such an environment a prophecy purporting to describe the potential annihilation of the Buddhist community could not but have found a willing audience.

But if the Dharma itself—or rather, the practice and teaching of the Dharma—is considered to be transitory, so indeed must be the individual sūtras in which its teachings are collected. And the

---

[1] The Chinese preference for the Mahāyāna wing of the Buddhist tradition appears to have emerged as early as the late 2nd century CE, and continued to hold sway throughout the rest of Chinese Buddhist history. This preference was shared by China's Tibetan and Khotanese neighbors (and was exported by the Chinese in turn to Korea and Japan), but not by the inhabitants of the rest of Central Asia (most of whom maintained their Sarvāstivādin identity until well into the T'ang period) or, for that matter, by Buddhists in many parts of India. The lack of Mahāyāna dominance in these regions during the early 7th century can be seen in the results of Hsüan-tsang's running census of the monastic population in the areas he visited; for a tabulation of the sectarian affiliation of these communities see Lamotte, *Histoire*, 596–601.

[2] The only other Mahāyāna version of the Kauśāmbī story available in Chinese prior to this time was the *Mahāmāyā-sūtra* (T No. 383), translated around the end of the 5th century (see above, pp. 168-70), and in fact this text was regularly cited by Chinese commentators. The *Mahāmāyā-sūtra* contains only a residual version of the Kauśāmbī prophecy, however, which may explain in part why its authority never equaled that of the *Candragarbha-sūtra*.

Candragarbha-sūtra is certainly no exception. From a peak of popularity in Central Asia during the late first and early second millennia CE, the *Candragarbha-sūtra* has sunk to a position of almost complete obscurity in modern Tibetan (and Mongolian) Buddhist thought. In East Asia, by contrast, the sūtra itself—though not, we should note, the Kauśāmbī story as such—remains an important point of reference for theories concerning the decline and ultimate disappearance of the Dharma and is of special importance to members of the Pure Land and Nichiren traditions.

To explain the divergent destinies of the *Candragarbha-sūtra* in these two regions requires first of all an awareness of the greater context within which the sūtra has been received. For Buddhist texts are not simply read by their devotees in isolation, but are received in the context of other scriptures and oral traditions that already serve as central points of orientation. To understand the way the *Candragarbha-sūtra* has been interpreted in Tibet and in East Asia, and to understand its eventual abandonment in Tibet in contrast to its ongoing influence in China and Japan, thus requires an examination of the general attitudes toward decline—or more broadly, toward history—that have been current in these different cultural areas.

Beginning with the Tibetan case, it is important first to recall that the Buddhist tradition received by the Tibetans from India lacked any explicit periodization of decline. Though Indian Buddhists eventually adopted the term *kali yuga* from their Hindu counterparts, the four-*yuga* theory appears only sporadically in Buddhist literature,[3] and it never became a central organizing

---

[3] The system of four *yugas* appears to be restricted to Hindu literature (with the corresponding Buddhist system being worked out in terms of kalpas, not *yugas*) until sometime during the Gupta period, when we begin to find references to the four-*yuga* scheme in Buddhist literature as well. A striking example of this usage appears in the tenth (*Sagāthakam*) chapter of the *Laṅkāvatāra-sūtra*, a section that almost certainly dates from just after the Gupta period. (The first, ninth, and tenth chapters of the *Laṅkāvatāra* are missing in the first Chinese translation of the text, completed in 443 CE, but are included in a later translation done in 513, and the late date of this section of the text is also confirmed by its reference to the Guptas themselves, who are to be followed by *mleccha* rulers, in verse 786.) Here we find the prediction that an "age of vice" (*kali yuga*) will follow the rule of "the Maurya, the Nanda, the Gupta, and then the Mleccha who are bad kings" (see D. T. Suzuki, trans., *The Lankavatara Sutra*, p. 286, verse 786). After this *kali yuga*, the text tells us, the True Dharma will no more prevail in the world. But the sūtra also

principle in Buddhist thinking. Moreover, though the Buddhists shared with the Hindus (and with Indian thinkers in general) the basic concept of decline, they never associated the course of the decline and disappearance of the Dharma of Śākyamuni with the astronomical numbers describing the duration of the *kali* age in Hindu literature. And the striking contrast between the vastness of these Hindu time schemes and the relatively brief figures for the duration of the Buddha's teachings (ranging from five hundred to five thousand years in Indian sources) points to an important difference in perspective: while Hindu decline mythology is clearly cosmic in scope—that is, it describes the decay of the universe as a whole—in Buddhist decline literature the focus is much narrower. Here the "decline of the Dharma" refers not to the decay of the order of the universe as such, but primarily to the fading away and eventual disappearance of the teachings of a specific historical figure. The proper Buddhist analogue of the Hindu four-*yuga* system is thus not the general theory of the decline of the Dharma, nor even the three-period time scheme current in East Asia, but the macrocosmic "oscillating universe" system presented in the *Abhidharmakośa*.[4]

---

enumerates the other three *yuga*s as well, for it states that "Not in the age of two (*dvāpara*), not in the age of triads (*tretā*), not in the age of vice (*kali*) . . . but in the golden age (*kṛta*) world-teachers will appear, and attain Buddhahood" (Suzuki, *Lankavatara*, p. 287, verse 804).

Less systematic treatments of the four-*yuga* system continue to appear in Buddhist literature from the Gupta period onward, yet it is fair to say that this time scheme was never fully domesticated within the Buddhist context. While the "golden age" (*kṛta yuga*) and the "age of fighting" (*rtsod-pa'i dus*, as the Tibetans regularly render the expression *kali yuga*; see *Mvy*. no. 8296) could be harmonized with pre-existing Buddhist concepts of history, the intervening periods were difficult to place, and wherever this fourfold system appears in the Buddhist sources its presence serves as direct evidence of the ongoing Hindu-Buddhist rapprochement that accelerated during the Gupta period. It also provides, however, important evidence of another sort. That Buddhist writers should have been forced to resort to this non-Buddhist time system to express a sense of the periodization of decline, and that references to this four-*yuga* system should continue to appear sporadically in Buddhist literature from the Gupta age to the Muslim period, clearly demonstrates that the Buddhists had no similar time scheme of their own. Were a periodization scheme comparable to that of the East Asian three-period system known in India, we would surely find Buddhist writers making use of that system instead of borrowing a four-period scheme from their Hindu rivals.

[4] See above, pp. 15–17. It is also important to point out, more specifically, that

In Tibet, then, as in India, we do not find commentators making extensive use of explicit periodization schemes for the disappearance of the Dharma. Not only is there no analogue of the East Asian concept of *mo-fa*, but even the term "reflection of the True Dharma" (Skt. *saddharma-pratirūpaka*, Tib. *dam-pa'i chos-kyi gzugs-brnyan*) was generally not understood as constituting a specific era in the history of the Dharma.[5] Rather, in South, Southeast, and Inner Asia the vision of decline was simply that of the gradual ebbing away of the Buddhist teachings, with few if any distinctive markers along the way. In such a context a prophecy of the demise of the Dharma such as that contained in the *Candragarbha-sūtra* could be read in only one way: as a prediction of the complete and total eradication of the Buddhist religion, together with a specific timetable for that event.

It is hardly surprising, then, that the Tibetan response to the impending expiration of this timetable was just what we have already seen in India: the abandonment of the timetable (and with it the Kauśāmbī story) in favor of a more extended figure. Thus the popularity of the *Candragarbha-sūtra*, with its 2,000-year timetable, during the time of Bu-ston (14th century CE) subsequently gave way to an almost total ignorance of the sūtra even among well educated Tibetans, who cite instead other timetables of 5,000 years or more.[6]

In China and Japan, by contrast, the sūtra was perceived in an entirely different light. By the time Narendrayaśas completed his

---

the *kali yuga* is not the functional equivalent of the East Asian notion of *mo-fa*. While both terms express a general sense of decline, the *kali yuga* is said to have begun well before the time of the Buddha (around 5000 BCE, according to some Hindu commentators), and thus could not be used to refer to a sub-period of the time since the Buddha's death (as *mo-fa* is). Moreover, while the onset of the period of *mo-fa* is frequently cited by East Asian writers as a justification for selecting certain "easy" practices appropriate to this decadent age, the notion of the *kali yuga* is more often used for precisely the opposite purpose: to point to the need for the more rigorous and demanding practices of tantra.

[5] On the use of the term *saddharma-pratirūpaka* in this non-periodized (i.e., inclusive) sense see above, pp. 75-78.

[6] As noted above (pp. 58–61), in Tibet the 2,000-year timetable found in the *Candragarbha-sūtra* was eventually replaced by a 5,000-year scheme, which in turn has been more or less overshadowed by the 5,104-year timetable found in the *Kālacakra-tantra*. The same approach was taken in the Theravāda countries of Southeast Asia, where a 5,000-year timetable propounded by Buddhaghosa has come to be accepted as standard (see above, pp. 56–59).

translation of the sūtra in 566 CE, the idea of a three-period system of "True Dharma" / "Semblance Dharma" / "End-Dharma" was already well on its way toward general acceptance in Chinese scholastic circles. The assumption of this time scheme thus resulted in an interpretation of the sūtra that differed markedly from that current in Tibet. Using the three-period system as their interpretive framework, East Asian Buddhist commentators began to treat the specific timetables found in the *Candragarbha-sūtra* and other decline texts not as references to the total duration of the Dharma, but only to the extent of the pre-*mo-fa* eras of the "True" and the "Semblance" Dharma. Beyond these relatively brief periods stretched the period of the "End-Dharma," which was expected to last for "ten thousand years and more." The very asymmetry of this system—in which the duration of *mo-fa* far exceeds that of either of the other two periods—points to what would eventually become a distinguishing characteristic of East Asian Buddhism: the primacy assigned to the task of learning to live in a prolonged (and for all practical purposes, unending) "evil age." Thus while in Tibet (as in India) a timetable that was believed to have expired could only serve to undercut the legitimacy of the ongoing Buddhist community—and thus had to be explained away, ignored, or (preferably) replaced by a longer timetable—in China and Japan the expiration of a given timetable could be interpreted simply as the definitive confirmation of the onset of *mo-fa*. And since *mo-fa* was understood (by grammatical analogy to the already familiar terms *cheng-fa* "True Dharma" and *hsiang-fa* "Semblance Dharma") not as the demise of the Dharma, but as a discrete period in the history of the Buddhist religion, the apparent expiration of any specific timetable could be viewed not (as was necessarily the case in India and Tibet) as a threat to the Buddhist community's very existence, but as an incentive to formulate new practices appropriate to this decadent age. And as we have seen, this challenge was taken up by a number of East Asian thinkers, who used it to construct new understandings of Buddhist doctrine and practice designed explicitly for this "Final Age."[7]

Yet it was not the Kauśāmbī story itself, but the more schematic timetables for the duration of the Dharma found in the same scripture, that were to fascinate East Asian readers of the *Candragarbha-*

---

[7] See above, pp. 137–39.

sūtra. Indeed, it was the system of five five-hundred year periods (found only in this sūtra) that was to become the dominant timetable in East Asian exegesis. And it was to point to this timetable, not to the narrative of the events at Kauśāmbī, that East Asian commentators appealed to this text.

What is surprising about the Kauśāmbī story, though—or rather, about the life history of the prophecy itself—is not that it was eventually eclipsed in favor of other, more flexible models for the duration and demise of the Dharma, but that it maintained its influence for as long as it did. For, to return to one of the questions posed in the opening chapter of this book, what could have motivated a Buddhist writer to produce such a seemingly pessimistic tale, and why did Buddhists preserve and transmit it with such persistence? Certainly the tale offers no consolation to the Buddhist believer in the form of promises of a Buddhist triumph over non-Buddhist forces, nor does it even paint a particularly flattering portrait of the Buddhist community. Rather, it does just the opposite: after describing a conflict among Buddhists at the highest level of the sangha, it predicts that the Buddhist religion (like all other conditioned things) will some day pass away. What possible comfort, inspiration, or encouragement could Buddhist believers have drawn from such a tale?

At this point we may take our cue not from the categories used in Buddhist Studies, but from a broader comparative perspective. For the proper analogy to the Buddhist decline myth—at least as expressed in the Kauśāmbī story—is not the apocalyptic literature of Judaism, Christianity, or Zoroastrianism, but the prophetic literature of earlier Hebrew texts. For it is here that we find religious thinkers speaking not to a persecuted or recently overthrown "righteous community," but to those who, under far more propitious conditions, are failing to live up to the opportunity to which they have been called. The Buddhist Kauśāmbī story, like the Jewish prophetic literature, offers not consolation but criticism of its own religious community, and not encouragement but exhortation.

Thus in the verse translation of the *Prophecy of Kātyāyana* we find the admonition to "be diligent, thinking about the great danger and fear to come,"[8] while in the prose translation of the same text the monk Kātyāyana tells his disciples, "Thus will be the events

---

[8] T No. 2029, 49.12b16.

of future evil transformations. Because the Buddha-Dharma continues today, as of old, you should be diligent and practice in it."[9] And though these are (according to the stemma constructed in chapter 8 above) the two oldest extant versions of the prophecy, this same message is maintained even in one of its latest recensions, for the version of the prophecy found in the Khotanese *Book of Zambasta* closes, just as the surviving text breaks off, with the exhortation to "Strive now, so that the [Buddha's] teaching . . . ."[10] Viewed from this perspective, the Kauśāmbī story can be read as a prophetic text in this comparative sense: that is, as a document that predicts dire events to take place in the future, but uses the very threat of these events to encourage its audience to make greater efforts in the present.

Such a perspective accords well with our earlier conclusions, described in chapter 8, concerning the provenance of the original Kauśāmbī prophecy. For the tale seems not to have been composed during a period of invasion or persecution, but during the "golden age" of prosperity and patronage experienced by Buddhists under Kushan rule. In contrast to apocalyptic literature, which is generally composed against a background of adversity (and, indeed, is frequently composed by a recently deposed elite),[11] the prophetic tradition—of which the Kauśāmbī story may be counted as an example—is instead a response to the complacency and even decadence that can come from overwhelming success.

That the debacle at Kauśāmbī takes place during a great feast, sponsored by the king himself, should not surprise us, nor should we find it curious that every surviving version of the tale is told

---

[9] T No. 2028, 49.9b20-22.

[10] Emmerick, trans., *Book of Zambasta*, p. 418, line 522. The English translation given here is adapted from that given by Emmerick on p. 419.

[11] For valuable information on the background of Hebrew apocalyptic literature see Paul D. Hanson, *The Dawn of Apocalyptic: The Historical and Sociological Roots of Jewish Apocalyptic Eschatology* (Philadelphia: Fortress Press, 1975). For comparative purposes I would suggest that we exclude from consideration those works that focus on a "heavenly journey" (or rather, that we give them a category of their own). Reserving the term "apocalyptic" for literature that predicts the triumph of the forces of good and the overthrow of the (previously victorious) forces of evil, we will have a category that is not only sociologically useful but valid for comparative study as well. My own working definition of "apocalyptic" is given above, p. 60, n. 84, and is discussed in greater detail in "The Meanings of the Maitreya Myth," pp. 42–44, notes 41–46.

from the perspective of members of the faction of the arhat Sūrata, and not of the king's preceptor Śiṣyaka. For it is precisely the threat of succumbing to the temptations of secular society that the author of this prophecy is arguing against. Read in this light, the Kauśāmbī story takes on clear significance as the plea of a traditionalist element within the Buddhist community not to give in to worldly temptations of ease and comfort.

Naturally there are vast differences in the worldviews that gave rise to the works of the Hebrew prophets, on the one hand, and to the Kauśāmbī story on the other. In the former case the prophets could appeal to divine sanctions if the Jewish people fail to live up to their special mission, while in the latter there is the constant reminder of the eventual and irreversible extinction of the Dharma, as expressed in the specific timetables that accompany every complete version of the tale.

But it is precisely this difference that points to a persistent theme in the Buddhist tradition, without which the full import of the Kauśāmbī story cannot be grasped. For in this very message of the transitoriness of all phenomena, Buddhists have seen not the insignificance of the present moment, but its unique and irreplaceable value. Just as Buddhist commentators have regularly pointed to the rarity of attaining a human rebirth, and the rarity of encountering the teachings of a Buddha, as incentives to diligent practice of the Dharma, so the Kauśāmbī story has been read by Buddhist exegetes as a call to take this opportunity seriously.

This, then, is the message of the Kauśāmbī story: that the Buddhist religious tradition is no less transitory than other worldly phenomena, and that the opportunity of encountering it is exceedingly rare. While human efforts can contribute to its preservation or can hasten its demise, they cannot provide it with an eternality that would contradict the very essence of its teachings. Thus the unique opportunity of living in the shadow of a Buddha's teaching should not be squandered, but should be used to the fullest toward the goal of final liberation.

Appendix

Proper Names in the Kauśāmbī Story

Listed below are the major proper names found in the versions of the Kauśāmbī story identified to date, with the exception of the *Mahāmāyā-sūtra* (which contains no proper names at all). This compilation has been carried out with two primary objectives in mind: first, to provide data useful for the reconstruction of the original Indian (Sanskrit or Prakrit) forms of the names; and second, to highlight the similarities and differences among the various textual "families," information which has been used in chapter 8 above to assist in reconstructing the relationships among the extant versions of the story.

In the texts included in this survey Indian proper names have been treated in two distinct fashions. In some cases the names are transliterated, while in others an attempt has been made to translate the significance of Indian names (via real or fictional etymologies) into Chinese or Tibetan terms. For translated names I have provided the corresponding English equivalents, together with the presumed Sanskrit (or Prakrit) antecedent. For transliterated names in Chinese I have provided the readings given in Karlgren's *Dictionary*, which (being based on the spoken language of north China in the 6th century) provide a closer approximation to the language of these texts than would any of the modern dialects. For transliterated names in Tibetan I have simply romanized the Tibetan spelling according to the Wylie system, and have (in cases where non-conformity with the common ancestor is likely) suggested a probable Indian antecedent. Finally, for the Khotanese names (all of which are transliterated) I have adopted the transcriptions given by Emmerick in his edition of *The Book of Zambasta*.

Abbreviations:

Mvbh.	*Mahāvibhāṣā* (T No. 1545, 27.918a18–b21)
Saṃ.	*Saṃyukta-āgama* (T No 99, 2.177b12–180a5)
Aś.	*Aśoka-avadāna* (T No 2042, 50.126c23–128b4)
Krmś.	*Karmaśataka* (Pek. No. 1007, *bam-po* 23, *mdo-sna-tshogs su* 279b2–290b4)
Kāt.(v)	*Prophecy of Kātyāyana* (verse) (T No. 2029, 49.9c20–12c2)
Kāt.(p)	*Prophecy of Kātyāyana* (prose) (T No. 2028, 49.7a21–9c14)
Tib. CG	*Candragarbha-[paripṛcchā]-sūtra* (Tun-huang ms., Stein No. J601.1)
Khot. CG	R. E. Emmerick, ed., *The Book of Zambasta* (pp. 398–419)
Ch. CG	*Candragarbha-sūtra* (T No. 397[15], 13.374c28–381c11)
Li'i yul	*Prophecy of [the Arhat of] Khotan* (Pek. No. 5699, *mdo-'grel nge*, 444a2–468a8)
Saṃgha.	*Prophecy of the Arhat Saṃghavardhana* (Pek. No. 5698, *mdo-'grel nge*, 435a8–444a2)
Lo-rgyus	*Religious Annals of Khotan* (Tun-huang ms., Pelliot No. 960)

1. "3 EVIL KINGS"

Mvbh.	(not named)[1]
Saṃ.	south: 釋迦 *śi̯äk-˛ka* (202, 342) < Skt. *śaka* "Saka"

[1] The *Mahāvibhāṣā* mentions a total of three kings, of whom two are portrayed as evil and the other (identified only as the "king in the east") as good. No ethnic name is associated with any of the three.

	north:	耶槃那 *꜀i̯a-[b'uân]-'nâ'* (226, 690,[2] 647) < Skt. *yavana* "Greek"
	west:	鉢羅婆 *puât-꜀lâ-꜀b'uâ* (707, 569, 753) < Skt. *pahlava* "Parthian"
	east:	兜沙羅 *꜀tə̯u-꜀ṣa-꜀lâ* (1017, 846, 569) < Skt. *tuṣāra*, for *tukhāra* "Kushan"[3]
Aś.	south:	釋拘 *śi̯äk-꜀ki̯u* (202, 484) < Skt. *śaka* "Saka"
	north:	閻無那 *꜀i̯äm-꜀mi̯u-'nâ'* (247, 1289, 647) < Skt. *yamunā*? (hypercorrection from *yavana* "Greek"?)
	west:	鉢羅擾 *puât-꜀lâ-'ńźi̯äu* (707, 569, 260[4]) < Skt. *pahlava* "Parthian"
Krmś.	south:	*sha-ka'i mi* "man of the Sakas" < Skt. *śaka* + ?
	west:	*ba-lhi-ka* < Skt. *bahlika*, "Bactrian" (hypercorrection from *pahlava*, "Parthian"[5])
	north:	*ya-ba-na* < Skt. *yavana* "Greek"
Kāt. (v)	front:	大秦 "Rome"[6]
	rear:	撥羅 *pi̯^{w}ɒt-꜀lâ* (Karlgren nos. 749, 569) "Parthia"[7]
	center:	安息 *꜀·ân-si̯ək* (4, 780) "Iran"[8]
Kāt. (p)	south:	耶來那 *꜀i̯a-꜀lâi-'nâ'* (226, 511,[9] 647) < Skt. *yavana* "Greek"

[2] The character 槃 does not appear in Karlgren's *Dictionary*, but cf. 般 *꜀puân*, 搬 *꜀buân* ~ *꜀puân*, and 盤 *꜀b'uân* listed under no. 690.

[3] See Lamotte, *Histoire*, 221, and MW 449c s.v. *tukhāra*. Note that the mention of the Kushans in this version does not in itself (*contra* Lamotte, *Histoire*, 221) require a later date for this recension than for the others of its group. See above, p. 152, n. 17.

[4] The reading 擾 (A. Ch. *'ńźi̯äu*; for this emendation see the addenda and corrigenda in Karlgren, *Dictionary*, 398) for Skt. *-va* is difficult to explain.

[5] In the blockprint editions of the Tibetan *Candragarbha-sūtra* the Tun-huang reading *pa-la-ba* is regularly emended to *ba-lhi-ka*.

[6] The term *ta-ch'in* is used in reference to the Roman Empire at least as early as the middle of the first century CE; see above, p. 158, n. 29.

[7] The Karlgren reading suggests an attempt to represent an original **pat-la* **pat-ra*, metathesis **parta* "Parthian" (for this derivation see above, p. 158, n. 30).

[8] The term *an-hsi* is derived from the name of the Parthian Arsacid dynasty (c. 248 BCE – 229 CE), but continued to be used even after the fall of that dynasty in reference to the territory of greater Iran (as opposed to that of Parthia, or East Iran, proper).

[9] The use of the character 來 *꜀lâi* for Skt. *va* has not been adequately explained.

	north:	(unnamed)
	[west]:	揵秋 [‘*g‘i̯on*’]-ˏ*ts‘i̯ə̯u* (373,[10] 1088) < Skt. ?
Tib. CG	first:[11]	*ya-bha-na* < Skt. *yavana* “Greek”
	second:	*pa-la-ba* < Skt. *pahlava* “Parthian”
	third:	*shag-ku-na* ~ *sheg-ku-na* < Skt. *śaka* “Saka” + ?
Khot. CG	first:[11]	*śśakaunä* < Skt. *śaka* “Saka” + ?
	second:	*yavanä* < Skt. *yavana* “Greek”
	third:	*palvalä* < Skt. *pahlava* “Parthian”
Ch. CG	south:	波羅帝 ˏ*puâ*-ˏ*lâ* (753, 569) < Skt. *pahlava* “Parthian” + Ch. 帝 “emperor”[12]
	west:	百祀 *pɒk-‘zi* (686, 808) < Skt. *pārsika* “Persian”?[13]
	north:	善意釋迦 “good thought Saka,” < Ch. 善意 “good thought” + *śi̯äk*-ˏ*ka* (202, 342) < Skt. *śaka* “Saka” + ?
Li’i yul		*ya-ba-na* ~ *ya-na-ba* (*la-sogs-pa*) “Greek, etc.”[14]
Saṃgha.	first:[11]	*stag-gzig* ~ *ta-zig* “Persian”
	second:	*drug-gu* ~ *dru-gu* “Turk”
	third:	*bod* “Tibetan”
Lo-rgyus	first:[11]	*rgya* “Chinese”
	second:	*bod* “Tibetan”
	third:	*hor* “Uighur”

2. MAHENDRASENA (“GREAT-LORD-ARMY”)[15]

Mvbh.	(not named)

---

[10] The character 揵 is not given in Karlgren, but cf. 建 *ki̯on*’, 健 *g‘i̯on*’, and 鍵 ‘*g‘i̯on* given at no. 373.

[11] The directions are not specified in this text.

[12] Read by Lamotte as a single word (“un roi du sud *Po-lo-ti*,” *Histoire*, 222), but given the unexpected nature of the final syllable, together with the mixture of translation and transliteration in the name of the Saka ruler in the same text, it seems preferable to read *ti* as a title and not as part of the name. Note also that *ti* 帝 is not one of the characters generally used to romanize Skt. *ti*.

[13] It is possible that *pɒk-‘zi* is the product of a metathesis of Skt. *pārsika* → **pa(r)sik* → **paksi*, but this is only a suggestion.

[14] Only one name is given in this text.

[15] See MW 802a, s.v. *mahendra*, and 1246b, s.v. *sena*.

Saṃ.	摩因陀羅西那 *˛muâ-˛·i̯ĕn-˛d'â-˛lâ-˛siei-'nâ'* (593, 273, 1011, 569, 776, 647)
Aś.	大軍 "great army" < Skt. *mahāsena* ?[16]
Krmś.	*dbang-chen-sde* "great-lord division"[17]
Kāt.(v)	(not named)
Kāt.(p)	(not named)
Tib. CG	*mhen-dra-se-na* ~ *men-drha-se-na*, *men-dra-se-na*
Khot. CG	*mahindraysenä*
Ch. CG	大軍 "great army" < Skt. *mahāsena* ?[16]
Li'i yul	(not named)
Saṃgha.	(does not appear)
Lo-rgyus	*man-'dre-seng-ge*

3. DUṢPRASAHA ("HARD TO BEAR")[18]

Mvbh.	(does not appear)
Saṃ.	難當 "hard to resist"
Aś.	難可看視 "hard to look at"
Krmś.	*bzod-par dka'-ba* "hard to tolerate"
Kāt.(v)	(does not appear)
Kāt.(p)	(does not appear)
Tib. CG	*drus-spra-sa-ha* ~ *du-spra-ba-sam*, *drus-sprha-lha-hra*
Khot. CG	*duṣpraysavä*[19]
Ch. CG	難看 "hard to look at"
Li'i yul	(does not appear)
Saṃgha.	*bzod-dka'*
Lo-rgyus	*'dre-spe-sad*

[16] But more likely, perhaps, the result of an intra-Chinese abbreviation from a three-syllable to a two-syllable name (cf. above, p. 158, n. 30).

[17] Skt. *mahendrasena*, but reading *sena* as "section, division" instead of "army" (see MW 1246b, s.v. *senā*).

[18] See MW 488a.

[19] For an explanation of the Khotanese rendering of Skt./Pkt. final *-ha* as *-va* (Khot. masc. nom. sg. *-vä*) see above, p. 178, n. 82.

4. AGNIDATTA ("FIRE-GIVEN")[20]

Mvbh.	(does not appear)
Saṃ.	阿耆尼達多 *˛·â-˛g'ji-˛nji-d'ât-˛tâ* (1, 340, 659, 956, 1006)
Aś.	大興 "great gift"[21]
Krmś.	*mes-sbyin* "given by fire"
Kāt.(v)	(does not appear)
Kāt.(p)	(does not appear)
Tib. CG	*ag-na-tra-ta*
Khot. CG	(does not appear)
Ch. CG	火施 "fire-almsgiving"
Li'i yul	(does not appear)
Saṃgha.	(does not appear)
Lo-rgyus	(does not appear)

5. ŚIṢYAKA ("ONE WHO HAS DISCIPLES")

Mvbh.	室史迦 *śi̯ĕt-'ṣi-˛ka* (1214, 885, 342); also given the epithet 般株, whose significance is unclear
Saṃ.	失沙 *śi̯ĕt-˛ṣa* (880,[22] 846) < Skt. *śiṣya*; also translated as 弟子 "disciple"
Aś.	多弟子 "[having] many disciples"
Krmś.	*slob-ma-can* "he who has disciples"
Kāt.(v)	尸師 *˛śi-˛ṣi* (878, 893) < Skt. *śiṣya* "disciple" ?
Kāt.(p)	尸依仇 *˛śi-˛·ei-˛g'i̯ə̯u* (878, 185, 399)
Tib. CG	*shir-sha-ka* ~ *shir-she-ka*, *shir-sha-ga*, *sher-she-ka*, *shir-she-kya*) < **śīrṣaka*[23]
Khot. CG	*śśärṣakä* < **śīrṣaka*[23]
Ch. CG	失師迦 *śi̯ĕt-˛ṣi-˛ka* (880, 893, 342) < **śīrṣaka* ?

---

[20] Cf. MW 5b.

[21] The character 大 "great" (found in the printed Taishō edition) is a copyist's error for 火 "fire."

[22] The character 失 (Karlgren no. 880, A. Ch. *śi̯ĕt*) may be an error for 矢 (Karlgren no. 881, A. Ch. *'śi*).

[23] For the confusion between Skt./Pkt. *śiṣyaka* and **śīrṣaka* see above, p. 179, n. 83.

Li'i yul	(does not appear)
Saṃgha.	*shir-sha-ka* < **śīrṣaka*
Lo-rgyus	*shir-zhag* ~ *zhir-shag* < **śīrṣaka*

6. SUDHANA ("VERY RICH," < *SU* "GOOD" + *DHANA* "WEALTH")[24]

Mvbh.	(does not appear)
Saṃ.	須陀那 *ˌsi̯u-ˌd'â-'nâ'* (839, 1011, 647)
Aś.	須達那 *ˌsi̯u-ˌd'ât-'nâ'* (839, 956, 647)
Krmś.	*nor-bzangs* "good goods"
Kāt.(v)	(does not appear)
Kāt.(p)	(does not appear)
Tib. CG	*s.hu-dha-ra-sh.ha-na*
Khot. CG	(does not appear)
Ch. CG	善財 "good goods"
Li'i yul	(does not appear)
Saṃgha.	(does not appear)
Lo-rgyus	(does not appear)

7. SŪRATA ("WELL-DISPOSED, COMPASSIONATE, TENDER")[25]

Mvbh.	蘇剌多 *ˌsuo-lât-ˌtâ* (823, 509, 1006)
Saṃ.	修羅他 *ˌsi̯ə̯u-ˌlâ-t'â* (257, 569, 223[26])
Aś.	須達 *ˌsi̯u-d'ât* (839, 956[27]), glossed 秦言善意 "in the Ch'in language, 'good intention' "; elsewhere 修陀羅 *ˌsi̯ə̯u-ˌd'â-ˌlâ* (257, 1011, 569) < **sudara*, metathesis < **surata* < Skt. *sūrata* ?
Krmś.	*des-pa* "of good nature"
Kāt.(v)	須賴 *ˌsi̯u-lâi*, second syllable earlier **-lâd*[28]
Kāt.(p)	須陀流 *ˌsi̯u-ˌd'â-ˌli̯ə̯u* (839, 1011, 564), glossed 晉言曰善 "in the Chin language, 'good' "
Tib. CG	*su-ra-ta* ~ *so-ra-da*

---

24 See MW 1225b.

25 See MW 1244b.

26 Var. 陀 *ˌd'â* (Karlgren no. 1011).

27 Contamination from *Sudhana*? (cf. no. 6 above).

28 For this spelling see above, p. 147, n. 6; and p. 159, n. 34.

Khot. CG	*sūratä* ~ *sūradä*
Ch. CG	涑羅多 [*ṣi̯əu'*]-*˛lâ*-*˛tâ* (910,[29] 569, 1006)
Li'i yul	(does not appear)
Saṃgha.	*su-ra-ta* ~ *su-ta-ra*
Lo-rgyus	*su-rag*[30]

8. AṄGADA ("A BRACELET WORN ON THE UPPER ARM")[31]

Mvbh.	(not named)
Saṃ.	安伽陀 *˛·ân⁻˛g'i̯a⁻˛d'â* (4, 342, 1011)
Aś.	噫伽度 *˛·i'-˛g'i̯a-d'uo'* (203,[32] 342, 1128)
Krmś.	*dpung-rgyan* "upper-arm ornament"
Kāt.(v)	阿斯 *˛·â-˛sie̯* (1, 816[33])
Kāt.(p)	上頭 "upper head"[34]
Tib. CG	*ag-na-dhe'i* ~ *a-gan-la* [*sic*]
Khot. CG	*aṃ-ggadī*
Ch. CG	鴦伽多 *˛i̯ang-˛g'i̯a-˛tâ* (210, 342, 1006) ~ 鴦伽 only
Li'i yul	(does not appear)
Saṃgha.	*a-kan-bi* ~ *a-gna-bi*
Lo-rgyus	*ang-ghan*

9. DADHIMUKHA ("SOUR-MILK FACE")[35]

Mvbh.	(does not appear)
Saṃ.	大提木佉 *d'âi'-˛d'iei-muk-k'i̯a* (952, 890, 643, 491[36])
Aś.	樂面 "joyful face"[37]

---

[29] The character 涑 does not appear in Karlgren; could this be an error for 漱 *ṣi̯əu'* (no. 910)?

[30] For an explanation of this form see above, p. 202, n. 149.

[31] See MW 7c.

[32] Error for 暗 *·âm'* or 喑 *˛·i̯əm* (Karlgren no. 277)?

[33] Error for one of the characters listed under Karlgren nos. 338 and 385?

[34] Not a personal name, apparently, but an epithet or monastic title (cf. above, p. 167 and n. 45).

[35] See MW 468a.

[36] Ordinarily read *˛k'i̯ʷo*, but read as *k'i̯a* when used to transcribed Skt. *kha* (see Karlgren, *Dictionary*, p. 163, no. 491).

[37] The character 樂 "joy" is presumably an error for 藥 "medicine" (note that *dadhi* or sour milk is regarded as a medicine in India).

Krmś.	*zho-gdong* "curd-face"
Kāt.(v)	(not named)
Kāt.(p)	(not named)
Tib. CG	*'dhid-rha-mu-kha*
Khot. CG	[*da*]*dämukhä*
Ch. CG	目佉檀提 *mi̯uk-k'i̯a-˛d'ân-˛d'iei* (644, 491,[38] 967, 890) < Skt. **mukha-dadhi* !
Li'i yul	(does not appear)
Saṃgha.	(does not appear)
Lo-rgyus	*'dra-dha-mu-ka*

10. *KEDĀRA[39]

Mvbh.	(does not appear)
Saṃ.	(does not appear)
Aś.	(does not appear)
Krmś.	(does not appear)
Kāt.(v)	(does not appear)
Kāt.(p)	(does not appear)
Tib. CG	*ge-rad*
Khot. CG	(does not appear)
Ch. CG	鶏多羅 *˛kiei-˛tâ-˛lâ* (126, 1006, 569)
Li'i yul	(does not appear)
Saṃgha.	*ka-ra-ta*
Lo-rgyus	(does not appear)

---

[38] See note 36.

[39] This reconstruction, which is based solely on the Tibetan and Chinese *Candragarbha* texts, is uncertain at best. For the rationale behind the choice of this spelling see above, p. 180, n. 84.

Bibliography

APTE, Vaman Shivaram. *The Practical Sanskrit-English Dictionary,* revised and enlarged edition. Poona, 1957; repr. Kyoto: Rinsen Book Company, 1978.

__________. *The Student's English-Sanskrit Dictionary*. 3rd rev. ed. 1920; repr. Delhi: Motilal Banarsidass, 1983.

BACOT, J., et al. *Documents de Touen-houang*. Paris: Paul Geuthner, 1940.

BAILEY, Sir H.W. "Hvatanica IV." *Bulletin of the School of Oriental and African Studies* 10 (1942), 880–924.

__________, ed. *Khotanese Texts*. London: Cambridge University Press, 1985.

BANERJEE, Biswanath, ed. *A Critical Edition of the Śrī Kālacakratantra-rāja (Collated with the Tibetan Version)*. Calcutta: The Asiatic Society, 1985.

BAREAU, André. *Les premiers conciles bouddhiques*. Saigon: École Française d'Extrême-Orient, 1955.

BASHAM, A. L., ed. *Papers on the Date of Kaniṣka*. Leiden: E.J. Brill, 1968.

BEAL, Samuel, trans. *Buddhist Records of the Western World*. 1884; repr. New York: Paragon, 1968.

BECHERT, Heinz, ed. *Die Sprache der ältesten buddhistischen Überlieferung*. Abhandlungen der Akademie der Wissenschaften in Göttingen, Phil.-Hist. Klasse, Dritte Folge, No. 117, 1980.

__________, ed. *Zur Schulzgehörigkeit von Werken der Hīnayāna-Literatur*, Part I. Göttingen: Vandenhoeck & Ruprecht, 1985.

BECKWITH, Christopher I. *The Tibetan Empire*. Princeton: Princeton University Press, 1987.

BENVENISTE, E. *Vessantara Jātaka. Texte sogdien édité, traduit et commenté*. Paris: Paul Geuthner, 1946.

BERNBAUM, Edwin. *The Way to Shambhala*. Garden City, NJ: Anchor Books, 1980.

BLOCH, Jules, ed. and trans. *Les inscriptions d'Asoka.* Paris: Société d'Édition "Les Belles Lettres," 1950.

BOYER, A. M., et al. *Kharoṣṭhī Inscriptions Discovered by Sir Aurel Stein in Chinese Turkestan,* Part II. Oxford: Clarendon Press, 1929.

BROUGH, John. *The Gāndhārī Dharmapāda.* London: Oxford University Press, 1962.

BULTMANN, Rudolf. *Primitive Christianity in Its Contemporary Setting,* trans. Reginald H. Fuller. New York: Meridian Books, 1956.

BUSWELL, Robert E., Jr., ed. *Chinese Buddhist Apocrypha.* Honolulu: University of Hawaii Press, 1990.

__________, ed. *Paths of Liberation: The Mārga and Its Transformations in Buddhist Thought.* Honolulu: University of Hawaii Press, 1991.

CARTER, John Ross. *Dhamma: Western Academic and Sinhalese Buddhist Interpretations, A Study of a Religious Concept.* Tokyo: The Hokuseido Press, 1978.

CHANDRA, Lokesh, ed. *Bu-ston's History of Buddhism. Tibetan Text from the Collection of Prof. Dr. Raghu Vira.* New Delhi: International Academy of India Culture, 1971.

CHAPPELL, David W. "Early Forebodings of the Death of Buddhism." *Numen* 27 (1980), 122–53.

__________. "Tao-ch'o (562–645), A Pioneer of Chinese Pure Land Buddhism." Ph.D. thesis, Yale University, 1976.

CHAVANNES, Édouard. "Le Voyage de Song Yun dans l'Udyāna et le Gandhāra." *Bulletin de l'École Française d'Extrême Orient* 3 (1903), 379–441.

CHILDERS, Robert Caesar. *A Dictionary of the Pali Language.* London, 1875; repr. Kyoto: Rinsen Book Company, 1976.

CONZE, Edward. *Buddhism: Its Essence and Development.* New York: Harper & Row, 1951.

__________. *Buddhist Wisdom Books.* 1958; repr. New York: Harper & Row, 1972.

__________. *The Short Prajñāpāramitā Texts.* London: Luzac & Co., 1973.

__________. *Vajracchedikā.* Serie Orientale Roma, No. 13. Rome, 1957.

CORLESS, Roger. *The Vision of Buddhism.* New York: Paragon House, 1989.

DANI, A. H. *Indian Paleography*. Oxford: Clarendon Press, 1963.

DAS, Sarat Chandra. *A Tibetan-English Dictionary*. Calcutta, 1902; repr. Kyoto: Rinsen Book Company, 1977.

DE BARY, Theodore M., ed. *Sources of Chinese Tradition*. New York: Columbia University Press, 1960.

DE JONG, J. W. "Buddha's Word in China." 28th George Ernest Morrison Lecture, Canberra, Australian National University, n.d. (c. 1960). Repr. in Gregory SCHOPEN, ed., *Buddhist Studies: Selected Essays of J. W. de Jong*, 77–101. Berkeley: Berkeley Buddhist Studies Series, 1979.

DEMIÉVILLE, Paul, et al., eds. *Hōbōgirin—dictionnaire encyclopédique du bouddhisme d'après les sources chinoises et japonaises*. 6 fasc. Tokyo: Maison Franco-Japonaise, 1929, 1930, 1974, 1967, 1979, 1983.

__________, Hubert DURT, and Anna SEIDEL, eds. *Répertoire du canon bouddhique sino-japonaise*. Fascicule annexe du Hōbōgirin. 2nd ed. Paris/Tokyo: Maison Franco-Japonaise, 1978.

DOLLARHIDE, Kenneth. *Nichiren's Senji-shō: An Essay on the Selection of the Proper Time*. New York: Edwin Mellen Press, 1982.

DUTT, Sukumar. *The Buddha and Five After-Centuries*. London: Luzac & Co., 1957.

__________. *Buddhist Monks and Monasteries of India*. London: George Allen and Unwin, 1962.

ETANI Ryūkai 恵谷隆戒. "Nangaku Eshi no Rissei ganmon wa gisaku ka 南岳慧思の立誓願文は偽作か [Is Nan-yüeh Hui-ssu's *Li shih-yüan wen* a forgery?]" *Indogaku Bukkyōgaku kenkyū* 6/2 (1958): 524–27.

EDGERTON, Franklin W. *Buddhist Hybrid Sanskrit Grammar and Dictionary*. Vol. II: *Dictionary*. New Haven, 1953; repr. Delhi: Motilal Banarsidass, 1977.

ELIADE, Mircea, ed. *The Encyclopedia of Religion*. New York: Macmillan, 1987.

EMMERICK, R. E., ed. and trans. *The Book of Zambasta: A Khotanese Poem on Buddhism*. London: Oxford University Press, 1968.

__________, ed. and trans. *Tibetan Texts Concerning Khotan*. London: Oxford University Press, 1967.

ENSINK, Jacob, ed. and trans. *The Question of Rāṣṭrapāla*. Zwolle: J. J. Tijl, 1952.

FRYE, Richard N. *The History of Ancient Iran*. München: Beck, 1983.

GEIGER, Magdalene and Wilhelm. *Pāli Dhamma: Vornehmlich in der kanonischen Literatur*. Abhandlungen der Bayerischen Akademie der Wissenschaften, Philosophisch-philologische und historische Klasse, Band XXXI, 1, May 1920 (München: Verlag der Bayerischen Akademie der Wissenschaften, 1920).

GÓMEZ, Luis O. and Jonathan A. SILK, eds. *Studies in the Literature of the Great Vehicle: Three Mahāyāna Buddhist Texts*. Ann Arbor: Collegiate Institute for the Study of Buddhist Literature, 1989.

GOOR, M. E. Lulius van. *De buddhistische Non, geschetst naar Gegevens der Pali-literatur*. Leiden, 1915.

GRANOFF, Phyllis, "Tobatsu Bishamon: Three Japanese Statues in the United States and an Outline of the Rise of This Cult in East Asia." *East and West* 20 (1970): 144–67.

HANSON, Paul D. *The Dawn of Apocalyptic: The Historical and Sociological Roots of Jewish Apocalyptic Eschatology*. Philadelphia: Fortress Press, 1975.

HARE, E. M., trans. *The Book of the Gradual Sayings*. Vol. 3. 1934; repr. London: Pali Text Society, 1973.

HARMATTA, J. [= Ya. Kharmatta], "K interpretatsii indiĭskikh nadpiseĭ na keramike iz Kara-tepe." In B. Ya. STAVISKII, gen. ed., *Buddiĭskie peshchery Kara-tepe v starom Termeze* [= *Kara Tepe*, 2], 32–39. Moscow: Nauka, 1969.

HARRISON, Paul. *The Samādhi of Direct Encounter with the Buddhas of the Present, An Annotated English Translation of the Tibetan Version of the Pratyutpanna-Buddha-Saṃmukhāvasthita-Samādhi-Sūtra*. Studia Philologica Buddhica Monograph Series, V. Tokyo: International Institute for Buddhist Studies, 1990.

__________. *The Tibetan Text of the Pratyutpanna-Buddha-Saṃmukhāvasthita-Samādhi-Sūtra*, Studia Philologica Buddhica Monograph Series, I. Tokyo: The Reiyukai Library, 1978.

HASTINGS, James, ed. *Encyclopedia of Religion and Ethics*. New York: Charles Scribners, 1908-26.

HENNING, W. B. "Argi and the 'Tokharians'." *Bulletin of the School of Oriental Studies* 9 (1938): 545–71.

HIRAKAWA Akira. "The Rise of Mahāyāna Buddhism and Its Relationship to the Worship of Stupas." *Memoirs of the Research Department of the Toyo Bunko*, No. 22 (1963): 57–106.

HOERNLE, A. F. Rudolf. *Manuscript Remains of Buddhist Literature Found in Eastern Turkestan*. London: Oxford University Press, 1916.

HOFFMANN, Helmut H. *The Religions of Tibet*. Translated from the German by Edward Fitzgerald. London: Allen & Unwin, 1961.

__________. *Tibet: A Handbook*. Bloomington, Indiana: Research Center for the Language Sciences, 1978.

__________. "Über ein wenig beachtetes Hilfswort zur Bezeichnung der Zukunft im Tibetischen." *Corolla Linguistica: Festschrift Ferdinand Sommer*. Wiesbaden: Harrassowitz, 1955.

HOPKINS, Jeffrey, ed. and trans. *The Kālachakra Tantra*. London: Wisdom Publications, 1985.

HORNER, I. B. *Women under Primitive Buddhism*. New York: E.P. Dutton and Co., 1930.

__________, trans. *Buddhavaṁsa*. London: Pali Text Society, 1975.

HUBBARD, James B. "Salvation in the Final Period of the Dharma: The Inexhaustible Storehouse of the San-chieh-chiao." Ph.D. thesis, University of Wisconsin, 1986.

HURVITZ, Leon, trans. *Scripture of the Lotus Blossom of the Fine Dharma*. New York: Columbia University Press, 1976.

INAGAKI Hisao. *A Dictionary of Japanese Buddhist Terms*. Kyoto: Nagata Bunshōdō, 1984.

JÄSCHKE, H. A. *A Tibetan-English Dictionary*. London, 1881; repr. Delhi: Motilal Banarsidass, 1975.

JAINI, Padmanabh S. *The Jaina Path of Purification*. Berkeley: University of California Press, 1979.

JONES, J. J., trans. *The Mahāvastu*. 3 vols. London: Luzac, 1949–1956.

KAJIYAMA Yūichi 梶山雄一 . *Shinran* 親鸞 . In NAGAO Gajin 長尾雅人 , YANAGIDA Seizan 柳田聖山 , and KAJIYAMA Yūichi, ed., *Daijō butten (Chūgoku–Nihon-hen)* 大乗仏典 中国・日本篇 [Mahāyāna Buddhist Texts: China and Japan], vol. 22. Tokyo: Chūō Kōronsha, 1987.

KANE, Mahāmahopādhyāya Pandurang Vaman. *History of Dharmaśāstra*. Poona: Bhandarkar Oriental Research Institute, 1946.

KARLGREN, Bernhard. *Analytic Dictionary of Chinese and Sino-Japanese*. 1923; repr. New York: Dover, 1974.

KAZUE Kyōichi 数江教一 . *Nihon no mappō shisō* 日本の末法思想 [*Mappō* thought in Japan]. Tokyo: Kōbundō, 1961.

KERN, H., trans. *Saddharmapuṇḍarīka or the Lotus of the True Law*. 1884; repr. New York: Dover, 1963.

__________, and B. Nanjio, eds. *Saddharmapuṇḍarīka*. Bibliotheca Buddhica, vol. X. 1912; repr. Osnabrück: Biblio Verlag, 1970.

KONOW, Sten, ed. *Kharoshṭhī Inscriptions, with the Exception of Those of Aśoka*. Corpus Inscriptionum Indicarum 2(1). Calcutta: Government of India, 1929.

KUMOI Shōzen 雲井昭善 . "Hōmetsu shisō no genryū 法滅思想の源流 [Origin of ideas concerning the extinction of the Dharma]." In ŌCHŌ Enichi, ed., *Hokugi bukkyō no kenkyū*, 287–97.

KVAERNE, Per. "Mongols and Khitans in a 14th-century Tibetan Bonpo Text." *Acta Orientalia* (Budapest) 34 (1980): 85–104.

LALOU, Marcelle. *Manuel élementaire de tibétain classique*. Paris: Imprimerie Nationale, 1950.

LA VALLÉE POUSSIN, Louis de., trans. *L'Abhidharmakośa de Vasubandhu*. Paris: Paul Geuthner, 1923–1926.

__________. *Catalogue of the Tibetan Manuscripts from Tun-huang in the India Office Library*. London: Oxford University Press, 1962.

LAI, Whalen. "The *Chan-ch'a ching*: Religion and Magic in Medieval China." In Robert E. BUSWELL, Jr., ed., *Chinese Buddhist Apocrypha*, 175–206. Honolulu: University of Hawaii Press, 1990.

LALOU, Marcelle. "Les textes bouddhiques au temps du roi Khri-sroṅ-lde-bcan." *Journal Asiatique* 241 (1953): 313–53.

__________. *Manuel élementaire de tibétain classique*. Paris: Imprimerie Nationale, 1950.

LAMOTTE, Étienne. "La critique de l'authenticité dans le bouddhisme." In *India Antiqua: A Volume of Oriental Studies Presented to Jean Philippe Vogel*, 213–22. Leiden: E. J. Brill, 1947.

_________. *Histoire du bouddhisme indien*. Louvain: Institut Orientaliste, 1958).

LANCASTER, Lewis. *The Korean Buddhist Canon: A Descriptive Catalogue*. Berkeley: University of California Press, 1979.

_________, gen. ed. "The Question of 'Apocryphal' Words in Chinese Buddhist Texts," unpublished paper presented at the annual meeting of the American Academy of Religion, Atlanta, Georgia, November 1986.

LEGGE, James, trans. *A Record of Buddhistic Kingdoms*. 1886; repr. New York: Dover, 1965.

LÉVI, Sylvain. "Notes chinoises sur l'Inde, V. Quelques documents sur le bouddhisme indien dans l'Asie Centrale (Première partie)." *Bulletin de l'École Française d'Extrême-Orient* 5 (1905): 262–84.

LIGETI, Louis. *Catalogue du Kanjur mongol imprimé*. Vol. I, *Catalogue*. Budapest: Société Kőrösi Csoma, 1942–1944.

MAAS, Paul. *Textual Criticism*, trans. Barbara Flower. Oxford: Clarendon Press, 1958.

MACDONNELL, Arthur Anthony. *A Practical Sanskrit Dictionary*. London: Oxford University Press, 1954.

MAGNIN, Paul. *La vie et l'oeuvre de Huisi* 慧思 *(515–577)* . Paris: École Française d' Extrême Orient, 1979.

MALALASEKERA, G. P. *Dictionary of Pāli Proper Names*. London: Luzac & Co., 1960.

MATHEWS, R. H. *A Chinese-English Dictionary*. Cambridge: Harvard University Press, 1943.

MCRAE, John R. "Encounter Dialogue and the Transformation of the Spiritual Path in Chinese Ch'an." In Robert E. BUSWELL, Jr., ed., *Paths of Liberation*, 274-300. Honolulu: University of Hawaii Press, 1991.

METZGER, Bruce M. *The Text of the New Testament*. New York: Oxford University Press, 1964.

MILLER, R. A. *Studies in the Grammatical Tradition in Tibet*. Amsterdam: John Benjamins B. V., 1976.

MOCHIZUKI Shinkō 望月信亨 . *Bukkyō daijiten* 仏教大辞典 [Encyclopedia of

Buddhism], 10 vols. Tokyo/Kyoto: Sekai Seiten Kankō Kyōkai, 1933–1936.

MONIER-WILLIAMS, Sir Monier. *A Sanskrit-English Dictionary*, rev. ed. 1899; repr. Oxford: Clarendon, 1964.

MOROHASHI Tetsuji 諸橋轍次. *Dai kanwa jiten* 大漢和辞典 [Chinese-Japanese Dictionary], 13 vols. Tokyo: Daishūkan Shoten, 1955–1960.

MURATA, Kiyoaki. *Japan's New Buddhism*. New York: Weatherhill, 1969.

NAKAMURA Hajime 中村 元. *Bukkyōgo daijiten* 仏教語大辞典 [Dictionary of Buddhist terms], 3 vols. Tokyo: Tōkyō Shoseki, 1975.

NATTIER, Jan. "The *Candragarbha-sūtra* in Central and East Asia." Ph.D. thesis, Harvard University, 1988.

__________. "Church Language and Vernacular Language in Central Asian Buddhism." *Numen* 37/2 (1990): 195-219.

__________, ed. and trans. "The *Kšanti qïlmaq nom bitig*, An Uighur Buddhist Confession Text for Laity." Unpublished manuscript, 1974.

__________. "The Meanings of the Maitreya Myth: A Typological Analysis." In Alan SPONBERG and Helen HARDACRE, eds., *Maitreya, the Future Buddha*, 23–47. Cambridge: Cambridge University Press, 1988.

NELSON, Andrew Nathaniel. *The Modern Reader's Japanese-English Character Dictionary*. 2nd revised ed. Rutland/Tokyo: Charles E. Tuttle, 1962.

NEWMAN, John R. "The Outer Wheel of Time: Vajrayāna Buddhist Cosmology in the Kālacakra Tantra," Ph.D. thesis, University of Wisconsin, 1987.

NORMAN, K. R., trans. *The Elders' Verses: Theragāthā*. London: Luzac & Co., 1969.

OBERMILLER, E., trans. *History of Buddhism (Chos-hbyung) by Bu-ston*. Heidelberg: Otto Harrassowitz, 1931.

ŌCHŌ Enichi 横超慧日, ed., *Hokugi bukkyō no kenkyū* 北魏仏教の研究 [Studies on Buddhism under the Northern Wei]: 287–97. Kyoto: Heirakuji Shoten, 1970.

PACHOW, W. *A Comparative Study of the Prātimokṣa*. Santiniketan: Sino-Indian Cultural Society, 1955.

PAUL, Diana Y. *Women in Buddhism*. 2nd ed. Berkeley, CA: Asian Humanities Press, 1985.

PELLIOT, Paul. "Notes à propos d'un catalogue du *Kanjur*." *Journal Asiatique* 4 (1914): 111–50.

POLLACK, David. *The Fracture of Meaning: Japan's Synthesis of China from the Eighth through the Eighteenth Centuries*. Princeton: Princeton University Press, 1986.

PREBISH, Charles S. *Buddhist Monastic Discipline*. University Park/London: Pennsylvania State University Press, 1975.

__________. "A Review of Scholarship on the Buddhist Councils." *Journal of Asian Studies*, 33/2 (1974): 239–54.

__________, and Janice J. NATTIER, "Mahāsāṃghika Origins: The Beginnings of Buddhist Sectarianism." *History of Religions* 16 (1977): 237–72.

PRZYLUSKI, Jean. *A-yu-wang-tchouan, Chronique des premiers siècles du bouddhisme*. Paris: Paul Geuthner, 1923.

__________. *La légende de l'empereur Açoka*. Paris: Paul Geuthner, 1923.

RERIKH, Yu. N. *Tibetsko-russko-angliiskiĭ slovar'*. 10 vols. Moscow: Nauka, 1983–1988.

RHODES, Robert. "Saichō's *Mappō-tōmyōki*." *The Eastern Buddhist*, n.s., 13/1 (1980): 79-103.

RHYS DAVIDS, C. A. F., trans. *The Book of Kindred Sayings*, vol. 1, 1917; repr. London: Pali Text Society, 1971.

RHYS DAVIDS, T. W., trans. *Dialogues of the Buddha*. 1899; repr. London: Pali Text Society, 1957.

__________, and Hermann OLDENBERG, trans. *Vinaya Texts*. 1885; repr. Delhi: Motilal Banarsidass, 1975.

__________, and William STEDE, eds. *The Pali Text Society's Pali-English Dictionary*. 1921–1925; repr. London: Routledge and Kegan Paul, 1972.

RICHARDSON, H. E. *A Corpus of Early Tibetan Inscriptions*. London: Royal Asiatic Society, 1985.

RINTCHEN. *Catalogue du tanjur mongol imprimé*. New Delhi: International Academy of Indian Culture, 1964– .

RÖHRBORN, Klaus, and Wolfgang VEENKER, eds. *Sprachen des Buddhismus in Zentralasien*. Wiesbaden: Harrassowitz, 1983.

ROSENFIELD, John M. *Dynastic Arts of the Kushans*. Berkeley: University of California Press, 1967.

RUEGG, David S. *The Life of Bu ston Rin po che*. Serie Orientale Roma, vol. 34. Rome: Istituto Italiano per il Medio ed Estremo Oriente, 1966.

SAGASTER, Karl, ed. and trans. *Die Weisse Geschichte*. Leipzig: Otto Harrassowitz, 1981.

SAKAKI Ryōzaburō 榊 亮三郎, et al., eds. *Mahāvyutpatti*. 2 vols. Kyoto: Shingonshū Kyōto Daigaku, 1916–1925.

SCHOPEN, Gregory. "The Manuscript of the Vajracchedikā found at Gilgit: An Annotated Transcription and Translation." In Luis O. Gómez and Jonathan A. Silk, eds. *Studies in the Literature of the Great Vehicle: Three Mahāyāna Buddhist Texts*, 89–139, Ann Arbor: Collegiate Institute for the Study of Buddhist Literature, 1989.

__________. "Filial Piety and the Monk in the Practice of Indian Buddhism: A Question of 'Sinicization' Viewed from the Other Side." *T'oung Pao* 70 (1984): 110–26.

__________, ed. *Buddhist Studies: Selected Essays of J. W. de Jong*. Berkeley: Berkeley Buddhist Studies Series, 1979.

SCHUBRING, Walther. *The Doctrine of the Jainas*, trans. Wolfgang Beurlen. Delhi: Motilal Banarsidass, 1962.

SIMS-WILLIAMS, N. "Indian Elements in Parthian and Sogdian." In Klaus Röhrborn and Wolfgang Veenker, eds. *Sprachen des Buddhismus in Zentralasien*. Wiesbaden: Harrassowitz, 1983.

SOOTHILL, William Edward, and Lewis HODOUS. *A Dictionary of Chinese Buddhist Terms*. London, 1937; repr. Delhi: Motilal Banarsidass, 1977.

SPEYER, J. S., ed. *Avadānaçataka*. Bibliotheca Buddhica, vol. 3. 1902–06; repr. Osnabrück: Biblio Verlag, 1970.

SPONBERG, Alan, "Attitudes toward Women and the Feminine in Early Buddhism." In José Ignacio CABEZÓN, ed., *Buddhism, Sexuality and Gender* (forthcoming, 1991).

__________, and Helen Hardacre, eds. *Maitreya, the Future Buddha*. Cambridge: Cambridge University Press, 1988.

STAVISKIĬ, B. Ya., gen. ed. *Buddiĭskie peshchery Kara-tepe v starom Termeze* [= *Kara Tepe*, 2]. Moscow: Nauka, 1969.

STEIN, Sir M. Aurel, trans. *Kalhaṇa's Rājataraṅgiṇī*. 1900; repr. New Delhi: Motilal Banarsidass, 1975.

STEIN, Sir M. Aurel. *Ancient Khotan*. 1907; repr. New York: Hacker Art Books, 1975.

STONE, Jackie. "Seeking Enlightenment in the Last Age: *Mappō* Thought in Kamakura Buddhism." *The Eastern Buddhist*, n.s., 18/1 (1985): 28–56 (Part 1) and 18/2 (1985): 35–64 (Part 2).

STRICKMANN, Michel. "Chinese Views of the End of the World." Unpublished paper presented at Harvard University, November 1979.

STRONG, John S. *The Legend of King Aśoka: A Study and Translation of the Aśokāvadāna*. Princeton: Princeton University Press, 1983.

SUZUKI, Daisetz T., trans. *The Lankavatara Sutra: A Mahayana Text*. London: Routledge & Kegan Paul, 1932.

_________, ed. *The Tibetan Tripitaka, Peking Edition. Catalogue*. Tokyo/Kyoto: Tibetan Tripitaka Research Institute, 1961.

TAKASAKI Jikido. *Introduction to Buddhism*, trans. Rolf W. Giebel. Tokyo: Tōhō Gakkai, 1987.

Taishō shinshū daizōkyō 大正新修大蔵経 , ed. and comp. by TAKAKUSU Junjirō 高楠順次郎 , WATANABE Kaigyoku 渡辺海旭 , et al. Tokyo: Taishō Issaikyō Kankōkai, 1924–1934.

Taishō shinshū daizōkyō sakuin 大正新修大蔵経索引 [Index to the Taishō Buddhist canon]. Tokyo: Research Association for the Terminology of the Taishō Tripiṭaka, 1964– .

TEKIN, Şinasi, ed. and trans. *Maitrisimit nom bitig. Die uigurische Übersetzung eines Werkes der buddhistischen Vaibhāṣika-Schule*. 2 vols. Berliner Turfantexte, IX. Berlin: Akademie Verlag, 1980.

THAPAR, Romila. *A History of India*, vol. 1. Baltimore: Penguin Books, 1966.

THOMAS, Edward J. *The Life of the Buddha as Legend and History*. New York: Alfred A. Knopf, 1927.

THOMAS, F. W. *Tibetan Literary Texts and Documents Concerning Chinese Turkestan*. 4 vols. London: Royal Asiatic Society, 1935–1963.

TUCCI, Giuseppe. *The Religions of Tibet*. Translated from the German and

Italian [*sic*] by Geoffrey Samuel. Berkeley/Los Angeles: University of California Press, 1980.

URAY, G. "Duplication, Gemination and Triplication in Tibetan." *Acta Orientalia* (Budapest) 4 (1954): 177–244.

__________. "The suffix *-e* in Tibetan." *Acta Orientalia* (Budapest) 3 (1953): 229–44.

VAIDYA, P. L., ed. *Gaṇḍavyūhasūtra*. Darbhanga: Mithila Institute, 1960.

VOGEL, J. "The Past Buddhas and Kāśyapa in Indian Art and Epigraphy." In Johannese SCHUBERT and Uleich SCHNEIDER, eds., *Asiatica, Festschrift Friedrich Weller*, 808–16. Leipzig: Harrassowitz, 1954.

VON GABAIN, Annemarie. *Alttürkische Grammatik*. 3rd ed. Wiesbaden: Harrassowitz, 1974.

VON HINÜBER, Oskar. "Die Bestimmung der Schulzgehörigkeit buddhistischer Texte nach sprachlichen Kritirien." In Heinz BECHERT, ed., *Zur Schulzgehörigkeit von Werken der Hīnayāna-Literatur*, Part I, 57–75. Göttingen: Vandenhoeck & Ruprecht, 1985.

__________. *A New Fragmentary Gilgit Manuscript of the Saddharmapuṇḍarīka-sūtra*. Tokyo: The Reiyukai, 1982.

WALDSCHMIDT, Ernst. "Central Asian Sūtra Fragments and their Relation to the Chinese Āgamas." In Heinz BECHERT, ed., *Die Sprache der ältesten buddhistischen Überlieferung*. Abhandlungen der Akademie der Wissenschaften in Göttingen, Phil.-Hist. Klasse, Dritte Folge, No. 117 (1980): 136–74.

WALLESER, Max, ed. *Manorathapūraṇī*. London: Oxford University Press, 1924.

WARREN, Henry Clarke. *Buddhism in Translations*. 1896; repr. New York: Atheneum, 1968.

WAYMAN, Alex. "Studies in Yama and Māra." *Iranian Journal* 3 (1959): 44–73 (Part 1) and 112–113 (Part 2).

WEINSTEIN, Stanley. *Buddhism under the T'ang*. Cambridge: Cambridge University Press, 1987.

WELLER, Friedrich, ed. *Tausend Buddhanamen des Bhadrakalpa*. Leipzig: Asia Major, 1928.

WHITNEY, William Dwight. *Sanskrit Grammar*. 2nd ed. Cambridge: Harvard University Press, 1889.

WOODWARD, F. L., trans. *The Book of the Kindred Sayings*, 5 vols. 1922–1934; repr. London: Pali Text Society, 1973.

YABUKI Keiki 矢吹慶輝 . *Sangaikyō no kenkyū* 三階教の研究 [Studies on the San-chieh-chiao]. Tokyo: Iwanami Shoten, 1927.

YAMADA Isshi, ed. *Karuṇāpuṇḍarīka, The White Lotus of Compassion*. New Delhi: Heritage Publishers, 1968.

YAMADA Ryūjō 山田龍城 . *Daijō bukkyō seiritsu ron josetsu* 大乗仏教成立論序説 [Introductory essays on the development of Mahāyāna Buddhism]. Kyoto: Heirakuji Shoten, 1959.

__________. "Mappō shisō ni tsuite 末法思想について [On *mappō* thought]." *Indogaku bukkyōgaku kenkyū* 4/2 (1956): 361–70.

__________. "Rengemen-gyō ni tsuite 蓮華面經について [On the *Lien-hua-mien ching*]." In *Yamaguchi Hakase kanreki kinen* 山口博士還暦記念 [Festschrift for Dr. Yamaguchi], 110–23. Kyoto: Hōzōkan, 1955.

__________. "The Logic of Crisis: The Mappō Theory in India, China and Japan." In *Proceedings of the IXth International Congress of the History of Religions, Tokyo and Kyoto 1958*, 459–62. Tokyo: Maruzen, 1960.

YAMAMOTO Kosho, trans. *The Mahayana Mahaparinirvana-Sutra*, 3 vols. Ube City: The Karinbunko, 1973–1975.

YARSHATER, Ehsan, ed. *The Cambridge History of Iran*, 3(2). London: Cambridge University Press, 1983.

YORITOMI Motohiro 頼富本宏 . *Chūgoku mikkyō no kenkyū* 中国密教の研究 [Studies in Chinese esoteric Buddhism]. Tokyo: Daitō Shuppansha, 1979.

YUYAMA, Akira. *A Bibliography of the Sanskrit Texts of the Saddharma-puṇḍarīkasūtra*. Canberra: Faculty of Asian Studies/Australian National University Press, 1970.

ZÜRCHER, Erik. *The Buddhist Conquest of China*. 2 vols. Leiden: E. J. Brill, 1959.

Index